**Microsoft** *Press*

# Inside
# ATL

**George Shepherd**
**Brad King**

PUBLISHED BY
Microsoft Press
A Division of Microsoft Corporation
One Microsoft Way
Redmond, Washington 98052-6399

Library of Congress Cataloging-in-Publication Data
Shepherd, George.
    Inside ATL / George Shepherd, Brad King.
        p.    cm.
    Includes index.
    ISBN 1-57231-858-9
    1. Application software--Development.    2. Active template library.
    I. King, Brad.    II. Title.
    QA76.76.D47S4897   1999
    005.26'8--dc21                                            98-44828
                                                                   CIP

Printed and bound in the United States of America.

1 2 3 4 5 6 7 8 9   QMQM   4 3 2 1 0 9

Distributed in Canada by Penguin Books Canada Limited.

A CIP catalogue record for this book is available from the British Library.

Microsoft Press books are available through booksellers and distributors worldwide. For further information about international editions, contact your local Microsoft Corporation office or contact Microsoft Press International directly at fax (425) 936-7329. Visit our Web site at mspress.microsoft.com.

**Acquisitions Editor:** Eric Stroo
**Project Editor:** Sally Stickney
**Technical Editor:** Jim Fuchs
**Manuscript Editors:** Sally Stickney, Rebecca McKay

*To Ted Shepherd, one most excellent guy.*

—George Shepherd

*To Matthew and Amanda. You are my greatest blessing.*

—Brad King

# BRIEF CONTENTS

# CONTENTS

## CHAPTER FOUR

# Getting Started: Implementing a Simple Object  **77**

**CHAPTER EIGHT**

## Advanced Class Composition Techniques  **191**

**CHAPTER THIRTEEN**

## Using ActiveX Controls in Different Development Environments   **327**

**CHAPTER FOURTEEN**

## ATL Window Classes   **341**

## CHAPTER FIFTEEN

# Enumerators and Collections   **367**

## CHAPTER SIXTEEN

# Writing Applications with ATL   **385**

**CHAPTER SEVENTEEN**

# ATL and Beyond  **399**

# ACKNOWLEDGMENTS

We both want to thank everyone at Microsoft Press and all the people who reviewed the manuscript for their kind support throughout this project. Eric Stroo, thanks for your patience as we completed the chapters (not always as fast as you wanted them). Sally Stickney and Rebecca McKay, thanks for your excellent job editing the manuscript and making it readable. Sally Stickney and John Pierce, thanks for managing the project. Jim Fuchs at Microsoft Press, Jason Whittington at DevelopMentor, and Rick Watson at RogueWave Software, thanks for doing technical reviews of our manuscript.

We also want to thank Steve Zimmerman for getting this book rolling. Steve was originally slated to write the book. Unfortunately, he was unable to finish the project because of time constraints. Steve contributed significantly to the early chapters.

Thanks also to Claire Horne for helping to manage the project. It was great working with you.

George has these individual acknowledgments: Wow—this is the third book project I've been involved in. I keep saying "never again," but I can't seem to resist. Each one has been an adventure of some sort, and this book was no exception. I'd like to thank the following people for their part in helping me finish this book.

Thanks to my son, Ted, an endless source of inspiration and enlightenment. Teddy is bountiful in his provision of wisdom. Once while sitting at dinner, Ted said to me, "Like, if you drew a graph of my brain, my knowledge would be this big [showing a small space between his thumb and forefinger] and my imagination would be this big [holding his hands far apart]." I said, "Good— you'll need that much imagination to understand ATL." Also thanks to Sandy Daston for tolerating my absences and my often grumpy disposition as I toiled on this project.

Thanks to Don Box for continuing to explain COM in ways that make sense. Also a big thanks to Mike Abercrombie at DevelopMentor for creating a wonderful environment for thinking about software—especially distributed objects. Thanks also to the folks at RogueWave—especially Jeff Boenig, Rick Watson, Bill Loeb, Jay Gopalkrishna, Jay Pitzer, Mike Jones, Ellen Cyr, Sam Robinson, Rob Oliver, Mark Isham, and Kate Dinardi—for the extra support and for bearing with my wackiness.

Thanks to Joe Flannigan at *Microsoft Systems Journal* and to Gwenn McKone at *Visual C++ Developers Journal* for working with me on your fine magazines.

Thanks to the many other folks who have touched this project, including those who attended my classes through DevelopMentor and my presentations at conferences as well as those who read *Microsoft Systems Journal* and *Visual C++ Developers Journal.*

And finally, a very special thanks to Brad King. Brad brought a tremendous amount of programming insight to this project, along with a really great sense of humor. Good job, Brad!

Brad has these individual acknowledgments: When George first planted the seed of coauthoring *Inside ATL*, I was both ecstatic and terrified. As a developer with a full-time job, I could hardly imagine making the commitment to write a book. Now the task is done. Thanks, George. You're infallible.

Thanks to my wife, Jenelle, for hot coffee brewed in the wee hours when I needed it. It's just one of the many manifestations of how awesome you are. Thanks to my son, Matthew, for calling me out to shoot some hoops once in a while and to my daughter, Amanda, for forgiving my absence from many important moments. Thanks to Mom and Dad for being there, each in your own way, throughout my 34 years. Thanks to Howard Keim Jr. for his inspirational living and faith. Thanks to Bill and Carol Sissel for your sacrifices for the kids.

Thanks to Mark Isham, Michael Jones, and Mike Blaszczak for various choice microbrew encounters. Thanks to Days of the New and Creed for great *Inside ATL* background tunes. Thanks to Walter Sullivan for putting up with Jones and me bugging him.

And last but not least, thanks to the ATL team at Microsoft for feeding us, the hungry C++ masses.

# PREFACE

One of the most interesting aspects of the industry we work in is the pace at which it evolves. Having software and computer technology progress so rapidly is both a blessing and a curse. It's a blessing for some obvious reasons: constantly improving tools can help us write faster and more powerful software, the rapid change can lead to better career opportunities if you choose to keep up with the technology, and the need to learn new things quickly can bring personal growth. In addition, the quick evolution of software and computer technology means there's always a lot of room for new and innovative ideas. But it's a curse because the pace of change often makes it seem so difficult to stay current. Every time we turn around, we're faced with something new to absorb. When do we have the time and opportunity to really master what we've just learned? Given that our chosen profession isn't going to change anytime soon, how can we as developers deal with this dual nature of our work? The answer, we think, is to find the best tools available to help you optimize the latest technology and minimize your learning curve.

Over the course of our careers, we've noticed a certain pattern in software development—perhaps you've observed it as well. When a new software technology emerges, it seems weird and bizarre, often a black art only a chosen few can master. Then folks develop higher-level abstractions that make the technology easier to work with.

In the beginning, there was assembly language—and it was good. Assembly language made implementing programs substantially easier than having to use machine language. Then computer languages, interpreters, and compilers replaced assembly language, and many more people were able to write programs.

When Microsoft Windows came along, it popularized the event-driven programming model. The event-driven programming model forced developers to completely overhaul their knowledge of programming. Writing Windows programs in the late 1980s and the early 1990s meant wrestling with the Windows SDK and the Microsoft C compiler—a lethal combination at the time, one that drove many developers to distraction. And then the Microsoft Foundation Class (MFC) library was created, making it unnecessary to write the same window procedure (that big switch statement) over and over again.

The Component Object Model (COM) saw the light of day in 1993—and it was good too. From the early 1990s (at the first OLE Professional Developers Conference) until 1996, however, the only real way to write COM-based software was using C++. More than anything, COM is a programming discipline known as interface-based programming. In interface-based programming, as many details as possible are hidden from the client code, making it easier to distribute software and integrate it at run time.

Programming raw COM with C++ involves myriad details. For example, implementing a COM class means creating a reference-counting mechanism and an interface-discovery mechanism for every object you implement. In addition, C++-based COM classes need another accompanying class object (sometimes called a class factory). Finally, writing a COM-based DLL in C++ means implementing the hooks that COM expects to see in a server (for exposing class objects) and often means managing a reference-counting mechanism for the server. Writing a COM-based EXE means exposing the class objects via an API function and implementing a lifetime control mechanism as well. Nearly the same code is duplicated from one project to another. That's why there's ATL.

The Microsoft Active Template Library (ATL) gets you to COM more quickly than using raw C++. By taking the boilerplate code necessary to get COM working and packaging it behind templates, classes, and utility functions, ATL saves you a lot of typing.

Knowing ATL doesn't replace your need to understand how COM works, though. In fact, the only way to really comprehend ATL is to get a firm grasp on COM. You'll find that ATL uses C++ templates extensively and, at first glance, you might think esoterically. Once you get the hang of ATL, however, you'll see that its design is quite elegant.

This book is intended to be a guide to using ATL. We cover topics such as COM by itself, C++ templates, ATL-based COM classes and servers, COM identity and class composition, ATL and ActiveX controls, the ATL wizards, ATL and persistence, ATL and connection points, ATL windowing support, and using ATL to write applications.

The target platform for this book is generally Microsoft Windows NT 4.0. Although the release of Microsoft Windows 2000 is just around the corner and some shops will adopt it right away, many shops will probably continue to use Windows NT 4.0 for some time. Windows 2000 brings some significant refinements to the COM programming model—the most important of which is the integration of Microsoft Transaction Server (MTS) into the programming model and the use of contexts and interception to help heterogeneous objects live in harmony. For example, in Windows NT 4.0, apartments are the main mechanism for protecting objects from concurrent access via multiple threads. In Windows 2000, the context is the main tool for protecting objects from concurrent access. (We cover this topic in Chapter 17.)

For now, the future is COM, and developing COM-based software in ATL is the fastest way to get there. Let's find out how.

```
if(YouWantAHistoryOfATL())
{
    ReadChapter1();
}
if(YouDontKnowCOM())
{
    ReadChapter2();
}
if(YouDontKnowTemplates())
{
    ReadChapter3();
}
ReadTheRestOfTheBook();
```

# System Requirements

To use this book, you'll need the following:

- A Pentium II–based computer or above
- 32 MB of memory minimum, 64 MB or more strongly recommended
- Windows NT 4.0 with Service Pack 4 or later, or Windows 95/98
- Microsoft Visual C++ 6.0 with Service Pack 2 or later
- ATL 3.0

# Using the Companion CD

To install the sample files, run Setup.exe in the root of the companion CD. This program copies the files to your hard drive and also clears the Read-Only flag on the files. If you're using a system with Windows NT 4.0 or Windows 2000, you'll need Administrator privileges in order to run the Setup program.

To uninstall the samples, follow these steps:

1. Open Add/Remove Programs.
2. Select "Inside ATL".
3. Click the Add/Remove button.

**NOTE** Some of the files on this CD have long filenames. If either your CD-ROM driver or your computer's BIOS doesn't support long filenames on CDs, you should install the book's files by running the Setup.exe program in the \Short directory. The files in this directory are all in 8.3 format; the Setup.exe program automatically restores long filenames after it copies the files to your hard drive.

In addition to the sample program code, the companion disc contains the complete text of the original print book in fully searchable electronic book format. For information on installation, including software, minimum requirements, and support for the electronic book, consult the Ebook\Readme.txt file.

## CHAPTER ONE

# ATL: The Past, Present, and Future

Unless you've been locked in a dungeon writing Fortran code for the last several years, you've undoubtedly heard about the Microsoft Component Object Model (COM). COM is arguably the most significant and promising personal computer software development technology to emerge since the release of the Microsoft Windows application programming interface (API). Unfortunately, although COM offers developers many benefits (which we'll review in Chapter 2), it has historically been difficult to master. In fact, some developers have maligned COM as the most difficult and nonintuitive programming model of our era. Although that characterization is certainly not entirely fair, many a developer has spent a late night or two (or two hundred!) pulling out his or her hair trying to understand the nuances of object linking and embedding (OLE), a powerful but wildly complicated set of services built on top of COM.

## COM Frameworks

Some tools are already available to help reduce the frustration induced by OLE and COM. For example, the Microsoft Foundation Class (MFC) framework is designed to make it as easy as possible for C++ developers to write applications and components that take advantage of OLE by providing a set of classes that encapsulate its use. Microsoft Visual Basic, the most popular Microsoft development tool, distances developers even further from the complexity of OLE. However, only with the release of the Visual Basic Custom Control Edition was it possible to develop COM objects using Visual Basic. Until then, Visual Basic had been a tool only for COM consumers, not for COM developers.

Certainly, developing COM objects using MFC and Visual Basic is much easier than trying to create them using raw C or C++. In fact, for all but the most advanced developers, attempting to face the wrath of COM without the shelter of a framework can be tantamount to developer suicide; those frameworks have been the only feasible approach. Along with the benevolent level of abstraction they provide, however, MFC and Visual Basic carry a fairly stiff penalty: they both saddle applications and components with a large run-time dynamic-link library (DLL). This extra freight inherent in MFC and Visual Basic has created a chasm between "lean and mean" COM development using straight C and C++ and the "fat, dumb, and happy" approach taken by those frameworks.

## Galileo

A few years ago, in an attempt to provide solutions to the problems facing COM developers within Microsoft, several members of the Visual C++ development team were formed into a new team created to design the Enterprise edition of Visual C++, code-named Galileo. The new team determined that internal corporate developers were adopting a multitiered strategy wherein application logic is divided into roughly three layers: user services, business services, and data services, as described in the following sidebar.

### Standard Three-Tier Client/Server Architecture

The three-tier architecture shown in Figure 1-1 has recently received a great deal of well-warranted publicity. Because this architecture is particularly applicable to COM and the Active Template Library (ATL), it is worth describing in some detail here. Basically, a client/server system can be divided into three basic architectural parts, or tiers. Although these tiers don't necessarily correspond to separate physical locations on a network, they represent a logical separation of functionality that gives developers a great degree of flexibility, scalability, and performance.

| Client Tier<br>(user services) | Middle Tier<br>(business services) | Data Source Tier<br>(data services) |
| --- | --- | --- |
| ActiveX, OLE | COM, DCOM,<br>Component Services | DBMS, SQL Server |

**Figure 1-1**
*The standard three-tier client/server architecture*

- The *client* tier provides the graphical user interface (GUI) for presenting and gathering information from the user. This tier, which resides on a local machine connected to the Internet, an intranet, or a LAN, is generally implemented using a custom front-end application or, increasingly, a set of Web pages displayed in a browser. Traditional COM-based technologies—Microsoft ActiveX controls, Microsoft Active Documents, and OLE servers and containers—reside almost exclusively in this tier. Development tools such as MFC, Visual Basic, Microsoft Visual FoxPro, and Microsoft Office are especially well suited for the client tier because of their rich support for user interfaces and OLE.

- The *middle* tier is a set of components that encapsulate the application logic and business rules of the system. These components respond to user requests by performing specific business tasks. This tier, which typically resides on one or more Microsoft Windows NT Server and Microsoft Windows 2000 Server machines, is the home of Microsoft Internet Information Server (IIS), Microsoft Active Server Pages (ASP), Microsoft Internet Server application programming interface (ISAPI) DLLs, lightweight COM objects, Microsoft Component Services—formerly known as Microsoft Transaction Server (MTS)—components, out-of-process COM servers, and Distributed COM (DCOM) servers. In our opinion, the middle tier is where the power and beauty of COM really shine! Not coincidentally, the middle tier is also the tier best suited for development with ATL.

- The *data source* tier defines, stores, and manages access to the system data. This tier, which may reside on a combination of servers and mainframe computers, is typically implemented using a database management system (DBMS) such as Microsoft SQL Server. By separating the services of the data source from the other components in the system, the structure and access to the data can be modified, scaled, or even re-architected with minimal effect on the client and middle tiers.

Naturally, the Galileo team decided that COM would be the most instinctive method of communication between the layers of logic. However, they concluded that the COM objects developed for the business services layer—the middle tier—would need to be built with size and speed (rather than ease of development) in mind, even if it meant an increase in the time required to develop those objects. Furthermore, the objects would need to be capable of supporting access from many clients simultaneously. Keep in mind that at that time the Microsoft tools for COM development were entirely focused on simplicity rather than performance. In other words, when it came to addressing the COM needs of multitiered, multithreaded business applications (to say nothing of the even stricter needs of Internet applications), MFC and Visual Basic simply couldn't cut it.

To provide a middle-ground solution between lethargic OLE-centric frameworks and no framework at all, the Galileo team designed and created a small C++ library that would simplify COM development without sacrificing component size and speed.

## The BaseCtl Framework

As tends to happen whenever developers on different teams strive to find better ways to solve the same sets of problems, another Microsoft team was simultaneously making similar inroads toward a lightweight C++-based COM framework. Specifically, members of the Visual Basic team were developing an in-house set of C++ classes for creating tight, quick OCXs (now known as ActiveX controls). Although their framework—eventually known as the ActiveX BaseCtl framework—was quite a bit more difficult to use than MFC (partially because BaseCtl wasn't really designed and documented for external use), it was still much easier to use than raw C++. Furthermore, its performance gains over MFC were impressive enough to warrant a great deal of excitement. Indeed, in early 1996, the BaseCtl framework was considered significant enough that it was released to the world as an undocumented (and unsupported) set of sample code.

## The Active Template Library

The Galileo team incorporated many of the aspects of the BaseCtl framework into their own C++ library and named the resulting code the Active Template Library (ATL). Actually, at one time ATL was called the ActiveX Template Library, but rumor has it that the "X" rating was removed to make ATL suitable for young developers!

At first, ATL was available only to a lucky few within Microsoft. After a short time, however, so many internal developers were asking for permission to use the code and providing suggestions for future enhancements that Microsoft decided to make ATL available to everyone. ATL 1.0 was released to the Visual C++ Web site at the end of April 1996, and ATL 1.1 (which included a number of bug fixes and an improved set of documentation and sample code) was made available shortly thereafter. Eventually, after further enhancements—including support for developing various flavors of ActiveX controls—ATL became the tool of choice for developing lightweight COM objects. In fact, ATL 2.1 was made an officially supported part of Visual C++ 5.0, and wizard support for it was added to Microsoft Developer Studio. As of this writing, the most recent release of ATL is version 3.0, which ships with Visual C++ 6.0.

# The Future of ATL and MFC

Although ATL certainly represents a significant milestone in the history of COM development, it doesn't signal the end of the line for MFC, despite the paranoia of some panic-stricken developers. When ATL was first released, nervous developers everywhere immediately began to ask some pointed questions: What is the future of MFC? Is Microsoft going to continue to improve and support MFC, or will ATL be positioned as its replacement? Because MFC has without question become the framework of choice for Windows development under C++, these are good questions. Indeed, because of the sheer number of developer-hours invested in MFC, any attempt to discontinue support for it would be met with a great deal of resistance, to say the least. Well, MFC developers can rest assured that Microsoft has no plans to abandon MFC anytime soon. The goals of MFC and ATL are different but complementary, so both should be around for a long time.

## The Benefits and Drawbacks of MFC

The goal of MFC is to make it as easy as possible for C++ developers to create robust Windows applications without sacrificing application performance. For that reason, the MFC class wrappers around the Windows API are, by design, wide and shallow. In other words, although it encapsulates many different APIs, the abstraction layer between the MFC classes and the native Win32 functions under the hood is noticeably thin. For example, the *CWnd::SendMessage* function does nothing more than call the *SendMessage* function exposed by the Windows API. Although this approach is frustrating to some developers—especially those who want to develop Windows-based applications without having to invest the time to understand the ins and outs of the Windows programming model—it is most often a good trade-off. It simplifies application development without selling out on speed. Of course, applications built using MFC will suffer some performance penalty compared to those built with the raw Windows

API, but for robust, large-scale applications, the maintainability of MFC code more than makes up for any slowdown in speed.

Unfortunately, MFC support for OLE and COM doesn't follow the same model as its support for the Windows API. Although MFC's window classes contain a substantial number of inline wrappers (à la *CWnd::SendMessage*), its OLE classes aren't nearly as lightweight. As a result, MFC is less suited for middle-tier COM object development than it is for Windows development or even OLE development. Until recently, the COM limitations of MFC have been largely forgivable—ActiveX controls developed with MFC are perfectly adequate for use in end-user applications written in Visual Basic and MFC. And when it comes to traditional OLE support—OLE document servers, compound documents, containers, and so on—MFC is the best choice. However, the recent trend toward client/server Internet applications and the three-tier architecture described earlier has exposed two problems. First, even the smallest components created using MFC are generally considered too large for use within a Web browser, especially considering the time it takes to download the associated DLLs. Second, MFC is not well suited for creating server components that provide no user interface but must simultaneously support multiple threads of execution. Thus, whereas MFC still has something to offer future Windows applications, it falls short when it comes to developing COM objects in the business services tier.

## ATL vs. MFC

In a way, ATL is to COM what MFC is to the Windows API. The goal of ATL is to provide a thin but effective wrapper around the most common COM interfaces without sacrificing component performance. Despite this similarity, however, the designs of MFC and ATL differ in several key ways:

- MFC contains an interconnected hierarchy of classes, whereas ATL is a set of disjoint templates. This difference means that with ATL you don't pay the size/speed penalty for a given feature unless your component actually uses it.

- MFC is linked to a project as a static library or a DLL, but ATL is compiled as source code. Because there are no OBJ files to link to, ATL requires no run-time DLL redistribution.[1]

---

1. Actually, you do have the option of linking dynamically to certain parts of ATL—several global functions and the Registry Scripting component—as explained in Chapter 4. More often than not, you'll find that you still link to the Visual C++ run-time routines, which you can do dynamically or statically. Fortunately, the choice is yours.

- MFC supports a single-inheritance model, whereas the functionality of an ATL component depends entirely on the use of multiple inheritance. Specifically, a component that supports several different COM interfaces will inherit from several different associated ATL templates.

- Over time, MFC has grown considerably. As the expectations placed on Windows applications have increased, so have the size and feature set of MFC. Although a similar progression is likely as the use of ATL becomes more prevalent, ATL's use of templates rather than regular inheritance will almost assuredly prevent class proliferation.

### A Framework by Any Other Name

If you were to study the scenery in the offices and cubicles of a thousand different Windows developers, you'd likely notice two recurring themes. First, you would see a shocking number of empty soda cans—after all, if the periodic table had been developed by programmers, it would have contained only three elements: carbonated water, sugar, and caffeine. Second, you would notice an abundance of MFC class hierarchy posters on the walls. These posters are likely as much status symbols as reference materials. MFC follows a very regimented, hierarchical, singly inherited class model. It doesn't take very long to see that just about everything inherits from *CWnd*, *CObject*, or *CCmdTarget*.

In stark contrast, ATL is composed almost entirely of independent base classes that are "templatized."(You hear that word a lot in the C++ community, even though our spelling checker doesn't like it.) It has been said that the best thing about the ATL framework is that it isn't a framework at all. Indeed, if an ATL poster is ever published, the class layout will be very, very flat.

## Conclusion

It seems clear that ATL has a bright, well-focused future as a tool for developing lightweight client controls and high-performance server-side objects. And because that's the direction in which the development world appears to be headed, you are wise to be reading this book. But before we jump into the details of ATL, we'll review the basic principles behind COM and C++ templates to make sure that you're up to speed. If you're already comfortable with those two topics, feel free to skim the next two chapters.

## CHAPTER TWO

# The Component Object Model

You're reading this book because you've decided to learn about the Microsoft Active Template Library (ATL). Maybe your project is headed in that direction. Perhaps you've heard the acronym and have decided that ATL is the next technology in which to bury yourself. Or maybe you just want to make sure you and your development team are buzzword-compliant. Whatever your reason, before you perch yourself in front of this or any other ATL book to learn how to work with the framework, you need to be sure that you understand exactly how the Microsoft Component Object Model (COM) works.

Developers sometimes misconstrue the purpose of ATL and hope that it will save them from having to learn COM. Nothing could be further from the truth. It's true that once you learn the core concepts of COM, ATL will save you from a lot of typing while letting you retain control over the COM classes you write. Under the hood, however, ATL is just another way to wire COM interfaces to their implementations. You can get by just pumping out COM classes using the ATL COM Object Wizard and adding interface methods and attributes using the ClassView pane. But you'll be able to go only so far before you start bumping into the important hardcore issues related to COM. For example, you'll need to understand the importance of separating implementations from their interfaces. And if you avoid working through the issue of COM apartments, you won't be able to work effectively with the different threading models in COM (and don't even think of touching the Free Threaded Marshaler check box in the ATL Object Wizard property page).

In this chapter, we'll explore Microsoft's binary object model (COM and Distributed COM, or DCOM), looking at the fundamental concepts behind the technology and examining how COM works in a distributed environment. Our focus is on how COM and DCOM work with Microsoft Windows NT 4.0. In Microsoft Windows 2000, some things change—we'll talk about those changes in Chapter 17. We'll go over COM interfaces, COM classes, class objects, and apartments. We'll cover COM from the C++ perspective because that's the only way to really understand how COM works. To begin, we'll take a look at why COM exists in the first place and then work through each of COM's atoms.

# The Software Game

The game of software has changed since the late 1980s and early 1990s. These days, robust software distribution (that is, objects everywhere—even on a network) is extremely important. For the past decade, developers have been writing applications using object-oriented languages and tools such as C++ and Delphi, among others. Using object-oriented programming languages has been a successful venture for most participants, giving rise to useful application frameworks and code libraries. These languages and tools are great for developing applications that exist on the desktop and that distribute information and functionality in limited ways.

Until now, sharing objects has traditionally been a source code proposition; that is, developing object-oriented software has involved confining the entire development team to a single development environment so that they could share the source code. With such a wide choice of languages and tools available to the contemporary developer, however, it doesn't make sense to use only one language to implement a large development project. For example, although tools such as C++ and the Microsoft Foundation Class (MFC) library are adequate for building user interfaces, they might not be the best tools for building infrastructure-type software. Microsoft Visual Basic is even better for writing user interfaces, but at the cost of losing some control. Raw C++ is a great language for writing infrastructure and lower-level software, but it makes writing user interfaces tedious.

Object models such as COM define *binary* standards so that different parts of an application can be developed independently. That way, an entire software project can be assembled from parts built using C, C++, Java, Visual Basic, or whatever language is popular at the moment.

In addition to software integration, COM is all about writing software that is easy to distribute—that's COM's primary function. COM basically takes the best parts of C++ and leaves out all the compiler-specific garbage imposed by the different compilers. In essence, COM formalizes the notion of interface-based programming.

# The Atoms of COM

COM can be broken down into several discrete chunks, or atoms. The atoms of COM include interfaces, implementations (COM classes and their associated class objects and servers), and apartments. Understanding each piece by itself is necessary for understanding COM as a whole. Let's start with interfaces—probably the single most important atom of COM.

## Interfaces

To help us understand the importance of interfaces, let's construct a hypothetical scenario. Imagine you're a late-night-up-in-the-room-above-the-garage developer trying to make it big by writing a component that almost everyone will want. You survey the computer landscape and notice that most of the computer users around are using office productivity applications such as word processors and spreadsheets. Imagine further that you've developed a spelling checker in C++ that is vastly superior to the ones that ship with the standard word processors and spreadsheets on the market.

### A Spelling-Checker Component Example

Because you're a C++ developer, you maintain the worldview that everybody else uses C++. So you decide to develop the spelling-checker component in C++, as shown in the following code. The class definition and body might look something like this:

```cpp
// checker.h
struct tagTEXTBLOB {
    unsigned long nSizeIs;
    char* pBuffer;
};

class CSpellChecker {
    static int m_nRefCount; // How many others are using this?
    LPTEXTBLOB m_lpText;    // LPTEXTBLOB is defined elsewhere.
public:
    CSpellChecker(LPTEXTBLOB lpText);
    virtual ~CSpellChecker();
    void CheckIt();
};

// checker.cpp
CSpellChecker:: m_nRefCount = 0;

CSpellChecker::CSpellChecker(LPTEXTBLOB lpText) {
    m_lpText = lpText;
}
CSpellChecker::~CSpellChecker() {
    m_lpText = NULL;
}
void CSpellChecker::CheckIt() {
    // Parse the text blob, looking up each word,
    //  making corrections when necessary.
}
```

11

*CSpellChecker* is a regular C++ class that has a constructor, a destructor, static member data, regular member data, and some member functions. There's nothing really special about it. Clients can use *CSpellChecker* as they do any other class. Here's an example of how a client might use the spelling-checker class to check the spelling in a view:

```
// EditView.h
#include "checker.h"
void CEditorView::OnCheckSpelling() {
    LPTEXTBLOB lpTextBlob = GetRawText();
    if (lpTextBlob) {
        CSpellChecker spellChecker(lpTextBlob);
        spellChecker.CheckIt();
    }
}
```

So far, there's nothing extraordinary about this code. It's just a regular C++ class like so many others you've probably seen. Once you've developed the C++ class, your next goal is to make it available to everyone else. If you're going to retire early, you've got to get as many folks as possible to use your spelling checker. But that's easy, right? With so many office productivity applications out there, tapping into this huge, receptive market should be a breeze. All you need to do is to get your spelling checker incorporated into some software and collect a small royalty for each copy sold. At this point, figuring out a decent distribution mechanism is your key to success.

## Try Static Linking

If you distribute your spelling-checker component as a library, office productivity vendors can use static linking to add your spelling-checker library to their applications. (This is the time-tested, traditional way.) However, distributing your library this way has two downsides.

The first disadvantage to the static-linking approach is redundancy. Because your spelling checker is so awesome, many vendors will undoubtedly decide to license it. Then as those vendors release their applications, customers will start buying the applications and installing them on their machines. If someone installs five different applications (each of which uses your spelling checker), that person has implicitly copied five copies of your spelling checker onto his or her disk. That's fine if you own some stock in the mass storage industry, but for most of us, this redundancy chews up valuable disk space that we'd rather use for games.

The second disadvantage to the static-linking approach is that the spelling checker becomes "glued" to your client's application. Static linking is fine until you have to change the spelling checker's functionality for some reason. Perhaps you've found a great way to enhance the spelling-checker algorithm.

Or perhaps, unfortunately, you've located a bug that causes your spelling checker to format the user's hard disk whenever certain words are encountered. Obviously, regardless of whether you're improving your product or fixing an error in it, you're going to need to release an updated version of your spelling checker. Your clients will have to rebuild and reissue their applications to accommodate the new version. From both a logistical and a marketing perspective, this situation is bad business and will likely make your clients very cranky.

Static linking has been used successfully for a long time as a way to distribute software. For example, most framework libraries were distributed that way until recently. Static linking used to be OK because a few years ago C++ libraries and frameworks were smaller than they are today. In addition, frameworks were much less popular than they are now. Linking library or framework code into an application wasn't a big deal back then because the libraries were smaller and most applications were written in the native language of Microsoft Windows: C and the Windows Software Development Kit (SDK).

These days, libraries and frameworks have assumed a prominent position in the typical software developer's toolbox. Major vendors use these libraries to get their applications out to market faster. (Just check out Microsoft's Paintbrush applet, which uses MFC, or Quyen's NetViz, which uses the Object Windows Library [OWL].)

Unfortunately, libraries are beginning to consume huge quantities of hard disk real estate. Such selfish resource consumption might be OK for one or two applications. But it's becoming a big problem now that many vendors are using the same (very large) libraries (such as your spelling checker).

Let's take MFC as an example. MFC as a framework can add significantly to the size of your code. A half-megabyte here and there isn't a whole lot these days—until you start multiplying it by the number of applications that use MFC. You can imagine what it would be like if each application carried around its own copy of MFC. Your hard disk would contain many redundant copies of MFC. Fortunately, most well-written applications aren't statically linked to MFC.

## Dynamic Linking to the Rescue

The solution to the problems inherent in static linking is a technology called *dynamic linking*. Dynamic linking isn't a new idea. In fact, it's the cornerstone of Windows itself. Windows is really just a collection of dynamic-link libraries (DLLs). DLLs are pieces of executable code that sit on your hard disk waiting to be called. When client code requires the services of a DLL, the client code can load the DLL and link to the functions at run time (instead of at compile time and link time). That way, only one copy of a given library resides on a disk at any particular time. All the clients of the DLL simply share that one copy of the library, freeing up disk space and memory resources for other things.

Traditionally, DLLs have exported single entry points. This entry-point system is exactly how the Windows API works. All those gazillion API functions listed in the SDK manuals really just describe entry points into one of the several DLLs in Windows. In addition, this arrangement involves the client in several housekeeping steps to use the DLL. For example, think about using a Graphics Device Interface (GDI) object such as a pen in a straight C/SDK application. You first have to call *CreatePen* to get a handle to a pen. Then you use the pen to draw stuff. Finally, you need to call *DestroyObject* when you're done with the pen.

But wait—C++ is supposed to resolve this sort of problem. Indeed, one of the main benefits of C++ is its ability to group functionality into related pieces called *classes*. That's what frameworks such as MFC and OWL do. (For example, the MFC class *CWnd* pretty much wraps all the HWND-based API functions.) In addition, C++ constructors and destructors are supposed to perform all the setup and cleanup functions (such as *CreatePen* and *DestroyObject*). Naturally, you'd like to provide your spelling checker's functionality through a C++ class so that your clients can take advantage of these C++ features.

## C++ and DLLs

Exporting the C++ class wholesale is probably the easiest way to expose the spelling-checker functionality. Inprise, Microsoft, and Symantec all support the following keywords for exporting entire classes from a DLL. The code for exporting the *CSpellChecker* class from a DLL looks like this:

```
class __declspec(dllexport) CSpellChecker {
    static int m_nRefCount;
    LPTEXTBLOB m_lpText; // LPTEXTBLOB is defined elsewhere.

public:
    CSpellChecker(LPTEXTBLOB lpText);
    virtual ~CSpellChecker();

    void CheckIt();
};
```

Notice that the only difference in this class definition is the addition of *__declspec(dllexport)*. When you export a class this way, all its member functions and static data members are added to the DLL's export list. Clients who want to use the *CSpellChecker* class need only include the header file in their source code and make sure the spelling-checker DLL is available in the path.

Wow, that was easy! Is there a hitch? Well, yes, a couple of problems arise.

## The Downside of Exporting C++ Classes

Imagine you start the marketing extravaganza for your spelling checker and someone licenses the DLL. You've written the DLL using Microsoft Visual C++. Your first client happens to develop software using Microsoft Visual C++ too, so you won't face a problem here. Then your next client wants to use Inprise's version of C++ as a development platform. Unfortunately, this client can't use the DLL. Here's why.

One of the strengths of C++ is that it employs type-safe linking to enable function overloading. When a C++ class is compiled into object code, the names of the class member functions become mangled; that is, the names become decorated with all kinds of information indicating their return types and signatures. C++ decorates the class members to ensure that the client code and the object code link correctly. This feature is known as *type-safe linking,* and it's a good thing. However, the folks in New Jersey (Bjarne et al.) only defined the language features (such as type-safe linking)—they couldn't force compiler vendors to implement a feature in a certain way. The folks in Santa Monica, Redmond, and Scotts Valley are free to implement type-safe linking any way they choose.

Here are examples of how each vendor mangles the function and static data symbols given in the class definition on the preceding page:

### Symantec's Mangling

```
??0CSpellChecker@@QAE@PAX@Z
??1CSpellChecker@@UAE@XZ
??4CSpellChecker@@QAEAAV0@ABV0@@Z
??_GCSpellChecker@@UAEPAXI@Z
??_RCSpellChecker@@QAEAAV0@ABV0@@Z
?CheckIt@CSpellChecker@@QAEXXZ
?m_nRefCount@CSpellChecker@@0HA
```

### Microsoft's Mangling

```
??0CSpellChecker@@QAE@ABV0@@Z
??0CSpellChecker@@QAE@PAX@Z
??1CSpellChecker@@UAE@XZ
??4CSpellChecker@@QAEAAV0@ABV0@@Z
??_7CSpellChecker@@6B@
??_ECSpellChecker@@UAEPAXI@Z
??_GCSpellChecker@@UAEPAXI@Z
?CheckIt@CSpellChecker@@QAEXXZ
?m_nRefCount@CSpellChecker@@0HA
```

### Inprise's Mangling

```
@CSpellChecker@$bctr$qpv
@CSpellChecker@$bdtr$qv
@CSpellChecker@CheckIt$qv
@CSpellChecker@m_nRefCount
```

The compilers and linkers use this scheme to make sure that all the parameters are passed correctly and safely. Obviously, trying to link the Inprise-built DLL with a Symantec-built client will result in linking errors because each compiler uses a different name-mangling scheme.

### Solving the Problem with Ordinals

One way around this name-mangling problem is to use ordinals. You can assign ordinal numbers to each exported member using a DEF file, thereby producing an import library for the compiler. Then the client code can refer to each member via its ordinal. This approach solves the problem of name mangling, but it introduces a huge maintenance overhead because you need to produce one import library for each compiler you support (because each compiler vendor probably uses a different name-mangling scheme).

### Oops—Some More Problems

The type-safe linkage problem isn't the only problem you need to tackle. Other problems arise as you evolve the class. For example, what if you decide to change the spelling checker, say, to add a feature that allows the user to cache the 10 most frequently looked-up words? To implement this optimization, you'll need to add some data to your class. Another interesting aspect of C++ comes into play when you make such a change.

Perhaps the new class definition now looks like this:

```
class __declspec(dllexport) CSpellChecker {
    static int m_nRefCount;
    LPTEXTBLOB m_lpText; // LPTEXTBLOB is defined elsewhere.
    LPSTR lpszFrequentWords[10];

public:
    CSpellChecker(LPTEXTBLOB lpText) {
        // Initialize.
    }
    virtual ~CSpellChecker() {
        // Tear down.
    }

    void CheckIt() {
        // Do the checking.
    }
```

```
    void AddToFrequentWordList(LPSTR lpszWord) {
        // Cache frequent words.
    }
};
```

By adding data to your class, you've changed the class's size. The class is now 40 bytes larger on an Intel-based machine. In addition, you've potentially changed the class's layout. The important point to keep in mind here is that when you write client code that uses a C++ class, the client is quietly aware of the class layout. Although C++ provides syntax for making members private, protected, or public, the semantics don't apply at run time. The client code isn't supposed to know anything about the C++ class layout, but it does. The client code understands the entire layout of the class even if the client can access only certain members using C++ code. Remember, older clients have already coded against the layout of a specific class. Using old client code and new DLL code (or new client code against old DLL code) will likely result in a horrific program crash, increased support costs, and lost sales. The upshot is that if you reissue the DLL, all your clients have to recompile their code and reissue their applications as well.

Unfortunately, this situation brings us back to the problem of distribution that we were trying to solve by using dynamic linking. This solution isn't really much better than static linking. What if one of your clients doesn't want to recompile its application, but the other ones do? That means the people who buy applications from multiple vendors have to maintain two copies of a DLL that do pretty much the same thing (except that the new one is a bit faster). And you might be faced with this problem every time you reissue the DLL to fix a bug or make an improvement.

Ever wonder why you might have a bunch of different versions of the MFC DLL (such as MFC30.DLL, MFC40.DLL, MFC42.DLL, and so on) on your machine? You have this assortment because the DLL versions of MFC use this technique of exporting classes wholesale. Every time the folks in Redmond change the class size and layout, they have to reissue a new DLL. In addition, if you develop your software using the Symantec or the Inprise version of C++, you need to ship the corresponding version of the MFC DLL with your application. (For example, Symantec has a DLL named SMFC42.DLL.)

So you seem to be stuck between a rock and some hard places at this point. If you make the spelling checker available through static linking, you bloat your client's applications. If you use DLLs in the normal manner (that is, one export per function), you impose a good deal of overhead on your clients in terms of setup and cleanup code (in addition to not taking advantage of the strong features of C++). Providing the spelling-checker functionality via a C++ class exported from a DLL is OK as long as (1) everybody agrees on a single C++ compiler, and (2) the class size and layout never change. Unfortunately, these two conditions don't exist in the real world. But don't worry. There's a better way to develop software than using standard *class-based programming*—namely, using a discipline called *interface-based programming*. As we just saw when we were trying to distribute C++ classes, class-based programming implicitly couples the client to the DLL in several ways; that is, name-mangling and class-layout issues come into play. Interface-based programming separates the interface of a class from its implementation, thereby reducing the coupling between the client code and the DLL.

## Interface-Based Programming

Although C++ has been a great tool for developing entire Windows-based applications during the past few years, it falls short when used to distribute object-oriented software components. The main reason for this limitation is that many C++ features are compiler-dependent and therefore source code bound. But remember that we're in the age of components now. We're trying to make it possible for anyone to purchase any component and be able to hook up to it easily.

When you export a class from a DLL, you explicitly export all the class's member functions, static data, and layout information to the client. You can probably get away with this method as long as you and all your clients are willing to use a single compiler forever. However, if your clients choose a different compiler or your compiler vendor decides to change the name-mangling scheme or class layout in memory, you're hosed. You'll have to recompile and redistribute everything.

**Computer science 101**   One of the first principles computer science instructors usually teach is the notion of establishing an interface and then holding it constant. If an interface is constant, you can switch the implementation around as much as you like without breaking code written to that interface. Although C++ has syntactic mechanisms for hiding various portions of C++ classes (using the public, private, and protected keywords), this mechanism breaks down as soon as you try to export the class from a DLL. When you export a class wholesale from a DLL, you implicitly provide all sorts of non-interface-related information to the client that can vary from compiler to compiler (or even from one version to another of a single compiler).

The problem we're trying to solve is to get the client's interface to a C++ class to remain constant so that we can exchange implementation details whenever we want to. For example, those implementation details might include a compiler vendor's name-mangling scheme or class layout in memory. In addition, we might want to shield ourselves from our own modifications to a C++

class that might inadvertently change the object's layout in memory. Fortunately, C++ has a mechanism for dealing with this situation: the abstract base class.

An *abstract base class* is simply a group of function signatures. In C++, pure abstract base classes—classes that have no data members and whose functions are all pure virtual—are expressed like this:

```
class PureAbstract {
    virtual Function1() = 0;
    virtual Function2() = 0;
};
```

These classes have three characteristics:

- Every function is virtual.

- Every function is without implementation. (That's what the " = 0" is for.)

- They don't contain any data members.

At first glance, abstract base classes are strange beasts. They are C++ classes, but you can't instantiate them. However, you can derive new classes from abstract base classes and instantiate the derived classes as long as you implement the functions defined in them.

For example, any self-respecting C++ compiler will complain if you try this:

```
class PureAbstract {
    virtual Function1() = 0;
    virtual Function2() = 0;
};

PureAbstract* pAbstract;
pAbstract = new PureAbstract;
```

But this is OK:

```
class PureAbstract {
    virtual Function1() = 0;
    virtual Function2() = 0;
};

class DerivedFromPureAbstract :
    public PureAbstract {
    virtual Function1();
    virtual Function2();
};

DerivedFromPureAbstract* pDerived;
pDerived = new DerivedFromPureAbstract;
```

You're probably wondering, "Why would I ever want to use these classes?" All the mainstream C++ literature tells us to take classes and inherit the functionality we need from them and tweak the new class to our liking. But an abstract base class by itself does nothing; it can't inherit functionality. In short, you don't get all the free functionality that C++ is famous for. So what good are these classes? It turns out that abstract base classes are the way to hold a class interface constant in C++ (which sounds like it might be useful for solving the funky DLL problem we're facing).

Let's see what it would take to hold the spelling-checker class's interface constant so that we can switch around the implementation without breaking the clients.

**Separating the interface from the implementation**   One way to separate the interface from its implementation is to describe a class simply as a collection of functions. After all, that's really what a C++ class is—just a bunch of functions that operate on data. Sure, in C++ we can expose data members publicly (even though it's often better design not to). We can always hold data in a C++ class and provide access to the data through accessor functions. So what we're really doing with C++ classes is describing functionality that might or might not have data associated with it.

Now imagine thinking hard about what you'd like to expose in a class and coming up with a complete set of functions that describes your C++ class. That set of functions becomes the abstract base class from which you derive your implementation.

Recall the spelling-checker implementation. (This is the code that goes in the DLL.)

```
// checker.h
__declspec(dllexport) class CSpellChecker {
    static int m_nRefCount; // How many others are using this?
    LPTEXTBLOB m_lpText;     // LPTEXTBLOB is defined elsewhere.

public:
    CSpellChecker(LPTEXTBLOB lpText);
    virtual ~CSpellChecker();

    void CheckIt();
};

// checker.cpp

CSpellChecker::m_nRefCount = 0;
```

```
CSpellChecker::CSpellChecker(LPTEXTBLOB lpText) {
    m_lpText = lpText;
}

CSpellChecker::~CSpellChecker() {
    m_lpText = NULL;
}

void CSpellChecker::CheckIt() {
    // Parse the text blob, looking up each word,
    //   making corrections when necessary.
}
```

By exporting the spelling-checker class wholesale from the DLL, the client can use the *new* operator to create an instance of the class. This approach works only if the stars are aligned, the gods aren't maligned, and both the client and the DLL were developed using the same compiler, because the client has coded to the entire class definition. We're trying to make it so that the client doesn't have to code to the class definition (because doing so brings in all the compiler-specific junk we're trying to avoid). To expose the class in a layout-independent and compiler-independent way, we need to develop a pure abstract base class representing the spelling-checker class to which the client can code.

For example, here's what the spelling-checker interface might look like:

```
// checkeri.h
class SpellCheckerInterface {
public:
    virtual void CheckIt() = 0;
};
```

Notice how the *SpellCheckerInterface* class differs from the original *CSpellChecker* class definition. Every function is virtual, the data members are absent, and an = 0; follows each function definition. To shield the client from all compiler-dependent types of things, the only functionality the client really needs is a way to call the *CheckIt* function. *SpellCheckerInterface* has neither a constructor nor a destructor because constructors and destructors introduce compiler dependencies. We'll see how to deal with those issues in a moment.

To attach the interface to some working C++ code, just derive the spelling-checker class from *SpellCheckerInterface* like this:

```
// checker.h
#include "checkeri.h"
class CSpellChecker : public SpellCheckerInterface {
    static int m_nRefCount; // How many others are using this?
    LPTEXTBLOB m_lpText;     // LPTEXTBLOB is defined elsewhere.
```

*(continued)*

```
public:
    CSpellChecker(LPTEXTBLOB lpText) {
        // Initialize.
    }
    virtual ~CSpellChecker() {
        // Tear down.
    }

    void CheckIt() {
        // Do what it takes.
    }
};
```

*CSpellChecker* is the concrete class that actually implements the spelling-checker functionality. The only difference between this class and the original *CSpellChecker* definition is that *CSpellChecker* now inherits from *SpellChecker-Interface*. This inheritance adds *SpellCheckerInterface*'s functions to *CSpellChecker* and promises the compiler an implementation of *CheckIt*.

**Construction and destruction**   We need to attend to one last detail: constructing and destroying the class. Consider again what we're trying to do: we're trying to move all the C++-specific details to the DLL side of the client/DLL boundary so that the client only needs to worry about accessing the pure functionality. C++ object construction and destruction both depend on compiler-specific C++ class information. For example, the *new* operator has to know how to call the object's constructor, which implies that the *new* operator must have knowledge about name mangling (a potential problem when going beyond DLL boundaries). In addition, the constructor has to know the address of the object's vtable so that it can put that address in the object's vpointer (an operation that requires class layout knowledge). As for the destructor, the name-mangling problem rears its ugly head again. So we still need to come up with some substitutes for the *new* operator and the *delete* operator and somehow manage the construction and destruction of objects.

What we really need to do is to move object construction and destruction behind the DLL wall so that all the compiler-dependent stuff stays in one place. The obvious way to handle object construction is to export a function from the DLL. For example, here's a bit of code that would work well as a constructor for the spelling checker. Notice that what the client receives is not the *CSpell-Checker* object itself but, rather, a pointer to the *SpellCheckerInterface*.

```
#include "checkeri.h"
#include "checker.h"
```

```
SpellCheckerInterface* ConstructSpellChecker(LPTEXTBLOB lpText) {
    return (SpellCheckerInterface*)
        new CSpellChecker(LPTEXTBLOB lpText);
}
```

The DLL exports this function. Clients can acquire a pointer to this function by calling the standard Windows API functions *LoadLibrary* and *GetProcAddress*. Once a client gets this function pointer, the client can call the function whenever it requires the spelling-checker functionality.

Before moving on, you need to understand an interesting bit of C++ chicanery that's going on here. Notice how the function casts the result of the *new* operator (which is a *CSpellChecker* pointer) to a pointer to the abstract base class (*SpellCheckerInterface\**). This cast might look a bit odd, but it's done for a reason. One not-so-well-known fact about C++ is that casting an object pointer to one of its pure abstract base class derivatives yields a pointer to that pure abstract base class, which is just a function table. Just what we want!

**Using the spelling-checker object**   Using the spelling checker requires going to the Win32 API and explicitly loading the DLL and calling the constructor function. Here's how a client might acquire and use the *SpellCheckerInterface*:

```
#include "checkeri.h"
  ⋮
typedef SpellCheckerInterface*
    (WINAPI* LPSPELLCHECKERCTOR)(LPTEXTBLOB);

void UseSpellChecker(LPTEXTBLOB lpText) {
    SpellCheckerInterface* pSpellChecker = NULL;
    LPSPELLCHECKERCTOR lpSpellCheckCtor = NULL;
    HINSTANCE hInstance;

    HInstance = LoadLibrary("c:\\spellingchecker.dll");

    lpSpellCheckCtor =
        GetProcAddress(hInstance, "ConstructSpellChecker");

    pSpellChecker = lpSpellCheckCtor(lpText);

    pSpellChecker->CheckIt();
}
```

This code doesn't venture beyond the realm of regular DLL coding techniques. *UseSpellChecker* first declares a pointer to a *SpellCheckerInterface* object. (The compiler sees this object simply as a function table.) In addition, *UseSpellChecker* declares a pointer to a function prototyped as the DLL's entry point used for obtaining spelling-checker interfaces. *UseSpellChecker* calls the Windows API function *GetProcAddress* to get the address of the DLL's *ConstructSpellChecker* function and then calls *ConstructSpellChecker* to get a *SpellCheckerInterface*. Once *UseSpellChecker* has the interface, it can use the interface to check the spelling of the block of text.

**Destroying the spelling-checker object**   As you can see from the code on the preceding page, the spelling-checker object is allocated but never freed. How do you handle object destruction in a case like this?

Destroying a C++ object isn't a simple prospect—it involves deallocating memory properly and calling the object's destructor. Again, memory allocation and object construction policies aren't something we want to share between client/DLL boundaries. We have to somehow ask the DLL to destroy the object. At first, it seems as though we might be able to export a single destructor function (as an analogue to the constructor function). However, that would be fairly inconvenient. A better way to handle the destruction is to add one more member function to the interface so that the client can ask the object to delete itself when it's done using the object. So the *SpellCheckerInterface* gets a new function named *DeleteMe*, as shown here:

```
// checkeri.h
class SpellCheckerInterface {
public:
    virtual void DeleteMe() = 0;
    virtual void CheckIt() = 0;
};
```

The implementation code looks like this:

```
void CSpellChecker::DeleteMe() {
    delete this;
}
```

This code might look funny, but it's perfectly legal C++ syntax. Calling *delete* with *this* simply calls the object's destructor and then deallocates any memory the object used in the normal C++ way. The important point to realize is that this activity is happening on the DLL side of the client/DLL boundary, thereby decoupling the DLL from the client.

Now let's finish the example. Here's how a client might use and destroy your spelling-checker object:

```
#include "checkeri.h"
void UseSpellChecker(LPTEXTBLOB lpText) {
    ⋮
    /* Use the exported function */
    /* to construct the object.  */
```

```
    pSpellChecker->CheckIt();
    pSpellChecker->DeleteMe();
}
```

**Immutable interfaces**    At this point, you know that an interface is just a collection of function signatures. (C++ represents these interfaces as abstract base
classes.) You also know that the only way for client code to talk to an object is
through the interface. Let's add one more ingredient—the idea that interfaces
should remain immutable. Once you've decided which functions to include
in the spelling-checker interface and clients start coding to the interface, the
spelling-checker interface should never change. Of course, this immutability
means that if a client can get a spelling-checker interface pointer, the client can
count on having a well-known way to talk to the spelling-checker object.

   Now you're probably thinking back and trying to recall the last project you
worked on whose programmatic interface didn't change eventually. You probably can't think of one. The notion of holding the interface constant is all well
and good: an ideal we should all aim for. But hey, we're in the real world, and
software changes. What should we do when we need to add functionality or
change an interface to a class?

   The answer is to create a completely new interface with a new name.
Imagine that you want to add a new function to your spelling-checker interface. To avoid breaking new clients by changing the existing interface, you simply
need to create a new interface. For example, let's say you want to add a function to get synonyms for a specific word:

```
class SpellCheckerInterface2 : SpellCheckerInterface {
public:
    // DeleteMe and CheckIt come from SpellCheckerInterface.
    virtual char* GetSynonyms(char* szWord) = 0;
};
```

   To implement this interface, you simply apply *SpellCheckerInterface2* to
the concrete class:

```
// checker.h
#include "checkeri.h"
class CSpellChecker : public SpellCheckerInterface2 {
    static int m_nRefCount; // How many others are using this?
    LPTEXTBLOB m_lpText;    // LPTEXTBLOB is defined elsewhere.

public:
    CSpellChecker(LPTEXTBLOB lpText) {
        // Initialize.
```

*(continued)*

25

```
    }
    virtual ~CSpellChecker() {
        // Tear down.
    }
    void CheckIt() {
        // Do what it takes.
    }
    void DeleteMe() {
        delete this;
    }
    char* GetSynonyms(char* szWord) {
        // Generate synonyms.
    }
};
```

The problem is that you've now enabled two ways to talk to the spelling-checker class: through the *SpellCheckerInterface* base class and through the *SpellCheckerInterface2* interface. To solve this problem, should you just add another entry point into the DLL (perhaps a function named *ConstructSpell-Checker2*) to get the second version of the interface?

The way to fix this problem is to provide a well-known way to get new interfaces from an existing interface. For example, imagine that *SpellChecker-Interface* and *SpellCheckerInterface2* look like this:

```
class SpellCheckerInterface {
public:
    virtual void* GetInterface(char* szInterfaceName) = 0;
    virtual void DeleteMe() = 0;
    virtual void CheckIt() = 0;
};

class SpellCheckerInterface2 : SpellCheckerInterface {
public:
    // GetInterface, DeleteMe, and CheckIt
    // come from SpellCheckerInterface.
    char* GetSynonyms(char* szWord);
};
```

Once the client gets a *SpellCheckerInterface*, the client has a way of navigating to a second interface on the object by calling *GetInterface*. For example, here's how some client code might use *GetInterface*:

```
void UseSpellChecker(SpellCheckerInterface* pSpellChecker) {
    pSpellChecker->CheckIt();
    SpellCheckerInterface2* pSpellChecker2;
    pSpellChecker2 =
        pSpellChecker->GetInterface("SpellCheckerInterface2");
```

```
        if (pSpellChecker2) {
            char* szSynonyms[256];
            pSpellChecker2->GetSynonyms("component");
        }
    };
```

When you think about it, this is a pretty good solution for the versioning problem we encountered earlier. Because *SpellCheckerInterface* never changes, clients can always count on certain function signatures in the interface. Older clients don't break. If you decide to add new functionality to the spelling-checker object, you just create a new interface. The *GetInterface* function (always available at the top of the interfaces) provides a way for you to acquire more interfaces as necessary.

Here's how you would implement the new version of the object:

```
// checker.h
#include "checkeri.h"
class CSpellChecker : public  SpellCheckerInterface2 {
    static int m_nRefCount; // How many others are using this?
    LPTEXTBLOB m_lpText;    // LPTEXTBLOB is defined elsewhere.

public:
    CSpellChecker(LPTEXTBLOB lpText) {
        // Initialize.
    }
    virtual ~CSpellChecker() {
        // Tear down.
    }
    void* GetInterface(char* pszInterfaceName) {
        if (stricmp(pszInterfaceName, "SpellCheckerInterface") {
            return static_cast<SpellCheckerInterface*>(this);
        } else if (stricmp(pszInterfaceName,
            "SpellCheckerInterface2") {
                return static_cast<SpellCheckerInterface2*>(this);
        } else {
            return 0;
        }
    }
    void CheckIt() {
        // Do what it takes.
    }
    char* GetSynonyms(char* szWord) {
        // Generate synonyms.
    }
};
```

The only difference in this implementation is the addition of the *Get-Interface* function. Notice how this function is implemented. *GetInterface* examines the string passed in by the client. If the object implements the interface that the client requested, the object performs a static cast on its own *this* pointer. This code looks kind of funny, but it's perfectly legal. By casting the pointer to a concrete class to one of its base classes, the C++ compiler *shears* into the object and retrieves that object's vptr (which just so happens to be a vtable representing the interface functions).

**Orthogonal interfaces**   Although at times you might want to extend an interface by adding or changing functions, at other times you need to add completely new independent interfaces to your class. For example, imagine you want to add an interface that persists the most frequently used words into a file. You might write an interface that looks like this:

```
class PersistMFUInterface {
public:
    virtual void* GetInterface(char* szInterfaceName) = 0;
    virtual void DeleteMe() = 0;
    virtual void PersistMFUWords(char* pszFileName) = 0;
};
```

Adding a new interface to an implementation is simply a matter of adding the abstract base class to the inheritance list and modifying *GetInterface* to work properly, like so:

```
// checker.h
#include "checkeri.h"
class CSpellChecker : public SpellCheckerInterface2,
                      public PersistMFUInterface {
    static int m_nRefCount; // How many others are using this?
    LPTEXTBLOB m_lpText;    // LPTEXTBLOB is defined elsewhere.

public:
    CSpellChecker(LPTEXTBLOB lpText) {
        // Initialize.
    }
    virtual ~CSpellChecker() {
        // Tear down.
    }
    void* GetInterface(char* pszInterfaceName) {
        if (stricmp(pszInterfaceName, "SpellCheckerInterface") {
            return static_cast<SpellCheckerInterface*>(this);
        } else if (stricmp(pszInterfaceName,
            "SpellCheckerInterface2") {
                return static_cast<SpellCheckerInterface2*>(this);
```

```
        } else if (stricmp(pszInterfaceName, "PersistMFUInterface") {
            return static_cast<PersistMFUInterface*>(this);
        } else {
            return 0;
        }
    }
    void CheckIt() {
        // Do what it takes.
    }
    char* GetSynonyms(char* szWord) {
        // Generate synonyms.
    }
    void PersistMFUWords(char* pszFileName) {
        // Save the most frequently used words to
        //  a file denoted by pszFileName.
    }
};
```

One interesting side effect of implementing C++ classes with multiple interfaces is that you create the potential for the client to refer to the C++ class more than once. Unfortunately, this possibility causes problems for the delete function. The problem is serious enough that we need to handle the object's lifetime a bit differently.

**Object lifetime**    The possibility that multiple interfaces can refer to a class causes a problem for the delete function. For example, consider the following code:

```
void UseSpellChecker(SpellCheckerInterface* pSpellChecker) {
    pSpellChecker->CheckIt();
    SpellCheckerInterface2* pSpellChecker2;
    pSpellChecker2 =
        pSpellChecker->GetInterface("SpellCheckerInterface2");
    if (pSpellChecker2) {
        char* szSynonyms[256];
        pSpellChecker2->GetSynonyms("component");
        // Should you call pSpellChecker2->DeleteMe here?
    }
    PersistMFUInterface* pPersistMFU;
    pPersistMFU = pSpellChecker->GetInterface("PersistMFUInterface");
    if (pPersistMFU) {
        pPersistMFU->PersistMFUWords("c:\\MFUWords.txt");
        // Should you call pPersistMFU->DeleteMe here?
    }
};
```

Unfortunately, it's unclear when the delete function should be called. One way to solve this problem is to use standard reference counting. So instead of including a delete function on the interface, you might include an *AddReference* function and a *ReleaseReference* function. Consider these new interfaces:

```
class SpellCheckerInterface {
public:
    virtual void* GetInterface(char* szInterfaceName) = 0;
    virtual void AddReference() = 0;
    virtual void ReleaseReference() = 0;
    virtual void CheckIt() = 0;
};

class SpellCheckerInterface2 : SpellCheckerInterface {
public:
    // GetInterface, AddReference, ReleaseReference,
    //  and CheckIt come from SpellCheckerInterface.
    virtual char* GetSynonyms(char* szWord) = 0;
};

class PersistMFUInterface {
public:
    virtual void* GetInterface(char* szInterfaceName) = 0;
    virtual void AddReference() = 0;
    virtual void ReleaseReference() = 0;
    virtual void PersistMFUWords(char* pszFileName) = 0;
};
```

The *AddReference* and the *ReleaseReference* functions are there to help the spelling-checker object know how many times it's being watched by the client.

The final version of the spelling checker (with the reference counting) now looks like this:

```
// checker.h
#include "checkeri.h"
class CSpellChecker : public SpellCheckerInterface2,
                      public PersistMFUInterface {
    static int m_nRefCount; // How many others are using this?
    LPTEXTBLOB m_lpText;    // LPTEXTBLOB is defined elsewhere.
    DWORD m_dwRefCount;

public:
    CSpellChecker(LPTEXTBLOB lpText) {
        m_dwRefCount = 0;
        // Initialize.
    }
    virtual ~CSpellChecker() {
        // Tear down.
    }
```

```
        void AddReference() {
            m_dwRefCount++;
        }

        void ReleaseReference() {
            m_dwRefCount--;
            if (m_dwRefCount == 0)
                delete this;
        }

        void* GetInterface(char* pszInterfaceName) {
            if (stricmp(pszInterfaceName, "SpellCheckerInterface") {
                AddReference();
                return static_cast<SpellCheckerInterface*>(this);
            } else if (stricmp(pszInterfaceName,
                "SpellCheckerInterface2") {
                    AddReference();
                    return static_cast<SpellCheckerInterface2*>(this);
            } else if (stricmp(pszInterfaceName, "PersistMFUInterface") {
                AddReference();
                return static_cast<PersistMFUInterface*>(this);
            } else {
                return 0;
            }
        }
        void CheckIt() {
            // Do what it takes.
        }
        char* GetSynonyms(char* szWord) {
            // Generate synonyms.
        }
        void PersistMFUWords(char* pszFileName) {
            // Save the most frequently used words to
            //  a file denoted by pszFileName.
        }
};
```

Notice that *AddReference* simply bumps the object's reference counter up by 1. *ReleaseReference* takes the reference counter down by 1. If the reference count is 0, the object deletes itself. The revised client code looks like this:

```
void UseSpellChecker(SpellCheckerInterface* pSpellChecker) {
    pSpellChecker->CheckIt();
    SpellCheckerInterface2* pSpellChecker2;
    pSpellChecker2 =
        pSpellChecker->GetInterface("SpellCheckerInterface2");
```

*(continued)*

```
if (pSpellChecker2) {
    char* szSynonyms[256];
    pSpellChecker2->GetSynonyms("component");
    pSpellChecker2->ReleaseReference();
}
PersistMFUInterface* pPersistMFU;
pPersistMFU = pSpellChecker->GetInterface("PersistMFUInterface");
if (pPersistMFU) {
    pPersistMFU->PersistMFUWords("c:\\MFUWords.txt");
    pPersistMFU->ReleaseReference();
}
};
```

Now instead of deleting the object wholesale, the client simply releases the interface pointers once the client has finished using them.

## The Upshot

So why would you ever want to spend the extra time writing abstract base classes? Wouldn't it be far more convenient simply to write a C++ class, export it from a DLL, and have the client link to the import library? This scenario actually works fine for small projects that are done in-house. In that setting, you can control which version of which compiler you choose. However, the operative word here is *small*. We've worked on projects where we've used the class-export technique and have found that it can cause significant problems on large projects (even when they're done in-house). When large projects use lots of DLLs that are coupled because of the DLL class-export mechanism, just adding one tiny variable to one tiny class can force a recompile of the entire project! That can sometimes take hours. (Sure is a great time to catch up on Dilbert, though!) And if you forget to compile one of the DLLs, your program might inadvertently crash because the client and the DLL don't agree on the layout of the class. Remember, for a program to work, all the bits and bytes have to be in *exactly* the right order.

These problems with DLLs (that is, trying to expose C++ classes from DLLs using the convenient *declspec(__dllexport)* statement) compound when you try to distribute your DLLs to other clients that might or might not share the same compiler, forcing you to create separate import libraries for each compiler. And this is in addition to the problems related to changing the size of the classes.

The technique outlined above (writing abstract base classes) might seem a bit extreme and might appear to introduce a bit of overhead into your DLLs. However, the benefits of not having to worry about recompiling huge libraries of code or breaking applications just because of a minor change in a DLL far exceed the up-front cost of somehow separating a C++ class's interface from its implementation.

If this programming technique involving abstract base classes makes sense to you, you're 85 percent of the way toward understanding COM. The entire basis of COM is this idea of separating an object's interface from its implementation and is a real key to object-oriented software components. You simply need to exercise a bit of discipline.

## COM Interfaces

COM is an integration and distribution technology based on the principle of interface-based programming. The main tenet of interface-based programming is that clients talk to software objects using well-defined interfaces (as opposed to talking to the software objects directly). For example, SDK-based Windows programming is a style of interface-based programming. Think about it—when you write software to talk to someone using an interface element on the screen, you don't talk to Windows directly. You communicate through a set of API functions, passing around a window handle. As a programmer, you don't know anything about what's behind that magic number represented by the window handle. However, you do have a well-defined way of making the software do what you want it to.

The C++ programming style of using abstract base classes is a style of interface-based programming. The client has a well-defined way of talking to the software. In this case, the interface is simply a table of function tables.

An interesting point to note is that C++ developers have always had the ability to write interface-based programs using C++ abstract base classes. COM just formalizes interface-based programming. Although the concept of interface-based programming is the most important point of COM, COM throws in some extra goodies. Those goodies are what we'll look at next.

**Interfaces are immutable**   When developing COM-based software, you'll spend a lot of your time concentrating on the interfaces that clients and objects are going to use to talk to each other. In COM, interfaces come first and then are followed up with implementations (as opposed to C++, where developers traditionally think about interfaces and implementation together). COM interfaces are expressed conveniently in C++ using abstract base classes—just as described earlier in this chapter.

As you saw in the spelling-checker example, COM defines a specific rule governing interfaces: interfaces are immutable. So once you create an interface and publish it (that is, the interface is used widely), you won't be able to change it. The advantage to this approach is that client code can count on an interface remaining constant. That way, clients don't break as a result of interface changes (because the interface never changes). Of course, software development is a dynamic process, and interfaces do change. At some point, you'll want to change your objects by changing an existing interface. In COM, you do that by adding a new interface. COM provides a way for the client to acquire those new interfaces—we'll go over that technique in a moment.

Just as in the spelling-checker example, COM interfaces are named. Instead of being named by human-readable strings, however, COM uses a numbering scheme to name interfaces. The numbers used to name interfaces are GUIDs.

**GUIDs**   When you work with interfaces, you must name them. Keep in mind these two points when it comes time to name your interfaces:

- Interfaces remain immutable for all time.
- Interfaces are going to be distributed all over the world.

These two facts mean that the naming scheme has to produce unique names. COM uses the Distributed Computing Environment (DCE) naming scheme. Specifically, COM borrows DCE's use of 128-bit numbers to identify unique elements. These 128-bit numbers are known as GUIDs—or globally unique identifiers. (GUIDs are also known as UUIDS, or universally unique identifiers.) For example, the following number is a GUID:

```
{1D5BA865-1F95-11d2-8CAA-E8C677 DDD893}
```

Whenever you need to name something uniquely within COM, you can use a GUID. (In fact, you can use a GUID whenever you need a unique name for anything—GUIDs are often a great way to name kernel objects.) GUIDs are pretty easy to come by. The Windows API includes a function named *CoCreateGuid* for generating GUIDs. In addition, Visual C++ comes with a useful utility named GUIDGEN.EXE that generates GUIDs in various formats.

The GUID-production algorithm first relies on the network card installed in the computer (generating numbers that are unique in space). The GUID-production algorithm also relies on the system clock (giving a number unique in time). Finally, the algorithm also uses a couple of other persistent counters that ensure the GUIDs are unique.

The first place you'll bump into GUIDs is in naming interfaces. Again, because interfaces are unique items, they're named by GUIDs. When you need interfaces, you'll ask for them using these GUIDs.

> **NOTE**   GUIDs are also called IIDs (interface IDs), CLSIDs (class IDs), LIBIDs (library IDs), and CATIDs (category IDs), depending on the item being identified. You'll run into some of these other terms later in the book.

***IUnknown*** Recall from the spelling-checker example that each interface started with a function named *GetInterface*. This function allows clients to widen their connections to objects at run time. In addition, each interface included a function to notify an object that new references are being made to it or that existing references are being removed. When you think about it, that's the kind of functionality all objects need in a binary object model. COM includes these facilities within a single well-known interface named *IUnknown*, which looks like this:

```
struct IUnknown {
    virtual HRESULT QueryInterface(REFIID riid, void** ppv) = 0;
    virtual AddRef() = 0;
    virtual Release() = 0;
};
```

Here's the trick to understanding *IUnknown*:

- Every COM object implements this functionality.
- Every COM interface makes this functionality available.

The first part is easy—every COM class you see will have code to handle *Query-Interface*, *AddRef*, and *Release*. The second part implies that every COM interface will start with these three functions.

Again, *IUnknown* embodies the functionality that more or less every object needs. The interface is called *IUnknown* because when you get a pointer to it, you don't know anything about the object behind the pointer. It's your job to query and find out about the interfaces the object supports. There are lots of ways to guess what's behind the pointer. For example, the vendor who provided this object might be able to give you some documentation telling you what interfaces the object supports.

**NOTE** You should keep in mind one detail about *QueryInterface*'s signature. Notice that the requested interface is returned as an out parameter (a parameter that a function uses to return information), not a conventional return value. The reason for the out parameter is that the COM remoting mechanism requires remotable functions to return HRESULTs. HRESULTs are 32-bit rich error codes that indicate success or failure of a method, the area in which a failure occurred (remote procedure call, or RPC; Automation; storage; and so on), and a specific error code.

The separation between interface and implementation is so fundamental to COM that there's even a separate language for describing interfaces: Interface Definition Language.

**Interface Definition Language (IDL)** Microsoft IDL (MIDL) exists to specifically describe interfaces in unambiguous terms. In conventional C and C++ development (nondistributed development), everybody's swimming in the same pool; that is, client software and object software share the same memory and resources such as the stack. These situations permit a lot more wiggle room, allowing for such conveniences as open-ended arrays.

Remember that one of COM's overriding goals is to make it easy to distribute software. We've looked only at the DLL distribution mechanism so far, but COM also makes it easy to write objects that can be distributed over a network. Obviously, when you've got client code sitting on one machine calling object code on another machine, the client and the object no longer share the same calling context. Something (in this case, the remoting layer) has to pick up the calling context of the client and transfer that calling context over to the object machine. This activity requires interfaces to be defined clearly and specifically. That's why IDL exists. When you describe interfaces using IDL, there's no wiggle room. You describe the calling context exactly so that it can be set up anywhere it needs to go.

IDL looks like an attribute-extended version of C. You describe "things" in IDL. "Things" in this context include interfaces, libraries, parameters, and so forth. Each "thing" in IDL can be preceded by an attribute. For example, when you describe interface functions, you can provide explicit instructions to the remoting layer about the size and direction of the parameters. We'll see an example in just a moment.

Microsoft's IDL compiler even uses the C preprocessor. IDL supports a rich set of primitive data types (short, long, *IUnknown\**, and so on). You can use IDL to compose your own structures out of the primitive data types. Although the primary purpose of IDL is to describe interfaces, IDL is also useful for describing what interfaces you can expect to find in a COM class.

Here's an example of some IDL—the spelling-checker interfaces described in IDL-ese:

```
import "oaidl.idl";

[
    uuid(457642F0-3914-11d1-8CB8-0080C73925BA),
    object,
    helpstring("Spelling Checker's Functionality")
]
interface ISpellChecker : IUnknown
{
    HRESULT SetText([in]BSTR bstrText);
    HRESULT CheckIt();
}
```

```
[
    uuid(457992F0-3914-11d1-8CB8-0080C73925BA),
    object,
    helpstring("Spell Checker 2 Functionality")
]
interface ISpellChecker2 : ISpellChecker
{
    HRESULT GetSynonyms([in]BSTR bstrWord, [out]BSTR* pbstrSynonyms);
}


[
    uuid(873542F0-3914-11d1-8CB8-0080C73925BA),
    object,
    helpstring("Persist Most Frequently Used Words")
]
interface IPersistMFU: IUnknown {
    HRESULT PersistMFUWords([in] BSTR* pbstrFileName);
};
[
    uuid(434532F5-3914-11d1-8CB8-0080C73925BA),
    helpstring("Spell checker library"),
    version(1.0),
    lcid(0)
]
library SpellChecker
{
    importlib("stdole32.tlb");
    [
        uuid(907A42F6-3914-11d1-8CB8-0080C73925BA),
        helpstring("Check the words")
    ]
    coclass CoSpellChecker
    {
        interface IUnknown;
        interface IPersistMFU;
        interface ISpellChecker2;
    }
}
```

This IDL file describes three distinct interfaces: *ISpellChecker, ISpell-Checker2,* and *IPersistMFU*. The first line of the IDL imports the standard COM definitions. This line is akin to including WINDOWS.H in your Windows program. Then come the interface definitions. Notice how each interface is preceded by attributes (found in the square braces). Each interface is named by a GUID. Also notice how the parameters have attributes applied to them that indicate the direction of the parameters. You'll see an interesting parameter type listed in some of the function signatures—the BSTR type. The BSTR type is a Unicode string preceded by length data. These parameters are used for Visual Basic compatibility.

Finally, the IDL code has a library statement. In IDL, the library statement tells the compiler to build a type library, or a binary database, including the interface definitions. The type library usually accompanies the DLL (or EXE) housing the COM classes. The *coclass* statement in IDL indicates which interfaces the client can reasonably expect to retrieve from the COM class.

When developing COM software, IDL is where you start. Again, one of the most important tenets of COM programming is that class implementations should be separated from their interfaces. You need to treat interfaces as separate entities, and having a separate language to define interfaces simply reinforces that requirement. In addition, compiling the IDL generates lots of useful products that your object will need throughout its lifetime. For example, compiling the IDL provides C/C++ header files you can use to implement the interfaces. (The header files include abstract base classes defining the interfaces.) Compiled IDL also produces a file containing symbolic definitions for the GUID mentioned in the IDL, the network glue and the type library so loved by the Java and Visual Basic clients.

**How clients use interfaces**   To see how COM interfaces are used, let's take a look at how we can alter the previous spelling-checker example by using the COM versions of the spelling-checker interfaces. COM's protocol for using interfaces goes like this: you first acquire an interface using some means (perhaps you call an API). You use the interface for as long as you need to. Then you release the interface. Here's an example of acquiring, using, and releasing interfaces:

```
void UseSpellChecker(ISpellChecker* pSpellChecker) {
    pSpellChecker->CheckIt();
    ISpellChecker2* pSpellChecker2;
    pSpellChecker->QueryInterface(IID_ISpellChecker2,
                                  (void**)&pSpellChecker2);
    if (pSpellChecker2) {
        BSTR bstrSynonyms;
        pSpellChecker2->GetSynonyms(&bstrSynonyms);
        SysFreeString(bstrSynonyms);
        PSpellChecker->Release();
    }
    PersistMFU* pPersistMFU;
    pSpellChecker->QueryInterface(IID_IPersistMFU,
                                  (void**) &pPersistMFU);
```

```
if (pPersistMFU) {
    BSTR bstrFile;
    bstrFile = SysAllocString(L"c:\\MFUWords.txt");
    pPersistMFU->PersistMFUWords(bstrFile);
    SysFreeString(bstrFile);
    pPersistMFU->Release();
}
};
```

As in the abstract base class example, the client only knows how to talk to the interfaces (instead of talking directly to the implementations). Notice that the *UseSpellChecker* function accepts a pointer to an *ISpellChecker* interface. Don't worry about how to acquire that pointer yet. We'll go over that shortly. Next up, we'll examine how to tie the interfaces to an implementation.

## Implementations (COM Classes)

Once you've defined your interfaces, you'll want to attach them to an implementation; that is, you'll want to write a COM class implementing those interfaces. COM classes are bodies of code that implement COM interfaces. A single COM class might implement several interfaces. In fact, a full-blown Microsoft ActiveX control implements more than a dozen COM interfaces.

As in the abstract base class example, the easiest way to attach the interfaces to a concrete class is to use multiple inheritance of the interfaces you want to implement. (This isn't the only way to wire up a COM class—we'll look at other ways when we cover advanced interface composition techniques in Chapter 8.) The formula for implementing a COM class is to inherit a concrete C++ class from the interfaces you want to implement. Then just implement the union of all interface functions on your C++ class, like so:

```
// checker.h
#include "checkeri.h" // From IDL compiler
#include "checker_i.c" // From IDL compiler
class CSpellChecker : public ISpellChecker2,
                      public IPersistMFU {
    BSTR m_bstrText; // LPTEXTBLOB is defined elsewhere.
    DWORD m_dwRefCount;

public:
    CSpellChecker(BSTR bstr) {
        m_dwRefCount = 0;
        // Initialize.
    }
```

*(continued)*

```
    virtual ~CSpellChecker() {
        // Tear down.
    }

    // From IUnknown
    ULONG AddRef () {
        return ++m_dwRefCount;
    }

    // From IUnknown
    ULONG Release () {
        m_dwRefCount--;
        if (m_dwRefCount == 0) {
            delete this;
            return 0;
        }
        return m_dwRefCount;
    }

    HRESULT QueryInterface(REFIID riid, void** ppv) {
        if (riid == IID_ISpellChecker) {
            *ppv = static_cast<ISpellChecker*>(this);
        } else if (riid == IID_ISpellChecker2) {
            *ppv = static_cast<ISpellChecker*>(this);
        } else if (riid == IID_IPersist) {
            *ppv = static_cast<*PersistMFU*>(this);
        } else if (riid == IID_IUnknown) {
            *ppv = static_cast<ISpellChecker*>(this);
        } else {
            *ppv = 0;
            return E_NOINTERFACE;
        }
        if (*ppv) {
            (reinterpret_cast<IUnknown*>(*ppv))->AddRef();
            return NOERROR;
        }
    }
    HRESULT CheckIt() {
        // Do what it takes.
    }
    HRESULT GetSynonyms(BSTR bstrWord, BSTR* pbstrSynonyms) {
        // Generate synonyms.
    }
    HRESULT PersistMFUWords(BSTR bstrFileName) {
        // Save the most frequently used words to
        //  a file denoted by pszFileName.
    }
};
```

This class is strikingly similar to the abstract base class. The only real change is that the interface function signatures return HRESULTs (so you can remote the interface if you choose to), and the name of the function for retrieving more interfaces is *QueryInterface*.

So far, you've seen how to implement COM classes using C++. Remember that the main precept in COM is the separation of the interface from its implementation. Once you understand that, your class is almost ready to participate in the COM infrastructure. For the spelling-checker object to work in the real world, it needs two more things: a class object and a server.

## Class Objects

COM classes are always paired with class objects. (This is a requirement for playing in the COM game.) Class objects are COM objects—they implement interfaces, as do all other COM classes. However, they have a special place inside the COM architecture.

You can think of a class object as a meta-class for your COM class. It's a singleton-type COM class that is paired with the real COM class. For example, imagine a COM server with three COM classes in it. That server would also contain three class objects—one for each kind of COM class in the server. COM class objects generally serve two purposes. First, COM class objects are usually responsible for activating the classes to which they're paired. They almost always accomplish this by implementing an interface named *IClassFactory*. Clients ultimately end up using the *IClassFactory* interface to create instances of COM classes.

The second purpose of COM class objects is to serve as the static data area for a COM class. The nature of the class object is that it is global and static. A COM class object's lifetime begins at the same time as the server's lifetime. A class object's life extends beyond the life of the COM object it represents. This longevity makes the class object the ideal place to store static data or implement a static interface (similar to the static modifier in C++).

Here's the definition of *IClassFactory*:

```
Struct IClassFactory : public IUnknown {
    HRESULT CreateInstance(IUnknown* pUnkOuter,
                           REFIID riid,
                           void** ppv);
    HRESULT LockServer(BOOL bLock);
};
```

The key function to notice within *IClassFactory* is the *CreateInstance* function. Notice how closely *CreateInstance* resembles *QueryInterface*—there's a GUID to identify the interface and a place to put the interface pointer. The first parameter to *CreateInstance* is called the *controlling unknown* used for COM aggregation. Don't worry about it now. We'll take a closer look at it when we look at COM identity and composing COM classes using ATL in Chapter 8. Here's an example of a class object for the spelling-checker object. This class object implements the *IClassFactory* interface.

```
class CSpellCheckerClassObject : public IClassFactory {
public:
    CSpellCheckerClassObject(LPTEXTBLOB lpText) {
    }

    // From IUnknown
    ULONG AddRef () {
        return 2;
    }

    // From IUnknown
    ULONG Release () {
        return 1;
    }

    HRESULT QueryInterface(REFIID riid, void** ppv) {
        if (riid == IID_IClassFactory) {
            *ppv = static_cast<IClassFactory*>(this);
        } else if (riid == IID_IUnknown) {
            *ppv = static_cast<ISpellChecker*>(this);
        } else {
            *ppv = 0;
            return E_NOINTERFACE;
        }
        if (*ppv) {
            (reinterpret_cast<IUnknown*>(*ppv))->AddRef();
            return NOERROR;
        }
    }
    HRESULT CreateInstance(IUnknown* pUnkOuter,
                           REFIID riid, void** ppv){
        *ppv = NULL;
        CSpellChecker* pSpellChecker = NULL;
        pSpellChecker = new CSpellChecker;
        if (!pSpellChecker)
            return E_NOMEMORY;

        pSpellChecker.AddRef();
        HRESULT hr = pSpellChecker.QueryInterface(riid, ppv);
        pSpellChecker.Release();
        return hr;
    }
```

```
    HRESULT LockServer(BOOL b) {
        // Depending on the parameter b, place or remove a lock on
        //  the server.
    }
};
```

This class object is just like the other COM classes we've seen except for the way reference counting is done. COM class objects are usually global to the server as opposed to being created on the heap. This means that a class object doesn't need to worry about deleting itself—it will go away when the server goes away.

So far, we've looked at how COM separates interfaces from their implementations and at how to attach a COM interface to a COM implementation (a COM class). We've also seen a COM class object—the instance-less area of a COM class. Our next stop is COM servers, where you'll find out how to house COM classes inside real code modules.

## COM Servers

COM objects obviously need to live somewhere—they live inside COM servers. One of the key features of COM is that it supports two fundamental localities:

- A lightweight in-process model (DLLs where the client and the object share the same address space)

- An out-of-process model (EXEs where the client and the object live in different process spaces)

Another key feature of COM is that clients call in-process objects as easily as they call remote objects. The remoting layer is well defined and completely invisible to the client. What's more, the same object code can live in either an in-process server or an out-of-process server. Because the differences necessary for supporting different localities are easily isolated, you can use the same source code to write in-process and out-of-process objects.

## The Client Side

Let's first look at COM servers from the client side. The client side is easy. Remember that COM is a binary object model. Instead of calling the *new* operator to create objects (as you do in C++), you call an API for activating objects, which COM supports.

Before calling any COM functions, a thread needs to call *CoInitialize* to load the COM infrastructure (and to enter an apartment, as we'll see in a moment). Once a thread calls *CoInitialize*, the thread is free to call COM APIs, including the activation APIs we're about to look at.

The first way to create COM objects is to retrieve the class object, ask for the *IClassFactory* interface, and call *CreateInstance* from the *IClassFactory* interface. Here's the prototype for *CoGetClassObject*:

```
HRESULT CoGetClassObject(REFCLSID rclsid, DWORD dwClsCtx,
                         COSERVERINFO *pcsi,
                         REFIID riid, void **ppvClsObj);
```

The first parameter for *CoGetClassObject* is the GUID of the implementation you're looking for. The second parameter represents the locality of the server. The locality is represented by some bitwise flags that can be any of the following values OR'd together: CLSCTX_INPROC_SERVER, CLSCTX_INPROC_HANDLER, CLSCTX_LOCAL_SERVER, CLSCTX_REMOTE_SERVER, CLSCTX_ALL, and CLSCTX_SERVER. The third parameter is a structure containing the name of the remote machine (if applicable) and authorization information. Finally, the last two parameters are the *QueryInterface* signature— a GUID naming an interface and a place to put the interface pointer. When clients want to talk to the class object, they usually (but not always) ask for the *IClassFactory* interface.

Here's how to use *CoGetClassObject*:

```
void CreateSpellChecker() {
    IClassFactory* pCF = NULL;
    IUnknown* pUnk = NULL;

    CoGetClassObject(CLSID_CoSpellChecker, CLSCTX_ALL, 0,
                     IID_IClassFactory, (void**)&pCF);
    if (pCF) {
        pCF->CreateInstance(NULL, IID_IUnknown, (void**)&pUnk);
        pCF->Release();
    }
    if (pUnk) {
        // Do stuff with the interface pointer and then release it.
        pUnk->Release();
    }
}
```

Using *CoGetClassObject* is the most flexible way to activate objects. Once you get the class object, you can request any interface you want (not just *IClassFactory*). That way, you can use other interfaces to activate the actual object. The downside of using *CoGetClassObject* is that it takes more than one round-trip to activate the object. If you want to create several instances of the spelling-checker object, the performance will be better if you get the class object once and then ask the class object to manufacture multiple objects for you.

COM provides a shortcut for activating objects—*CoCreateInstance*. *CoCreateInstance* wraps the calls to *CoGetClassObject* and *IClassFactory:: CreateInstance*. Here's the prototype for *CoCreateInstance*:

```
HRESULT CoCreateInstance(REFCLSID rclsid,
                         IUnknown *pUnkOuter,
                         DWORD dwClsCtx,
                         REFIID riid,
                         void **ppvObj);
```

As with *CoGetClassObject*, the first parameter for *CoCreateInstance* is the GUID of the implementation you're looking for. The second parameter is the controlling unknown used for aggregation. The third parameter represents the locality requested by the client. Finally, the fourth and fifth parameters are the *Query-Interface* signature (a GUID representing the requested interface and a place to put the interface pointer).

Here's how you create the spelling-checker object using *CoCreateInstance*:

```
void CreateSpellChecker() {
    IUnknown* pUnk = NULL;

    CoCreateInstance(CLSID_CoSpellChecker, NULL, CLSCTX_ALL,
                     IID_IClassFactory, (void**)&pUnk);
    if (pUnk) {
        // Do stuff with the interface pointer and then release it.
        pUnk->Release();
    }
}
```

This means of activating objects is less flexible because it creates only a single object. However, it takes only one round-trip to create the object. If you want to create several instances of the spelling-checker object, the performance will languish.

So just what happens behind *CoGetClassObject* and *CoCreateInstance*? These two functions are responsible for locating and activating the servers the client requests. They work somewhat differently depending on the locality of the server requested, but the client doesn't care.

Now let's take a closer look at how COM servers work.

## The Server Side: DLLs

A COM server is simply a code module that houses a COM class and its class object. Again, COM servers come in two flavors: DLLs and EXEs. Although the actual code for the COM classes doesn't vary much, the code for the server will vary depending on whether it's a DLL or an EXE. Let's start with DLL servers.

Four exported functions distinguish a COM DLL from a normal, everyday DLL: *DllGetClassObject, DllCanUnloadNow, DllRegisterServer*, and *DllUnregisterServer*. Of these four functions, only *DllGetClassObject* is absolutely required. If you want to be a good COM citizen when you write servers, however, you'll implement all of them. (Your ATL-based COM servers will implement all these functions.)

When a client calls *CoGetClassObject* using the GUID that identifies your object, the service control manager (SCM) searches the Registry for that GUID. COM looks under the Registry key HKCR (HKEY_CLASSES_ROOT) for the CLSID (short for class ID) key. The CLSID key contains all the COM classes registered on the machine. This key is just a list of GUIDs. If the GUID representing the spelling-checker class is listed and the GUID has a subkey named *InProcServer32* that contains a value that points to a DLL, COM assumes that is the DLL containing the implementation. The SCM loads the DLL and looks for a distinguished entry point named *DllGetClassObject*. Here's the signature for *DllGetClassObject*:

```
HRESULT DllGetClassObject(REFCLSID rclsid,
                          REFIID riid,
                          void **ppv);
```

The SCM simply forwards the CLSID and the interface ID (IID) requested by the client and the pointer to the interfaces. It's the DLL's responsibility to provide an interface to the class object if the requested class object and interface are available. Here's how you might implement *DllGetClassObject* for the spelling-checker object:

```
// Source code for the server

CSpellCheckerClassObject spellCheckerCO; // Global class object
                                         // is always available.

STDAPI DllGetClassObject(REFCLSID rclsid, REFIID riid, void** ppv) {
    if (rclsid == CLSID_CoSpellChecker)
        return spellCheckerCO.QueryInterface(riid, ppv);
    else
        return CLASS_E_CLASSNOTAVAILABLE;
}
```

Notice that the spelling-checker object is a global variable in the DLL source code. This is fine because it suits the purpose of the class object—to be the static area of a COM class. When the SCM calls into *DllGetClassObject*, *DllGetClassObject* rips through the list of available COM classes (there's only one in this case) and queries it for the interface the client requested.

The other issue to tackle with the COM DLL is the issue of lifetime management. When you've got a client process space that's loaded with DLLs, that client will often want to remove DLLs when they're no longer needed. The Win32 API includes a function named *FreeLibrary* that complements the call to *LoadLibrary* used to load the COM DLL into the client's process space. Keep in mind, however, that a COM DLL might be serving multiple objects simultaneously. It would be very rude (and would crash the system) to remove a DLL via *FreeLibrary* while the DLL is still in use. For this reason, COM has a specific unloading scheme for its DLLs. That's where the second distinguished entry point, *DllCanUnloadNow*, comes in.

COM DLLs usually maintain a global reference count on themselves. This count goes up in three cases:

■ When the DLL hands out a reference to a class object

■ When the DLL hands out a reference to an object

■ When the client calls *IClassFactory::LockServer*, passing in a value of TRUE

The count goes down in three cases:

■ When the client releases a reference to a class object

■ When the client releases the last interface pointer to an object

■ When the client calls *IClassFactory::LockServer*, passing in a value of FALSE

*DllCanUnloadNow* examines this global reference count and returns S_OK if the reference count is 0 (the DLL is not serving any objects) or returns S_FALSE if the reference count is nonzero.

The system calls *DllCanUnloadNow* whenever a client calls the COM API function *CoFreeUnusedLibraries*. *CoFreeUnusedLibraries* goes to each DLL that's loaded and asks the DLL if it can unload by calling into *DllCanUnload-Now*. If the DLL can unload, the system frees the library.

The last two functions that distinguish a COM DLL from a regular DLL are *DllRegisterServer* and *DllUnregisterServer*. By implementing these two functions, you turn your DLL into a self-registering DLL. "Self-registering" means that the DLL is responsible for putting the required interfaces into the Registry. So far, the only entry we've seen is the HKCR\CLSID\{Some Guid}\InProcServer32 key. We'll see others as we move further into ATL.

*DllRegisterServer* and *DllUnregisterServer* are usually called by installation programs. *DllRegisterServer* and *DllUnregisterServer* exercise the Win32 Registry API to insert and remove Registry entries.

### The Server Side: EXEs

COM objects residing within EXEs are activated in a slightly different way than are COM objects residing within DLLs. Let's take a look at how COM EXE servers work under the hood.

Again, the client activates COM objects residing within EXEs in the same way it activates COM objects residing within DLLs. The client just calls *CoGet-ClassObject* or *CoCreateInstance*. When the SCM looks for the EXE version of the server, however, the SCM searches the Registry for the LocalServer32 key under the requested CLSID. When the SCM finds the path to the server, the SCM launches the server. The first task the server performs once it's launched is to register the class objects with the SCM by calling the Win32 API *CoRegister-ClassObjects*. This run-time registration makes the class objects available to the SCM so that the SCM can hand interfaces to class objects over to the client. Then the client uses the class object to activate the real object (or whatever). Once the EXE server has registered its class objects with the SCM, the server spins a message pump until it receives a WM_QUIT message.

As with DLL servers, EXE servers must manage their own lifetimes. The main difference between DLL lifetimes and EXE lifetimes is that the server gets a lock on an EXE lifetime by calling *CoRegisterClassObject*. This call is equivalent to the DLL putting a lock on the server every time a reference to a class object is made. Remember that the SCM is going to hold on to the class object. Otherwise, the server increments its reference count every time it hands out an interface pointer.

Unlike DLL servers, which need to be unloaded from the outside, EXE servers are responsible for removing themselves when they are no longer needed. EXE servers self-delete by posting a WM_QUIT message to themselves at the appropriate time (when the server reference count drops to 0). This message causes the EXE server to fall out of the message pump, revoke its class objects, and clear out.

Here's the infrastructure of an EXE server:

```
// EXE server
CSpellCheckerClassObject spellCheckerCO;
//  Global; class object is always available.

int WINAPI WinMain(HINSTANCE, HINSTANCE, LPSTR, int) {
    DWORD dwSpellChecker;
    CoInitialize(0);  // Join the main single-threaded apartment.
```

```
CoRegisterClassObject(CLSID_CoSpellChecker, & spellCheckerCO,
                      CLSCTX_LOCAL_SERVER,
                      REGCLS_MULTIPLEUSE, &dwQuux);
MSG msg; // Allow a single-threaded apartment to dispatch calls.
while (GetMessage(&msg, 0, 0, 0))
    DispatchMessage(&msg);
CoRevokeClassObject(dwSpellChecker);
CoUninitialize();
return 0;
}
```

Notice how the thread first calls *CoInitialize*, registers the spelling checker's class object, and then runs the message loop. Before the server ends, it revokes the class object registration from the SCM by calling *CoRevokeClassObject*.

Finally, EXE servers are responsible for publishing the correct entries in the Registry. They do this by looking for /RegServer on the command line when they run. If an EXE server detects the /RegServer switch on the command line, the EXE server just plugs the proper entries in the Registry and leaves—the server doesn't run a message pump or engage in any other activity.

The final issue we'll explore is how COM handles threading and remote communication.

## Apartments

COM is all about allowing as many different kinds of developers as possible to share software. This goal is no small feat, given the variety of development tools and environments in use. For example, it's perfectly reasonable to expect a Visual Basic program to use components written in C++, and vice versa. That kind of sharing is already a done deal because Visual Basic provides a mapping between the Visual Basic language and COM interfaces. Some other issues come into play, however, when developers using other development languages want to share software. One of those issues is thread safety, or making sure data and objects don't get messed up when accessed by multiple threads.

**NOTE**  The information we cover here is relevant to Windows NT 4.0. The apartment story changes a bit in Windows 2000, in which contexts handle most of the threading issues.

Consider all the different kinds of developers out there. Some technophiles are very concerned with writing threads and are used to dealing with the issues involved in running concurrent threads of execution. To them, a responsive interface might be a software requirement, in which case threads are extremely useful. Other developers don't want to deal with threads and their related issues. For many, worrying about that stuff is a waste of clock cycles. What if the second kind of software developer starts writing components that the first kind of software developer decides he or she wants to use? Chaos will likely ensue because the components are probably not thread-safe.

## COM and Threads

Recall that one of the major issues that arises with multithreaded applications is concurrent data access. When two threads of execution have access to the same piece of data, you have to pretend that the two threads are touching the data at the same time. (In fact, the two threads might actually be running concurrently on a multiprocessor machine.) This problem also occurs when multiple threads can access a single COM object.

Now imagine you're a developer who lives for multithreading. When your latest issue of *Windows Tech Journal* comes in the mail, you open it to page 42. Staring you in the face is an advertisement for a COM-based component (perhaps an ActiveX control) that solves a sticky problem you've been having. Because you're COM savvy, you know that this component is a black box. You're not supposed to know any of its implementation details (such as whether it's thread-safe).

Let's say that for some reason you want to use this component from two threads at the same time. Because of the black box nature of the component, however, you have no idea whether it's safe to have two threads access the COM object at the same time. For example, the component might contain some global data that must be preserved between method calls. If the component hasn't taken appropriate precautions (that is, used critical sections to control access to the data), that data could be easily corrupted if a thread manipulating the object was preempted. Does this possibility mean that you have to throw your hands up and write your own guaranteed-to-be-thread-safe version of the component?

Thankfully, the answer is "no." COM provides some built-in facilities for restricting or allowing concurrent access to components. That facility is a set of abstractions collectively known as COM's *threading models*. These abstractions are sometimes referred to as *apartment* models, and we'll get to them in a moment.

Just as COM clients don't have to understand what kind of language or what kind of tool a certain component uses, COM protects client code from having to know anything about whether a component is thread-safe. COM does this by placing components into apartments. In some cases, COM lets multiple threads access the object (the object had better be thread-safe), and in other cases, COM lets objects be touched by one and only one thread (the object doesn't need to be thread-safe). In either case, the client doesn't need to concern itself with those details—it's the component developer who decides whether to make the class thread-safe. If the object isn't thread-safe, COM will protect the object from concurrent access.

## Just What Is an Apartment?

Apartments are strange when you first encounter them because they are basically abstractions. Apartments don't have handles (as windows do), and the only apartment-related API calls are *CoInitialize*, *CoUninitialize*, *CoInitializeEx*, *OleInitialize*, and *OleUninitialize*. Despite some of their odd characteristics, however, COM apartments are fundamental to COM remoting, and you need to understand them if you hope to understand COM remoting. Keep these two points in mind as you think about apartments:

- Threads live in apartments.

- Objects live in apartments. Sometimes an object shares the same apartment as the thread that created it, and sometimes an object lives in a different apartment than the thread that created it.

COM currently defines two kinds of apartments: a *single-threaded apartment* (often abbreviated STA) and a *multithreaded apartment* (often abbreviated MTA). The names are pretty self-explanatory. A single-threaded apartment houses a single thread, and a multithreaded apartment houses multiple threads. A single process has at most one MTA, but it might have many STAs.

## Moving into an Apartment

A thread moves into an apartment by calling one of three COM API functions: *CoInitialize*, *CoInitializeEx*, and *OleInitialize*. Calling *CoInitialize* or *Ole-Initialize* moves the thread into a new STA. *CoInitializeEx* gives you the option of moving your thread into the multithreaded apartment by passing COINIT_APARTMENTTHREADED as the second parameter. Calling the corresponding revoke function (*CoUninitialize* or *OleUninitialize*) causes a thread to leave an apartment. Calling one of these initialization functions (such as *CoInitialize*) in a thread is required before calling any COM-related APIs or object method calls.

## Interface Pointers and Apartments

So, calling one of the initialization functions causes a thread to move into an apartment. But how do apartments relate to objects and interfaces? When you call a COM API function or a method on an interface to an object, the thread that invoked the API call or method determines the apartment to which the resulting interface pointer belongs. If the call returns a pointer to the actual object, the object itself resides in the calling thread's apartment. You'll see an example of this arrangement if you call *CoCreateInstance* to create an in-process object. The interface pointer you get back is in the same process space as your client because the object lives in a DLL.

In other cases, the object can't reside in the caller's apartment for various reasons. The obvious reason is that the object might already exist in a different process or host machine. In this case, the object has to live in another apartment (because the server is in a whole other process space). Another reason is that the object's concurrency requirements are incompatible with the client's apartment (as indicated by some Registry settings we'll see shortly), in which case the client will depend on operating system support to synchronize calls into an object. In these cases, the client receives a pointer to a proxy instead of the real object. This proxy pattern is the basis of the COM remoting architecture.

## COM Remoting

When a calling thread needs to live in a different apartment from the object, COM needs some mechanism for allowing interfaces to be exported from one apartment (making internal interfaces visible outside a certain apartment) and imported into another (making external interfaces visible inside an apartment). When client code imports an interface, the client talks to a pointer to a proxy. The proxy looks, tastes, and feels like the interface pointer the client expects. Rather than implementing the actual functionality of the object, however, the proxy is managing some sort of cross-apartment communication mechanism. Another part of the proxy's job is to ensure that all method calls execute in the correct apartment. This process is called *remoting*.

## Marshaling

If you've worked with COM for more than a few weeks, you've probably come across the term *marshaling*. Marshaling refers to the technique for passing data—often data that includes function parameters—across apartment boundaries. Although the remoting layer has to get well-defined data structures across apartment boundaries, the more interesting case is marshaling interface pointers. Marshaling an interface pointer simply means writing enough information into a byte stream to uniquely identify the object and its owning apartment. For example, this information might include the machine's network address and some other information, such as the thread ID. This byte stream allows any apartment to import the interface pointer and make method calls on the object.

Interface pointers are normally marshaled silently as COM performs its magic. The marshaling all happens under the hood, and you don't even know what's happening when programming at higher levels. Most of the work involved in marshaling interface pointers happens within the two main marshaling APIs: *CoMarshalInterface* and *CoUnmarshalInterface*.

*CoMarshalInterface* exports a COM interface from an apartment by writing the information necessary to establish a connection to a byte stream represented by COM's *IStream* interface. *CoUnmarshalInterface* reads the information out of the byte stream and sets up the connection between the client thread and the object. Although *CoMarshalInterface* and *CoUnmarshalInterface* are usually called silently by the remoting layer, you might want to call these functions manually from time to time, say, if you want to share interface pointers between two threads in different apartments.

## The Default Protocol: COM ORPC

Once a client thread connects to a COM object in another apartment, COM uses the COM Object Remote Procedure Call (ORPC) communications protocol by default for remoting. COM ORPC is layered over MS-RPC, a DCE derivative. Because MS-RPC is a protocol-independent communications mechanism, you can easily extend it to support new transport protocols (via dynamically loadable transport DLLs). COM is smart enough to use the most efficient transport protocol available based on the proximity and types of the importing and exporting apartments. For example, COM favors the User Datagram Protocol (UDP) when communicating off-host (although most common network protocols are also supported). COM uses one of several other transports optimized for a particular apartment type when communicating locally. The key is that the remoting mechanism is sufficiently abstract and indirect that the actual communication mechanism can be substituted on the fly.

## Apartments, DLLs, and the Apartment Registry Entries

Because the reason for all this apartment business is to allow the client to remain ignorant about the goings-on inside an object, it's your job as an object implementor to decide the kind of apartment in which you want your object to execute. If you're writing an out-of-process server, you choose your apartment type explicitly by calling *CoInitializeEx* with the appropriate second parameter. The story for in-process servers is a bit different. In the in-process case, the client will have already called *CoInitializeEx* by the time the object is created. Because in-process objects don't have the opportunity to state their apartment preference at run time, COM uses the Registry to mark apartment types. COM allows the in-process server subkey under the CLSID key to have its own distinct threading model that is advertised in the local Registry using the *ThreadingModel* named value, as shown in Figure 2-1.

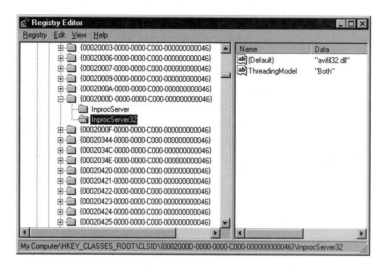

**Figure 2-1**
*The object's apartment preference stored in the Registry*

COM currently allows four possible threading models for a CLSID:

- ThreadingModel="Both" indicates that instances of the class can execute in either an MTA or an STA.

- ThreadingModel="Free" indicates that instances of the class can execute only in an MTA.

- ThreadingModel="Apartment" indicates that instances of the class can execute only in an STA.

- ThreadingModel="Absent" implies that instances of the class can run only in the main STA or the first STA initialized in the process.

The most efficient scenario is that the client's apartment is compatible with the CLSID's threading model. In this case, in-process activation requests for that CLSID will instantiate the object directly in the apartment of the client. This procedure is efficient because the remoting layer isn't used (that is, no intermediate proxy is created).

Things slow down if the client's apartment is incompatible with the CLSID's threading model. Even though an activation request might be in-process, the value associated with the CLSID might force COM to silently instantiate the object in a separate apartment, in which case the client gets back a pointer to the proxy instead of a pointer to the real object.

When an STA-based client activates a class marked as "Free," the class object and subsequent instances of the class execute in the MTA. When an MTA-based client activates a class marked "Apartment," COM creates a new STA in which the class object and subsequent instances of the class can execute. Whenever either type of client activates a class without a threading model named value (implicitly marked as a main STA-based class), the class object and subsequent instances of the class execute in the process's main STA. If the thread that activated the object is the main STA thread, the object will be accessed directly. Otherwise, the client accesses a proxy. If no STAs exist in the process (that is, if no threads have called *CoInitializeEx* with the COINIT_APARTMENT-THREADED flag), COM will create a new STA to act as the main STA for the process.

### What the Models Mean to the COM Developer

If you don't want to bother with threading issues (such as the data contention that can happen if multiple threads access your apartment), you can leave the threading model value blank. If you leave it blank, the DLL will be accessed only from the main STA.

By marking a class as apartment threaded, you're telling COM that only one thread can access instances of the class for the lifetime of the object. In this case, you don't need to protect instance data—only data shared by multiple instances of the class (that is, static class data and data global to the DLL). By marking a class as either "Free" or "Both," you're telling COM that instances of the class can run in the MTA. Be careful here—a single instance of the class can be accessed concurrently. In this case, you need to protect all data used by a single instance from concurrent access. In addition to protecting shared data as you would for classes marked as apartment threaded (static class data and global DLL data), you also need to protect instance data members. For example, dynamic objects that live and die by their reference counts need to implement *AddRef* and *Release* by calling *InterlockedIncrement* and *InterlockedDecrement*.

### The Whole Picture

That's basically the story behind COM's apartment threading models. From a developer's standpoint, it's really just about deciding how to handle concurrent access to your object. But don't minimize the importance of understanding apartments; if you really understand apartments, you'll have a much deeper knowledge of the inner workings of COM—especially the remoting aspect. Figure 2-2 illustrates the whole picture of how COM manages threads and apartments.

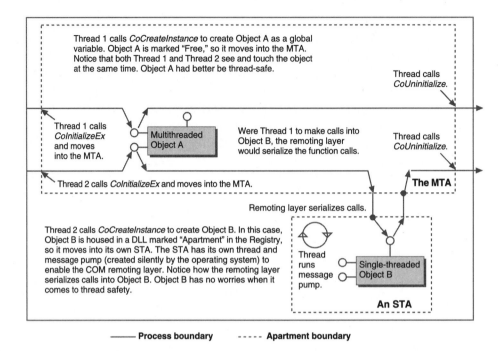

**Figure 2-2**
*Threads creating COM objects in different apartments*

# Conclusion

So there you have it—the basic atoms of COM. These are the fundamental concepts to understand in COM:

- The separation of interface and implementation
- COM classes (attaching interfaces to code that actually does the work)
- Class objects (static, instance-less areas for COM classes)
- COM DLL and EXE servers
- COM apartments

With the exception of COM's apartment and remoting support, everything in COM is really just a matter of exercising some discipline. C++ programmers have always had the option of separating the implementations from their interfaces. Most of us were brainwashed into accepting the mantra of implementation inheritance. Not that implementation inheritance is bad in itself—it can be very useful within certain contexts. It's just that when you take advantage of implementation inheritance you implicitly couple base classes with their derived classes. Interface-based programming lends itself to a different kind of software philosophy—here software parts exist as real decoupled components.

As you examine ATL throughout the rest of this book, keep in mind that ATL is doing exactly what we covered in this chapter—even though here we've given you only an overview of the most important parts of COM. We'll uncover more nuances of COM (such as identity and threading issues) as we dig through ATL.

## CHAPTER THREE

# C++ Templates

After reading Chapter 2, you should have a pretty firm grasp of COM, and you should be sold on its benefits (we hope). Recall that COM is really just Microsoft's brand of interface-based programming. The primary distinction between interface-based programming and class-based programming (the kind C++ programmers have been doing for the last decade) is that in interface-based programming a class's implementation is separated from its interface.

One downside of COM is that getting a COM class up and running requires substantial amounts of boilerplate code. To write a COM class, you need to perform the following tasks:

- Write the COM class, implementing *IUnknown* correctly.
- Add *IDispatch* (or a dual interface) if the object is to be available to a scripting environment.
- Write a class object (which implements *IClassFactory* in most cases).
- Add a reference-counting mechanism to the server.
- Add self-registration code to the server.
- Add the correct entry points if the server is a DLL: *DllGetClassObject*, *DllCanUnloadNow*, *DllRegisterServer*, and *DllUnregisterServer*.
- Add calls to *CoRegisterClassObject* if the server is an EXE.

As you can see, just as writing a regular Win32 SDK–type application requires reams of infrastructure code, so does writing a COM DLL or EXE involve a huge amount of infrastructure code that stays mostly the same from one COM class to another.

Code reuse has been the mantra of programmers since time began. Why should we have to retype lots of code for lots of different classes when most of the code is going to be the same in every class? With C++ templates, we don't have to.

Developers are always looking for ways to reduce the amount of typing they need to do. C and C++ developers have been using preprocessor macros to abstract and generalize code for years. If you write a macro, the preprocessor simply substitutes the code the macro defines whenever the macro is used in the code. Macros basically save you a whole bunch of typing. The biggest problem with macros is that they are often difficult to get right and to debug. C++ templates are like macros in that they also facilitate abstracting and generalizing C++ code. However, templates are C++ language–specific and are handled by the compiler (rather than the preprocessor) and so are type-safe.

In this chapter, we'll cover the philosophy behind C++ templates and explain how to use them. This information is important for you to know because Microsoft Active Template Library (ATL) is based heavily on C++ templates.

# When Inheritance Isn't Enough

The invention of the C++ class has been a great boon for developers. Using C++ and the notion of a class, we can model the world as classes; that is, we can factor functionality into layers and achieve a reasonable amount of code reuse. For example, some classes will have a lot of the same functionality. C++ lets you factor that functionality into some base classes.

The canonical example is to model certain kinds of animals using C++ classes, such as dog and cat classes. The seasoned C++ developer will naturally create a hierarchy of classes. In the classic animal examples, the most basic functionality might be implemented in a base class named *CAnimal*:

```
class CAnimal {
public:
    CAnimal() {
    }
    ~CAnimal() {
    }
    void Eat();
    void Sleep();
    CAnimal* Procreate();
};

class CMammal : public CAnimal {
    HAIRFOLLICLES m_hair[1000000];
public:
    CMammal() {
    }
    ~CMammal() {
    }
```

```
    void ProduceMilk();
};

class CCat: public CMammal {
public:
    CCat() {
    }
    virtual ~CCat();
    virtual void MakeNoise() {
        // "Meow"
    }
};

class CDog : public CMammal {
public:
    CDog() {
    }
    virtual ~CDog();
    virtual void MakeNoise() {
        // "Woof"
    }
};
```

The power of C++ comes from the fact that you don't have to type the source code for common functions over and over again. Instead, you override the behavior of these functions only when necessary. Although the inheritance and encapsulation capability of C++ is very powerful, at times it isn't quite enough. In some situations, inheritance might even be inappropriate.

Inheritance implies an "is a" relationship between two classes. For example, deriving the *CDog* class from the *CMammal* class implies that a dog "is a" mammal. That approach works great for such broad generalizations. However, sometimes we'd like to generalize about a "has a" relationship between two classes. For example, a dog has certain body organs, such as a heart, lungs, a stomach, and so on. It wouldn't make sense to derive a *CDog* class from these parts. But it would make sense to say a dog is composed of these parts. Furthermore, a dog isn't composed of just any old body parts, but of dog body parts. Templates give you a way to generalize the "has a" relationships between your classes. When inheritance and encapsulation won't solve your problems for one reason or another, you can turn to C++ templates.

Like C++ inheritance, C++ templates represent a way to abstract and generalize C++ code. To illustrate the use of C++ templates, we'll look at an all-too-common example—what happens when you write a really great class and debug it thoroughly, only to find out that your pointy-haired boss says you need to change it so that it works on a new kind of data.

## A Canonical Template Example

In writing this book, we discovered that federal law requires us to provide this example when talking about C++ templates. Maybe that claim is stretching the truth a bit, but the following example does express the letter and the spirit behind C++ templates.

Imagine that you are required to write some code that represents a self-managing array of integers. Let's say that the array is a C++ class with a data member representing the array of integers and member functions that let you add and remove elements. All the code for allocating, reallocating, and destroying the array is encapsulated inside the class. The class will look something like this:

```
class DynIntArray {
public:
    DynIntArray();   // Allocates memory
    ~DynIntArray(); // Cleans up and does memory management
    int Add(int n); // Adds an element and does
                    //  memory management
    void Remove(int nIndex) // Removes an element and
                            //  does memory management
    int GetAt(nIndex) const;
    int GetSize();
private:
    int* m_pIntArray;
    int m_nArraysize;
};
```

If you've been programming for a while, you've undoubtedly written a class that resembles this one. Why should you write *malloc* and *free* statements all over the place to resize the array when you can easily package all that stuff into a C++ class? C++ lets you encapsulate these operations and hide them from the client.

So let's say you've spent a considerable amount of time debugging this class and perfecting it. Just as you're adding the finishing touches, your clueless boss comes in and says he needs you to write the class so that it represents an array of floating numbers. Should you be alarmed? Just what is the difference between the class you wrote to manage integers and the class you need to write to manage an array of floating point numbers? The answers to these questions are, respectively, "No" and "Very little." The only difference between the two classes is the type of data being managed.

Your first reaction to needing to retool the class might be simply to take the class you wrote for integers and use editor inheritance to implement a dynamic array of floating numbers (that is, use copy and paste). A better way to transition the class, however, is to use C++ templates. C++ templates provide a way to generalize your code to work with many data types. The following code shows how you might use C++ templates to generalize the dynamic array to work with multiple data types:

```
template <typename T>
class DynArray {
public:
    DynArray();
    ~DynArray(); // Cleans up and does memory management
    int Add(T Element); // Adds an element and does
                        //  memory management
    void Remove(int nIndex) // Removes an element and
                            //  does memory management
    T GetAt(nIndex) const;
    int GetSize();
private:
    T* TArray;
    int m_nArraysize;
};
```

Templates look a bit weird at first glance. But you'll get used to them quickly once you understand the syntax. C++ template syntax involves using the keyword *template* before describing a data type. In the preceding example, notice that the keyword *template* appears before the *DynArray* class declaration. This keyword tells the compiler that whatever data type description follows uses the template. The second part of the template syntax uses angle braces, which indicate the template's parameters to the compiler.

The preceding example also illustrates generalizing the *DynArray* on the data type managed by the class. Notice that instead of hard-coding the int data type, the *DynArray* manages a data type represented by the capital letter *T*. (The template syntax doesn't require you to use the capital letter *T*—it's just tradition.) Here's how you would use the *DynArray* class:

```
void UseDynArray() {
    DynArray<int> intArray;
    DynArray<float> floatArray;

    intArray.Add(4);
    floatArray.Add(5.0);

    intArray.Remove(0);
    floatArray.Remove(0);

    int x = intArray.GetAt(0);
    float f = floatArray.GetAt(0);
}
```

Notice how using the *DynArray* involves instantiating instances of the *DynArray* based on a *type*. The client code isn't limited to using floating point numbers or integers. It can specify any simple data type, structure, or class and the *DynArray* will work just fine. In many ways, using templates in this way is like using macros and is virtually the same as writing a version of the *DynArray* for each data type the client needs to manage. The critical difference is that templates are type-safe. The preprocessor does a straight substitution when it sees a macro. Templates are a bit different from macros, however, because they have to go through the compiler and are subject to all the rigorous type checking the compiler imposes.

C++ templates can be applied to solve many programming problems, and they turn out to be especially useful when cranking out COM code. As we just saw, templates are useful for writing one piece of source code that works with any type of data. They're also handy for writing smart pointers, creating parameterized algorithms, and mixing functionality into your class. Let's examine these various uses, starting with pointers.

## "Dumb" Pointers

Consider a regular C++ pointer. The traditional C++ literature calls the pointers built into C++ "dumb" pointers. That name might not be very nice, but it does accurately describe them. Normal C++ pointers don't do much except point to things. The client is often responsible for seeing to such details as pointer initialization.

To illustrate the problems with dumb pointers, let's study the example shown here, which uses a C++ class to model a musician:

```
class CMusician {
protected:
    CMusician(){} // Never use a default constructor.
public:
    CMusician(char* szInstrument) {
        strcpy(m_szInstrument, szInstrument);
    }
    ~CMusician() {
        MessageBox(NULL,
            "Elvis has just left the building",
            NULL, MB_OK);
    }
    virtual void Play() {
        MessageBox(NULL, "Makin' music. Drums set up?",
                    m_szInstrument, MB_OK);
    }
```

```
    char m_szInstrument[256];
};
```

The musician objects are constructed using the name of the instrument each musician plays. (A more complete example would probably do more than simply label the musician as someone who plays a particular instrument.) Notice that the *CMusician* class has a function to play music—the *Play* function. Now imagine some client code that looks like this:

```
void UseMusician() {
    CMusician* pMusician;

    // You need to initialize the musician pointer at
    //  some time. But what if you forget to do it now,
    //  and then later do something like this:
    if (pMusician) {
        // Get ready for fireworks because pMusician is
        //  NOT NULL, but it points to some random data.
        pMusician->Play();
    }
}
```

In this case, the client code forgot to initialize the *pMusician* pointer to NULL. (Of course, this never happens in real life!) Because *pMusician* contains a non-NULL value (it's actually whatever value happened to be on the stack at the time), the test to make sure the pointer is valid succeeds (when in fact it should fail). The client gleefully proceeds, believing all is right in the world. At best, the client will experience unexpected results; at worst, the client will crash. The unpredictable consequences are possible because the client is "calling into darkness." (Who knows where *pMusician* is pointing—probably not to anything even resembling a musician.) Naturally, we'd like a mechanism for ensuring that pointers are initialized. We'll see one technique for making sure this happens—using "smart" pointers—in a moment.

Now imagine a second scenario. Perhaps you'd like to plug a little extra code into the musician class to perform an operation common to all musicians. For example, let's say you'd like all the musicians to help the drummer unload and set up his equipment before they begin playing. And maybe the musicians should also help the drummer clean up after the gig is over. Consider the musician example above. When the client calls the *Play* function, the musician starts playing before the drummer has set up properly, leaving the poor client unable to dance. What we'd like to do is add a generic hook to the musician class so that it can make sure the drummer is set up before the rest of the band begins to play.

The C++ solution to coping with these problems is called a *smart pointer*.

# Smart Pointers

A smart pointer is a C++ class for wrapping "dumb" pointers. By wrapping a pointer in a class (and specifically in a template), you can make sure certain mundane, boilerplate-type operations are taken care of automatically instead of deferred to the client. One good example of such an operation involves making sure pointers are initialized correctly so that embarrassing calls through randomly assigned pointers don't happen. Another is making sure certain initialization tasks are accomplished before function calls are made through a pointer.

## Inventing a Smart Pointer

Let's invent a smart pointer for the musician model described on the previous page. First we'll consider several types of musicians based on the *CMusician* class, as shown here:

```
class CGuitarist : public CMusician {
public:
    CGuitarist() : CMusician("Guitar") {}
    CGuitarist(char* szInstrument) :
        CMusician(szInstrument) {
    }
    void PlayLead() {
        MessageBox(NULL, "Play in a boring style",
                   "Joe Guitarist", MB_OK);
    }
};

class CDrummer : public CMusician {
public:
    CDrummer() : CMusician("Drums") {}
    CDrummer(char* szInstrument) :
        CMusician(szInstrument) {
    }
    void BangAway() {
        MessageBox(NULL, "Play in a boring style",
                   "Joe Drummer", MB_OK);
    }
};

class CVocalist : public CMusician {
public:
    CVocalist() : CMusician("Vocals") {}
    CVocalist(char* szInstrument) :
        CMusician(szInstrument) {
    }
    void Sing() {
```

```
        MessageBox(NULL, "Sing in a boring style",
                    "Joe Singer", MB_OK);
    }
};

class CBassist : public CMusician  {
public:
    CBassist(): CMusician("Bass") {}
    CBassist(char* szInstrument) :
        CMusician(szInstrument) {
    }
    void ThumpAway() {
        MessageBox(NULL, "Play in a boring style",
                    "Joe Bassist", MB_OK);
    }
};
```

Once you grasp the different musician types, consider a template-based class named *SmartMusician* that can wrap a musician object, as shown here:

```
template <class T>
class CSmartMusician {
    T* m_pT;
public:
    CSmartMusician(T& rT) {
        m_pT = &rT;
        HelpDrummerSetup();
    }
    ~CSmartMusician() {
        HelpDrummerCleanup();
    }
    void HelpDrummerCleanup() {
        MessageBox(NULL, "Helping drummer clean up",
                    NULL, MB_OK);
    }
    void HelpDrummerSetup() {
        MessageBox(NULL, "Carry them drums",
                    NULL, MB_OK);
    }
    CSmartMusician& operator=(const CSmartMusician& rMusician) {
        return *this;
    }
    T* operator->() const {
        MessageBox(NULL,
                    "Dereferencing pointer. Everyone happy?",
                    NULL, MB_OK);
        return m_pT;
    }
};
```

This *CSmartMusician* template class wraps a pointer of type *CMusician*. Because the *CSmartMusician* class is based on a template, the class can provide generic functionality regardless of the type of data associated with the class.

We want the smart pointer to handle all musicians, including guitarists, bass players, vocalists, and drummers. We accomplish this flexibility by placing the *template* *<class T>* statement right before declaring the class. The *CSmartMusician* template class includes a pointer to the type of musician for which the class will be defined. (The pointer is a data member named *m_pT*.) The *CSmartMusician*'s constructor takes a pointer to that type as a parameter and assigns the parameter to *m_pT*.

In addition to wrapping a pointer, the *CSmartMusician* class implements several operators. The most important one is the -> operator (the indirection operator). This operator is the workhorse of any smart pointer class, and overloading the pointer operator is what turns a regular class into a smart pointer class. Normally, using the pointer-based member-selection operator on a regular C++ dumb pointer tells the compiler to select a member belonging to the class or structure being pointed to. By implementing the pointer-based member-selection operator, you provide a way to hook into memory dereference operations and have some boilerplate code called every time the client calls a method. In the musicians example, the smart constructor makes sure the drummer's equipment is set up before the band begins playing. This example is contrived, though it does illustrate the point: in real life, you might want to put in some other kind of hook.

Adding the -> operator to the class causes the class to behave like the pointers built into C++. To act like native C++ pointers in other ways, smart pointer classes need to implement the other standard operators, such as the dereferencing and assignment operators.

## Using Smart Pointers

Using smart pointers is similar to using the regular built-in C++ pointers. To illustrate this similarity, let's check out this example of a client using the plain-vanilla musician classes:

```
void UseDumbMusicians() {
    MessageBox(NULL, "Not using smart pointers yet",
               NULL, MB_OK);

    CGuitarist guitarist("Guitar");
    CDrummer drummer("Drums");
    CBassist bass("Bass");
```

```
    guitarist.Play();
    drummer.Play();
    bass.Play();
}
```

No surprises here—executing this code causes the musicians simply to come in and play. Running this function causes three message boxes to be displayed, each indicating that a different musician is playing. The poor drummer doesn't get any help setting up his stuff. However, we want to use the smart musicians—the ones who help the drummer set up before playing. The following code wraps the musician objects in the smart pointer class:

```
void UseSmartMusician() {
    MessageBox(NULL, "Using smart pointers now...",
            NULL, MB_OK);

    CGuitarist guitarist("Guitar");
    CDrummer drummer("Drums");
    CBassist bass("Bass");

    CSmartMusician<CMusician> smartguitarist(guitarist);
    CSmartMusician<CMusician> smartdrummer(drummer);
    CSmartMusician<CMusician> smartbass(bass);

    smartguitarist->Play();
    smartdrummer->Play();
    smartbass->Play();
}
```

Instead of letting the musicians behave in their standard unhelpful way (as the previous example did), this example wraps the guitarist, bassist, and drummer objects using the smart pointer template. When the client asks the smart musicians to do the work, the smart musicians will automatically help the drummer set up before they begin to play.

This example illustrates one use for C++ templates—wrapping C++ classes so that certain generic setup and tear-down code executes. C++ also lets you override the -> operator as a hook to make sure everything is kosher before making function calls.

As it turns out, smart pointers aren't the only use for templates. You can also use templates to provide client code with an easy way to specialize the behavior of a class by passing in algorithms as template parameters. Let's see how.

# Parameterized Algorithms

If you use C++ templates to model musicians but don't use smart pointers, you'll find that the "coded" musicians behave like real-life musicians—the guitarist, the bass player, and the vocalist are off drinking beer while the drummer is left to carry in all his equipment and to set up before and clean up after the band plays. When modeled using smart pointers, the musicians put down their beers and help the drummer carry in his stuff, set it up, tear it down, and load it again when the band is done playing. Let's take templates a step further and see how to use them to let the client easily change the musicians' behavior; that is, let's use templates to parameterize algorithms performed by the musicians.

In real life, you have to sift through a number of issues when you're starting a band. For example, you'll need to audition prospective band members. In choosing musicians for the band, you'll need to consider all sorts of factors, including the style of each instrumentalist. For example, if you find a guitarist who's really flashy but not a solid rhythm guitarist, you'll need to weigh how that will affect the band's sound. In the example that follows, we'll use C++ templates to model a band that the client (the one putting together the band) can easily modify by applying different template parameters.

## Putting Together a Band

To begin, let's consider how the client might put together a band. One way to model a band is to write a template class that accepts types of musicians as template parameters. The *CRockBand* class would then have a public function to get the musicians to play together. The *CRockBand* class might look something like this:

```
template<class TGuitar, class TBass,
        class TDrums, class TVocals>
class CRockBand {
    TGuitar guitar;
    TBass bass;
    TVocals vocals;
    TDrums drums;
public:
    void PlayMusic(void) {
        guitar.PlayLead();
        bass.ThumpAway();
        drums.BangAway();
        vocals.Sing();
    }
};
```

The rock band class is pretty straightforward. It takes a drummer, a bass player, a vocalist, and a guitarist as template parameters. The *PlayMusic* function simply causes each musician to play his own instrument in his own particular style. The client might use the *CRockBand* class as shown here:

```
void ListenToRockBand() {
    CRockBand<CGuitarist, CBassist,
            CDrummer, CVocalist> NoName;

    MessageBox(NULL, "A non-name band is on",
            NULL, MB_OK);
    NoName.PlayMusic();
}
```

Notice in this example that the client pieces together the band using average Joe musicians off the street.[1] When you execute this function, four message boxes come up, each indicating that the four musicians are using their own boring styles. What if the client wants to move away from the boring and forge a rock band from more notable players? We want to give the client the option of forming that kind of band too. To provide the client with this option, we first need to define classes to represent some more interesting players.

## Finding World-Class Musicians

Let's start by inventing classes to represent some famous musicians. This class will derive ultimately from *CMusician* and will represent each player's style through the appropriate member function. The following code presents world-class musicians from the bands Rush and Van Halen:

```
class CEddieVanHalen : public CGuitarist {
public:
    CEddieVanHalen() :
        CGuitarist("Guitar") {
    }
    void PlayLead() {
        MessageBox(NULL,
                "Use hammer-ons",
                "Eddie Van Halen", MB_OK);
    }
};
```

*(continued)*

---

1. We use the term "Joe" the same way Mike Myers uses it in the movie *Wayne's World*—to indicate the mundane and the average.

```
class CGaryCherone : public CVocalist {
public:
    CGaryCherone() :
        CVocalist("Vocals") {
    }
    void Sing() {
        MessageBox(NULL,
                    "Sounds like Extreme",
                    "Gary Cherone", MB_OK);
    }
};

class CAlexVanHalen : public CDrummer {
public:
    CAlexVanHalen() :
        CDrummer("Drums") {
    }
    void BangAway() {
        MessageBox(NULL,
                    "Look at the flaming bass drum",
                    "Alex Van Halen", MB_OK);
    }
};

class CMichaelAnthony : public CBassist {
public:
    CMichaelAnthony() :
        CBassist("Bass") {
    }
    void ThumpAway() {
        MessageBox(NULL,
                    "Play the Jack Daniels bass",
                    "Michael Anthony", MB_OK);
    }
};

class CAlexLifeson : public CGuitarist {
public:
    CAlexLifeson() :
        CGuitarist("Guitar") {
    }
    void PlayLead() {
        MessageBox(NULL,
                    "Use lots of textures",
                    "Alex Lifeson", MB_OK);
    }
};
```

```
class CGeddyLee : public CVocalist, CBassist {
public:
    CGeddyLee() :
        CBassist("Bass"),
        CVocalist("Vocals") {
    }
    void Sing() {
        MessageBox(NULL,
                    "High and screechy",
                    "Geddy Lee", MB_OK);
    }

    void ThumpAway() {
        MessageBox(NULL,
                    "Intricate bass lines",
                    "Geddy Lee", MB_OK);
    }
};

class CNeilPeart : public CDrummer {
public:
    CNeilPeart() :
        CDrummer("Drums") {
    }
    void BangAway() {
        MessageBox(NULL,
                    "Really inventive style",
                    "Neil Peart", MB_OK);
    }
};
```

Each player has a particular style that is represented through a member function. For example, Eddie Van Halen is well known for popularizing two-handed tapping, so when he's called on to play a lead, he does it with lots of hammer-ons. Neil Peart has a distinctive drumming style that is very inventive, which is represented through his *BangAway* function.

Once the world-class musicians are in place, we can model different bands through the *CRockBand* class and mix in various musicians.

# Mixing Functionality

Once all this groundwork is in place, it becomes easy to create different kinds of bands. In this example, the difference between bands is really just who plays the instruments. We can create different kinds of rock bands by mixing in different musicians. The code on the following page shows how four bands distinguish themselves by the musicians who participate.

```
void ListenToRockBands() {
    CRockBand<CGuitarist, CBassist,
            CDrummer, CVocalist> NoName;
    CRockBand<CAlexLifeson, CGeddyLee,
            CNeilPeart, CGeddyLee> Rush;
    CRockBand<CEddieVanHalen, CMichaelAnthony,
            CAlexVanHalen, CGaryCherone> VanHalen;
    CRockBand<CEddieVanHalen, CGeddyLee,
            CNeilPeart, CGeddyLee> WhatsThis;

    MessageBox(NULL,
            "A non-name band is opening",
            NULL, MB_OK);
    NoName.PlayMusic();
    MessageBox(NULL,
            "Rush is on second",
            NULL, MB_OK);
    Rush.PlayMusic();
    MessageBox(NULL,
            "Van Halen is on third",
            NULL, MB_OK);
    VanHalen.PlayMusic();
    MessageBox(NULL,
            "What's This is on fourth",
            NULL, MB_OK);
    WhatsThis.PlayMusic();
}
```

Remember that the original goal of this exercise was to let the client form the rock band. Here's where the templates come in. When the client wants to form a band, the client creates an instance of the *CRockBand* class based on a particular set of musicians, as shown in the preceding code.

After looking at this code for a bit, you should realize just what a cool, flexible tool templates are. If you chose to, you could implement a whole host of musicians to use as template parameters for the rock band. Templates add the ability to mix types. But what does all this have to do with COM and ATL?

# Applying C++ Templates to COM

The examples we've covered in this chapter were inspired by ATL. We'll investigate how templates are useful to COM developers as we proceed through the book. For now, however, we'll present a couple of highlights.

One way ATL uses templates is to parameterize its implementations of *IUnknown*. *IUnknown* is the single interface that every COM class must implement. *IUnknown* describes two areas of functionality: interface type coercion

(*QueryInterface*) and object lifetime control (*AddRef* and *Release*). *AddRef* and *Release* might work differently depending on what threading model is used. For example, if an object is meant to run in a single-threaded apartment, *AddRef* and *Release* might be implemented using the more efficient increment (++) and decrement (--) operators. An object meant to run within the multithreaded apartment should use the thread-safe (and less efficient) *InterlockedIncrement* and *InterlockedDecrement* functions. ATL provides two template classes, *CComSingleThreadModel* and *CComMultiThreadModel,* for specializing the reference-counting behavior of an ATL-based COM class. ATL's base class for implementing *AddRef* and *Release* is *CComObjectRootEx.* As a template class, *CComObjectRootEx* takes a class with member functions for references counting as a template parameter. Here is ATL's core class for implementing *IUnknown::AddRef* and *IUnknown::Release*:

```
template <class ThreadModel>
class CComObjectRootEx : public CComObjectRootBase {
    typedef ThreadModel _ThreadModel;
public:
    ULONG InternalAddRef() {
        return _ThreadModel::Increment(&m_dwRef);
    }
    ULONG InternalRelease() {
        return _ThreadModel::Decrement(&m_dwRef);
    }
};
```

Notice how the *CComObjectRootEx* class maintains a variable of the *ThreadModel* type passed in as the template parameter. *CComObjectRootEx*'s *AddRef* and *Release* implementations simply delegate to the template parameter.

Another way in which templates are useful to COM developers is within implementations of *IClassFactory::CreateInstance.* What's the difference between one implementation of *IClassFactory* and another? Very little, except for the *type* of C++ object produced during the invocation of *CreateInstance.* Coding a class that can return different types of objects is a perfect use for a C++ template. For example, you might write a generic templatized version of *IClassFactory* like so:

```
template <class T>
class CoGenericClassFactory : IClassFactory {
public:
    // Other members were deleted for clarity.
    STDMETHODIMP CreateInstance(IUnknown* pUnk,
                                REFIID riid,
                                void** ppv) {
```

*(continued)*

```
                    *ppv = 0;
                    if (pUnkOuter != 0)
                        return CLASS_E_NOAGGREGATION;
                    T* pT = new T;
                    if (!pT)
                        return E_OUTOFMEMORY;
                    pT->AddRef( );
                    HRESULT hr = pT->QueryInterface(riid, ppv);
                    pT->Release( );
                        return hr;
                }
                // Other members were deleted for clarity.
            };
```

The code is parameterized so that the *new* operator creates the type of class factory for a particular COM-based C++ class. Whenever a client calls *CoCreateInstance*, control flow ends up in *IClassFactory*, which creates the right kind of class.

Finally, ATL does have its own version of smart pointers, named *CComPtr* and *CComQIPtr*. They work much like the smart pointer we looked at earlier in this chapter. They hold interface pointers as data members. They overload the ->, *, and & operators, allowing clients to treat them as pointers. Because these are COM pointers, they call *Release* during their constructors. In addition, their assignment operators are overloaded to call *Release* on the old pointer data member and *AddRef* on the new assignee.

# Conclusion

Templates are making their way into the programming world in a big way. Many developers restrict their use of templates to implementing collections and smart pointers, but templates are often useful for other purposes as well. In this chapter, we examined a way to employ templates that allow clients to change the behavior of a C++ class simply by passing in a template parameter when the template-based object is created. This capability is a testament to the power and flexibility of C++ when it's used correctly. Now that you're sufficiently grounded in templates, all the ATL source code that we'll sift through in the remainder of the book will make much more sense.

## CHAPTER FOUR

# Getting Started: Implementing a Simple Object

Throughout this book, we'll spend most of our time focusing on the under-the-hood aspects of ATL—how it works, what it does well, and what aspects of the library might still need a bit of improvement. With that goal in mind, we'll dedicate little print space to screen shots and hand-holding tutorials. That said, we still think you need to have a general sense of what ATL has to offer before we dive into the details of its implementation. In this chapter, we'll show you an overview of how to create a simple ATL-based COM object as a springboard for the details we'll examine in subsequent chapters. If you're already somewhat versed in ATL, you could skip directly to Chapter 5. (We'll also discuss the ATL wizards again in Chapter 9, in much more detail, so if you choose to read this chapter, don't be surprised if some of the material in Chapter 9 seems familiar.) But be aware that as this chapter unfolds, we'll resolve several misconceptions and answer some frequently asked questions about ATL as we discuss the following topics:

- The build configurations generated by the ATL COM AppWizard
- The proxy/stub makefile
- How the clients you decide to support affect component design choices
- How to use an ATL component in other applications
- How to enhance the functionality of a component through proper versioning

Throughout the chapter, we'll use ATL to develop a simple COM object, a "Tip of the Day" component that provides random quotes similar to those found in the startup dialog boxes of various Microsoft applications. (See

Figure 4-1.) As far as we know, there aren't any widely used "Tip of the Day" COM components in existence, so the code for these types of dialog boxes is typically reinvented or replicated from application to application. Indeed, the implementation of such functionality is generally language specific, framework specific, and user interface specific.

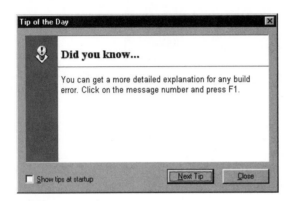

**Figure 4-1**
*The Tip Of The Day dialog box found in Visual C++ 6.0*

**NOTE** Microsoft Visual C++ can generate the code required to support limited "Tip of the Day" functionality via its Components and Controls gallery, but code generation is a much less effective form of reuse and encapsulation than the language-independent, interface-based approach offered by COM components.

A better approach is to leverage the benefits of COM to create a *TipOfTheDay* component that could be used from browser-independent Web pages via Microsoft Active Server Pages (ASP), Microsoft Visual Basic projects, and traditional Microsoft Foundation Class (MFC) applications. Figure 4-2 shows this component added to a Web application. To support these clients, the *TipOfTheDay* component must have the following characteristics:

- Expose an interface that supports both interpreted (scripting) languages and compiled languages. This requirement points to the use of a dual interface.

- Not predetermine the user interface that will be used to display each tip. In other words, the *TipOfTheDay* component will provide the tip text but not the associated user interface.

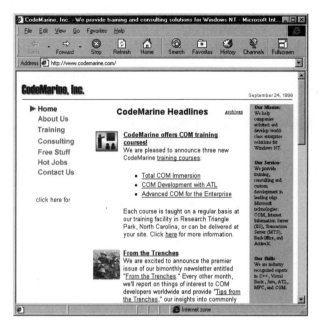

**Figure 4-2**
*The* TipOfTheDay *component used in a Web application*

# The ATL COM AppWizard

One of the best—and worst—features of Visual C++ are its many code-generation wizards. (See Figure 4-3.) Wizards help developers kick-start new projects, components, and classes by providing ready-to-compile starter code. The "new project" wizards generate fully functional projects complete with source files, resource files, and a makefile containing various build configurations that specify appropriate default compiler and linker settings. The downside to the wizards is that they lull novice developers into a false sense of security. Wizards provide an adequate starting point, but they don't supply information about how to get to the finish line. Developers who don't understand the generated code and how it works will find themselves in trouble as soon as the requirements of their application diverge from the educated guesses made by the wizards.

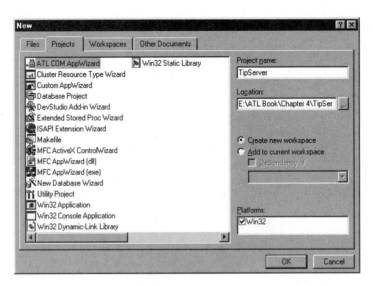

**Figure 4-3**
*The Visual C++ "new project" wizards*

> **NOTE** Although we recommend the ATL COM AppWizard to de-
> velopers of all skill levels, we think it's a good idea to create an ATL
> project from scratch at least once, if only to force yourself to recog-
> nize that the wizard makes a number of design decisions for you,
> including apartment model, marshaler, type library name, build con-
> figurations, compiler settings, and preprocessor symbols.

The ATL COM AppWizard is no exception. Because the ATL syntax and
semantics are sophisticated, with an abundance of complex templates and tricky
macros, the ATL COM AppWizard is essentially a required starting point for
new ATL projects. But without a solid understanding of COM, you'll have a
hard time even answering the questions the wizard poses, let alone developing effective COM-based applications. For example, Step 1 of the ATL COM AppWizard
expects you to know about proxies and stubs and whether or not they should be
merged into the component you're developing. (See Figure 4-4.) Online help
provides some insights, but it's certainly not a replacement for a basic compre-
hension of COM. Clearly, wizards aren't much help unless you understand the
implications of the choices they offer. For that reason, we've dedicated an entire chapter (Chapter 9) to an explanation of the various ATL wizard options
and their implications for your components.

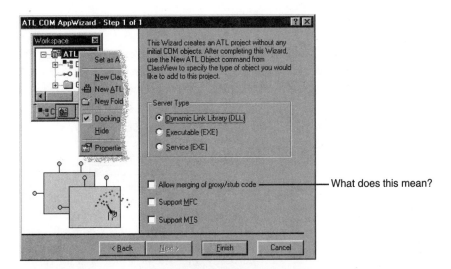

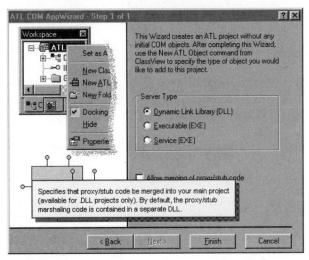

**Figure 4-4**

*A potentially confusing check box in the ATL COM AppWizard and its online help*

As you can see in Figure 4-3 and Figure 4-4, we accepted the default ATL COM AppWizard choices to create an empty DLL-based (in-process) COM server named TipServer.DLL. We might have instead chosen an EXE server or a Microsoft Windows NT service, but we felt that an in-process server was better suited for use in conjunction with Microsoft Internet Information Server (IIS) and eventual use within the Microsoft Transaction Server (known as Microsoft Component Services in Windows 2000) environment. Table 4-1 explains the reasons you might choose one server option over another.

**Table 4-1  The Three Types of COM Server**

| Server Type | Explanation |
| --- | --- |
| In-process DLL | This type offers the best performance of any server type because an object running inside the same apartment as its clients requires no marshaling overhead. Microsoft ActiveX controls must be housed in in-process servers. In-process servers currently offer the best potential for throughput; the version of Microsoft Component Services available at the time of this writing supports only in-process servers. |
| Out-of-process EXE | This type has reduced performance compared to in-process servers because all method calls require method remoting. The strengths of out-of-process servers are that they offer increased fault isolation, separate security credentials, and the benefit of distributed computation. |
| Out-of-process Windows NT service | This type is similar to an out-of-process server, but a Windows NT service can execute using the built-in System account.* |

\* It is our experience that most developers choose the Windows NT service option in the ATL COM AppWizard for two reasons: as a way of ensuring that a COM server remains running even when no objects are active, and as a means of providing a standard way for administrators to shut down or restart the server when something goes wrong. Only the second reason carries any weight, since the preferred way to keep a server running is simply to keep its lock count above zero.

Recall from the COM overview in Chapter 2 that a COM server is a binary module that houses one or more COM classes. The ATL COM AppWizard generates all the code necessary to compile and register a COM server, but it doesn't actually add any coclasses to the server. That addition is the responsibility of the ATL Object Wizard, as we'll describe later in this chapter. Figure 4-5 shows the wizard-generated TipServer workspace along with its accompanying project files.

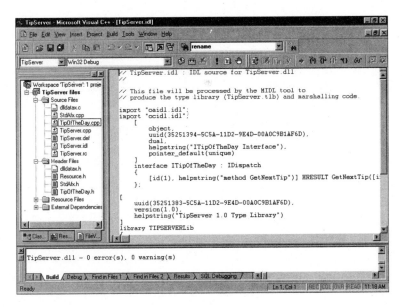

**Figure 4-5**
*The wizard-generated TipServer project*

# Wizard-Generated Build Configurations

As with the other AppWizards, the ATL COM AppWizard creates a project file that contains several build configurations, each tuned to a different set of goals and needs. The nuances of the ATL preprocessor symbols defined by the various ATL build configurations are quite possibly the most misunderstood aspect of ATL. Table 4-2 summarizes the build configurations we'll be covering in this section.

## _ATL_MIN_CRT

Visual C++ lets you decide how to link the C run-time functions into your application, whether statically, dynamically, or not at all. Static linking means that the run-time code will be linked directly into your application. Dynamic linking means that your application will contain only references to the run-time functions. The implementation of those functions will reside in a DLL (MSVCRT.DLL) that your application links to at run time. For your application to run, that DLL must be present. Even when dynamically linking to the

### Table 4-2  Wizard-Generated Build Configurations

| Build Configuration | Description | Preprocessor Symbols | Dependencies |
|---|---|---|---|
| Win32 Debug | Used exclusively for testing and debugging. Compiler optimizations are disabled, and the linker generates debug information. | _DEBUG | Implicit link to *CoCreateInstance* of Registrar component |
| Win32 Release MinSize | Aims to generate the smallest possible component footprint. Compiler optimizations are set to Minimum Size. | NDEBUG _ATL_DLL _ATL_MIN_CRT | Explicit link to ATL.DLL |
| Win32 Release MinDependency | Aims to reduce dependencies on other modules. Compiler optimizations are set to Minimum Size. | NDEBUG _ATL_STATIC_ REGISTRY _ATL_MIN_CRT | None |
| All configurations | Links to static version of run-time library. C++ exception handling and Run Time Type Information (RTTI) are disabled. Exception handling must be enabled to use the Standard Template Library (STL). | N/A | N/A |
| Unicode configurations | Links to Unicode versions of all Win32 APIs and treats TCHAR as wchar_t. For use only with components running exclusively under Windows NT and Windows 2000. | _UNICODE | Windows NT |

run-time DLL, some run-time functions require the existence of statically linked startup code. If you use those functions, the link to the C run-time library—whether static or dynamic—causes the linker to add startup code to your application, significantly increasing its size. This startup code, provided by the run-time library, calls constructors on global objects and initializes data structures used by the run-time library. Not all the run-time functions require the startup code—*memcpy* and *strlen* are typical examples—but many of them do. The following functions require statically linked startup code:

- String comparison routines
- Memory allocation routines
- Global objects with constructors
- C++ exception handling

**NOTE** The startup code adds only about 25 KB to your application footprint. This amount is negligible in traditional stand-alone applications built with MFC or Visual Basic. But when you're trying to create lean, mean COM servers (that *is* why you're using ATL, right?), 25 KB is a big, big deal.

Because the goal of ATL is to develop components that are as small as possible, ATL provides alternate implementations for several of the commonly used run-time functions that would otherwise require costly startup code. The _ATL_MIN_CRT preprocessor symbol controls the use of the ATL versions of these run-time functions. The _ATL_MIN_CRT symbol doesn't prevent you from using C run-time functions in your application. It simply tells the linker not to include the run-time library–provided startup code. Thus, if _ATL_MIN_CRT is defined and you attempt to use a function that requires the run-time startup code but doesn't have an ATL replacement, you'll get a link error stating that the *_main* function is unresolved. The error message makes sense: you've attempted to link to a function that requires startup code, but you've told the linker not to provide the startup code. The most effective approach is to define _ATL_MIN_CRT and then go about your merry business until you use a run-time function that produces the infamous *_main* link error. At that point, you can simply remove the _ATL_MIN_CRT preprocessor symbol and pay the associated code-size penalty. You can't define ATL_MIN_CRT if you want to use C++ exception handling or the Standard Template Library (STL), because both require the run-time startup code.

## ATL.DLL

Like the C run-time library, ATL provides functionality that resides in a shared-code DLL—aptly if unimaginatively named ATL.DLL. (In early versions of ATL, the shared-code DLL was named REGISTER.DLL, a name that was neither apt nor imaginative.) This file contains basically two things: global functions used by various ATL classes and templates, and the Registrar component, which we'll explain in detail in Chapter 7. Like the C run-time library, ATL is structured such that the code contained in the shared DLL can be linked to your component statically or dynamically. The method of linking to the ATL shared code depends on the absence or existence of two preprocessor symbols, _ATL_DLL and _ATL_STATIC_REGISTRY. The usage of these two symbols determines whether the ATL.DLL must be redistributed and registered along with the component. Table 4-3 explains the linkage implications of the _ATL_DLL and _ATL_STATIC_REGISTRY symbols. As you can see from the table, the only combination of these two symbols that doesn't create a run-time dependency on ATL.DLL is to define _ATL_STATIC_REGISTRY and *not* define _ATL_DLL.

**Table 4-3  Preprocessor Symbols That Control Linkage to ATL.DLL**

| Preprocessor Symbol | Explanation |
| --- | --- |
| _ATL_DLL | The existence of this symbol indicates that ATL will dynamically link to its global functions (as exported by ATL.DLL) rather than statically linking them directly into the module. |
| _ATL_STATIC_REGISTRY | The existence of this symbol indicates that ATL will not use *CoCreateInstance* to instantiate the Registrar component housed in ATL.DLL. Rather, ATL will statically link that functionality directly into the module. |

The process of installing and registering the ATL shared-code DLL is complicated by the fact that there are two different versions of ATL.DLL—one for Microsoft Windows 95 and Windows 98 (ANSI) and one for Windows NT and Windows 2000 (Unicode). If your application targets both operating systems, your setup program must include both versions of the DLL and take special precautions to ensure that the proper DLL is installed and registered, depending on the operating system that resides on the target machine.

**NOTE** ATL.DLL should reside in the windows\system32 folder. If that file already exists on the target machine, you should perform a version comparison before copying the file to make sure that the version of ATL.DLL that you're installing is newer than the one that already exists. After copying the file, you must register it using REGSVR32.EXE or by loading the DLL and calling its exported *DLLRegisterServer* function.

---

### Previous Versions of ATL: ATL.DLL

On the Visual C++ 5.0 installation CD, the Unicode and ANSI versions of ATL.DLL reside in the \devstudio\vc\redist and \devstudio \vc\redist\ansi folders, respectively. On the Visual C++ 6.0 CD, these two files reside in the \os\system and \os\system\ansi folders, respectively. The version of ATL.DLL that ships with Visual C++ 6.0 is backward compatible to ATL projects developed with Visual C++ 5.0.

---

## Win32 Debug

The Win32 Debug build configuration is used exclusively for testing and debugging. Generally, you shouldn't redistribute components built with the Debug configuration. Compiler optimizations are turned off, and the linker uses the static, debug version of the multithreaded run-time library. Because the Debug configuration doesn't define the _ATL_STATIC_REGISTRY symbol, it is dependent on the Registrar component that resides in ATL.DLL.

## Win32 Release MinSize

The Win32 Release MinSize build configuration attempts to create the smallest COM server possible. It does this by defining _ATL_DLL, which causes the project to link dynamically to ATL.DLL, and _ATL_MIN_CRT. Because most developers aren't in the habit of building the release versions of their components until far along in the development cycle, they typically suffer from the *_main* link error described earlier when they first attempt to compile the Release MinSize (and Release MinDependency) build. If you're faced with that situation, you have two options: you can remove the _ATL_MIN_CRT definition from the configuration, or you can replace all references to the C run-time functions that require run-time startup code with Win32 API equivalents (if available). The former is a much simpler process, but the latter is a worthwhile exercise, especially when you're trying to develop the smallest component possible.

Interestingly, the MinSize configuration links to the static rather than the dynamic version of the C run-time DLL. For components that make liberal use of the C run-time library, a reduction in footprint might be gained by instead linking to the run-time library dynamically. (See Figure 4-6.)

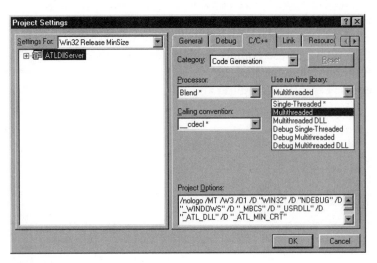

**Figure 4-6**
*Visual C++ allows you to specify whether to link to the C run-time library statically or dynamically*

## Win32 Release MinDependency

The Win32 MinDependency build takes the opposite tack of the MinSize configuration. It favors lack of dependency over reduced footprint. For developers who are willing to pay a small code-size price for the luxury of not having to redistribute the ATL.DLL or MSVCRT.DLL files, the MinDependency build is the best choice. This configuration defines _ATL_STATIC_REGISTRY and _ATL_MIN_CRT, and it links to the static version of the C run-time library.

## All Configurations

All the ATL COM AppWizard–generated build configurations share common characteristics. Notably, they don't enable C++ exception handling or Run Time Type Information (RTTI). Having no C++ exception handling or RTTI is an acceptable default setting because it encourages the use of the two COM practices that differ from the traditional C++ usage model. First, although it's acceptable to throw exceptions within the body of an interface method, it violates the rules of COM to throw an exception that crosses a component boundary. To pass errors from one component to another, COM instead uses HRESULTs and the *ISupportErrorInfo* and *IErrorInfo* interfaces. Second, when dealing with interface pointers, you must use *QueryInterface* rather than *dynamic_cast* to convert from one pointer type to another. The reason is that it's perfectly legal for a COM object to use composition rather than inheritance as its means of supporting multiple interfaces.

Because exception handling and RTTI are used less frequently in light-weight COM objects than in traditional stand-alone C++ applications, and because these options can increase footprint size and memory usage, they are disabled in all the wizard-generated configurations. If you want to use the *dynamic_cast, type_id,* or *type_info* operators, you must enable RTTI. If you want to use the STL in your ATL project, you must manually enable exception handling for all configurations, but you should take precautions to ensure that exceptions thrown by the STL don't cross the boundaries of your interface's methods. The following code is taken from a COM collection object:

```
class CAnimals :
    public CComObjectRootEx<CComSingleThreadModel>,
    public CComCoClass<CAnimals, &CLSID_Animals>,
    public ISupportErrorInfoImpl< &IID_IAnimals >,
    public IDispatchImpl<IAnimals, &IID_IAnimals, &LIBID_ANIMALSERVERLib>
{
    ⋮
    std::vector<IAnimal*> m_itemList;
    STDMETHOD(Item)(VARIANT index, IDispatch** ppItem)
    {
        // Oops! An out-of-range index throws an exception!
        return m_itemList.at(index)->QueryInterface(
            IID_IDispatch, (void**)ppItem);
    }
    ⋮
};
```

In the preceding code, the STL vector class throws an *out_of_range* exception if an invalid index is passed into the *vector::at* method. Under the rules of traditional C++, it might have been acceptable to let the exception percolate up the call stack, but under the COM model it isn't. Visual Basic clients, for which collection classes were invented, don't know how to handle C++ exceptions, so the *Animals* collection is doomed to failure unless one of two things happens:

- A change is made to prevent the exception from being thrown:

```
STDMETHODIMP CAnimals::Item(long index, IDispatch** ppItem)
{
    if(index < 0 || index >= m_itemList.size())
        return Error("Index out of range ");
    return m_itemList.at(index)->QueryInterface(
        IID_IDispatch, (void**)ppItem);
}
```

- The exception is handled within the bounds of the method:

```
STDMETHODIMP CAnimals::Item(long index, IDispatch** ppItem)
{
    try
    {
    return m_itemList.at(index.iVal)->QueryInterface(
        IID_IDispatch, (void**)ppItem);
    }
    catch (std::out_of_range& error)
    {
        return Error(error.what());
    }
}
```

In case you're wondering, the *CComCoClass::Error* method used in the code snippets shown above sets up the *IErrorInfo* interface to provide error information to the client.

All the wizard-generated configurations link statically to the C run-time library. As described earlier, you can both define _ATL_MIN_CRT and link statically to the run-time library: the settings aren't mutually exclusive. The combination of these settings simply means that C run-time functions not provided by ATL will be linked statically and must not require startup code.

## Unicode Configurations

The wizard-generated project includes Unicode versions of the three basic build configurations described earlier: Debug, Release MinSize, and Release MinDependency. The Unicode configurations are for use only with components that will run exclusively under Windows NT and Windows 2000 because Unicode isn't supported under Windows 95 or Windows 98. Under Windows NT and Windows 2000, the system DLLs export two versions of many of the Win32 APIs—one version for single-byte characters and another for double-byte

Unicode characters. Whereas the non-Unicode configurations define the _MBCS preprocessor symbol, the three Unicode build configurations define the _UNICODE preprocessor directive, which causes an application to link to the wide versions of the Win32 APIs. Here's the pseudocode for the *MessageBox* function:

```
WINUSERAPI int WINAPI
MessageBoxA(HWND hWnd, LPCSTR lpText, LPCSTR lpCaption, UINT uType);
WINUSERAPI int WINAPI
MessageBoxW(HWND hWnd, LPCWSTR lpText, LPCWSTR lpCaption, UINT uType);
#ifdef _UNICODE
#define MessageBox  MessageBoxW
#else
#define MessageBox  MessageBoxA
#endif // !UNICODE
```

Most often, you'll simply use the generic *MessageBox* function in your code, but it's translated to the appropriate exported system function based on the presence or absence of the _UNICODE directive.

# The Proxy/Stub Makefile

As described in Chapter 2, COM defines an abstraction, called an *apartment*, for managing concurrent access to components. An apartment is a grouping of objects that share the same threading requirements. A single-threaded apartment (STA) can house one and only one thread. The multithreaded apartment (MTA) can house any number of threads. Every thread that wants to gain direct access to a given COM object must reside in an apartment—the same apartment, in fact, in which the COM object resides. Before accessing the object, a thread must call *CoInitialize* or *CoInitializeEx*, whereby it specifies which type of apartment it wants to enter. When a thread creates an instance of a COM object, that object might or might not reside in the same apartment as the creating thread, depending on the apartment preference specified by the object itself. Because a thread can directly access only the objects that reside in its own apartment, communication with objects residing in other apartments can occur only by means of a proxy. A *proxy* is an object that resides in the apartment of the calling thread that behaves as if it were the object itself. The proxy forwards method calls from one apartment to another—a technique known as *method remoting*—ensuring that all calls are made by threads running in the object's apartment. On the server side, a special *interface stub* object that runs in the address space of the callee unmarshals the parameters for that interface and makes the requested method call. The proxy and stub typically communicate with one another using Object Remote Procedure Call (ORPC) requests.

The beauty of the apartment model is that a client can remain blissfully ignorant about the threading limitations of the COM object, treating those requirements as essentially an implementation detail.

**NOTE** This information on apartments and threading is specific to Windows NT 4.0. The apartment story changes with Windows 2000.

## Marshaling Methods

Method remoting not only expedites communication between apartments, it also facilitates communication between objects running in different processes and on different machines via a technique known as *marshaling*.[1] The three marshaling techniques are described in Table 4-4.

### Table 4-4　Marshaling Techniques

| Technique | Description |
| --- | --- |
| Custom | Object implements the *IMarshal* interface and handles its own cross-apartment communication. This technique is used only in the rare cases in which the COM-provided marshaling techniques don't suffice. |
| Type library | Uses OLEAUT32.DLL to marshal the interface. The type library marshaler provides marshaling only for the Automation data types. The component specifies type library marshaling using the [oleautomation] or [dual] Interface Definition Language (IDL) attributes. Type library marshaling supports marshaling between 16-bit and 32-bit applications. |
| Standard | COM looks in the Registry to find the correct proxy/stub DLL for marshaling the interface. The object must define custom data types in IDL and provide registered proxy/stub objects for each marshaled interface. More than one proxy/stub object can reside in the same server DLL. |

As you can see from Table 4-4, type library marshaling is used with Automation-compliant interfaces and uses the built-in proxy/stub objects the system provides. Type library marshaling is an appropriate choice for dual interfaces or

---

1. Chapter 2 contains a brief, high-level overview of the concepts of apartments, method remoting, and marshaling but doesn't attempt to substitute for a thorough explanation. No book on the planet does a better job of describing the details of these concepts than *Essential COM* by our friend and colleague Don Box (Addison-Wesley, 1998). We highly recommend it.

interfaces with methods that use only the primitive VARIANT-compatible Automation data types. Standard marshaling is much more flexible because it allows you to create sophisticated data structures in IDL, but it requires you to build and register in-process proxy/stub objects.

> **NOTE** It's not a strict requirement that interfaces marked with the [dual] keyword use the type library marshaler. In theory, there's nothing to prevent you from registering a custom proxy/stub DLL for dual interfaces, but that is rarely done in practice.

## Building the Proxy/Stub

Along with the workspace and project files, the ATL COM AppWizard generates a makefile that you can use to create an in-process DLL containing the proxy and stub objects required to marshal the interfaces exposed by your COM server by means of the standard marshaler. This makefile, named <projname>PS.MK, is placed in the same folder as the wizard-generated workspace. If you're not planning to use the standard marshaler, or if you know that your component will never be accessed by a thread residing in a separate apartment, you might never need to compile the proxy/stub DLL. Otherwise, here's how to register the proxy:

1. Build the component, causing the MIDL compiler to generate the files that will be linked into the proxy/stub DLL. Obviously, if your component doesn't use the standard marshaler, the MIDL compiler won't generate the files necessary to build the DLL.

2. Make sure that the Visual C++ environment variables are registered either at setup or by explicitly running VCVARS32.BAT from the command line.

3. From the command line, compile the makefile in the project directory, like so:

   ```
   nmake -f TipServerps.mk
   ```

4. Register and redistribute the resulting DLL, using REGSVR32.EXE or your setup program.

   ```
   regsvr32.exe TipServerps.dll
   ```

**NOTE** If your component rolls its own *IMarshal* interface or if your component exposes dual interfaces, you can simply leave the proxy/stub makefile alone. Otherwise, you should always build, redistribute, and register the proxy/stub DLL. If an interface marshaled by means of the standard marshaler resides in an EXE server, the proxy/stub is always required. Even if the interface resides in a DLL, chances are good that a client will try to access the interface from a background thread. Redistribute and register the proxy/stub!

## Merging the Proxy/Stub DLL

The proxy object must reside in an in-process server DLL rather than an EXE server because it must be loaded into the same apartment—and hence the same process—as the client thread. The same principle applies to the relationship between the stub and the server thread. When cross-apartment communication is required on a single machine that hosts both the client application and the server component, the proxy/stub objects for each marshaled interface must be registered on that machine. When the communication crosses machine boundaries, the proxy/stub DLL must be registered on both the client and server machines.

If you're developing an in-process server, the ATL COM AppWizard provides an option that allows you to house the proxy/stub objects within the same DLL as the server itself, thereby reducing the number of files that must be redistributed with your component. (Refer to Figure 4-4 on page 81.) Choosing the Allow Merging Of Proxy/Stub Code wizard option still creates a separate proxy/stub makefile, so it doesn't preclude you from housing the proxy/stub objects in a separate DLL. But selecting the merge option creates extra code that will merge the proxies into the component server if you define the _MERGE_PROXYSTUB preprocessor symbol.

If you're developing an in-process server and you're fairly certain that your component will always reside on the same machine as its clients, merging the proxy/stub objects into the server is probably a good idea. Merging them reduces the number of modules you must compile, register, and redistribute, and the footprint will be smaller than the combined footprint of separate server and proxy/stub DLLs. If you're planning to deploy your in-process server on a remote machine under the auspices of a surrogate, however, merging the two DLLs might not be such a good idea. Because you must register the proxy/stub object on the client machine, merging will mean that the implementation code for your component must be installed on the client machine even though the code runs on a separate machine.

# The ATL Object Wizard

Now that we've described various aspects of the AppWizard-generated makefiles, it's time to proceed with our development of the *TipOfTheDay* component. Sometimes the words *component* and *server* are used interchangeably, but they probably shouldn't be. Technically speaking, a COM component is a COM class (or coclass) that exposes one or more COM interfaces. A COM server is a binary module in which one or more components reside. The ATL COM AppWizard creates an empty COM server, and the ATL Object Wizard is the productivity tool that helps you create coclasses. In our sample, the *TipOfTheDay* component will reside in a COM server named TIPSERVER.DLL and will expose (among others) an interface named *ITipOfTheDay*.

As shown in Figure 4-7, the ATL Object Wizard provides handy starter templates for several different types of commonly created components. With the release of Visual C++ 6.0, the APIs required to add your own starter object to the Object Wizard are now documented. Because the *TipOfTheDay* component is a simple object that exposes no user interface, we chose Simple Object and filled out the wizard options, as shown in Figure 4-8.

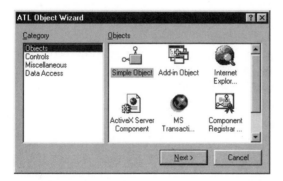

**Figure 4-7**
*The ATL Object Wizard*

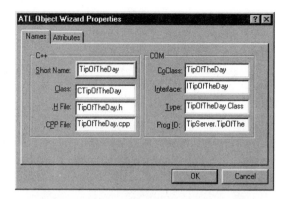

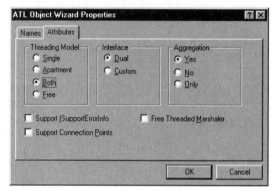

**Figure 4-8**
*The properties for the new* TipOfTheDay *component*

For now, we'll make only a few observations regarding the *TipOfTheDay* properties. In Chapter 9, we'll provide in-depth information about nearly all the options the ATL wizards offer, along with their implications for developers.

## ThreadingModel=Apartment

The apartment model (or models) supported by an in-process component is determined by its ThreadingModel Registry setting. Although the wizard makes it easy for you to choose any one of these models, you shouldn't make this decision lightly. If you specify an STA—which, somewhat confusingly, maps to ThreadingModel=Apartment in the Registry—you're guaranteed that instances of your component will be accessed by only a single thread. That means you must protect access to global data but not to instance data. If you specify the MTA (ThreadingModel=Free), you must protect access to both global and instance data. Because we're not sure whether the *TipOfTheDay* component will maintain per-instance state, we'll initially mark it as ThreadingModel=Apartment to be on the safe side. After we've completed the implementation, we'll reexamine the issue to see whether individual instances of the *TipOfTheDay* component can handle concurrent access by multiple threads. If so, it might make sense to choose ThreadingModel=Both instead.

## Dual Interfaces

As mentioned earlier, we plan to use our *TipOfTheDay* component from within an ASP application as well as from MFC. Because existing scripting languages don't support vtable interfaces, the *TipOfTheDay* component must expose a dispinterface. This leaves us with three choices:

- Expose a dispinterface only

- Expose a dispinterface and a separate vtable interface

- Expose a dual interface—a vtable interface derived from *IDispatch*

Depending on the circumstances, any one of these options might be appropriate. For an in-process server such as the *TipOfTheDay* component, the overhead associated with routing method calls through *IDispatch* is significant. For an EXE server, the relative overhead would be less significant but still an issue we would need to consider. Dispatch interfaces are less C++-friendly than vtable interfaces, but they work well in rapid application development (RAD) environments such as Visual Basic and Microsoft Visual InterDev. The default choice in the Object Wizard is the dual interface option. It's an appropriate choice if you must support both scripting clients and vtable-aware clients and if the interface methods use only simple, VARIANT-compatible data types as parameters. Because the *ITipOfTheDay* interface fits those two criteria, that's the option we chose.

The Object Wizard adds an implementation class to the project and an empty interface—that is, one with no methods—to the IDL file. (See Listing 4-1.) To add a method to the newly created interface, we must do three things:

- Add a method entry to the *ITipOfTheDay* interface, as defined in the IDL file.

- Add the method declaration to the *CTipOfTheDay* header file. *CTipOfTheDay* is the class that will provide an implementation of the *ITipOfTheDay* interface.

- Add the method definition (implementation) to the *CTipOfTheDay* source file.

```
// TipServer.idl : IDL source for TipServer.dll
//

// This file will be processed by the MIDL tool to
// produce the type library (TipServer.tlb) and marshaling code.

import "oaidl.idl";
import "ocidl.idl";
    [
        object,
        uuid(C8FC12DF-47ED-11D2-B387-006008A667FD),
        dual,
        helpstring("ITipOfTheDay Interface"),
        pointer_default(unique)
    ]
    interface ITipOfTheDay : IDispatch
    {
    };

[
    uuid(C8FC12D1-47ED-11D2-B387-006008A667FD),
    version(1.0),
    helpstring("TipServer 1.0 Type Library")
]
library TIPSERVERLib
{
    importlib("stdole32.tlb");
    importlib("stdole2.tlb");

    [
        uuid(C8FC12E0-47ED-11D2-B387-006008A667FD),
        helpstring("TipOfTheDay Class")
    ]
    coclass TipOfTheDay
    {
        [default] interface ITipOfTheDay;
    };
};
```

**Listing 4-1**
*Object Wizard–generated IDL for the* ITipOfTheDay *interface and the*
TipOfTheDay *coclass*

## Adding a Method

Fortunately, Visual C++ provides a handy Add Method dialog box that performs these three steps quickly and easily. To use the Add Method dialog box, right-click on the interface in the ClassView pane and choose the Add Method option from the context menu. (See Figure 4-9.) Using this timesaving approach, we added a *GetNextTip* method to the *ITipOfTheDay* interface. The autogenerated IDL for the *GetNextTip* method looks like this:

```
interface ITipOfTheDay : IDispatch
{
        [id(1), helpstring("method GetNextTip")]
        HRESULT GetNextTip([in, out] VARIANT* pvCookie,
                            [out, retval] BSTR* pbstrText);
};
```

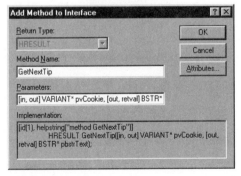

**Figure 4-9**
*The Add Method dialog box*

The *GetNextTip* method will allow the calling client to iterate through the tips provided by the component. To facilitate the iteration, this method uses a cookie.

**NOTE**  We're not sure who coined the word *cookie* in the context of storing component state, but it's certainly not a very descriptive choice. Perhaps a word like *bookmark* would have been more intuitive, if less entertaining. In short, a cookie is a tidbit of state-identifying information (an index, perhaps) passed from a server to its client so that the server can recall the state it was in when the client accesses it again sometime in the future. The client doesn't comprehend the format or meaning of the information and therefore can do nothing with the cookie other than pass it back to the server. By sharing the responsibility of state management with its clients, a server can often achieve greatly increased scalability. Trust us on this one, though: if you hand either of us a chocolate chip cookie, we'll know exactly what to do with it and you'll never get it back.

Because the component must operate in the ASP environment, we used a VARIANT as the data type for the cookie parameter. Although it's generally undesirable to use VARIANTs because of the degree of effort required to work with them in C++, this choice was necessary because ASP supports only the VARIANT data type. When *GetNextTip* is called, the cookie parameter specifies the tip to be retrieved. At the end of the method invocation, the cookie is set to a new value that identifies the next tip in the sequence.

**NOTE**  Had the cookie variable been an [in] parameter, we could have declared it as a long instead of a VARIANT. When you pass by value, Visual Basic, Scripting Edition (VBScript) can perform automatic type conversion from VARIANT to any of the standard types that the VARIANT encapsulates. When you pass by reference (as is the case with [out] parameters), no such conversion can be made.

As mentioned previously, the wizard generates the skeleton C++ code for the implementation of the newly added method in addition to the IDL:

```
class ATL_NO_VTABLE CTipOfTheDay :
    ⋮
{
    ⋮
// ITipOfTheDay
public:
    STDMETHOD(GetNextTip)(/*[in, out]*/ VARIANT* pvCookie,
                          /*[out, retval]*/ BSTR* pbstrText);
};
    ⋮
STDMETHODIMP CTipOfTheDay::GetNextTip(VARIANT *pvCookie,
    BSTR *pbstrText)
```

```
{
    return S_OK;
}
```

## Separation of Interface from Implementation

As we've said before, one of the key benefits of COM is its separation of interface from implementation. When a coclass exposes an interface, it makes a contract with its clients regarding the syntax and semantics of its entry points, but it doesn't specify how those methods will be implemented. The implementation details, whether they be coded in C++, Java, Visual Basic, or COBOL, are hidden from the user of the coclass. In the case of the *TipOfTheDay* component, its clients have no idea how or where the text for each tip is stored—whether in memory, in a sequential file, or in a sophisticated distributed database. The powerful combination of encapsulation and polymorphism means that the implementation of the *TipOfTheDay* component can change over time without requiring any changes to its clients.

Despite its productivity benefits, the Add Method dialog box does have one drawback. It encourages developers to create interfaces and their associated implementations simultaneously. This two-birds-with-one-stone approach is by no means a fatal blow to solid COM development, but it does blur the line between two phases of software development that are best treated distinctly: interface design and interface implementation. Although we don't discourage the use of the Add Method and Add Property dialog boxes, we don't think they are a good substitute for thoughtful interface design, which is best achieved through careful whiteboard modeling of the interactions between the components in the system.

As shown in Listing 4-2, the initial implementation for our *TipOfTheDay* component uses a simple, static array as the mechanism for storing the tips. Obviously, a more sophisticated version of the component would have stored the tips in a file or a database rather than hard-wiring them into the code, thereby allowing administrators to add, configure, or edit the tips after deployment. Fortunately, our use of COM would allow us to make that transition behind the scenes, without requiring changes to existing clients.

```
// TipOfTheDay.cpp : Implementation of CTipOfTheDay

#include "stdafx.h"
#include "TipServer.h"
#include "TipOfTheDay.h"
```

**Listing 4-2**                                          *(continued)*
*A simple implementation of the* ITipOfTheDay *interface*

**Listing 4-2** *continued*

```
///////////////////////////////////////////////////////////////////////
// CTipOfTheDay

#define TIP_COUNT     7
static LPWSTR gTipText[TIP_COUNT] =
{
    L"You should avoid strangers",
    L"Good things come to those who wait",
    L"Lay off the code; your love life is hurting",
    L"Do a good turn today",
    L"You win some, you lose some",
    L"COM is love?",
    L"All's fair in love and war"
};

STDMETHODIMP CTipOfTheDay::GetNextTip(VARIANT *pvCookie,
    BSTR *pbstrText)
{
    if(!pvCookie || !pbstrText)
        return E_POINTER;

    ::VariantChangeType(pvCookie, pvCookie, 0, VT_I4);
    if(pvCookie->lVal < 0 || pvCookie->lVal >= TIP_COUNT)
        return E_INVALIDARG;

    *pbstrText = SysAllocString(gTipText[pvCookie->lVal]);
    if(++(pvCookie->lVal) == TIP_COUNT)
        pvCookie->lVal = 0;

    return S_OK;
}
```

# Using the Component

Now it's time to take a look at how we can use the *TipOfTheDay* component from other applications. Although we won't delve into the details of how each language implements COM clients, we will show you sample code that uses the component from ASP, Visual Basic, and MFC and provide a couple of high-level insights.

## Active Server Pages

Active Server Pages currently supports two scripting languages: VBScript and Microsoft JScript. As of this writing, neither of those languages supports early (vtable) binding of COM interfaces, so coclasses invoked in those environments must implement the *IDispatch* interface. Furthermore, VBScript—by far the most commonly used language within ASP—supports only a single data type: the VARIANT. As described earlier in the chapter, the *TipOfTheDay* component was designed with these two constraints in mind. Specifically, we made two design decisions to accommodate ASP. First, the *ITipOfTheDay* interface inherits from *IDispatch* rather than *IUnknown*, resulting in a dual interface. Second, the *GetNextTip* method uses a VARIANT [in, out] parameter to pass the updated cookie back to the caller. The accompanying trade-offs are that the component is more difficult to version (as you'll see shortly) and C++ clients have to coerce their data types to and from a VARIANT.

Listing 4-3 shows the sample code for a simple ASP page that leverages the *TipOfTheDay* component to embed a tip within the HTML that gets delivered to the browser. The bookmark required by the *ITipOfTheDay::GetNextTip* method is stored on the client machine using a browser cookie, as facilitated by using the *Request* and *Response* objects provided by the ASP run-time environment. Each time the user clicks the browser Refresh button while viewing this page, the cookie will be updated and a new tip will be shown.

```
<%@ LANGUAGE="VBSCRIPT" %>
<%
If Request.Cookies("TipOfTheDay") = "" Then
    Response.Cookies("TipOfTheDay") = "0"
End If
set tipOfDay = Server.CreateObject("TipServer.TipOfTheDay")
lCookie = Request.Cookies("TipOfTheDay")
tipText = tipOfDay.GetNextTip(lCookie)
Response.Cookies("TipOfTheDay") = lCookie
Response.Cookies("TipOfTheDay").Expires = #December 31, 1999#
%>

<HTML>
<BODY>

<P>The tip for the day is:</P>

<P><FONT color=blue>
<% Response.Write tipText & "<br>" %>
</FONT></P>

<P>(Click refresh to see the next tip).</P>

</BODY>
</HTML>
```

**Listing 4-3**
*An ASP page that uses the* TipOfTheDay *component*

## Visual Basic

Visual Basic supports both vtable and dispatch interfaces. It can also support simple structures in addition to the primitive data types encapsulated by the VARIANT. Were it not for the need to support ASP clients, the *ITipOfTheDay* interface could have been derived from *IUnknown* instead of *IDispatch*. Furthermore, the *GetNextTip* method could have used a long instead of a VARIANT, like so:

```
interface ITipOfTheDay : IDispatch
{
        [id(1), helpstring("method GetNextTip")]
        HRESULT GetNextTip([in, out] long* pvCookie,
                           [out, retval] BSTR* pbstrText);
};
```

Although versions of Visual Basic previous to 4.0 didn't support vtable binding, Visual Basic can now call interface methods directly, without having to wade through the overhead of *IDispatch*. In this code snippet, the method calls are made via *IDispatch*:

```
Dim lCookie
Dim tip As Object

Private Sub Form_Load()
    lCookie = 0
    Set tip = CreateObject("TipServer.TipOfTheDay")
    tipText = tip.GetNextTip(lCookie)
End Sub

Private Sub nextTip_Click()
    tipText = tip.GetNextTip(lCookie)
End Sub
```

In the following code snippet, method calls are resolved using early binding and thus are made directly via the vtable:

```
Dim lCookie
Dim tip As ITipOfTheDay

Private Sub Form_Load()
    lCookie = 0
    Set tip = New TIPSERVERLib.TipOfTheDay
    tipText = tip.GetNextTip(lCookie)
End Sub

Private Sub nextTip_Click()
    tipText = tip.GetNextTip(lCookie)
End Sub
```

As you can see, the difference between the two snippets is subtle, but the second is significantly more efficient than the first.

**NOTE**   To support early binding, the type library for the TipServer DLL must be registered in the Visual Basic References dialog box.

## Visual C++/MFC

To show the use of our component from within MFC, we created a simple SDI application using the AppWizard and added the Visual C++ "Tip of the Day" component. Then we ripped out the automatically generated tip storage code and replaced it with calls to the *TipOfTheDay* COM component, as shown in Listing 4-4.

```
#import "../TipServer/TipServer.tlb" no_namespace

class CTipDlg : public CDialog
{
protected:
    variant_t vtCookie;
    ITipOfTheDayPtr m_tipOfDay;
    :
};

static const TCHAR szSection[] = _T("Tip");
static const TCHAR szIntStartup[] = _T("StartUp");
static const TCHAR szCookie[] = _T("Cookie");

CTipDlg::CTipDlg(CWnd* pParent /*=NULL*/)
    : CDialog(IDD_TIP, pParent)
{
    //{{AFX_DATA_INIT(CTipDlg)
    m_bStartup = TRUE;
    //}}AFX_DATA_INIT

    CWinApp* pApp = AfxGetApp();
    m_bStartup = !pApp->GetProfileInt(szSection, szIntStartup, 0);
    vtCookie = (long)pApp->GetProfileInt(szSection, szCookie, 0);

    HRESULT hResult =
        m_tipOfDay.CreateInstance("TipServer.TipOfTheDay");
    if(SUCCEEDED(hResult))
        GetNextTipString(m_strTip);
}
```

**Listing 4-4**                                                                                    *(continued)*
*Modifying the Tip Of The Day dialog box to use our COM component*

**Listing 4-4** *continued*

```
CTipDlg::~CTipDlg()
{
    CWinApp* pApp = AfxGetApp();
    ::VariantChangeType(&vtCookie, &vtCookie, 0, VT_I4);
    pApp->WriteProfileInt(szSection, szCookie, vtCookie.lVal);
}

void CTipDlg::GetNextTipString(CString& strNext)
{
    strNext = (BSTR)(m_tipOfDay->GetNextTip(&vtCookie));
}
```

The application is still responsible for rendering the text within the fancy dialog box (see Figure 4-10), but the same engine ASP and Visual Basic use can be shared by the MFC program. Now that's code reuse!

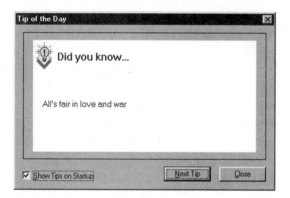

**Figure 4-10**
*The MFC application using the* TipOfTheDay *component*

# Versioning the Coclass

Over time, the complexity and sophistication of software increases. Users request more features, new technologies facilitate more features, and developers invent more features. This progression is the nature of the business, and it's generally good for software consumers. COM facilitates software progression by helping developers limit the impact that changes in a component have on the client applications that use it. Once you've published an interface, COM doesn't allow you to make any modifications to that interface that would change its syntax or significantly alter its semantics. So how do you allow your component to progress over time or increase in sophistication? You expose another interface. You can either inherit from the existing interface or develop a completely new one, as long as the old interface still remains available to legacy clients.

If the new interface is simply a superset of an old interface, you'd be smart to have the new interface inherit from the old one, like so:

```
[ object, uuid(93ED133D-3DA3-11D2-B380-006008A667FD) ]
interface IBuckDog : IUnknown
{
    HRESULT Bark([out, retval] BSTR* pbstr);
    HRESULT Sniff();
    HRESULT NeedsWalk([out, retval] BOOL *pVal);
};

[ object, uuid(93ED1341-3DA3-11D2-B380-006008A667FD) ]
interface IBuckDog2 : IBuckDog
{
    HRESULT RollOver();
    HRESULT HasFleas([out, retval] BOOL *pVal);
};
```

In this IDL, the new interface, *IBuckDog2*, exposes all the methods found in *IBuckDog* in addition to two new ones. It makes sense to derive *IBuckDog2* from *IBuckDog* and update your implementation to support both interfaces—the new methods as well as the old.

In other cases, we might be wiser to expose an additional interface not derived from one that currently exists. Take our *TipOfTheDay* component: it currently exposes a single interface that allows its users to iterate through each tip in the pool. It would be nice if the component also supported an interface that allowed administrators or sophisticated users to add new items to the tip pool. Obviously, adding this type of functionality would require significant changes in the internal implementation of the original component, because the current implementation uses a global array. Fortunately, COM allows you to make these changes (perhaps storing the tips in a SQL Server database) completely unbeknownst to the component's clients. So if we do want to allow certain users to add their own tips, we probably want to expose another interface entirely rather than add unrelated methods to the existing interface signature. Thus, we might end up with the following:

```
interface ITipOfTheDay : IDispatch
{
    [id(1), helpstring("method GetNextTip")]
    HRESULT GetNextTip([in, out] long* pvCookie,
                       [out, retval] BSTR* pbstrText);
};
```

*(continued)*

```
interface ITipManager : IDispatch
{
    [id(1), helpstring("method AddTip")]
    HRESULT AddTip([in] BSTR bstrText,
                   [out, retval] long lCookie);
};
```

In both cases, the result is that a single coclass exposes two interfaces. Old clients that expected only the original interface wouldn't be negatively affected by the new one. They wouldn't even know it had been added. New clients would be able to take advantage of the functionality of both interfaces by calling *QueryInterface* to get back a pointer to either one.

## The Dual Interface Dilemma

Unfortunately, this approach doesn't work with dual or dispatch interfaces because a component can expose only a single set of methods and properties via the *IDispatch* interface. So instead of being able to expose a second interface and take advantage of the power of dynamic discovery (à la *QueryInterface*), components that expose dual or dispatch interfaces must change the existing interface to create an encompassing superset of both the old and the new methods, as shown here:

```
interface ITipOfTheDay : IDispatch
{
    [id(1), helpstring("method GetNextTip")]
    HRESULT GetNextTip([in, out] long* pvCookie,
                       [out, retval] BSTR* pbstrText);
};

interface ITipManager : IDispatch
{
    [id(1), helpstring("method GetNextTip")]
    HRESULT GetNextTip([in, out] long* pvCookie,
                       [out, retval] BSTR* pbstrText);
    [id(2), helpstring("method AddTip")]
    HRESULT AddTip([in] BSTR bstrText,
                   [out, retval] long* plCookie);
};

coclass TipOfTheDay
{
    [default] interface ITipManager;
    interface ITipOfTheDay;
};
```

In the class declaration, both interfaces would be supported, and vtable-aware clients could call *QueryInterface* to get at both interfaces. To support scripting clients (which don't use *QueryInterface* and can thus see only a single dispinterface per component), however, the conceptual integrity of the *ITipManager* interface would be compromised. It would have to encompass the functionality of the unrelated *ITipOfTheDay* interface and thus implement the *GetNextTip* method:

```
class ATL_NO_VTABLE CTipOfTheDay :
public CComObjectRootEx<CComSingleThreadModel>,
public CComCoClass<CTipOfTheDay, &CLSID_TipOfTheDay>,
public IDispatchImpl<ITipOfTheDay, &IID_ITipOfTheDay,
    &LIBID_TIPSERVERLib>,
public IDispatchImpl<ITipManager, &IID_ITipManager,
    &LIBID_TIPSERVERLib>
{
    :
    BEGIN_COM_MAP(CTipOfTheDay)
    COM_INTERFACE_ENTRY(ITipOfTheDay)
    COM_INTERFACE_ENTRY(ITipManager)
    COM_INTERFACE_ENTRY2(IDispatch, ITipManager)
    END_COM_MAP()
    :
// ITipOfTheDay
public:
    STDMETHOD(AddTip)(/*[in]*/ BSTR bstrTest,
                      /*[out, retval]*/ long* plCookie);
    STDMETHOD(GetNextTip)(/*[in, out]*/ VARIANT* pvCookie,
                          /*[out, retval]*/ BSTR* pbstrText);
    :
};
```

# Threading Revisited

After a careful examination of the implementation of the TipOfTheDay coclass, we confirmed our original suspicions: we were able to design the component such that it doesn't store global data, per-class data, or even per-instance data. The state of the component is entirely determined by the cookie parameter stored by the client application, so restricting object access to a single thread is unnecessary. Because the *TipOfTheDay* component doesn't use worker threads, there's no reason we wouldn't allow it to be created in an STA, so it makes sense to support both threading models. We'll change the Registry setting from ThreadingModel=Apartment to ThreadingModel=Both by editing the TIPOFTHEDAY.RGS file that the ATL Object Wizard created and added to the project.

```
InprocServer32 = s '%MODULE%'
{
    val ThreadingModel = s 'Both'
}
```

We'll also need to change some wizard-generated code to reflect the threading model. Replace

```
#define _ATL_APARTMENT_THREADED
Public CComObjectRootEx<CComSingleThreadModel>
```

with

```
#define _ATL_FREE_THREADED
Public CComObjectRootEx<CComMultiThreadModel>
```

> **NOTE** It wouldn't be accurate to say that the *TipOfTheDay* component is stateless, because the call history does indeed affect the data returned by the *GetNextTip* method. A client that calls *GetNextTip* three times will get a different result than a client that calls *GetNextTip* four times. More precisely, our component can be called "state estranged." A separate entity manages and stores its state.

# Conclusion

The choices you make when you use the ATL COM AppWizard, the ATL Object Wizard, and the Add Method dialog box significantly impact the architecture and implementation of your COM components. Although each of these productivity features is beneficial, they all must be used judiciously and with an understanding of the effect they have on the outcome of your components. In this chapter alone, we've discussed several key concepts you'll need to understand when creating components with ATL:

- The ATL preprocessor symbols
- The AppWizard-generated build configurations
- The choice of a threading model
- The advantages and drawbacks of dual interfaces
- The support needs of clients built using different languages, including ASP, Visual Basic, and Visual C++

In the next chapter, we'll see how ATL also makes *using* COM objects a little more painless with its client-side helper classes.

## CHAPTER FIVE

# Client-Side ATL

As you saw in Chapter 2, COM is a beautiful, logical model for component-based development. The underlying concepts that define the COM model—such as encapsulation, abstraction, and polymorphism—are essentially simple principles. Despite the simplicity of the model itself, however, many developers find COM development under C++ tedious. Many developers (ourselves included) complain that a significant portion of day-to-day C++ COM development is spent implementing repetitive, low-level details. In this chapter, we'll focus on the client-side use of COM and take an in-depth look at the ATL classes that make client-side COM easier. Specifically, we'll look at the ATL smart pointer classes *CComPtr* and *CComQIPtr*, the data conversion classes *CComBSTR* and *CComVariant*, and the handy *CComDispatchDriver* class.

## Is COM Tedious?

With COM, every time you decide to implement a new interface, you must provide much more than just the implementation code for the methods exposed by that interface. Because every interface must inherit from *IUnknown*, you must also supply an implementation for *IUnknown*'s *AddRef*, *Release*, and *QueryInterface* methods. Typically, you must also provide an associated class object that implements the methods defined by the *IClassFactory* interface. If the new interface must behave effectively in C++, Microsoft Visual Basic, and scripting environments such as Microsoft Active Server Pages, you'll probably want to declare the interface as a dual interface—meaning that it is derived from *IDispatch*—so you'll have to supply an implementation of the four *IDispatch* methods as well. The great thing about COM development using C++ is that you have complete control over the implementation of each of these interfaces and methods. In other languages, such as Visual Basic, you don't. In some cases, you must have a high level of coding control, especially when you're developing code that defines your application's business logic. But in many cases, the code for the *IDispatch*, *IClassFactory*, and *IUnknown* interfaces—among others—is boilerplate; that is, the implementation code for those interfaces is essentially the same for each of your custom interfaces. Certainly, to be a productive COM developer, you must have a solid understanding of the role of each of those core interfaces. But having to reimplement "stock" interfaces unnecessarily over and over again can reduce your efficiency and introduce coding errors.

The tendency toward tedium found in C++ COM development is compounded by the fact that the code required to work with COM objects on the client side is often both ugly and error prone. Compare the code shown in Listings 5-1 and 5-2. Both listings show the code required to automate a COM-based application. Listing 5-1 shows the code required in Visual Basic, and Listing 5-2 shows the code required in Microsoft Visual C++. As you can see, the Visual Basic code couldn't be simpler—but the C++ code isn't a pretty picture. Why is the Visual Basic code so much cleaner? Three fundamental reasons account for the simplicity of the Visual Basic code:

- Visual Basic automatically manages dynamic interface discovery and object lifetime, meaning that the client code never explicitly calls any of the *IUnknown* methods *QueryInterface*, *AddRef*, and *Release*.

- Visual Basic inherently supports the BSTR and VARIANT data types.

- Visual Basic hides the details required to make calls to *IDispatch*-based methods.

```
Dim App As Object
Private Sub Form_Load()
    Set App = CreateObject("MSDEV.Application")
    App.Visible = True
    App.Quit
End Sub
```

**Listing 5-1**
*Visual Basic client code*

```
HRESULT CountArgsInFormat(LPCTSTR pszFmt, UINT FAR *pn);
LPCTSTR GetNextVarType(LPCTSTR pszFmt, VARTYPE FAR* pvt);
HRESULT CreateObject(LPOLESTR pszProgID,
    IDispatch FAR* FAR* ppdisp);

void OnFormLoad()
{
    CoInitialize();

    CLSID clsid;
    CLSIDFromProgID(L"MSDEV.APPLICATION", &clsid);
    IDispatch* pdisp = NULL;
    hr = CoCreateInstance(clsid, NULL, CLSCTX_SERVER,
        IID_IDispatch, (void**)&pdisp);

    Invoke(pdisp, DISPATCH_PROPERTYPUT, NULL, NULL, NULL,
        OLESTR("Visible"), "b", VARIANT_TRUE);
    Invoke(pdisp, DISPATCH_METHOD, NULL, NULL, NULL,
        OLESTR("Quit"), NULL);
    pdisp->Release();
    CoUninitialize();
}

HRESULT Invoke(LPDISPATCH pdisp, WORD wFlags, LPVARIANT pvRet,
    EXCEPINFO FAR* pexcepinfo, UINT FAR* pnArgErr,
    LPOLESTR pszName, LPCTSTR pszFmt, ...)
{
    va_list argList;
    va_start(argList, pszFmt);
    DISPID dispid;
    HRESULT hr;
    VARIANTARG* pvarg = NULL;

    if(pdisp == NULL)
        return E_INVALIDARG;

    hr = pdisp->GetIDsOfNames(IID_NULL, &pszName, 1,
        LOCALE_USER_DEFAULT, &dispid);
    if(FAILED(hr))
        return hr;
```

**Listing 5-2**
*Visual C++ client code*

*(continued)*

**Listing 5-2** *continued*

```
DISPPARAMS dispparams;
_fmemset(&dispparams, 0, sizeof dispparams);
if(pszFmt != NULL)
    CountArgsInFormat(pszFmt, &dispparams.cArgs);

DISPID dispidNamed = DISPID_PROPERTYPUT;
if(wFlags & DISPATCH_PROPERTYPUT)
{
    if(dispparams.cArgs == 0)
        return E_INVALIDARG;
    dispparams.cNamedArgs = 1;
    dispparams.rgdispidNamedArgs = &dispidNamed;
}


if(dispparams.cArgs != 0)
{
    pvarg = new VARIANTARG[dispparams.cArgs];
    if(pvarg == NULL)
        return E_OUTOFMEMORY;
    dispparams.rgvarg = pvarg;
    _fmemset(pvarg, 0, sizeof(VARIANTARG) * dispparams.cArgs);
    LPCTSTR psz = pszFmt;
    pvarg += dispparams.cArgs - 1;   // Parameters go in
                                     //  opposite order.
    while (psz = GetNextVarType(psz, &pvarg->vt))
    {
        if(pvarg < dispparams.rgvarg)
        {
            hr = E_INVALIDARG;
            goto cleanup;
        }
        switch (pvarg->vt)
        {
        case VT_I2:
            V_I2(pvarg) = va_arg(argList, short);
            break;
        case VT_I4:
            V_I4(pvarg) = va_arg(argList, long);
            break;
        case VT_R4:
            V_R4(pvarg) = va_arg(argList, float);
            break;
        case VT_DATE:
```

```
case VT_R8:
    V_R8(pvarg) = va_arg(argList, double);
    break;
case VT_CY:
    V_CY(pvarg) = va_arg(argList, CY);
    break;
case VT_BSTR:
    V_BSTR(pvarg) = SysAllocString(va_arg(argList,
        OLECHAR FAR*));
    if(pvarg->bstrVal == NULL)
    {
        hr = E_OUTOFMEMORY;
        pvarg->vt = VT_EMPTY;
        goto cleanup;
    }
    break;
case VT_DISPATCH:
    V_DISPATCH(pvarg) = va_arg(argList, LPDISPATCH);
    break;
case VT_ERROR:
    V_ERROR(pvarg) = va_arg(argList, SCODE);
    break;
case VT_BOOL:
    V_BOOL(pvarg) = va_arg(argList, BOOL) ? -1 : 0;
    break;
case VT_VARIANT:
    *pvarg = va_arg(argList, VARIANTARG);
    break;
case VT_UNKNOWN:
    V_UNKNOWN(pvarg) = va_arg(argList, LPUNKNOWN);
    break;

case VT_I2|VT_BYREF:
    V_I2REF(pvarg) = va_arg(argList, short FAR*);
    break;
case VT_I4|VT_BYREF:
    V_I4REF(pvarg) = va_arg(argList, long FAR*);
    break;
case VT_R4|VT_BYREF:
    V_R4REF(pvarg) = va_arg(argList, float FAR*);
    break;
case VT_R8|VT_BYREF:
    V_R8REF(pvarg) = va_arg(argList, double FAR*);
    break;
```

*(continued)*

**Listing 5-2** *continued*

```
        case VT_DATE|VT_BYREF:
            V_DATEREF(pvarg) = va_arg(argList, DATE FAR*);
            break;
        case VT_CY|VT_BYREF:
            V_CYREF(pvarg) = va_arg(argList, CY FAR*);
            break;
        case VT_BSTR|VT_BYREF:
            V_BSTRREF(pvarg) = va_arg(argList, BSTR FAR*);
            break;
        case VT_DISPATCH|VT_BYREF:
            V_DISPATCHREF(pvarg) = va_arg(argList,
                LPDISPATCH FAR*);
            break;
        case VT_ERROR|VT_BYREF:
            V_ERRORREF(pvarg) = va_arg(argList, SCODE FAR*);
            break;
        case VT_BOOL|VT_BYREF:
            {
                BOOL FAR* pbool = va_arg(argList, BOOL FAR*);
                *pbool = 0;
                V_BOOLREF(pvarg) = (VARIANT_BOOL FAR*)pbool;
            }
            break;
        case VT_VARIANT|VT_BYREF:
            V_VARIANTREF(pvarg) = va_arg(argList,
                VARIANTARG FAR*);
            break;
        case VT_UNKNOWN|VT_BYREF:
            V_UNKNOWNREF(pvarg) = va_arg(argList,
                LPUNKNOWN FAR*);
            break;

        default:
            {
                hr = E_INVALIDARG;
                goto cleanup;
            }
            break;
        }

        --pvarg; // Get ready to fill the next argument.
    } //while
} //if
```

```
        if(pvRet)
            VariantInit(pvRet);
        hr = pdisp->Invoke(dispid, IID_NULL, LOCALE_USER_DEFAULT,
            wFlags, &dispparams, pvRet, pexcepinfo, pnArgErr);

cleanup:
        // Clean up any arguments that need cleaning up.
        if(dispparams.cArgs != 0)
        {
            VARIANTARG FAR* pvarg = dispparams.rgvarg;
            UINT cArgs = dispparams.cArgs;

            while (cArgs--)
            {
                switch (pvarg->vt)
                {
                case VT_BSTR:
                    VariantClear(pvarg);
                    break;
                }
                ++pvarg;
            }
        }
        delete dispparams.rgvarg;
        va_end(argList);
        return hr;
}

HRESULT CountArgsInFormat(LPCTSTR pszFmt, UINT FAR *pn)
{
    *pn = 0;

    if(pszFmt == NULL)
        return NOERROR;

    while (*pszFmt)
    {
        if(*pszFmt == '&')
            pszFmt++;

        switch (*pszFmt)
        {
```

*(continued)*

**Listing 5-2** *continued*

```
            case 'b':
            case 'i':
            case 'I':
            case 'r':
            case 'R':
            case 'c':
            case 's':
            case 'e':
            case 'd':
            case 'v':
            case 'D':
            case 'U':
                ++*pn;
                pszFmt++;
                break;
            case '\0':
            default:
                return E_INVALIDARG;
        }
    }
    return NOERROR;
}

LPCTSTR GetNextVarType(LPCTSTR pszFmt, VARTYPE FAR* pvt)
{
    *pvt = 0;
    if(*pszFmt == '&')
    {
        *pvt = VT_BYREF;
        pszFmt++;
        if(!*pszFmt)
            return NULL;
    }
    switch (*pszFmt)
    {
        case 'b':
            *pvt |= VT_BOOL;
            break;
        case 'i':
            *pvt |= VT_I2;
            break;
        case 'I':
            *pvt |= VT_I4;
            break;
```

```
        case 'r':
            *pvt |= VT_R4;
            break;
        case 'R':
            *pvt |= VT_R8;
            break;
        case 'c':
            *pvt |= VT_CY;
            break;
        case 's':
            *pvt |= VT_BSTR;
            break;
        case 'e':
            *pvt |= VT_ERROR;
            break;
        case 'd':
            *pvt |= VT_DATE;
            break;
        case 'v':
            *pvt |= VT_VARIANT;
            break;
        case 'U':
            *pvt |= VT_UNKNOWN;
            break;
        case 'D':
            *pvt |= VT_DISPATCH;
            break;
        case '\0':
            return NULL;      // End of format string
        default:
            return NULL;
    }
    return ++pszFmt;
}
```

Admittedly, the sample code in Listing 5-1 and Listing 5-2 represents an extreme example of the difference between the client-side COM support provided by Visual Basic and by Visual C++, but it does illustrate the difficulty of using COM objects from C++. If you're a big fan of C++, you don't need to get defensive. A framework such as Visual Basic, which takes care of all the details, is like valet service for your car. It's a great convenience if you're in a hurry, but it requires a degree of trust and a significant overhead expense.

In an ideal world, C++ developers would have complete control over any details considered necessary—which might change from object to object—but also have a lightweight, unobtrusive framework to handle any details deemed unnecessary behind the scenes. For example, because nearly all the code shown in Listing 5-2 consists of helper functions that can be used in every COM application that makes calls to an *IDispatch* interface, encapsulating those functions within a reusable class makes sense. That's where ATL comes in. It takes care of many of the messy COM details yet leaves you a great degree of flexibility and control. For most C++ developers, ATL represents an ideal trade-off. It provides a lean, optimized, default implementation of many tedious COM idioms while still allowing you the ability to override, replace, or ignore any of those idioms. (In case you're wondering, ATL encapsulates the lengthy code in Listing 5-2 in a handy *CComDispatchDriver* class.)

# Smart Pointers

One of the most confusing concepts for the developer just getting started with COM is the notion of per-interface reference counting. The idea is really quite simple and can be summed up in two statements:

- A COM object manages its own lifetime by keeping track of the number of clients that reference it.

- A COM object must be notified whenever a client reference (that is, an interface pointer) comes into or goes out of existence.

Reference counting is a powerful, elegant concept, but it does add a certain degree of complexity to C++ client code that uses COM objects. The use of *CoCreateInstance* (or other COM object–creation mechanisms), *AddRef*, and *Release* represents a syntactic paradigm shift from the commonly used *new* and *delete* keywords that are familiar to C++ developers. In other words, a C++ developer must treat interface pointers differently than other pointers. To illustrate, let's consider the following pseudocode:

```
CMyClient::CMyClient()
{
    m_pBuffer = new CBuffer();
    m_pArray = new CArray();
    m_pInterface = SomeCreationMechanism();
}

CMyClient::~CMyClient()
{
    delete m_pBuffer;
    delete m_pArray;
    delete m_pInterface;    // Oops!
}
```

Obviously, if *m_pInterface* represents a COM interface pointer, this code will fail miserably. Why? Because the destructor should call *m_pInterface->Release* instead of trying to free the pointer using the C++ *delete* keyword. The fact that interface pointers must be handled with different cleanup syntax than other pointers makes it easy for programmers unaccustomed to COM to introduce bugs into their code. This potential hot spot is similar to another common C++ cleanup error. The following code contains a subtle bug:

```
CMyCode::CMyCode()
{
    m_pArray = new CString[256];
    m_pBuffer = new TCHAR[256];
}

CMyCode::~CMyCode()
{
    delete m_pArray;    // Oops!
    delete m_pBuffer;   // Oops!
}
```

What's the problem with this code? C++ coding rules specify that when deleting an array of objects, the *delete* keyword must be followed by a bracket pair to tell the compiler to perform the necessary heap cleanup on each object in the array, like so:

```
CMyCode::~CMyCode()
{
    delete [] m_pArray;    // That's better!
    delete [] m_pBuffer;   // This bracket pair is technically
                           //  required too!
}
```

Even though the improper use of the *delete* keyword (without the necessary brackets) in the cleanup of the *m_pBuffer* variable doesn't cause a memory leak under Visual C++, it's still technically a bug, albeit a benevolent one. The Visual C++ compiler will clean up the mistake where *m_pBuffer* is not destroyed using *delete []*. The improper deletion of *m_pArray*, an array of *CStrings*, does result in a memory leak. Cleaning up COM interface pointers is similar to deleting arrays because it also represents a special case, one that you must keep in mind—consciously at first, subconsciously after a bit of practice—when writing code.

Having to remember to call *AddRef* and *Release* instead of *delete* shouldn't be a big deal once you learn the rules, right? Well, theoretically that's true, but C++ exception handling adds a significant degree of complexity to the picture. Recall that when you use exceptions in your code, the C++ compiler will automatically generate the necessary code to unwind the stack back to the *catch* block.

For example, study the following pseudocode:

```
try
{
    ⋮
    IFortuneCookie* pCookie;
    CoCreateInstance(clsid, NULL, CLSCTX_ALL,
        IID_IFortuneCookie, (void**)&pCookie;
    HRESULT hr = pCookie->SetSeed(FALSE);
    if(hr != S_OK)
        throw hr;
}
catch(HRESULT hr)
{
    TCHAR szErrorDesc[256];
    ::FormatMessage(FORMAT_MESSAGE_FROM_SYSTEM, NULL, hr,
        MAKELANGID(LANG_NEUTRAL, SUBLANG_NEUTRAL),
        szErrorDesc, sizeof(szErrorDesc), NULL);
    ::MessageBox(NULL, szErrorDesc, "HRESULT Failure", MB_OK);

    // Oops! I just leaked pCookie!
}
```

In this code, the client creates an instance of a COM object and calls one of its methods. Following the rules of proper COM development, the object doesn't throw an exception from within the called method when an error occurs. Rather, it returns an error in HRESULT that the client code throws. The code above attempts to recover elegantly from the error by displaying the text-based description of the error to the user before continuing program execution. The problem with this code is that because *pCookie* is a dynamically allocated interface pointer rather than a stack variable, the compiler won't release *pCookie* when the thrown exception causes it to go out of scope. Because *pCookie* isn't defined in the context of the catch block, the code can't call *pCookie->Release*. As a result, if the COM object is implemented as an out-of-process server, the server won't shut down when the client code terminates because of the outstanding reference to the object.

In the preceding example, we could easily restructure the code so that the scope of *pCookie* encompasses the *catch* block—calling *pCookie->Release* would then be possible. For typical applications, though, writing code to handle a situation like this one would be challenging if not impossible. To solve this problem, some programming languages—specifically Visual Basic and Java—perform automatic garbage collection and *IUnknown* encapsulation so that the developer doesn't have to manually code calls to the *AddRef, Release*, and *QueryInterface* interface methods. Consider the following Visual Basic code:

```
Private Sub Form_Load()
    Dim cookie As IFortuneCookie
    Dim cookie2 As IFortuneCookie2
    Set cookie = New FortuneCookie
    Set cookie2 = cookie
    cookie2.SetSeed(77)
End Sub
```

This code creates an instance of a *FortuneCookie* COM class, calls *QueryInterface* at least twice—once each for the *IFortuneCookie* and *IFortuneCookie2* interfaces— and automatically handles the reference counting of each interface. Because of the inherent COM run-time support found in Visual Basic and Microsoft Visual J++, developers using those languages are somewhat more able than C++ developers to focus on the problems their software must solve rather than on syntax.

## The *CComPtr* and *CComQIPtr* Classes

To provide a level of syntactic convenience that more closely approaches the code shown in Listing 5-1, but without the associated overhead expense Visual Basic imposes, ATL provides two smart pointer classes—*CComPtr* and *CComQIPtr*— that implement automatic reference counting. (See Chapter 2 for more details about smart pointers.) The term *smart pointer*—a common but rather controversial notion in the COM community—refers to a lightweight templatized C++ wrapper class that manages the lifetime of an interface pointer. The basic idea behind smart pointers is to encapsulate the calls to *AddRef* and *Release* such that the constructor and destructor call them automatically, as shown in this pseudocode:

```
template <class P>
class CSmartPtr
{
    P* p;
public:
    CSmartPtr(P* ptr) { p = ptr; if(p) p->AddRef(); }
    ~CSmartPtr() { if(p) p->Release(); }
};
```

As you'll see later in this chapter, this technique introduces its own set of complications, but it has two benefits. First, the client code no longer needs to call *AddRef* and *Release* when using an instance of the pointer. Second, the client code can represent the interface using a *CSmartPtr* stack variable instead of a dynamically allocated pointer, which means that *Release* will automatically be called from within the *CSmartPtr* destructor when the variable goes out of scope.

The ATL smart pointer classes are much more sophisticated than the implementation shown in the preceding pseudocode example. Using the ATL

*CComPtr* and *CComQIPtr* classes, the C++ version of the Visual Basic code at the top of the previous page would look like this:

```
void OnLoad()
{
    CComPtr<IFortuneCookie> cookie;
    cookie.CoCreateInstance(OLESTR("FortuneLib.Cookie"));
    CComQIPtr<IFortuneCookie2> cookie2(cookie);
    cookie2->SetSeed(77);
}
```

Although the C++ version of the *OnLoad* code is still syntactically more complex than the Visual Basic code it mimics, it can be expressed in fewer lines. Even more important, because *cookie* and *cookie2* are implemented as stack variables rather than pointers, the interfaces they encapsulate are automatically released when *OnLoad* terminates, whether as a result of normal execution or a thrown exception.

---

### Previous Versions of ATL: *CComPtr* and *CComQIPtr*

The *CComPtr* and *CComQIPtr* classes were significantly improved from ATL 2.1 to ATL 3.0. As we describe later in this chapter, one of the chief disadvantages of smart pointer encapsulation is that inadvertent calls made directly to the *IUnknown::AddRef* and *IUnknown::Release* methods can cause unexpected and disastrous results. To prevent this problem, the ATL 3.0 versions of the *CComPtr* and *CComQIPtr* classes include special provisions that prevent users of those classes from calling *AddRef* and *Release* using the overloaded indirection operator ( -> ). ATL 3.0 also introduces several new methods to the smart pointer classes, as you'll see in Table 5-1 on page 130.

---

Let's take a look at how the ATL smart pointers work. The source for the *CComQIPtr* class is defined in atlbase.h and is shown in Listing 5-3. The *CComPtr* and *CComQIPtr* classes differ only slightly, so the code in Listing 5-3 essentially represents the functionality of both classes. Because of this similarity, we'll refer to the ATL smart pointer classes as *CComPtr* unless we're specifically describing the extra methods implemented by *CComQIPtr*. As shown in boldface in the listing, *CComQIPtr* has an optional templatized parameter and two methods not found in *CComPtr*.

**NOTE**   In day-to-day development, we use *CComQIPtr* almost exclusively because it contains a superset of the functionality exposed by *CComPtr*.

```
template <class T>
class _NoAddRefReleaseOnCComPtr : public T
{
private:
    STDMETHOD_(ULONG, AddRef)()=0;
    STDMETHOD_(ULONG, Release)()=0;
};

template <class T, const IID* piid = &__uuidof(T)>
class CComQIPtr
{
public:
    typedef T _PtrClass;
    CComQIPtr()
    {
        p=NULL;
    }
    CComQIPtr(T* lp)
    {
        if((p = lp) != NULL)
            p->AddRef();
    }
    CComQIPtr(const CComQIPtr<T,piid>& lp)
    {
        if((p = lp.p) != NULL)
            p->AddRef();
    }
    CComQIPtr(IUnknown* lp)
    {
        p=NULL;
        if(lp != NULL)
            lp->QueryInterface(*piid, (void **)&p);
    }
```

**Listing 5-3**                                                    *(continued)*
*Source listing for the* CComQIPtr *class*

**Listing 5-3** *continued*

```
    ~CComQIPtr()
    {
        if(p)
            p->Release();
    }
    void Release()
{
        IUnknown* pTemp = p;
        if(pTemp)
        {
            p = NULL;
            pTemp->Release();
        }
    }
    operator T*() const
    {
        return p;
    }
    T& operator*() const
    {
        ATLASSERT(p!=NULL); return *p;
    }
    // The assert on operator& usually indicates a bug. If the
    // assertion is really what is needed, however, take the
    // address of the p member explicitly.
    T** operator&()
    {
        ATLASSERT(p==NULL);
        return &p;
    }
    _NoAddRefReleaseOnCComPtr<T>* operator->() const
    {
        ATLASSERT(p!=NULL);
        return (_NoAddRefReleaseOnCComPtr<T>*)p;
    }
    T* operator=(T* lp)
    {
        return (T*)AtlComPtrAssign((IUnknown**)&p, lp);
    }
    T* operator=(const CComQIPtr<T,piid>& lp)
    {
        return (T*)AtlComPtrAssign((IUnknown**)&p, lp.p);
    }
```

```
T* operator=(IUnknown* lp)
{
    return (T*)AtlComQIPtrAssign((IUnknown**)&p, lp, *piid);
}
bool operator!() const
{
    return (p == NULL);
}
bool operator<(T* pT) const
{
    return p < pT;
}
bool operator==(T* pT) const
{
    return p == pT;
}
// Compare two objects for equivalence.
bool IsEqualObject(IUnknown* pOther)
{
    if(p == NULL && pOther == NULL)
        return true; // They are both NULL objects.

    if(p == NULL || pOther == NULL)
        return false; // One object is NULL
                      //  but the other isn't.

    CComPtr<IUnknown> punk1;
    CComPtr<IUnknown> punk2;
    p->QueryInterface(IID_IUnknown, (void**)&punk1);
    pOther->QueryInterface(IID_IUnknown, (void**)&punk2);
    return punk1 == punk2;
}
void Attach(T* p2)
{
    if(p)
    p->Release();
    p = p2;
}
T* Detach()
{
    T* pt = p;
    p = NULL;
    return pt;
}
```

*(continued)*

**Listing 5-3** *continued*

```
    HRESULT CopyTo(T** ppT)
    {
        ATLASSERT(ppT != NULL);
        if(ppT == NULL)
            return E_POINTER;
        *ppT = p;
        if(p)
            p->AddRef();
        return S_OK;
    }
    HRESULT SetSite(IUnknown* punkParent)
    {
        return AtlSetChildSite(p, punkParent);
    }
    HRESULT Advise(IUnknown* pUnk, const IID& iid, LPDWORD pdw)
    {
        return AtlAdvise(p, pUnk, iid, pdw);
    }
    HRESULT CoCreateInstance(REFCLSID rclsid,
        LPUNKNOWN pUnkOuter = NULL, DWORD dwClsContext = CLSCTX_ALL)
    {
        ATLASSERT(p == NULL);
        return ::CoCreateInstance(rclsid, pUnkOuter, dwClsContext,
            __uuidof(T), (void**)&p);
    }
    HRESULT CoCreateInstance(LPCOLESTR szProgID,
        LPUNKNOWN pUnkOuter = NULL, DWORD dwClsContext = CLSCTX_ALL)
    {
        CLSID clsid;
        HRESULT hr = CLSIDFromProgID(szProgID, &clsid);
        ATLASSERT(p == NULL);
        if(SUCCEEDED(hr))
            hr = ::CoCreateInstance(clsid, pUnkOuter, dwClsContext,
                __uuidof(T), (void**)&p);
        return hr;
    }
    template <class Q>
    HRESULT QueryInterface(Q** pp)
    {
        ATLASSERT(pp != NULL && *pp == NULL);
        return p->QueryInterface(__uuidof(Q), (void**)pp);
    }
    T* p;
};
```

The template parameter *T*—used to specify the type of the interface pointer being encapsulated—is required to allow the *CComPtr* class to be strongly typed. This strong typing means that rather than using a generic *void\** type, the class has a member variable of type *T\** that holds the interface pointer. This technique offers more than just type safety. It allows the wrapper class to act as if it were a pointer to the interface *T* when dereferenced using the indirection operator ( -> ), like so:

```
CComPtr<IBuckDog> smartPtr(pDogPtr);
pDogPtr->Bark();    // This calls the IBuckDog::Bark method.
smartPtr->Bark();   // So does this!
```

In this code snippet, *pDogPtr* is a pointer to an *IBuckDog* interface, so using the indirection operator to call its *Bark* method is obvious and fully expected. What isn't immediately clear to the novice is how calling *smartPtr->Bark* ends up calling the *Bark* method in light of the fact that *smartPtr* doesn't inherit from *IBuckDog*, nor is it a pointer! The answer to this puzzle is that the *CComPtr* class overloads the indirection operator, as shown in the following pseudocode:

```
T* CComPtr::operator->() const
{
    return m_ptr;  // Where m_ptr is a member variable of type T*
}
```

The elegance of C++—combined with the use of templates—allows the *CComPtr* class to leverage operator overloading to make seamless, type-safe calls to the interface pointer, at the expense of a negligible layer of method invocation.

Using the *CComPtr* class has several benefits. The *CComPtr* class allows you to manage the lifetime of an interface pointer as if it were a class pointer by encapsulating the calls to *AddRef* and *Release* in its constructors and destructor, respectively. Because smart pointers are typically automatic variables rather than dynamically allocated variables, they are automatically cleaned up when they go out of scope. The use of *CComPtr* and *CComQIPtr* simplifies the syntax of the application by reducing the calls to *AddRef*, *Release*, and *QueryInterface* sprinkled throughout the code.

Aside from the benefits mentioned above, the *CComPtr* class provides helper methods that make it even more convenient to use. Several of these methods, introduced in ATL 3.0, are shown in Table 5-1.

## Table 5-1   Frequently Used *CComPtr* Methods

| *CComPtr* Method | Description |
| --- | --- |
| *IsEqualObject* | Compares two interface pointers to see whether they represent the same object. According to the rules of COM, whether two interface pointers represent the same object can be determined only by comparing *IUnknown* pointers. This function isn't the same as the == operator, which simply performs a mathematical comparison of the value of two pointers. |
| *Attach* | Attaches a pointer to the class without incrementing its reference count. Presumably, if the pointer is valid, its reference count is already nonzero via a previous call (whether directly or indirectly) to *AddRef*. If the class already encapsulates a valid pointer, that pointer will be released before being overwritten. |
| *Detach* | Returns the encapsulated pointer and sets the internal copy to NULL without calling *Release*. |
| *CoCreateInstance* | Creates an instance of a coclass specified by its CLSID or its progID, requesting the interface of type *T*. This method simply calls the global *::CoCreateInstance* function, but it does so in a type-safe manner. This method provides default arguments for the outer aggregate and class context. |
| *QueryInterface* | Allows the client to make *QueryInterface* calls on the encapsulated pointer in a type-safe manner. |

Although there is no inheritance relationship between *CComPtr* and *CComQIPtr*, the *CComQIPtr* class is essentially a superset of the functionality provided by *CComPtr*. The chief difference between the two classes is that *CComQIPtr* provides additional constructor and assignment operators that automatically call *QueryInterface* when passed an interface pointer. As mentioned earlier, these methods are displayed in boldface in Listing 5-3. *CComQIPtr* allows you to assign one pointer to another—even if the two pointers represent different interfaces—by making a call to *QueryInterface* under the hood during the assignment.

```
CComPtr<IUnknown> ptrUnk;
HRESULT hr = ptrUnk.CoCreateInstance(OLESTR("MSDEV.Application"));
hr = OleRun(ptrUnk);

CComQIPtr<IDispatch> ptrDisp(ptrUnk);      // QI under the hood!
CComQIPtr<IApplication> ptrApp;
ptrApp = ptrUnk;                           // QI under the hood!
```

```
if(!application)
    // Failed
```

In this code, *CComQIPtr* makes a call to *QueryInterface* in the *dispTest* constructor and also in the *ptrApp* assignment. To allow you to determine whether a smart pointer represents a valid interface pointer, the smart pointer overloads the logical NOT operator, returning true if the pointer is NULL:

```
bool CComPtr::operator!() const
{
    return (p == NULL);
}
```

## The Mr. Hyde of Smart Pointers

So far, we've described the advantages of using the *CComPtr* and *CComQIPtr* classes. Obviously, they offer a level of convenience and information hiding that makes their use attractive. Smart pointers are not without a dark side, however. They can potentially introduce several problems into your application.

The smart pointer classes provide a *CoCreateInstance* method that encapsulates a call to the COM API of the same name. This method is helpful in many situations, especially because it has two overloaded implementations: one that takes a progID parameter and another that accepts a CLSID. The ATL smart pointer classes also encapsulate the casting of the interface pointer to a *void\*\** (as required by the global *::CoCreateInstance* API), thus reducing the errors generally associated with that cast's lack of type safety. The drawback is that the *CoCreateInstance* method calls *::CoCreateInstance* rather than *::CoCreateInstanceEx*, so you can't use it when you need to explicitly specify the name and activation security context of the remote machine on which the object will be created. Furthermore, you can't always use the *CoCreateInstance* method when instantiating Automation servers. Some servers require you to call the *::OleRun* API to transition the object into a running state before calling *QueryInterface* for the desired interface.

> **NOTE** Microsoft Developer Studio is an example of such an Automation server. Because you must first call *QueryInterface* for *IUnknown*, call *OleRun*, and then call *QueryInterface* for *IApplication*, the *CComPtr<IApplication>::CoCreateInstance* method won't work correctly. Incidentally, the Visual C++ run-time library implements a smart pointer class named *_com_ptr* that automatically performs these steps in its *CreateInstance* method.

As mentioned earlier in the chapter, the *CComQIPtr* class automatically calls *QueryInterface* on an incoming pointer used during construction or assignment.

This feature is convenient, but it hides the return value from the hidden call. Here is the equivalent pseudocode for the assignment operator:

```
T* CComQIPtr::operator=(IUnknown* lp)
{
    IUnknown* pTemp = p;      // p is the member pointer.
    p = NULL;
    if(lp != NULL)
        lp->QueryInterface(riid, (void**)&p);
    if(pTemp)
        pTemp->Release();
    return p;
}
```

Notice that the HRESULT returned by the call to *QueryInterface* is completely ignored! For objects created in the same apartment or process as the client, this "cold shoulder" is probably not a big deal because *QueryInterface* simply returns S_OK upon success or E_NOINTERFACE upon failure. But when the call to *QueryInterface* crosses apartment or process boundaries, a wide range of HRESULTs might be returned because of the existence of the remote procedure call (RPC) layer. The client code can use the logical NOT operator to test the validity of the pointer, but it has no way of knowing what specifically caused the error.

 *CComPtr* also includes an implicit type cast operator, which generates a fairly common error. The cast allows smart pointers to be assigned to raw pointers. For example, examine the following code:

```
void (IBuckDog* pDog)
{
    CComPtr<IBuckDog> dog;
    GetObject(&dog);
    *pDog = dog;
}
```

ATL's implementation allows the last line of the function to compile. However, no *AddRef* occurs, which is bad.

 The last problem that can occur with smart pointers has to do with the use of the *CComPtr* and *CComQIPtr* classes being a stylistic preference rather than a necessity. It isn't uncommon to find two developers working on the same project—perhaps even the same routines—who don't both use the smart pointer classes. One developer might prefer using these classes, but the other might be accustomed to calling *AddRef* and *Release*. In versions of ATL prior to 3.0, you could directly call the *IUnknown::AddRef* and *IUnknown::Release* methods exposed by the encapsulated pointer by using the overloaded indirection operator ( -> ), as shown in this pseudocode:

```
void CMyClass::OnLoad()
{
    CComPtr<ITimeServer> ptrApp;
    CoCreateInstance(CLSID_TimeServer, NULL, CLSCTX_ALL,
        IID_ITimeServer, (void**) &ptrApp);
    ptrApp->Release();    // Oops! This is gonna cause problems!
}
```

This code leads to disastrous results because the reference count for the interface pointer will have already been manually reduced to 0 before the smart pointer destructor calls *Release*. Fortunately, the architects of ATL 3.0 found a tricky way to prevent this from happening, so the code shown here will no longer compile. We'll leave it as an exercise for you to figure out how they did it.

## Data Conversion Classes

Because COM is a language-independent model for software development, in the early years of its use, developers tried to standardize on the primitive data types that would be passed from component to component. In COM, text characters are represented using the 16-bit OLECHAR data type. The architects of COM decided to use a 2-byte character instead of the 8-bit character representation more familiar to C and C++ developers so that COM could support all existing code pages, including Unicode. OLECHAR strings can be represented by using a buffer in which the end of the string is specified with a terminating null value, similar to single-byte character strings. (See Figure 5-1.) The only difference is that each character—including the null character—is represented using 2 bytes instead of 1.

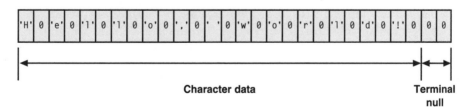

**Character data**    **Terminal null**

**Figure 5-1**
*Format of an OLECHAR string*

The use of simple null-terminated OLECHAR arrays isn't the preferred technique for passing text from one component to another. Instead, the de facto standard is to use the BSTR type, an array of OLECHARs that is length-prefixed as well as null-terminated. It is popular because the BSTR type, which stands

133

for "Basic STRing," is the string data type both Visual Basic and the Java *java.lang.String* class use. Although the widespread use of the BSTR type in rapid application development (RAD) languages makes it a good choice for usage as a COM data type, the BSTR type is foreign to most C and C++ developers. The first four bytes of a BSTR are used as a length prefix that indicates the length of the text string. This approach is advantageous because it allows developers to encode NULL characters inside the BSTR, but it poses an interesting problem. Because the first four bytes of a BSTR represent its length rather than the first two characters in the array, how are BSTRs and OLECHAR arrays used interchangeably in display functions? The answer is that the COM-provided BSTR allocation APIs—*SysAllocString* and *SysReallocString*—return a pointer to the first character in the string, not the first byte in the allocated array, as shown in Figure 5-2.

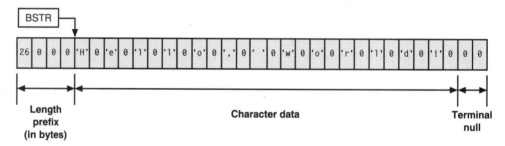

**Figure 5-2**
*Format of a BSTR*

This technique turns out to be a mixed blessing for C++ developers. On one hand, it means that a BSTR can be passed into most functions that take a pointer to an OLECHAR array. On the other hand, BSTRs can't be created, freed, and manipulated using the familiar C++ run-time functions. Functions such as *malloc*, *free*, *new*, *delete*, *lstrcat*, and *lstrlen* don't currently work when applied to BSTRs. The use of BSTR as the standard string data type in COM makes sense because it allows components developed in C++, Visual Basic, and Visual J++ to share text information, but it means extra work for C++ developers. Just as you must treat an interface pointer differently than a class pointer, you must treat a BSTR differently than a TCHAR*.

## The *CComBSTR* Class

Fortunately, ATL provides support for dealing with BSTRs. The *CComBSTR* class encapsulates the functionality of a BSTR in much the same way as the MFC

*CString* class encapsulates a TCHAR array, albeit with fewer features. Table 5-2 describes several of the most pertinent methods of this class.

**Table 5-2   Frequently Used *CComBSTR* Methods**

| CComBSTR Method | Description |
|---|---|
| *CComBSTR* | Various overloaded constructors allocate a new BSTR given an LPCOLESTR, an LPCSTR, or another *CComBSTR*. |
| *~CComBSTR, Empty* | Frees the encapsulated BSTR. |
| *Attach, Detach* | Attaches an existing BSTR to the class, or detaches it such that the destructor won't free it when the class goes out of scope. *Detach* is helpful when using the *CComBSTR* class to assign an [out] parameter. |
| *operator BSTR, operator&* | Allows the BSTR to be accessed directly. *operator BSTR* allows *CComBSTR* to be used in place of BSTR as an [in] parameter. *operator&* allows *CComBSTR* to be used in place of a BSTR* as an [out] parameter. |
| *operator=, operator+=, operator<, operator==, operator>* | Overloaded operators provide assignment, concatenation, and simple comparison of BSTRs. |
| *LoadString* | Allows you to initialize a BSTR with text stored in a string resource. |
| *ToLower, ToUpper* | Converts the BSTR to all uppercase or all lowercase using the language-safe *CharLower* and *CharUpper* Microsoft Win32 APIs, respectively. |
| *WriteToStream, ReadFromStream* | Reads or writes the BSTR to and from an *IStream* interface. |

To developers transitioning from MFC to ATL, the *CComBSTR* class is frustrating because it doesn't offer nearly as many convenient features as does the *CString* class. A list of notable omissions is shown in Table 5-3. Simply stated, *CComBSTR* isn't meant as a full-blown replacement for string manipulation. It is simply a convenience class for converting from an LPCTSTR to a BSTR and for treating a BSTR as a class rather than with the COM *SysXXXXString* APIs. If you need to perform sophisticated string manipulation—which we'll conveniently define as any operation shown in Table 5-3—you should instead use the *wstring* class provided by the Standard Template Library (STL). Admittedly, the syntax of the STL string classes is quite different from *CString*, so they take some getting used to, but time spent mastering STL is a good investment.

**Table 5-3  Notable *CComBSTR* Omissions**

| Features Not Included in *CComBSTR* | Explanation |
|---|---|
| LPCSTR extraction | Several of the *CComBSTR* methods take an LPCSTR as input, allowing you to convert from a single-byte character string to a BSTR. However, there are no methods that allow you to convert back to an LPCSTR. The need to convert back to an LPCSTR often occurs in non-Unicode projects when you want to pass the string to a Win32 API that takes an LPCTSTR. The solution when developing for Microsoft Windows NT is to explicitly specify the Unicode version of the API, such as *MessageBoxW* instead of *MessageBox*, so that no conversion is required. Under Microsoft Windows 95 and Windows 98, or if your situation otherwise requires you to convert from BSTR to LPCSTR, you can use the *_bstr_t* class provided by the Visual C++ runtime library, which provides an LPCTSTR extraction operator. |
| String manipulation (including *Replace*, *Insert*, *Delete*, *Remove*, *Find*, *Mid*, *Left*, *Right*, and so on) | *CComBSTR* doesn't support these methods because they are beyond the scope of its role. To perform string manipulation on an array of wide characters, use the *wstring* class provided by STL. |
| Language-sensitive collation | The string comparison functions provided by *CComBSTR* (<, >, ==) perform byte-by-byte comparisons rather than language-specific collation. To perform collation, use the *wstring* class. |

The following pseudocode shows the typical use of *CComBSTR*:

```
HRESULT CMyObject::MyMethod(IOtherObject* pSomething)
{
    CComBSTR bstrText(L"Hello");
    bstrText += " again";                    // LPCSTR conversion
    bstrText.ToUpper();
    pSomething->Display(bstrText);           // [in] parameter
    MessageBoxW(0, bstrText, L"Test", MB_OK); // Assumes Windows NT
}
```

### CComBSTR Gotchas

As you can see, *CComBSTR* significantly simplifies the use of BSTRs. Four uses of *CComBSTR*, however, require special care:

- Freeing the BSTR explicitly
- Using *CComBSTR* as an [out] parameter
- Using a *CComBSTR* automatic variable in right-side assignments
- Using a *CComBSTR* member variable in right-side assignments

Because *CComBSTR* exposes an *operator BSTR* method, there's nothing to prevent you from explicitly freeing the underlying BSTR, as shown here:

```
HRESULT CMyObject::MyMethod1()
{
    CComBSTR bstrText(L"This is a test");
    ::SysFreeString(bstrText);
    ⋮
    MessageBoxW(NULL, bstrText, L"Test", MB_OK);
}
```

In this code, the BSTR beneath *bstrText* has already been freed, but there's nothing to stop you from still using it because *bstrText* hasn't yet gone out of scope. When it finally does go out of scope, *SysFreeString* will be called a second time. Preventing this "gotcha" would require removing the *operator BSTR* method from the class—but that would render *CComBSTR* nearly useless because you couldn't use it in place of BSTR for [in] parameters.

When passing a *CComBSTR* as an [out] parameter in place of a BSTR*, you must first call *Empty* to free the contents of the string, as shown here:

```
HRESULT CMyObject::MyMethod2(ISomething* p, /*[out]*/ BSTR* pbstr)
{
    CComBSTR bstrText;
    ⋮
    bstrText = L"Some assignment";    // BSTR is allocated.
    ⋮
    bstrText.Empty();                 // Must call empty before
    pSomething->GetText(&bstrText);   //  using as an [out] parameter.
    if(bstrText != L"Schaller")
        bstrText += "Hello";          // Convert from LPCSTR.
}
```

Calling *Empty* before passing the *CComBSTR* as an [out] parameter is required because—following the COM rules for [out] parameters—the called method doesn't call *SysFreeString* before overwriting the contents of the BSTR. If you forget to call *Empty*, the contents of the BSTR immediately preceding the call will be leaked.

The third *CComBSTR* gotcha is also fairly obvious, but it's much more dangerous than the first two. Examine the following code:

```
HRESULT CMyObject::MyMethod3(/*[out, retval]*/ BSTR* pbstr)
{
    CComBSTR bstrText(L"Hello");
    bstrText += " again";
    *pbstr = bstrText;          // No! Call Detach instead!
}
```

The pointer to the BSTR encapsulated by *bstrText* is passed as an [out] parameter in the *\*pbstr = bstrText* assignment statement. When *bstrText* goes out of scope just before returning from *MyMethod3*, the BSTR will be freed by the call to *SysFreeString* in the *CComBSTR* destructor. The caller will get a pointer to an already freed buffer, causing extremely undesirable results. Because *bstrText* is about to go out of scope, you must instead assign *\*pbstr* to the output of your choice of the *CComBSTR Copy* or *Detach* methods. *CComBSTR Copy* makes a copy of the string; *Detach* simply removes the BSTR from the auspices of the wrapper class so that it won't be deleted when *bstrText* goes out of scope:

```
HRESULT CMyObject::MyMethod4(/*[out, retval]*/ BSTR* pbstr)
{
    CComBSTR bstrText(L"Hello");
    bstrText += " again";
    //*pbstr = bstrText.Copy();    // Better!
    *pbstr = bstrText.Detach();    // Much better!
}
```

In this case, you'd be better off calling *Detach* instead of *Copy* for reasons of efficiency. *Detach* doesn't incur the unneeded overhead of creating an extra copy of the string. However, *Copy* is required when the contents of *CComBSTR* must still be used after making the assignment.

The final *CComBSTR* gotcha is the most subtle. In the following code, the *CStringTest* class uses *CComBSTR* as a member variable to store a BSTR property. The *put_Text* and *get_Text* interface methods allow the value to be modified.

```
class CStringTest
{
    ⋮

    CComBSTR bstrText;

// IStringTest
public:
    STDMETHOD(put_Text)(/*[in]*/ BSTR newVal)
```

```
    {
        m_bstrText = newVal;
        return S_OK;
    }
    STDMETHOD(get_Text)(/*[out, retval]*/ BSTR *pVal)
    {
        *pVal = m_bstrText;    // Oops! Call m_bstrText.Copy
                               //  instead.
        return S_OK;
    }
};
```

Can you see the bug? Because *m_bstrText* doesn't go out of scope at the end of the *get_Text* method, you might think you can reasonably assume that you don't need to call *Copy* when making the *pVal = m_bstrText* assignment. This is not the case. According to the rules of COM, the caller is responsible for freeing the contents of an [out] parameter. Because *pVal* points to the BSTR encapsulated by *m_bstrText* instead of a copy, both the caller and the *m_bstrText* destructor will attempt to delete the string.

---

### Previous Versions of ATL: *CComBSTR*

The *CComBSTR* class was enhanced from ATL 2.1 to ATL 3.0. The *ToLower*, *ToUpper*, and *LoadString* methods are new, as are the operator overloads (+=, <, ==, and >). It's possible that future versions of ATL will continue to extend the functionality of *CComBSTR* until it approaches the feature set provided by *CString*, but we doubt it. The STL *wstring* class is the preferred alternative to *CString* when performing string manipulation.

---

## The *CComVariant* Class

In addition to the BSTR, ATL provides support for another popular but less-than-C++-friendly COM data type called the VARIANT (or alternatively, VARIANTARG). A VARIANT is a catchall data structure used to represent all Automation-compatible data types including (but not limited to) floating point numbers, longs, dates, strings, interface pointers, and arrays. Structurally, a VARIANT consists of a union and a type variable that specifies which member of the union is in use. The VARIANT structure also contains three unused data members reserved for future use. The chief benefit of the VARIANT is that it allows RAD and scripting languages to treat all data types polymorphically, meaning that you can perform operations on a VARIANT without being concerned with the actual data type it represents. If necessary, those languages automatically call the COM-provided *VariantChangeType* API to perform the required conversion. Here's an example from Visual Basic:

```
Sub Form_OnLoad
    Dim myValue
    set myValue = "132"
    myValue = myValue + 68
    myValue = myValue & " dollars"
    MsgBox myValue      ' Displays "200 dollars"
End Sub
```

This flexibility is appropriate for scripting languages because a single data type can intermittently be treated as both a number and a string. The necessary conversions required to make this code work correctly are conveniently hidden from the developer.

Unlike scripting languages, C++ puts a higher priority on type safety and correctness than on flexibility and ease of use. C++ developers are encouraged to use strongly typed data rather than catchall types whenever possible. However, the genesis of COM, strongly influenced by what was then known as OLE Automation, has resulted in the need to support the VARIANT.

**NOTE** OLE is a rich but complicated implementation of compound document–based features that uses COM as its underlying technology. At one time, OLE stood for *object linking and embedding*. Later, it stood for nothing. It is our completely unfounded belief that once the marketing types at Microsoft learned that the word *olé* in Spanish means "bravo!" or "good," they decided that the term "OLE Automation" was an oxymoron and so dropped the "OLE," leaving simply Automation.

Because the VARIANT can represent any one of a number of data types, the tasks of variable initialization, assignment, and comparison are especially tedious under C++. To offer some relief, ATL provides a *CComVariant* class that wraps the VARIANT in a manner similar to the way *CComBSTR* wraps the BSTR, except that *CComVariant* uses inheritance rather than composition. In other words, *CComVariant* inherits from VARIANT rather than having a VARIANT data member. This inheritance allows you to use *CComVariant* anywhere a VARIANT is required, which is a good thing. But be aware that *CComVariant* is subject to the same misuse as the *CComBSTR* class, as shown here:

```
void CMyObject::MyMethod()
{
```

```
CComVariant vtText(L"This is a test");
::VariantClear(&vtText);
ThisMethodTakesAVariant(vtText);    // Oops, already freed!
// vtText destructor calls ::VariantClear again!
}
```

Because much of the functionality of *CComVariant* is the result of over-loaded constructors and assignment operators, we won't provide an exhaustive list of its members. Instead, in Table 5-4 we've outlined the services provided by *CComVariant*.

**Table 5-4**  *CComVariant* **Functionality**

| *CComVariant* Functionality | Description |
| --- | --- |
| Overloaded constructors | *CComVariant* provides a type-specific constructor for each of the basic data types supported by the VARIANT. Notable exceptions are the DATE and SAFEARRAY types. |
| Assignment operators (*operator=*) | *CComVariant* provides type-specific assignment operator overloads for each of the data types supported by its constructors. |
| Comparison operators (*operator==*) | *CComVariant* provides a comparison operator that implements a switch statement on the union type. When comparing VARIANT BSTRs, *operator==* performs a string comparison, not a pointer comparison. When comparing VARIANT-encoded *IDispatch* and *IUnknown* interfaces, *operator==* performs a simple pointer comparison. Because the COM specifications expressly allow an object to return a different (but equivalent) *IDispatch* pointer value every time *QueryInterface* is called, it is possible that *operator==* will return FALSE when comparing *IDispatch* VARIANTs that point to the same object. |
| Type changing | *CComVariant* exposes a *ChangeType* method that allows the VARIANT type to change during its lifetime by calling the global *VariantChangeType* API. |
| Stream serialization | *CComVariant* implements *ReadFromStream* and *WriteFromStream* serialization support. If the underlying VARIANT represents an *IDispatch* or *IUnknown* pointer, the *ReadFromStream* method queries the pointer for *IPersistStream*. If *IPersistStream* is supported, *CComVariant* uses the *OleSaveToStream* and *OleLoadFromStream* APIs to handle object serialization. |

# Simplifying *IDispatch::Invoke*

As we mentioned at the beginning of this chapter, C++ lacks the built-in support for Automation that Visual Basic provides. When dealing with the Visual Basic–centric Automation data types BSTR and VARIANT, C++ code can get a bit messy. But nowhere is the "impedance mismatch" between Automation and C++ more obvious than when you're using the *IDispatch* interface. Recall this Visual Basic code, which first appeared as Listing 5-1:

```
Dim App As Object
Private Sub Form_Load()
    Set App = CreateObject("MSDEV.Application")
    App.Visible = True
    App.Quit
End Sub
```

As shown in Listing 5-2 on page 113, the equivalent functionality in C++ requires over 250 lines of code. Fortunately, working directly with *dispinterfaces* (groupings of methods and properties exposed via the *IDispatch* interface) is not frequently required because vtable interfaces have become the norm. Still, at times you'll need to work with dispinterfaces, especially when hosting Microsoft ActiveX controls.

## The *CComDispatchDriver* Class

To simplify the occasional but necessary client use of the *IDispatch* interface, ATL provides the *CComDispatchDriver* class. You can think of *CComDispatchDriver* as a simplified specialization of the *CComQIPtr* class described earlier in the chapter, with a few additional helper methods that simplify the syntax required to call methods and properties using the *IDispatch* interface. The following pseudocode will serve as an example:

```
try
{
    CComPtr<IUnknown> unk;
    HRESULT hr = unk.CoCreateInstance(OLESTR("MSDEV.Application"));
    OleRun(unk);

    CComDispatchDriver disp(unk);    // QI for IDispatch
    if(!disp)                        // Is pointer NULL?
        throw(E_NOINTERFACE);

    // Calling IDispatch methods directly
```

```
    DISPID dispid;
    LPOLESTR lpStr[] = {L"Visible", NULL};
    disp->GetIDsOfNames(IID_NULL, lpStr, 1,
        LOCALE_USER_DEFAULT, &dispid);

    CComVariant vtVisible(VARIANT_TRUE);
    DISPPARAMS dispparams = {NULL, NULL, 1, 1};
    dispparams.rgvarg = &vtVisible;
    DISPID dispidPut = DISPID_PROPERTYPUT;
    dispparams.rgdispidNamedArgs = &dispidPut;

    disp->Invoke(dispid, IID_NULL, LOCALE_USER_DEFAULT,
        DISPATCH_PROPERTYPUTREF, &dispparams, &vtVisible,
        NULL, NULL);

    // Using helper functions

    disp.PutPropertyByName(L"Visible", &CComVariant(VARIANT_FALSE));
    disp.Invoke0(L"Quit");
}
catch(HRESULT hr)
{
    // Handle HRESULT
}
```

*CComDispatchDriver* has an overloaded constructor that takes an *IUnknown* pointer argument and queries for *IDispatch*. Similar to *CComQIPtr< IDispatch>*, *CComDispatchDriver* implements the necessary operator overloading that allows it to be used anywhere *IDispatch\** is required:

```
class CComDispatchDriver
{
    ⋮
    operator IDispatch*() {return p;}
    IDispatch& operator*() {ATLASSERT(p!=NULL); return *p; }
    IDispatch** operator&() {ATLASSERT(p==NULL); return &p; }
    IDispatch* operator->() {ATLASSERT(p!=NULL); return p; }
    ⋮
};
```

---

## Previous Versions of ATL: *CComDispatchDriver*

In versions of ATL previous to 3.0, the *CComDispatchDriver* class provided only the *GetProperty* and *PutProperty* helper functions. The *GetPropertyByName*, *PutPropertyByName*, and *InvokeX* methods were introduced in version 3.0.

---

When using *CComDispatchDriver*, you can call *IDispatch* methods directly using the overloaded indirection operator ( -> ) or one of several simplified helper methods defined by the class, as shown in Table 5-5.

**Table 5-5   Frequently Used *CComDispatchDriver* Methods**

| CComDispatchDriver Method | Description |
|---|---|
| *GetProperty, PutProperty* | Get or set a dispinterface property using its DISPID. For convenience, static-member versions of these functions exist that take an *IDispatch\** parameter, allowing you to call these methods without having to construct a *CComDispatchDriver* variable. |
| *GetPropertyByName, PutPropertyByName* | Similar to the *GetProperty* and *SetProperty* methods, except that these methods allow you to invoke a property by name rather than by DISPID. The implementation of these methods simply calls *IDispatch::GetIDsOfNames* under the hood and forwards the returned DISPID to the *GetProperty* and *PutProperty* methods described in the first row of this table. Because this algorithm doesn't cache the DISPID to improve the performance of repeated calls to these methods, you should use *GetProperty* and *PutProperty* directly if you repeatedly invoke the same property. |
| *Invoke0, Invoke1, Invoke2* | Simplify the parameter list required to call *IDispatch::Invoke*. |

# Visual C++ Native COM Support

Ever since the 5.0 release, Visual C++ has provided several COM helper classes as part of its run-time library. These classes—including *_com_ptr_t*, *_bstr_t*, and *_variant_t*—provide support similar to the *CComPtr*, *CComBSTR*, and *CComVariant* classes described in this chapter. How do you decide whether to use the run-time classes or the C++ classes? Both sets of classes perform nearly identically, with a few exceptions:

■ Unlike *_bstr_t*, *CComBSTR* provides an operator overload that allows it to be used as an [out] parameter in place of a BSTR*. *_bstr_t* allows you to extract an LPCTSTR, and it implements a reference-counting technique that makes it generally more efficient than *CComBSTR*.

■ Unlike *CComPtr::CoCreateInstance*, the equivalent *_com_ptr_t::CreateInstance* method follows a three-step process for returning the desired pointer:

1. Call *::CoCreateInstance*, asking for *IUnknown*.

2. Call *::OleRun*.

3. Call *QueryInterface* for the desired interface.

This algorithm is less efficient, especially when dealing with remote servers, but it's more friendly to Automation servers that require a call to *OleRun*.

■ The Visual C++ run-time classes throw *_com_error* exceptions instead of returning error codes. Although this technique is desirable when you're using the run-time classes in COM client code, you must take special precautions when using the run-time classes in COM server code because the COM specification expressly forbids throwing an exception across the boundaries of a COM server.

■ The *#import* keyword, a powerful extension to the Visual C++ compiler, optionally generates code that uses the run-time support classes. If you're using the *#import* keyword, you might prefer the run-time classes over the ATL classes.

■ The ATL classes are, at least in theory, more portable because they don't depend on special extensions to the C++ compiler. At the time of this writing, however, only the Microsoft Visual C++ compiler supports ATL.

■ The run-time COM classes don't depend on ATL, so they might be more appropriate than the ATL classes for use in MFC applications.

Neither set of classes is clearly preferable, so the decision is up to you. It's likely that Microsoft will continue to support both sets of classes for some time. In fact, you can use both the run-time classes and the ATL client classes in a single application. For fairly obvious reasons, however, we recommend using the run-time classes from within MFC applications and the ATL classes within an ATL project.

# Conclusion

Future versions of COM might make it easier for C++ developers to work with Automation and its associated data types. The COM+ run-time library, not available at this writing, will likely allow the Visual C++ compiler to inherently support COM interface pointers, BSTRs, VARIANTs, and dispinterfaces with a degree of ease and simplicity approaching that of Visual Basic and Java. Even if the client-side ATL classes we've discussed in this chapter—*CComPtr*, *CComQIPtr*, *CComBSTR*, *CComVariant*, and *CComDispatchDriver*—are someday superseded by the COM+ run-time library, you still need to understand the concepts of Automation. Furthermore, client code written using the ATL classes will still function correctly long after the COM+ run-time library is made available.

## CHAPTER SIX

# Fundamentals of ATL COM Objects

Creating COM objects in ATL takes a little getting used to. The Object Wizard is a great place to start, but the generated code isn't exactly intuitive. In this chapter, we'll explain the generated code and explore the following classes, which form the foundation of ATL COM object implementations:

- *CComThreadModel* and *CComCriticalSection*
- *CComObjectRoot*
- *CComObject*
- *IDispatchImpl*

We'll also see how these classes help with ATL debugging.

Let's start by looking at the header file for a simple object, *CSimple1*, as generated by the Object Wizard using the wizard's default settings:

```
// Simple1.h : Declaration of the CSimple1

#ifndef __SIMPLE1_H_
#define __SIMPLE1_H_

#include "resource.h"       // Main symbols

/////////////////////////////////////////////////////////////////////
// CSimple1
class ATL_NO_VTABLE CSimple1 :
    public CComObjectRootEx<CComSingleThreadModel>,
    public CComCoClass<CSimple1, &CLSID_Simple1>,
    public IDispatchImpl<ISimple1, &IID_ISimple1,
        &LIBID_FUNOBJECTSLib>
```

*(continued)*

```
{
public:
    CSimple1()
    {
    }

DECLARE_REGISTRY_RESOURCEID(IDR_SIMPLE1)

DECLARE_PROTECT_FINAL_CONSTRUCT()

BEGIN_COM_MAP(CSimple1)
    COM_INTERFACE_ENTRY(ISimple1)
    COM_INTERFACE_ENTRY(IDispatch)
END_COM_MAP()

// ISimple1
public:
};

#endif // __SIMPLE1_H_
```

The header file shown here is all the application-specific code you need to implement a functional COM object that supports *IUnknown*, *IDispatch*, and the dual
interface generated by the Object Wizard, *ISimple1*. Of course, a fair amount
of ATL code is under the sheets. Our *CSimple1* object derives from several ATL
classes to inherit implementations of *IUnknown* and *IDispatch* and to properly
handle concurrency issues and aggregation. Figure 6-1 shows where the *CSimple1*
class fits into the ATL inheritance tree for the object.

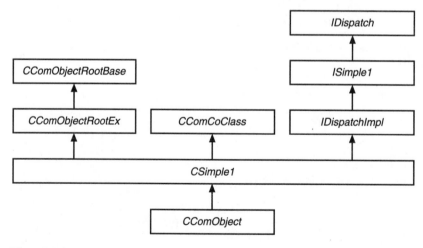

**Figure 6-1**
*The* CSimple1 *class hierarchy*

In general, the *CComObjectRootEx* and *CComObject* classes work together to implement *IUnknown* for the object, although *CComObject* doesn't enter the picture until the object is actually created. *CComCoClass* defines the class factory behavior, which we discuss in detail in Chapter 7, along with the object map and registration. *IDispatchImpl* supplies the *IDispatch* part of the *ISimple1* dual interface. The individual *ISimple1* methods are left for us to implement.

As we'll soon see, many of the class variations that ATL implements for us depend on the choices we make for threading-model and aggregation support. First, though, we need to take a brief look at the critical-section and threading-model classes, which are used by the root classes.

# ATL Critical-Section Classes

ATL critical-section classes wrap a Win32 critical-section synchronization object. These fairly simple classes rely on the standard *InitializeCriticalSection*, *EnterCriticalSection*, *LeaveCriticalSection*, and *DeleteCriticalSection* APIs. The following code shows the *CComCriticalSection* class from ATLBASE.H:

```
class CComCriticalSection
{
public:
    void Lock() {EnterCriticalSection(&m_sec);}
    void Unlock() {LeaveCriticalSection(&m_sec);}
    void Init() {InitializeCriticalSection(&m_sec);}
    void Term() {DeleteCriticalSection(&m_sec);}
    CRITICAL_SECTION m_sec;
};
```

This implementation requires calling *Init* after construction. *CComAutoCritical-Section* calls *Init* in the constructor and *Term* in the destructor, freeing you from the need to remember to call them yourself. The price for this convenience is that you might need the CRT startup code if you use *CComAutoCriticalSection* in a static class member or global.

*CComFakeCriticalSection* doesn't wrap a Win32 critical section. In fact, all its methods are empty implementations. By declaring this type, ATL enables the reuse of the same semantics for both multithreaded and single-threaded object locking.

Although not seen in the inheritance tree in Figure 6-1, an ATL COM object is indirectly associated with a critical section through the threading-model class. You can also use *CComCriticalSection* and *CComAutoCriticalSection* as general-purpose critical sections outside the context of an object. In this chapter, we limit the discussion of critical sections to their application in the threading-model classes, which we examine next.

# ATL Threading-Model Classes

The threading-model class determines how your object will be reference counted and which critical-section class will be used to protect key areas from concurrent access if necessary. This choice is initially made in the Object Wizard, as we describe in Chapter 4, but can be modified post-wizard at any time. An ATL COM object specifies its threading model as a template parameter to the *CComObjectRootEx* class. Each of the threading-model classes implements an *Increment* and *Decrement* function and declares a typedef for the critical-section class appropriate for the threading model. Table 6-1 lists ATL's threading-model classes, their methods of reference counting, and their associated critical-section classes.

**Table 6-1  The ATL Threading-Model Classes**

| Class | Increment/Decrement | Critical Section |
|---|---|---|
| *CComSingleThreadModel* | Uses C++ operators ++ and -- | *CComFakeCriticalSection* |
| *CComMultiThreadModel* | *InterlockedIncrement/ Decrement* | *CComAutoCriticalSection* |
| *CComMultiThreadModelNoCS* | *InterlockedIncrement/ Decrement* | *CComFakeCriticalSection* |

If an object is created for the single-threading or apartment-threading model, *CComSingleThreadModel* is used. The *Both* and *Free* threading models use *CComMultiThreadModel*. *CComMultiThreadModelNoCS* is a hybrid of the two threading models, for cases in which an object can be accessed by multiple threads but doesn't require synchronization in its methods. In the following code, notice that the methods of the threading-model classes are static:

```
class CComSingleThreadModel
{
public:
    static ULONG WINAPI Increment(LPLONG p) {return ++(*p);}
    static ULONG WINAPI Decrement(LPLONG p) {return --(*p);}
    typedef CComFakeCriticalSection AutoCriticalSection;
    typedef CComFakeCriticalSection CriticalSection;
    typedef CComSingleThreadModel ThreadModelNoCS;
};
```

Static members allow *CComObjectRootEx* to utilize these methods for reference counting without ever actually instantiating a threading-model class.

ATL defines two additional classes for threading, *CComObjectThreadModel* and *CComGlobalsThreadModel*. These are not new classes but typedefs that are defined based on one of the following threading preprocessors:

```
#if defined(_ATL_SINGLE_THREADED)
    typedef CComSingleThreadModel CComObjectThreadModel;
    typedef CComSingleThreadModel CComGlobalsThreadModel;
#elif defined(_ATL_APARTMENT_THREADED)
    typedef CComSingleThreadModel CComObjectThreadModel;
    typedef CComMultiThreadModel CComGlobalsThreadModel;
#else
    typedef CComMultiThreadModel CComObjectThreadModel;
    typedef CComMultiThreadModel CComGlobalsThreadModel;
#endif
```

By default, an ATL server will have the _ATL_APARTMENT_THREADED preprocessor defined in stdafx.h. You can use *CComObjectThreadModel* as your object's threading-model class, allowing the change from single-thread to multithread access by changing the preprocessor to _ATL_FREE_THREADED. Following this path forces the same threading model on all objects in a server that use *CComObjectThreadModel*. ATL uses *CComGlobalsThreadModel* internally to protect the module lock count and class object reference count.

Let's now look at how the threading-model class is used in an ATL COM object implementation through the *CComObjectRoot* classes.

# *CComObjectRoot* Classes

ATL objects inherit from *CComObjectRootEx* or *CComObjectRoot*. *CComObjectRoot* is just a typedef for *CComObjectRootEx<CComObjectThreadModel>*. *CComObjectRootEx* has the advantage of allowing each object to declare its own threading model. Using *CComObjectRoot* applies the global *CComObjectThreadModel* to your object. When we examine the following class definition, we can see how the threading model ties in to the reference-counting scheme:

```
template <class ThreadModel>
class CComObjectRootEx : public CComObjectRootBase
{
public:
    typedef ThreadModel _ThreadModel;
    typedef _ThreadModel::AutoCriticalSection _CritSec;
    typedef CComObjectLockT<_ThreadModel> ObjectLock;
```

*(continued)*

```
    ULONG InternalAddRef()
    {
        ATLASSERT(m_dwRef != -1L);
        return _ThreadModel::Increment(&m_dwRef);
    }
    ULONG InternalRelease()
    {
        ATLASSERT(m_dwRef > 0);
        return _ThreadModel::Decrement(&m_dwRef);
    }

    void Lock() {m_critsec.Lock();}
    void Unlock() {m_critsec.Unlock();}
private:
    _CritSec m_critsec;
};
```

The threading model is maintained as a typedef *ThreadModel* whose static *Increment* and *Decrement* members are called on to handle safe reference counting. An instance of the critical section determined by the threading-model class is instantiated as the *m_critsec* data member, which is delegated in the *Lock* and *Unlock* implementations. Other ATL base classes can use the *ObjectLock* typedef as a mechanism for calling *Lock / Unlock* by creating an instance of the *ObjectLock* type. *CComObjectLockT* simply calls *Lock* on the object in the constructor and *Unlock* in the destructor.

The base class *CComObjectRootBase* keeps the actual reference count for the object as a data member. It also handles *QueryInterface* method calls, which are forwarded from the *CComObject* classes through the COM map and eventually to *InternalQueryInterface* in *CComObjectRootBase*. We'll look at the routing shortly, when we discuss *CComObject*. *InternalQueryInterface* delegates to *AtlInternalQueryInterface*, which loops through the COM map to find the requested interface. *CComObjectRootBase* also handles reference counting and *QueryInterface* for aggregated and tear-off objects by maintaining a pointer to the outer *IUnknown* and implementing *OuterAddRef*, *OuterRelease*, and *OuterQueryInterface*.

## *CComObject* Classes

At the bottom of an ATL object instance inheritance tree you'll find *CComObject* or some variation of it. *CComObject* classes are the entry point for all the *IUnknown* methods on an object. Because the implementation of *QueryInterface* varies depending on whether the object is being aggregated, the particular flavor of *CComObject* you use is determined based on the object's declared aggregation support and the context in which the creation occurs. Aggregation support is declared statically with one of a set of aggregation macros. Table 6-2 shows the available aggregation macros, the corresponding *CComObject* class that is used as the base class for the object, and the resulting ATL base class used with the associated aggregation macro. In most cases, the base class varies depending on whether the object is instantiated as an aggregate.

**Table 6-2  Aggregation Macros**

| Macro | Normal Case | Aggregated Case |
|---|---|---|
| DECLARE_NOT_AGGREGATABLE | *CComObject* | Not supported |
| DECLARE_AGGREGATABLE | *CComObject* | *CComAggObject* |
| DECLARE_ONLY_AGGREGATABLE | Not supported | *CComAggObject* |
| DECLARE_POLY_AGGREGATABLE | *CComPolyObject* | *CComPolyObject* |

Each macro declares a typedef for the creator class that is used in normal and aggregated cases. Creators work with class objects to create an object instance when a client requests it. (Creators and class objects are covered in more detail in Chapter 7.) By default, objects inherit DECLARE_AGGREGATABLE from *CComCoClass*. You can override the default by inserting one of the other macros in your object header file or by making a choice other than "Yes" for aggregation on the Attributes tab in the Object Wizard. By implementing *QueryInterface*, *AddRef*, and *Release*, the *CComObject* classes relieve us from writing the boilerplate code over and over again, and they also offer free aggregation support. *CComObject* also handles incrementing and decrementing the module count when the object is created and destroyed—that's more boilerplate code you don't have to write.

Each *CComObject* class has a static *CreateInstance* member that is used to create the object. If the object is created by means of *CoCreate*, the class object makes the call in its *IClassFactory::CreateInstance* method. If you're creating objects internally, however, you can also call this function directly and bypass the class object entirely. *CreateInstance* returns a pointer to a newly created *CComObject*, as shown here:

```
template <class Base>
HRESULT WINAPI CComObject<Base>::CreateInstance(CComObject<Base>** pp)
{
    ATLASSERT(pp != NULL);
    HRESULT hRes = E_OUTOFMEMORY;
    CComObject<Base>* p = NULL;
    ATLTRY(p = new CComObject<Base>())
```

*(continued)*

```
    if(p != NULL)
    {
        p->SetVoid(NULL);
        p->InternalFinalConstructAddRef();
        hRes = p->FinalConstruct();
        p->InternalFinalConstructRelease();
        if(hRes != S_OK)
        {
            delete p;
            p = NULL;
        }
    }
    *pp = p;
    return hRes;
}
```

You can then use the returned object as you would any other COM object. Notice that *CreateInstance* doesn't call *AddRef* on the object, so you might want to call *QueryInterface* after creation to get the automatic deletion when the reference count reaches 0. The following code shows how you can use *CreateInstance* directly:

```
CComObject<CSimpleObject> *pObj;
HRESULT hr = CComObject<CSimpleObject>::CreateInstance(&pObj);
if(SUCCEEDED(hr))
{
    CComPtr<ISimpleObj> pISimple;
    hr = pObj->QueryInterface(&pISimple);
    if(SUCCEEDED(hr))
        pISimple->Test();
}
```

The use of the *CComObject QueryInterface* override allows the use of a typedef pointer. Using *CComObject* as shown in the preceding code does save some cycles by not creating a class object through the *CoCreate* mechanism. Even so, this process is somewhat tedious for a stack-based object. ATL provides the *CComObjectStack* class to simplify object creation and usage within a stack frame. We can write the same code using *CComObjectStack*.

```
CComObjectStack<CSimpleObject> Obj;
Obj.Test();
```

Use *CComObjectStack* when the lifetime of the object is contained in a stack frame. When an object's lifetime is contained in a stack frame, reference counting isn't required and therefore isn't implemented. *QueryInterface* isn't allowed on *CComObjectStack* instances.

ATL has several other variations of *CComObject* to handle specific reference counting, module locking, and *QueryInterface* cases. These variations and their descriptions are listed here:

- **CComObjectCached** This class doesn't increment the module lock count until the reference count reaches 2 and thus allows an instance of an object to exist without keeping the module loaded. ATL wraps DLL class objects in this way to provide faster access via the cached instance. We'll look at this more in Chapter 7 when we examine class objects and module locks.

- **CComObjectNoLock** This class does no module locking whatsoever. ATL uses it for class objects in EXE servers, which can't allow a class object instance to keep the module running.

- **CComObjectGlobal** This class doesn't keep an internal reference count separate from the module lock count. The object's lifetime must be managed externally. ATL uses this class in its singleton implementation, holding the single object instance wrapped in *CCom-ObjectGlobal*.

- **CComTearOffObject** This class delegates its *QueryInterface* calls to an owner object. *CComTearOffObject* allows a separate implementation for an interface, which is created only when a client requests the interface through *QueryInterface*. The tear-off is reference counted and deleted when the reference count is 0. When created, the tear-off object calls *AddRef* on its owner to ensure that the owner object doesn't delete itself with an outstanding tear-off reference.

- **CComCachedTearOffObject** This class reuses a tear-off object instance once an instance is created. Using *CComTearOffObject* results in a new object being created every time the tear-off interface is queried for.

One of the fundamental tasks of the *CComObject* classes is to appropriately route *QueryInterface*. Our next step is to look more closely at the implementation of *QueryInterface* once *CComObject* hands it off. We'll start by examining how ATL uses the COM map to manage the list of interfaces available from an object.

# The ATL COM Map

When a client calls *QueryInterface* on an ATL object, the internal call stack goes like this:

1. *CComObject::QueryInterface*

2. *YourClass::_InternalQueryInterface*

3. *CComObjectRootBase::InternalQueryInterface*

4. *AtlInternalQueryInterface*

This progression utilizes the COM map in the object, starting with step 2. *_InternalQueryInterface* is implemented in an object by the BEGIN_COM_ _MAP macro. This macro is inserted by default in the object header file when the ATL Object Wizard generates the code. *_InternalQueryInterface* is implemented like this:

```
HRESULT _InternalQueryInterface(REFIID iid, void** ppvObject)
{
    return InternalQueryInterface(this, _GetEntries(),
        iid, ppvObject);
}
```

Notice that the *this* pointer and the *_GetEntries* parameter are passed to *CComObjectRootBase::InternalQueryInterface*. *_GetEntries*, another static function implemented by BEGIN_COM _MAP, returns a pointer to an array of _ATL_INTMAP_ENTRY structures. The entries that populate the array depend on the interfaces the object supports for *QueryInterface*. ATL provides a slew of macros that you can use to make these entries; just insert any of the macros after BEGIN_COM_MAP. Here's a simple COM map that declares *QueryInterface* support for *ISimple1* and *IDispatch*:

```
BEGIN_COM_MAP(CSimple1)
    COM_INTERFACE_ENTRY(ISimple1)
    COM_INTERFACE_ENTRY(IDispatch)
END_COM_MAP()
```

COM_INTERFACE_ENTRY is defined like this:

```
#define COM_INTERFACE_ENTRY(x)\
    {&_ATL_IIDOF(x), \
    offsetofclass(x, _ComMapClass), \
    _ATL_SIMPLEMAPENTRY},
```

The _ATL_INTMAP_ENTRY structure that COM_INTERFACE_ENTRY populates is defined like this:

```
struct _ATL_INTMAP_ENTRY
{
    const IID* piid;        // The interface ID (IID)
    DWORD dw;
    _ATL_CREATORARGFUNC* pFunc; // NULL:end, 1:offset, n:ptr
};
```

The structure holds a pointer to the interface ID, a DWORD offset of the interface implementation from the base class, and a final *pFunc* entry that is defined as the constant _ATL_SIMPLEMAPENTRY (1). This is the most common case—COM_INTERFACE_ENTRY is used to add a map entry. This macro calculates the inherited class offset using the _ComMapClass typedef and the ATL *offsetofclass* function. *ComMapClass* is just another alias for the object class name passed into the BEGIN_COM_MAP macro. The end of the array is marked if the *pFunc* member is 0. END_COM_MAP populates an _ATL_INTMAP-_ENTRY for you that is all 0s. The *pFunc* argument serves multiple purposes. Instead of the constant 1 or 0, the *pFunc* argument can be a function pointer if the interface implementation isn't in the base class inheritance tree, which is the case with tear-off interfaces and aggregates. The *pFunc* argument can delegate to debugging code as well, as we'll see in the macro descriptions that follow. The DWORD member *dw* serves as an extra argument to *pFunc* in this case, not an offset. The content of *dw* depends on the function pointed to in *pFunc*. You can even create your own function that is called every time *QueryInterface* is called on a particular interface. This multiple use of structure members is somewhat confusing but efficient.

The first entry in the map is special in that it must be a simple map entry. The *QueryInterface* implementation relies on this simple map entry to ensure that COM identity is maintained for the object. The macros that define this type of entry and their descriptions are listed here:

- **COM_INTERFACE_ENTRY(*x*)** The object derives directly from the implementation of this interface or from the interface itself. The interface's ID will be obtained using _ _*uuidof(x)*.

- **COM_INTERFACE_ENTRY_IID(*iid, x*)** This macro is the same as COM _INTERFACE _ENTRY except that the interface ID is explicitly specified. COM_INTERFACE_ENTRY_IID is useful in cases in which _ _*uuidof* isn't supported.

- **COM_INTERFACE_ENTRY2(*x, x2*)** Use this macro for interfaces that appear in multiple base classes. Most often this occurs for *IDispatch* when inheriting from multiple dual interfaces. *x* is the interface that is entered into the array; *x2* is the immediate base class the object derives from. _ _*uuidof(x)* is used to obtain the interface ID.

■ **COM_INTERFACE_ENTRY2_IID(*iid, x, x2*)**   This macro is the same as COM_INTERFACE_ENTRY2, with the addition of the explicit interface ID parameter for *x*.

All of the preceding macros meet the simple interface requirement and can be used as the first map entry. Let's have a look at the remaining macros before we continue with our *QueryInterface* investigation.

■ **COM_INTERFACE_ENTRY_BREAK(*x*)**   This macro causes a debug break in execution whenever *QueryInterface* is called for the interface *x*.

■ **COM_INTERFACE_ENTRY_NOINTERFACE(*x*)**   This macro results in an E_NOINTERFACE return value whenever *QueryInterface* is called for the interface *x*.

■ **COM_INTERFACE_ENTRY_FUNC(*iid, dw, func*)**   This macro allows you to set up any function to be the delegate for handling *QueryInterface* for interfaces of type *iid*. The function must have the following signature:

```
HRESULT WINAPI func(void* pv, REFIID riid, LPVOID* ppv,
    DWORD dw);
```

The final DWORD parameter is the same *dw* specified in the macro.

■ **COM_INTERFACE_ENTRY_FUNC_BLIND(*dw, func*)**   When you use this macro, querying for any interface other than *IUnknown* will delegate to *func*, regardless of the interface ID.

■ **COM_INTERFACE_ENTRY_TEAR_OFF(*iid, x*)**   When you use this macro, ATL creates a new tear-off object by creating class *x*.

■ **COM_INTERFACE_ENTRY_CACHED_TEAR_OFF(*iid, x, punk*)**   This macro delegates to a *CComCachedTearOff* derived class instance identified by *punk* to handle *QueryInterface*.

■ **COM_INTERFACE_ENTRY_AGGREGATE(*iid, punk*)**   This macro delegates *QueryInterface* for *iid* to the inner unknown, *punk*.

■ **COM_INTERFACE_ENTRY_AGGREGATE_BLIND(*punk*)**   If the interface hasn't been found in the COM map by the time this entry is evaluated, the query will be delegated to the inner unknown, regardless of *iid*.

- ■ **COM_INTERFACE_ENTRY_AUTOAGGREGATE(*iid, punk, clsid*)**   If *punk* is not NULL, this macro works just like COM_INTERFACE-_ENTRY_AGGREGATE. If *punk* is NULL, ATL creates an aggregate on the fly using *clsid* and delegates to its *IUnknown*.

- ■ **COM_INTERFACE_ENTRY_AUTOAGGREGATE_BLIND(*punk, clsid*)**   This macro works the same way as AUTOAGGREGATE except that no interface ID comparison is made.

- ■ **COM_INTERFACE_ENTRY_CHAIN(*classname*)**   This macro causes the COM map of an object's base class to be searched for any requested interface.

We look at each of these macros in detail in Chapter 8.

The order of macro placement in the map is important, especially for delegating and chaining. Top entries are evaluated first, followed by the entries below in the interface map.

At the beginning of this section, the COM map entered the picture when *CComObject* called _*InternalQueryInterface*. This is a static member declared by the BEGIN_COM_MAP macro. *InternalQueryInterface* delegates to *CComObjectRootBase::InternalQueryInterface* (which injects some debugging hooks that we'll see in the next section) and then delegates to *AtlInternalQueryInterface*. This is where the COM map is enumerated and *QueryInterface* is resolved or routed to any functions specified by the individual map macros. Before enumerating the map, *AtlInternalQueryInterface* checks to make sure that the first map entry is a simple map entry. As we said earlier, ATL uses this first entry for any queries for the *IUnknown* interface. The *InlineIsEqualUnknown* function just compares the interface ID to IID_IUnknown, as shown here:

```
ATLINLINE ATLAPI AtlInternalQueryInterface(void* pThis,
    const _ATL_INTMAP_ENTRY* pEntries, REFIID iid,
    void** ppvObject)
{
    ATLASSERT(pThis != NULL);
    // First entry in the COM map should be a simple map entry
    ATLASSERT(pEntries->pFunc == _ATL_SIMPLEMAPENTRY);
    if(ppvObject == NULL)
        return E_POINTER;
    *ppvObject = NULL;
    if(InlineIsEqualUnknown(iid)) // Use first interface
    {
        IUnknown* pUnk = (IUnknown*)((int)pThis+pEntries->dw);
        pUnk->AddRef();
        *ppvObject = pUnk;
        return S_OK;
    }
```

If *IUnknown* isn't what the client is looking for, the code falls through to a loop that enumerates the COM map entries. If the map entry doesn't specify an *iid*, it's considered a blind entry. If the entry is blind or its interface ID matches the one the client is looking for, one of two things happens:

- If the entry has a *pFunc* of 1 (_ATL_SIMPLEMAPENTRY), the interface is part of the object itself and can be found at the offset specified in the *dw* member of the _ATL_INTMAP_ENTRY structure.

- If the entry has a *pFunc* that points to a real function, ATL delegates to that function.

The loop code in *AtlInternalQueryInterface* is shown here:

```
while (pEntries->pFunc != NULL)
{
    BOOL bBlind = (pEntries->piid == NULL);
    if(bBlind || InlineIsEqualGUID(*(pEntries->piid), iid))
    {
        if(pEntries->pFunc == _ATL_SIMPLEMAPENTRY) // Offset
        {
            ATLASSERT(!bBlind);
            IUnknown* pUnk =
                (IUnknown*)((int)pThis+pEntries->dw);
            pUnk->AddRef();
            *ppvObject = pUnk;
            return S_OK;
        }
        else // Actual function call
        {
            HRESULT hRes = pEntries->pFunc(pThis,
                iid, ppvObject, pEntries->dw);
            if(hRes == S_OK || (!bBlind && FAILED(hRes)))
                return hRes;
        }
    }
    pEntries++;
}
return E_NOINTERFACE;
```

That's it for *QueryInterface*. For more information on tear-off interfaces and aggregation, look ahead to Chapter 8.

# Supporting *IDispatch*

*IDispatch* enables an object to expose properties and methods to clients that don't have access to type information at compile time or that perhaps aren't compiled languages. The client might be a scripting language such as Microsoft VBScript, or it might be a control container that must support any control that is inserted at run time. Scripting languages lack the ability to include a description of the interfaces the object supports. Containers can't predict which controls the user will want to insert at run time. *IDispatch* solves this problem by providing a predefined interface with a mechanism for invoking methods by integer ID, commonly called a dispatch ID, or dispid. If the ID for a method isn't known, it can be discovered by name. You can create an object that exposes its properties and methods through *IDispatch* only or through a dual interface. Dual interfaces allow either vtable binding or dynamic binding by inheriting from *IDispatch*. ATL objects are generated with a dual interface by default. The implementation for *IDispatch* on a dual interface is provided in the ATL *IDispatchImpl* base class, which your object derives from, and is defined as here:

```
class ATL_NO_VTABLE CAtlSimple :
    public CComObjectRootEx<CComSingleThreadModel>,
    public CComCoClass<CAtlSimple, &CLSID_AtlSimple>,
    public IDispatchImpl<IAtlSimple, &IID_IAtlSimple,
        &LIBID_ATLSIMPLESVRLib>
```

*IDispatchImpl* implements the four *IDispatch* methods, which are described in Table 6-3.

#### Table 6-3   The Four *IDispatch* Methods

| Method | Description |
|--------|-------------|
| *GetTypeInfoCount* | Retrieves the number of type information interfaces the dual interface supports (0 or 1) |
| *GetTypeInfo* | Gets the type information that describes the dual interface |
| *GetIDsOfNames* | Converts a string method name to an integer ID to be used in *Invoke* |
| *Invoke* | Calls a method on the dual interface |

Implementing *IDispatch* on a dual interface relies on the type library that describes the object. *IDispatchImpl* receives the GUID for the type library as a template parameter, so it can load the type library and delegate two of the four *IDispatch* methods to the type library parser. In particular, the type library parser COM provides in OLEAUT32.DLL implements *Invoke* and *GetIDsOfNames*, which are accessed via an *ITypeInfo* pointer. *IDispatchImpl* maintains a contained *CComTypeInfoHolder* object to interface with the type library parser and procure an *ITypeInfo* pointer. *IDispatchImpl* delegates to *CComTypeInfoHolder* for all methods except *GetTypeInfoCount*, which simply returns 1. The *CComTypeInfoHolder* class name is actually a default template parameter to *IDispatchImpl*. Although this scenario is unlikely, if necessary, you can provide a type description through some other mechanism by specifying a different class name. The *IDispatchImpl* class is shown here:

```
template <class T, const IID* piid, const GUID* plibid =
    &CComModule::m_libid, WORD wMajor = 1,
    WORD wMinor = 0, class tihclass = CComTypeInfoHolder>
class ATL_NO_VTABLE IDispatchImpl : public T
{
public:
    typedef tihclass _tihclass;
// IDispatch
    STDMETHOD(GetTypeInfoCount)(UINT* pctinfo)
    {
        *pctinfo = 1;
        return S_OK;
    }
    STDMETHOD(GetTypeInfo)(UINT itinfo, LCID lcid,
        ITypeInfo** pptinfo)
    {
        return _tih.GetTypeInfo(itinfo, lcid, pptinfo);
    }
    STDMETHOD(GetIDsOfNames)(REFIID riid, LPOLESTR* rgszNames,
        UINT cNames, LCID lcid, DISPID* rgdispid)
    {
        return _tih.GetIDsOfNames(riid, rgszNames, cNames,
            lcid, rgdispid);
    }
    STDMETHOD(Invoke)(DISPID dispidMember, REFIID riid,
        LCID lcid, WORD wFlags, DISPPARAMS* pdispparams,
        VARIANT* pvarResult, EXCEPINFO* pexcepinfo,
        UINT* puArgErr)
    {
        return _tih.Invoke((IDispatch*)this, dispidMember,
            riid, lcid, wFlags, pdispparams, pvarResult,
            pexcepinfo, puArgErr);
    }
```

```
protected:
    static _tihclass _tih;
    static HRESULT GetTI(LCID lcid, ITypeInfo** ppInfo)
    {
        return _tih.GetTI(lcid, ppInfo);
    }
};
```

As you can see, the static *CComTypeInfoHolder* member *_tih* does the brunt of the work. Before *CComTypeInfoHolder* can do anything, it must load the type library and get the *ITypeInfo* pointer from the parser for the dual interface. This is accomplished in *CComTypeInfoHolder::GetTI*, part of which is shown here:

```
ITypeLib* pTypeLib;
hRes = LoadRegTypeLib(*m_plibid, m_wMajor, m_wMinor,
    lcid, &pTypeLib);
if(SUCCEEDED(hRes))
{
    CComPtr<ITypeInfo> spTypeInfo;
    hRes = pTypeLib->GetTypeInfoOfGuid(*m_pguid, &spTypeInfo);
    ⋮
}
```

The member variables *m_pguid*, *m_plibid*, *m_wMajor*, and *m_wMinor* are initialized statically from the *IDispatchImpl* template parameters. The variable *m_pguid* is the interface ID for the dual interface. The variable *m_plibid* is the type library ID. Although not obvious, major and minor library version information is also specified in the *IDispatchImpl* template. The version numbers default to 0 and 1, respectively. Because type libraries can contain information about several interfaces, enumerations, and coclasses, *GetTypeInfoOfGuid* is used to single out the information for the dual interface specified in the template. The resulting *ITypeInfo* pointer is cached in *CComTypeInfoHolder::m_pInfo*, where it can be retrieved by an *IDispatchImpl::GetTypeInfo* request or used internally to access the parser. *GetTI* is called to load the library and cache the pointer only once: the first time *IDispatchImpl* delegates a call to *CComTypeInfoHolder*. That means the locale ID specified in *GetTypeInfo*, *GetIDsOfNames*, or *Invoke* is ignored after the first call because the type info has already been loaded. *GetTI* also caches an array of method names and their corresponding dispatch IDs to speed up *GetIDsOfNames* access. Finally, when an *Invoke* call is received, *CComTypeInfoHolder* can simply delegate to the type library parser, as shown here:

```
HRESULT Invoke(IDispatch* p, DISPID dispidMember,
    REFIID /* riid */, LCID lcid, WORD wFlags,
    DISPPARAMS* pdispparams, VARIANT* pvarResult,
    EXCEPINFO* pexcepinfo, UINT* puArgErr)
```

*(continued)*

```
{
    HRESULT hRes = EnsureTI(lcid);
    if(m_pInfo != NULL)
        hRes = m_pInfo->Invoke(p, dispidMember, wFlags,
            pdispparams, pvarResult, pexcepinfo, puArgErr);
    return hRes;
}
```

In the preceding code segment, *EnsureTI* loads the type library (using *GetTI*) if it hasn't been loaded already.

We're done talking about *IDispatch*. That's the last foundation topic we'll cover except for the debugging support we get for free by using the ATL framework.

# Debugging Tips

ATL can provide you with run-time feedback in the output window that displays the results of *QueryInterface*, *AddRef*, and *Release* on any interface in your server project. These features are not enabled by default, even in debug builds, and there is no way to enable them through the user interface in Microsoft Visual C++. Instead, you enable debug output by defining macros in stdafx.h. Currently two options are available: *QueryInterface* debugging, which is enabled by the _ATL_DEBUG_QI preprocessor, and reference-count debugging, which is enabled by the _ATL_DEBUG_INTERFACES preprocessor. Both options can be used at the same time or independently, but remember that the options apply to all objects in a server. After inserting either or both of these in stdafx.h (prior to atlbase.h), you'll need to recompile for ATL to conditionally include the debugging points.

## Debugging *QueryInterface*

You can watch the results of *QueryInterface* calls by defining the _ATL_DEBUG_QI preprocessor in your server. A debug string is sent to the output window for every call to *QueryInterface* that occurs in the server. The string contains the name of the class followed by the name of the interface on which *QueryInterface* was called. If the interface name isn't found in the Registry, the interface ID is shown instead. If *QueryInterface* fails, the output is appended with a "failed" suffix. Figure 6-2 shows the output from _ATL_DEBUG_QI in the Visual C++ Output window when a simple object is created.

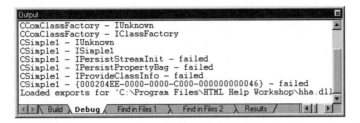

**Figure 6-2**
*The _ATL_DEBUG_QI output*

Figure 6-3 shows a Microsoft Visual Basic application creating the object.

**Figure 6-3**
*A Visual Basic client creating a simple ATL object*

The *QueryInterface* debug feature relies on all *QueryInterface* calls ending up in *CComObjectRootBase::InternalQueryInterface*, in which a macro is called to dump the results of the call. *InternalQueryInterface* is shown here:

```
static HRESULT WINAPI InternalQueryInterface(void* pThis,
    const _ATL_INTMAP_ENTRY* pEntries, REFIID iid,
    void** ppvObject)
{
    ATLASSERT(pThis != NULL);
    // First entry in the COM map should be a simple map entry
    ATLASSERT(pEntries->pFunc == _ATL_SIMPLEMAPENTRY);
#if defined(_ATL_DEBUG_INTERFACES) || defined(_ATL_DEBUG_QI)
    LPCTSTR pszClassName = (LPCTSTR) pEntries[-1].dw;
#endif // _ATL_DEBUG_INTERFACES
    HRESULT hRes = AtlInternalQueryInterface(pThis, pEntries,
        iid, ppvObject);
#ifdef _ATL_DEBUG_INTERFACES
    _Module.AddThunk((IUnknown**)ppvObject, pszClassName, iid);
```

*(continued)*

165

```
#endif // _ATL_DEBUG_INTERFACES
    return _ATLDUMPIID(iid, pszClassName, hRes);
}
```

The very last line of code is the source of our output, using _ATLDUMPIID. This macro is conditionally compiled based on the presence or lack of the _ATL_DEBUG_QI macro, shown here:

```
#ifdef _ATL_DEBUG_QI
#define _ATLDUMPIID(iid, name, hr) AtlDumpIID(iid, name, hr)
#else
#define _ATLDUMPIID(iid, name, hr) hr
#endif
```

If you're not debugging *QueryInterface*, the macro simply resolves to the HRESULT returned by *AtlInternalQueryInterface*; otherwise, it generates a call to *AtlDumpIID*, passing in the interface ID, the class name, and the result of *QueryInterface*. *AtlDumpIID* outputs the class name and attempts to look up the interface ID in the Registry to get the interface name. If the name isn't found under HKCR\Interfaces or HKCR\CLSID, the string IID itself is output.

*AtlDumpIID* is also used for tracing reference counts on interfaces, although the method of getting there is more complex.

## Reference-Count Debugging

ATL provides you with the ability to trace reference counts on a per-interface basis. To enable this feature, you just define the preprocessor _ATL_DEBUG_INTERFACES. Any time *AddRef* or *Release* is called on an interface, the reference count, class name, and interface name are sent to the Output window, as shown in Figure 6-4.

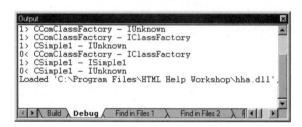

**Figure 6-4**
*The _ATL_DEBUG_INTERFACES output*

Lines of output with a greater than symbol (>) indicate *AddRef*, and lines with a less than symbol (<) indicate *Release*. ATL generates the debug output by creating a structure for each interface supported in your object. The structure has code that intercepts calls into that interface and injects debug output into the process. The interception process begins when the client calls *QueryInterface* on a particular interface, resulting in a call to *CComObjectRootBase::InternalQueryInterface* in an ATL object, just as we saw in *QueryInterface* debugging. However, this time we're interested in the *AddThunk* call in *InternalQueryInterface*, shown here:

```
#ifdef _ATL_DEBUG_INTERFACES
    _Module.AddThunk((IUnknown**)ppvObject, pszClassName, iid);
```

In this case, *thunking* refers to adding a level of indirection to a virtual function call sequence for the purpose of adding the debug output. After the debug output is complete, the call is forwarded to its original target function. If the call isn't to *AddRef* or *Release*, it passes through the thunk code to the target object. *AddThunk* creates a new _QIThunk structure for the interface being queried for if one doesn't exist for that COM identity. _QIThunk caches the interface pointer for the object and has vtable entries for all of the *IUnknown* methods and room for more than a thousand other methods supported by the interface. Once the _QIThunk is created, *AddThunk* returns *IUnknown* for the thunk to *CComObjectRootBase*. Any calls on that interface will go through the thunk first. Because ATL doesn't know the signature for any methods on the interface except the obligatory *IUnknown* methods, other methods are forwarded by one of the 1024 vtable placeholders in _QIThunk (minus the space for the *IUnknown* entries). The extra entries are declared with placeholder methods, as shown here:

```
STDMETHOD(f3)();
    :
STDMETHOD(f1023)();
STDMETHOD(f1024)();
```

Each placeholder has a corresponding implementation, defined by a matching IMPL_THUNK macro, shown here:

```
IMPL_THUNK(3)
    :
IMPL_THUNK(1023)
IMPL_THUNK(1024)
```

IMPL_THUNK expands to inline assembly code to forward the method call on to its correct vtable entry on the real object, like this:

```
#define IMPL_THUNK(n)\
__declspec(naked) inline HRESULT _QIThunk::f##n()\
{\
    __asm mov eax, [esp+4]\
    __asm cmp dword ptr [eax+8], 0\
    __asm jg goodref\
    __asm call atlBadThunkCall\
    __asm goodref:\
    __asm mov eax, [esp+4]\
    __asm mov eax, dword ptr [eax+4]\
    __asm mov [esp+4], eax\
    __asm mov eax, dword ptr [eax]\
    __asm mov eax, dword ptr [eax+4*n]\
    __asm jmp eax\
}
```

In this function, the esp register is modified to hold the *QIThunk* cached *pUnk* interface pointer to the real object, and the vtable entry is then calculated using the offset *n* passed in as the macro parameter in IMPL_THUNK. This code relies on the cached *IUnknown* pointer to the target object (*pUnk*) as the first data member in _QIThunk, which puts it first in memory after the vtable pointer.

The familiar *AddRef* and *Release* methods are not handled through IMPL-_THUNK. Instead, they are forwarded directly to the object and then *AtlDump-IID* is called on to create the debug output. *_QIThunk::AddRef* is shown here:

```
STDMETHOD_(ULONG, AddRef)()
{
    if(bBreak)
        DebugBreak();
    pUnk->AddRef();
    return InternalAddRef();
}
ULONG InternalAddRef()
{
    if(bBreak)
        DebugBreak();
    ATLASSERT(m_dwRef >= 0);
    long l = InterlockedIncrement(&m_dwRef);
    ATLTRACE(_T("%d> "), m_dwRef);
    AtlDumpIID(iid, lpszClassName, S_OK);
    if(l > m_dwMaxRef)
        m_dwMaxRef = l;
    return l;
}
```

Although the IMPL_THUNK code isn't specifically used in *AddRef* and *Release*, it enables ATL to intercept *AddRef* and *Release* on a given interface by forwarding the non-*IUnknown* methods, which aren't of interest for reference-count debugging.

# Conclusion

ATL hides much of an object's internal architecture behind useful abstractions. These abstractions are rooted in the foundation classes described in this chapter. Critical-section and threading-model classes ensure that the object is thread-safe in the model you choose to support in the Object Wizard. *CComObjectRoot* classes utilize the threading classes and provide a basis for reference counting. *CComObject* classes derive from your object class and provide the entry point for *IUnknown* methods in aggregated and normal object instances. The COM map describes the interfaces for which your object supports *QueryInterface* by means of a series of macros. The COM map also describes how to access the interfaces. *IDispatchImpl* uses type information to implement *IDispatch* for an object with a dual interface. ATL uses a thunking mechanism to produce debug output for per-interface reference counting.

In this chapter, we focused on the details of ATL COM object implementation. In Chapter 7, we'll take a step back and examine the housings that contain COM objects, also known as servers. As we'll see, ATL handles much of the boilerplate code necessary to build a fully functional server.

## CHAPTER SEVEN

# Fundamentals of ATL COM Servers

In Chapter 6, we examined the architecture of an ATL COM object. In this chapter, we'll look at the necessary support structure that ATL provides for serving COM objects to a client. ATL COM objects are contained in DLL or EXE modules. DLL modules are loaded in the process of the client, which is why they're called in-process (or in-proc) servers. An EXE module, which is sometimes called an out-of-process (or out-of-proc) server, runs in its own distinct process. In addition to the code for the COM objects themselves (which is your main focus as a developer), the module must provide the necessary infrastructure for the following concepts:

- Self-registration
- Class objects
- Server lifetime management

Fortunately, ATL provides a lot of code to help out in these areas. The ATL COM AppWizard uses this code to generate fully functional server modules to house your objects. In this chapter, we'll look at some of the wizard-generated code along with a lot of undocumented ATL features to determine how ATL handles the boilerplate grunge that the "cut and paste" approach typically generates in classic COM development.

Let's start by examining the heart of an ATL-based server: *CComModule*.

## The *CComModule* Class

The ATL COM AppWizard relies on the ATL *CComModule* class for much of the required server implementation. *CComModule* is implemented in atlbase.h, which is included in stdafx.h. Regardless of your choice of server (DLL or EXE), an instance of *CComModule* will be created in your main .cpp file with the name

*_Module*. EXE servers use a derivative of *CComModule* that we'll look at when we discuss server lifetime. ATL classes are tightly coupled to the *_Module* instance name, so you must not change the name. A pointer to this single instance is also cached in atlbase.h in the *_pModule* global variable so that other classes implemented in atlbase.h (such as *CComBSTR*) can get to the module instance.

At a bare minimum, you need calls to *_Module.Init* and *_Module.Term* in your module. These calls bracket the usable lifetime for ATL in your project. In DLL servers, *Init* is called from the entry point *DllMain* when the client process is attached, and as you might guess, *Term* is called when the process is detached. In EXE servers, *Init* and *Term* are called in the *_tWinMain* entry point between *CoInitialize* and *CoUninitialize* calls. *Init* takes three arguments and gives the module a chance to cache the HINSTANCE for the module and a pointer to the object map, which is described later in this chapter. The prototype for *Init* is shown here:

```
HRESULT Init(_ATL_OBJMAP_ENTRY* p, HINSTANCE h,
    const GUID* plibid = NULL)
```

The ID for the server type library, which you need for self-registration, is passed in as the last argument to *Init*. *Term* performs the necessary cleanup work before COM is uninitialized.

We'll be looking at areas of *CComModule* specific to self-registration, server lifetime, and class objects throughout this chapter.

## Self-Registration

Self-registration involves adding keys and values to the Registry to let COM know that your server module is available and how to launch it. Well-behaved servers also remove those entries when the object is no longer available. ATL supports this capability through the functions *CComModule::RegisterServer* and *CComModule::UnregisterServer*. This abstraction is used for both DLL and EXE modules through the *_Module* global instance. EXE servers register themselves when they are run with the */RegServer* option on the command line and unregister themselves when invoked with */UnregServer*. DLL servers perform these functions when the exported functions *DllRegisterServer* and *DllUnregisterServer* are called. The ATL COM AppWizard generates the necessary code in either case. The following code shows the registration and cleanup for a DLL server:

```
STDAPI DllRegisterServer(void)
{
    // Registers object, typelib and all interfaces in typelib
    return _Module.RegisterServer(TRUE);
}
```

```
STDAPI DllUnregisterServer(void)
{
    return _Module.UnregisterServer(TRUE);
}
```

*CComModule::RegisterServer* takes a BOOL as its first argument. If the argument is TRUE, the type library for the server should be registered along with the coclasses and interfaces for the objects themselves. The Microsoft Interface Definition Language (MIDL) compiler generates the type library from the project IDL file when the project is compiled. The IDL file for the project is listed in the FileView tab under Source Files. We won't get into the details of IDL here, but be aware that by default ATL uses the helper function *Atl-ModuleRegisterTypeLib* to perform the necessary registration for your type library. *CComModule::RegisterServer* has an optional second argument—the CLSID (class ID) of the object to register. By default, all objects in the object map are registered, so normally this argument isn't necessary. If you specify a CLSID, only the object that has a matching CLSID will be registered. The same rule applies to *CComModule::UnregisterServer*, which takes a CLSID as its only argument.

## Registry Scripts

Let's examine a section of the ATL COM AppWizard–generated registration code for an EXE server in *_tWinMain*.

```
if(lstrcmpi(lpszToken, _T("UnregServer"))==0)
{
    _Module.UpdateRegistryFromResource(IDR_ATLExeServer, FALSE);
    nRet = _Module.UnregisterServer(TRUE);
    bRun = FALSE;
    break;
}
if(lstrcmpi(lpszToken, _T("RegServer"))==0)
{
    _Module.UpdateRegistryFromResource(IDR_ATLExeServer, TRUE);
    nRet = _Module.RegisterServer(TRUE);
    bRun = FALSE;
    break;
}
```

In addition to the expected *_Module.RegisterServer* and *_Module.Unregister-Server* entries, notice the calls to *_Module.UpdateRegistryFromResource*. When executed, this helper function adds or removes Registry entries based on a resource script. A *resource script* is a custom resource that is a text-based representation of the entries to make for an object or an application. The first argument to *_Module.UpdateRegistryFromResource* is the resource ID of the script, and the second argument indicates whether the entries should be registered (TRUE) or unregistered (FALSE). The script for the preceding code section looks like this:

```
HKCR
{
    NoRemove AppID
    {
        {EA5E30E1-C133-11D2-B18B-D0554FC10001} = s 'ATLExeServer'
        'ATLExeServer.EXE'
        {
            val AppID = s {EA5E30E1-C133-11D2-B18B-D0554FC10001}
        }
    }
}
```

The script shown adds the Registry key HKEY_CLASSES_ROOT\AppID if one doesn't exist. The NoRemove attribute ensures that the key won't be removed during the unregistration process. This is a good thing, since many applications depend on the presence of the *AppID* key. Under this key, a new GUID subkey is made, representing the AppID for this EXE module. This key is then given the default string value "ATLExeServer." So far we've covered the script down to the "ATLExeServer.EXE" line. The next three lines create another subkey, HKCR\AppID\ATLExeServer.EXE, and add a named string value (AppID) under the new subkey with the GUID as a string value.

Your compiled project contains Registry scripts as resources, and they can be viewed from the FileView tab under Resource Files or in the ResourceView tab under the custom type "REGISTRY". ATL COM projects have a separate script resource for each object contained in the server. EXE servers have an additional script for the AppID, similar to the one shown earlier.

**NOTE** The ATL team didn't invent a new notation for Registry scripts. Registry scripts are in Backus-Naur form (BNF), a standard notation used to describe syntax for interpretation. This is but one application of BNF.

## Object Registration Macros

The *Module.RegisterServer* function registers individual object scripts during its activity. Now that you're armed with the knowledge that *_Module.Update-RegistryFromResource* will interpret a Registry script, the DECLARE_REGISTRY_RESOURCEID macro in a default ATL Object Wizard–generated header file should make more sense.

```
#define DECLARE_REGISTRY_RESOURCEID(x)\
    static HRESULT WINAPI UpdateRegistry(BOOL bRegister)\
    {\
    return _Module.UpdateRegistryFromResource(x, bRegister);\
    }
```

Just as you saw in _tWinMain_, the macro expands to a static function, _UpdateRegistry_, which delegates to _Module.UpdateRegistryFromResource_. Table 7-1 lists other registration macros that you can also use.

### Table 7-1 **Registration Macros**

| Macro | Description |
|---|---|
| DECLARE_REGISTRY_RESOURCE(*x*) | *x* is a string identifier for a script resource. |
| DECLARE_REGISTRY(*class*, *pid*, *vpid*, *nid*, *flags*) | Inserts and removes the five basic keys for your object. No script is used. |
| DECLARE_NO_REGISTRY() | Doesn't make any Registry entries. |

If the mechanisms described above don't meet your needs, you can forgo the macros and write your own custom version of the static _UpdateRegistry_ member function. Simply use the same signature as the macro expansion shown in the preceding code.

**NOTE** Chapter 9 examines the ATL Object Wizard in detail.

## The ATL Registry Component (Registrar)

_CComModule::RegisterServer_ and _CComModule::UnregisterServer_ need a way to parse the Registry scripts in a server and add or remove the necessary entries. ATL provides the Registrar component for this purpose. The Registrar is available to your application as a prebuilt COM component in ATL.DLL or as statically linked code. Two preprocessors control the option: _ATL_STATIC_REGISTRY and _ATL_DLL. _ATL_STATIC_REGISTRY forces the inclusion of the Registrar code (statreg.h) into atlbase.h, which ends up in your stdafx.h. The absence of _ATL_STATIC_REGISTRY results in the use of the parser in ATL.DLL, which means you must distribute ATL.DLL with your application and register it during installation. ATL.DLL serves two purposes:

- It contains the COM version of the parser _CDLLRegObject_.

- It exports global ATL functions to optimize your server for size.

Linkage to ATL.DLL is enabled with the _ATL_DLL preprocessor. The ReleaseMinSize build uses this option to build the smallest server possible, removing the global implementations from the ATL source and instead using the DLL versions. Using _ATL_DLL and _ATL_STATIC_REGISTRY together results in a compiler error. The key to understanding this problem lies in statreg.h.

```
#if defined(_ATL_DLL) | defined(_ATL_DLL_IMPL)
class ATL_NO_VTABLE CRegObject
    : public IRegistrar
#else
class CRegObject
#endif
```

When _ATL_STATIC_REGISTRY is defined, *CComModule::Update-RegistryFromResource* attempts to instantiate a *CRegObject*. This will fail if _ATL_DLL is also defined because of the ATL_NO_VTABLE optimization shown in the preceding code. ReleaseMinDependency builds have the ATL_STATIC_REGISTRY preprocessor and therefore include the Registrar code directly in your server. To completely remove dependencies on ATL.DLL, you must remove the _ATL_DLL preprocessor and add _ATL_STATIC_REGISTRY. Table 7-2 summarizes the preprocessors and the resulting project dependencies.

**Table 7-2  ATL Preprocessors**

| _ATL_STATIC_REGISTRY | _ATL_DLL | Result |
|---|---|---|
| No | No | No linkage to ATL.DLL but uses ATL.DLL for the COM version of the parser |
| No | Yes | Linkage to ATL.DLL and uses COM version of the parser |
| Yes | No | No ATL.DLL dependencies whatsoever |
| Yes | Yes | Not allowed; build failure |

To make this information concrete, let's look at how *CComObject* uses the parser in the default debug build configuration, which has neither _ATL_DLL nor _ATL_STATIC_REGISTRY. Recall that *CComModule::UpdateRegistryFromResource* is where ATL does the real registration work, either when called by itself or as the result of the DECLARE_REGISTRY_RESOURCEID($x$) macro and *CComModule::RegisterServer*. Atlbase.h defines *UpdateRegistryFromResource* differently depending on the _ATL_STATIC_REGISTRY preprocessor. Here are the macro definitions for static and DLL linkage:

```
#ifdef _ATL_STATIC_REGISTRY
#define UpdateRegistryFromResource UpdateRegistryFromResourceS
#else
#define UpdateRegistryFromResource UpdateRegistryFromResourceD
#endif
```

Because we don't have _ATL_STATIC_REGISTRY in the debug build, we'll use *UpdateRegistryFromResourceD*. This function delegates to *AtlModule-UpdateRegistryFromResourceD*, which uses good old *CoCreateInstanceEx* to instantiate the Registrar component from ATL.DLL.

```
ATLINLINE ATLAPI AtlModuleUpdateRegistryFromResourceD(
    _ATL_MODULE* pM, LPCOLESTR lpszRes, BOOL bRegister,
    struct _ATL_REGMAP_ENTRY* pMapEntries, IRegistrar* pReg)
{
    USES_CONVERSION;
    ATLASSERT(pM != NULL);
    HRESULT hRes = S_OK;
    CComPtr<IRegistrar> p;
    if(pReg != NULL)
        p = pReg;
    else
    {
        hRes = CoCreateInstanceEx(CLSID_Registrar, NULL,
            CLSCTX_INPROC_SERVER, IID_IRegistrar, (void**)&p);
    }
⋮
    if(bRegister)
        hRes = p->ResourceRegister(pszModule,
            ((UINT)LOWORD((DWORD)lpszRes)), szType);
⋮
}
```

*ResourceRegister* handles parsing the entire script and making all of the requested Registry entries. You can look at statreg.h in the ATL include directory for all of the gory parser details. As you can see, ATL has a significant amount of code to support self-registration.

# Class Objects

A class object is a COM object that typically implements the *IClassFactory* interface to create instances of objects of a particular CLSID. *CoCreateInstanceEx* depends on the class object's *IClassFactory::CreateInstance* method to create the object of the requested type (CLSID) and return an interface pointer to the new instance. At that point, the class object is no longer needed, so *CoCreateInstanceEx* releases it. The class object can be obtained directly with *CoGetClassObject* in case you have other functionality in the class object that you need to access, or if you want to optimize creation of many objects of the same type.

## ATL Support for Class Object Creation

ATL supports the COM idiom of a class object that implements *IClassFactory* through *CComClassFactory*. By default, all of your ATL objects use *CCom-ClassFactory* as a common class object implementation. Your object inherits this behavior by deriving from *CComCoClass*. Inside *CComCoClass* (atlcom.h), the following macro is declared:

```
DECLARE_CLASSFACTORY()
```

This macro expands to

```
DECLARE_CLASSFACTORY_EX(CComClassFactory)
```

and finally results in the following typedef in *CComCoClass* (for EXE servers):

```
typedef CComCreator< CComObjectNoLock< CComClassFactory > >\
    _ClassFactoryCreatorClass;
```

For DLL servers, the following typedef is used instead:

```
typedef CComCreator< CComObjectCached< CComClassFactory > >\
    _ClassFactoryCreatorClass;
```

In both cases, your object inherits a typedef for *_ClassFactoryCreatorClass* from *CComCoClass*. The derivation from *CComObjectCached* or *CComObject-NoLock* is related to server lifetime, which will be discussed later in this chapter. For now, let's stick to the task at hand—object creation. At the bottom of the typedef chain is *CComCreator*. The entire class is shown here:

```
template <class T1>
class CComCreator
{
public:
    static HRESULT WINAPI CreateInstance(void* pv,
        REFIID riid, LPVOID* ppv)
    {
        ATLASSERT(*ppv == NULL);
        HRESULT hRes = E_OUTOFMEMORY;
        T1* p = NULL;
        ATLTRY(p = new T1(pv))
        if(p != NULL)
        {
            p->SetVoid(pv);
            p->InternalFinalConstructAddRef();
            hRes = p->FinalConstruct();
            p->InternalFinalConstructRelease();
```

```
            if(hRes == S_OK)
                hRes = p->QueryInterface(riid, ppv);
            if(hRes != S_OK)
                delete p;
        }
        return hRes;
    }
};
```

Notice that *CComCreator* has a single static *CreateInstance* function that creates a new instance of the templatized type *T1*, which will be *CComObjectxxx- <CComClassFactory>*. This is where the actual creation of the class object occurs. It might seem like a lot of work simply to create a class object; but consider that through this mechanism, ATL uses a single implementation of a class object to create all types of objects. Also, the DECLARE_CLASSFACTORY macro that started this expansion declares the most common class object type configuration. You can override this default declaration by inserting one of the macros described in Table 7-3 directly into your object header file.

### Table 7-3  Class Factory Macros

| Macro | Description |
| --- | --- |
| DECLARE_CLASSFACTORY2(*lic*) | Declares a class object that implements *IClassFactory2* for licensed components |
| DECLARE_CLASSFACTORY-_AUTO_THREAD() | Allows objects in EXE servers to be created in multiple apartments |
| DECLARE_CLASSFACTORY-_SINGLETON(*obj*) | Allows only a single instance of your object to be created in the process that contains it |

Because the default DECLARE_CLASSFACTORY macro is declared in *CComCoClass*, any macro declared in your derived class will create a *_ClassFactory- CreatorClass* typedef that overrides the *CComCoClass* version as long as your object class name is used to reference it. Regardless of the macro used, a class object can be created from your object class using this syntax:

```
CMyObject::_ClassFactoryCreatorClass::CreateInstance(…);
```

## Enabling *CComClassFactory::CreateInstance*

A class object needs to know how to create objects of a particular type. So far, we've learned how to create a generic *CComClassFactory* object. Now let's look at how this class object creates an instance of a specified type. First we need to look more closely at *CComCreator::CreateInstance*.

```
static HRESULT WINAPI CreateInstance(void* pv,
    REFIID riid, LPVOID* ppv)
{
    ATLASSERT(*ppv == NULL);
    HRESULT hRes = E_OUTOFMEMORY;
    T1* p = NULL;
    ATLTRY(p = new T1(pv))
    if(p != NULL)
    {
        p->SetVoid(pv);
    }
    ⋮
}
```

Notice that the *void* *pv* parameter in the preceding code is passed up to the class factory in *SetVoid*. *CComClassFactory::SetVoid* reveals that *void* * is actually a function pointer, shown here:

```
void SetVoid(void* pv)
{
    m_pfnCreateInstance = (_ATL_CREATORFUNC*)pv;
}
_ATL_CREATORFUNC* m_pfnCreateInstance;
```

You'll see *m_pfnCreateInstance* again in the *IClassFactory::CreateInstance* implementation in *CComClassFactory,* shown here:

```
STDMETHOD(CreateInstance)(LPUNKNOWN pUnkOuter,
    REFIID riid, void** ppvObj)
{
    ⋮
    hRes = m_pfnCreateInstance(pUnkOuter, riid, ppvObj);
    ⋮
    return hRes;
}
```

Because this same code is executed for all class objects when the client calls *IClassFactory::CreateInstance,* or executed by COM inside *CoCreateInstanceEx,* *m_pfnCreateInstance* must be able to create a specific object type. Therefore, *m_pfnCreateInstance* resolves to *yourobject::_CreatorClass::CreateInstance,* which is the next typedef we need to look at. In addition to the DECLARE_CLASS-FACTORY macro, *CComCoClass* has the DECLARE_AGGREGATABLE(T) macro, which creates the *_CreatorClass* typedef shown here:

```
typedef CComCreator2< CComCreator<CComObject<x>>,\
    CComCreator< CComAggObject<x>>> _CreatorClass;
```

The template parameter *x* is your object class name, as passed in to *CComCo-Class*. *CComCreator2* is very much like *CComCreator*, which is used for class objects, except that *CComCreator2* creates an aggregated component if an outer unknown is passed in to its *CreateInstance* method. The *CComCreator2* class is shown here:

```
template <class T1, class T2>
class CComCreator2
{
public:
    static HRESULT WINAPI CreateInstance(void* pv,
        REFIID riid, LPVOID* ppv)
    {
        ATLASSERT(*ppv == NULL);
        return (pv == NULL) ?
            T1::CreateInstance(NULL, riid, ppv) :
            T2::CreateInstance(pv, riid, ppv);
    }
};
```

*T1* and *T2* are the *CComCreator<CComObject<YourObject>>* and *CCom-Creator<CComAggObject<YourObject>>* parameters from the DECLARE-_AGGREGATABLE macro. Like the class factory macros, other macro choices are available, depending on whether aggregation is allowed or required by your component. Aggregation isn't the focus of this discussion, so we'll continue on the track of object creation. Assuming we're not aggregated, a call to *YourClass:: CreatorClass::CreateInstance* results in the static *CComCreator2::CreateInstance* (shown above) function calling *T1::CreateInstance*, where *T1* is *CComCreator-<CComObject<YourObject>>*. *CComCreator::CreateInstance* finally creates a new instance of your object using the *new* operator. That sequence, starting with *IClassFactory::CreateInstance*, is:

1. *CComClassFactory::CreateInstance*

2. *CComCreator2::CreateInstance*

3. *CComCreator::CreateInstance*

After you create your object, it is initialized and clients call *QueryInterface* for the requested interface. (*T1* is your object class name.) The complete code for *CComCreator* is shown on pages 178–179.

# The ATL Object Map

ATL servers keep track of the objects they contain in the object map. The map is declared in the main .cpp file for your project and begins with the BEGIN-_OBJECT_MAP(*x*) macro. A typical object map with one object in it might look like this:

```
BEGIN_OBJECT_MAP(ObjectMap)
OBJECT_ENTRY(CLSID_MyObj, CMyObj)
END_OBJECT_MAP()
```

The relevant macros are defined in atlcom.h:

```
#define BEGIN_OBJECT_MAP(x) static _ATL_OBJMAP_ENTRY x[] = {
#define END_OBJECT_MAP()    {NULL, NULL, NULL, NULL, NULL,\
    NULL, NULL, NULL}};
#define OBJECT_ENTRY(clsid, class) {&clsid, class::UpdateRegistry,\
    class::_ClassFactoryCreatorClass::CreateInstance,\
    class::_CreatorClass::CreateInstance, NULL, 0,\
    class::GetObjectDescription, class::GetCategoryMap,\
    class::ObjectMain },
#define OBJECT_ENTRY_NON_CREATEABLE(class) {&CLSID_NULL,\
    class::UpdateRegistry, NULL, NULL, NULL, 0, NULL,\
    class::GetCategoryMap, class::ObjectMain },
```

An object map is an array of _ATL_OBJMAP_ENTRY structures, the first element of which is identified by the name passed to BEGIN_OBJECT_MAP. This name (ObjectMap by default) is passed in to the *Module.Init* call, where ATL caches it in the *CComModule::m_pObjMap* member. The map is used whenever ATL needs to iterate over the objects contained in the server, particularly for registration and class object initialization.

There is one OBJECT_ENTRY per class of object in the server, defined by the individual OBJECT_ENTRY macros between the beginning and ending macros. OBJECT_ENTRY fills an _ATL_OBJMAP_ENTRY structure based on the CLSID of your object and its C++ implementation class name. The structure is defined as follows:

```
struct _ATL_OBJMAP_ENTRY
{
    const CLSID* pclsid;
    HRESULT (WINAPI *pfnUpdateRegistry)(BOOL bRegister);
    _ATL_CREATORFUNC* pfnGetClassObject;
    _ATL_CREATORFUNC* pfnCreateInstance;
    IUnknown* pCF;
    DWORD dwRegister;
    _ATL_DESCRIPTIONFUNC* pfnGetObjectDescription;
    _ATL_CATMAPFUNC* pfnGetCategoryMap;
```

```
        HRESULT WINAPI RevokeClassObject()
        {
            return CoRevokeClassObject(dwRegister);
        }
        HRESULT WINAPI RegisterClassObject(DWORD dwClsContext,
            DWORD dwFlags)
        {
            IUnknown* p = NULL;
            if(pfnGetClassObject == NULL)
                return S_OK;
            HRESULT hRes = pfnGetClassObject(pfnCreateInstance,
                IID_IUnknown, (LPVOID*) &p);
            if(SUCCEEDED(hRes))
                hRes = CoRegisterClassObject(*pclsid, p,
                    dwClsContext, dwFlags, &dwRegister);
            if(p != NULL)
                p->Release();
            return hRes;
        }
// Added in ATL 3.0
        void (WINAPI *pfnObjectMain)(bool bStarting);
};
```

Many of these elements relate directly to the registration and class objects discussed earlier in the chapter. The structure is more familiar if we look at it in terms of the OBJECT_ENTRY macro definition in Table 7-4.

### Table 7-4   _ATL_OBJMAP_ENTRY Structure Data Members

| _ATL_OBJMAP_ENTRY Member | OBJECT_ENTRY Macro Part |
|---|---|
| const CLSID* pclsid | &clsid |
| HRESULT (WINAPI *pfnUpdateRegistry) (BOOL bRegister) | Class::UpdateRegistry (BOOL bRegister) |
| _ATL_CREATORFUNC* pfnGetClassObject | Class::_ClassFactoryCreator-Class::CreateInstance |
| _ATL_CREATORFUNC* pfnCreateInstance | Class::_CreatorClass::CreateInstance |
| IUnknown* pCF | NULL |
| DWORD dwRegister | 0 |
| _ATL_DESCRIPTIONFUNC* pfn-GetObjectDescription | Class::GetObjectDescription |
| _ATL_CATMAPFUNC* pfnGetCategoryMap | class::GetCategoryMap |
| void (WINAPI *pfnObjectMain)(bool bStarting) | class::ObjectMain(bool bStarting) |

*UpdateRegistry* is the same registration function we looked at in self-registration. The *_CreatorClass* typedefs are used to create a class object and initialize it with a function that creates this kind of object, as outlined in the previous section on class objects. *IUnknown\* pCF* is a cached pointer to the class object. DLL servers create the class object for an object the first time it is requested in *DllGetClassObject*, initializing *pCF* in the process. EXE servers leave this member NULL and instead use *CoRegisterClassObject* to maintain an instance. The other *class::* entries use the same pattern we've seen before, in which ATL calls static initialization functions on your object. Only EXE servers use the *RegisterClassObject* and *RevokeClassObject* functions (along with the *dwRegister* member), as we'll see in the next section.

The object map is a vital piece of the ATL module support, enabling efficient enumeration of the items needed to bring objects into existence.

# Activation

When a client needs to use an object, it relies on COM to find the necessary information to load the DLL or start the EXE server that contains the object. In most cases, the client can remain unaware of which housing contains the object and use *CoCreateInstanceEx* or *CoGetClassObject* to instantiate an object.

Server implementors have the task of following the activation protocol required by the COM service control manager (SCM) to make the instantiation process transparent to the client. Although the mechanisms differ for DLL and EXE servers, ATL makes handling the different mechanisms as painless as possible by utilizing the object map and *CComModule* to perform much of the work.

## DLL Server Activation

When a client requests an object that resides in a DLL, COM loads the DLL into the client's process and calls the *DllMain* entry point with DLL_PROCESS-_ATTACH, in which *_Module.Init* is called. The most important service *_Module.Init* performs for activation is to cache the object map pointer.

Once the DLL is initialized and *DllMain* has returned, *DllGetClassObject* will be called to retrieve the class object for the desired object CLSID. A one-line call to *_Module.GetClassObject* completes the task. The implementation of *CComModule::GetClassObject* uses the cached object map pointer to iterate over the object map, looking for an entry with the same CLSID as the one requested. If the entry is found, the following code executes:

```
if(pEntry->pCF == NULL)
{
    EnterCriticalSection(&pM->m_csObjMap);
    if(pEntry->pCF == NULL)
        hRes = pEntry->pfnGetClassObject(
            pEntry->pfnCreateInstance, IID_IUnknown,
            (LPVOID*)&pEntry->pCF);
    LeaveCriticalSection(&pM->m_csObjMap);
}
if(pEntry->pCF != NULL)
    hRes = pEntry->pCF->QueryInterface(riid, ppv);
break;
```

Remember that the _ATL_OBJMAP_ENTRY structure has an *IUnknown**
*pCF* member. The first time a class object for a certain CLSID is requested, ATL
creates the class object and caches its *IUnknown* pointer in *pCF*. ATL maintains
the class object instance internally for the lifetime of the server. This cached
instance won't keep the server alive, as we'll see in the section "Server Lifetime
Management" below. The cached pointer is then used to query the class object
for the requested interface—usually *IClassFactory*.

## EXE Server Activation

Because an EXE server is itself a process, that process must be launched by COM
if it isn't already running. Unlike DLL servers, EXE servers have no equivalent
of *DllGetClassObject* that the SCM can call. Instead, the server adds its class
objects to a map maintained by the SCM using *CoRegisterClassObject*. An ATL
EXE server can register all its class objects using *_Module.RegisterClassObjects*.
The ATL COM AppWizard adds this call to your *_tWinMain* function:

```
hRes = _Module.RegisterClassObjects(CLSCTX_LOCAL_SERVER,
            REGCLS_MULTIPLEUSE);
```

This function delegates to *AtlModuleRegisterClassObjects*, which loops
through the object map calling *RegisterClassObject* on each entry.

```
ATLINLINE ATLAPI AtlModuleRegisterClassObjects(_ATL_MODULE* pM,
    DWORD dwClsContext, DWORD dwFlags)
{
    ATLASSERT(pM != NULL);
    if(pM == NULL)
        return E_INVALIDARG;
    ATLASSERT(pM->m_pObjMap != NULL);
    _ATL_OBJMAP_ENTRY* pEntry = pM->m_pObjMap;
    HRESULT hRes = S_OK;
```

*(continued)*

```
while (pEntry->pclsid != NULL && hRes == S_OK)
{
    hRes = pEntry->RegisterClassObject(dwClsContext,
        dwFlags);
    pEntry = _NextObjectMapEntry(pM, pEntry);
}
return hRes;
}
```

As promised in our earlier object map discussion, the *RegisterClassObject* member of the _ATL_OBJMAP_ENTRY structure is called on to actually do the *CoRegisterClassObject* API call. Once the class objects are registered, the SCM happily continues with the activation as requested by the client.

## Server Lifetime Management

DLL server lifetime is ultimately tied to the client that uses the objects it contains. When a client wants to remove a server from memory, it calls *CoFree-UnusedLibraries*, typically during idle processing. This results in the server receiving a call to the exported function *DllCanUnloadNow*. The server returns S_OK if the DLL can be freed, S_FALSE otherwise. The DLL can be freed if no outstanding references to objects are contained in the server (including class objects) and no outstanding locks are on the server via *IClassFactory::LockServer*. The implementation of *DllCanUnloadNow*, shown in the following code, reveals that *CComModule* maintains a global reference count that keeps the DLL loaded as long as it is nonzero.

```
STDAPI DllCanUnloadNow(void)
{
    return (_Module.GetLockCount()==0) ? S_OK : S_FALSE;
}
```

The lock count is incremented and decremented using *_Module.Lock* and *_Module.Unlock*, which increment or decrement *CComModule::m_nLockCnt*. As you might expect, the lock count initially starts at 0. Typically, *Lock* is called when an object in the server is created and *Unlock* is called when it is destroyed. Class objects have slightly different behavior. Recall that the object map maintains an *IUnknown* pointer to the class objects it creates the first time they are requested. If construction of a class object incremented the lock count, the server would never be released. Thus class objects are created using *CComObjectCached*, which locks the server only when the object reference count reaches 2 and unlocks only when the count falls below 2. *IClassFactory::LockServer* also locks or unlocks the server, as implemented in *CComClassFactory*.

EXE servers have different requirements for shutting down. Class objects are registered with COM using *CoRegisterClassObject*. The SCM holds a reference to the class object until *CoRevokeClassObject* is called. ATL places a call to *_Module.RevokeClassObjects* at the end of an EXE server's *_tWinMain* entry point. Once again, the object map is iterated, this time to remove the class object references. *RevokeClassObject* is called on each map entry, which calls *CoRevokeClassObject* using the *dwRegister* cookie received from *CoRegisterClassObject*. When *_Module.RevokeClassObjects* is executed, the server is already shutting down, implying that class objects can't keep an EXE server running. That's why class objects in an ATL EXE server are created with *CComObjectNoLock*. The choice to use *CComObjectNoLock* in the typedef for *_ClassFactoryCreatorClass* is selected based on the type of server you're creating. The following code shows how the typedef is defined for DLL and EXE servers:

```
#if defined(_WINDLL) | defined(_USRDLL)
#define DECLARE_CLASSFACTORY_EX(cf) typedef CComCreator<\
    CComObjectCached< cf > > _ClassFactoryCreatorClass;
#else
// Don't let class factory refcount influence lock count
#define DECLARE_CLASSFACTORY_EX(cf) typedef CComCreator<\
    CComObjectNoLock< cf > > _ClassFactoryCreatorClass;
#endif
```

As the name implies, *CComObjectNoLock* does no module locking whatsoever. That leaves outstanding object references and explicit *IClassFactory::LockServer* locks to keep the server running. Once all objects have been released and the lock removed, the server can shut down. Because EXE servers run in their own process space, some signaling method must be used to initiate shutdown when the module lock count reaches 0. The ATL COM AppWizard provides the signaling mechanism by inserting a *CComModule* derived class in your application in stdafx.h. The derived class implements *Unlock* and adds some new members as well, shown here:

```
class CExeModule : public CComModule
{
public:
    LONG Unlock();
    DWORD dwThreadID;
    HANDLE hEventShutdown;
    void MonitorShutdown();
    bool StartMonitor();
    bool bActivity;
};
extern CExeModule _Module;
```

Before starting the message pump, _Module.StartMonitor is called to create a Win32 event and start a worker thread. All of the related code is in the server main .cpp file, shown here:

```
bool CExeModule::StartMonitor()
{
    hEventShutdown = CreateEvent(NULL, false, false, NULL);
    if(hEventShutdown == NULL)
        return false;
    DWORD dwThreadID;
    HANDLE h = CreateThread(NULL, 0, MonitorProc, this, 0,
        &dwThreadID);
    return (h != NULL);
}
```

The thread procedure *MonitorProc* begins executing immediately and delegates to *MonitorShutdown,* shown here:

```
void CExeModule::MonitorShutdown()
{
    while (1)
    {
        WaitForSingleObject(hEventShutdown, INFINITE);
        DWORD dwWait=0;
        do
        {
            bActivity = false;
            dwWait = WaitForSingleObject(hEventShutdown,
                dwTimeOut);
        } while (dwWait == WAIT_OBJECT_0);
        // Timed out
        if(!bActivity && m_nLockCnt == 0)
        {
#if _WIN32_WINNT >= 0x0400 & defined(_ATL_FREE_THREADED)
            CoSuspendClassObjects();
            if(!bActivity && m_nLockCnt == 0)
#endif
                break;
        }
    }
    CloseHandle(hEventShutdown);
    PostThreadMessage(dwThreadID, WM_QUIT, 0, 0);
}
```

This code is constantly running on the background thread, looking for the *hEventShutdown* event to be signaled. The event is signaled from the main thread when the module lock count reaches 0, as shown here:

```
LONG CExeModule::Unlock()
{
    LONG l = CComModule::Unlock();
    if(l == 0)
    {
        bActivity = true;
        SetEvent(hEventShutdown);
    }
    return l;
}
```

After seeing the shutdown event and a period of time with no activity, the wait loop exits and a WM_QUIT message is posted to the main thread, causing the message loop to terminate. The *_tWinMain* function continues on to revoke the class objects before a graceful end.

# Conclusion

In this chapter, we examined the support ATL provides for building fully functional COM servers in DLL and EXE modules. Registration is simplified by using Registry script resources and the Registrar component. Class objects are implemented in *CComClassFactory* for all object types, with unique creation functions provided through typedefs. Creator classes are used as object factories for both class objects and the target objects themselves. The object map is maintained as a collection of object information that can be iterated to locate specific registration and activation methods for all classes of objects or a specific object class. ATL effectively handles module locking to control server lifetime in DLL and EXE housings.

## CHAPTER EIGHT

# Advanced Class Composition Techniques

We've covered a lot of ground so far. You now know the basics of COM and how it solves certain software distribution and integration problems. You know how to create a COM server from scratch and how to add COM classes to your server by driving ATL's Object Wizard. However, there's more than one way to compose a COM class. This chapter will show you some of the details of composing more complex COM classes using ATL's interface maps. First we'll go over the meaning of COM identity. Understanding COM identity is central to understanding the various techniques for composing COM classes. Then we'll present some alternative techniques for composing COM classes. These techniques include composing classes with dual interface implementations as well as some more esoteric composition techniques, such as tear-off interfaces and aggregation. Let's start with a comprehensive examination of COM identity.

## Object Identity

Before tackling COM identity, let's consider the meaning of identity for a normal C++ class. When you want an instance of a C++ class, you simply call on operator *new* to produce one for you. If operator *new* succeeds, you get back a pointer to the top of the object, after which the compiler lets you access any of the public data members and functions. In the following example, notice how operator *new* gives you a pointer to the object in its entirety:

```
class CSomeClass {
public:
    short x;
    void DoIt();
    void DoItAgain();
};
```

*(continued)*

```
CSomeClass* pSomeClass = new CSomeClass;
pSomeClass->x = 42;
pSomeClass->DoIt();
pSomeClass->DoItAgain();
```

In the example above, *pSomeClass* represents the object's identity; that is, *pSomeClass* represents the whole object and nothing but the object. If you need to know the identity of the C++ object, you can cast the pointer to the object using *void\**, like this:

```
CSomeClass* pSomeClass = new CSomeClass;
void* pvIdentity = NULL;
pvIdentity = (void*) pSomeClass;
```

Doing this establishes the C++ object's position in memory, which turns out to represent the object's run-time identity.

Recall that a COM object is just some piece of code (remember—a COM object is a component, so the internal workings should be left as implementation details). What distinguishes the COM object from random memory is that the COM object implements a COM interface (a function table) named *IUnknown*. *IUnknown* includes three functions, which can be expressed in C++ like this:

```
struct IUnknown {
    virtual HRESULT QueryInterface(REFIID riid,
        void** ppv) = 0;
    virtual ULONG AddRef() = 0;
    virtual ULONG Release() = 0;
};
```

As you saw in Chapter 2, the key to grasping *IUnknown* is to understand these points:

- A COM object needs to implement these three functions.

- All COM interfaces you'll ever encounter begin with these three functions.

Remember that there's no *this* pointer when it comes to binary objects, which means that *IUnknown* establishes the identity of a COM object.

Most C++ developers are comfortable writing client code that talks directly to a C++ object. In COM—unlike normal C++—you never talk to an actual object. Instead, you talk to one of the object's interfaces. For example, a similar COM-based example of working with an object might look like this:

```
struct ISomeInterface  : IUnknown {
    virtual void DoIt() = 0;
};
```

```
ISomeInterface* pSomeInterface;
CoCreateInstance(CLSID_CoSomeClass,
    NULL,
    CLSCTX_ALL,
    ISomeInterface,
    (void**)&pSomeInterface);
if(pSomeInterface) {
    pSomeInterface->DoIt();
    pSomeInterface->Release();
}
```

When the client code talks to *pSomeInterface,* the client isn't touching the actual instance of *CoSomeClass*—it's touching an interface attached to the *CoSome-Class* object. Now imagine that *CoSomeClass* implements another interface named *IAnotherInterface.* Once the client obtains an interface (any interface) to the object, the client can try to (arbitrarily) widen its connection to the object, like this:

```
struct IAnotherInterface : IUnknown {
    void DoItAgain();
}

void UseSomeInterface(ISomeInterface *pSomeInterface) {
    IAnotherInterface* pAnotherInterface = 0;
    pSomeInterface->QueryInterface(IID_IAnotherInterface,
        (void**)&pAnotherInterface);
    if(pAnotherInterface) {
        pAnotherInterface->DoItAgain();
        pAnotherInterface->Release();
    }
}
```

The client can do this because *QueryInterface* (a member of the *IUnknown* interface) is the first function of every COM interface you'll ever see.

At this point, we're staring the notion of COM and object identity right in the face. Remember the lollipop diagrams that appear so often throughout the COM literature? Each lollipop represents an interface, and the rounded rectangle represents the body of code implementing the interface.

## Switching Interfaces

COM's *IUnknown* interface allows objects to have multiple personalities. *Co-SomeObject* understands how to implement two interfaces—*ISomeInterface* and *IAnotherInterface.* A client can hold a pointer to *ISomeInterface* and a pointer to *IAnotherInterface,* and both pointers might be pointing to the same object.

By permitting this functionality (the mechanism for arbitrarily widening the connection to an object at run time), COM effectively provides a means for extending objects arbitrarily without breaking old clients. Older clients that understand the existing interfaces remain content because the interfaces still exist. Clients that want to use the newer interfaces simply have to ask for a new interface.

In COM, *IUnknown* represents a pointer to an object; that is, *IUnknown* denotes an object's identity. COM establishes some basic rules about COM identity. At first, these rules seem unimportant and perhaps a bit pointless. However, once you understand these rules, you can use them to your advantage and compose COM classes by a variety of means.

## COM's Identity Rules

To help remember COM's rules of identity, just remember three letters: STR. *IUnknown::QueryInterface* is symmetric, transitive, and reflexive.

COM interfaces are *symmetric*. For example, if you're using the *ISomeInterface* pointer on *CoSomeObject,* and you call *QueryInterface* to successfully retrieve *IAnotherInterface*, you should be able to call *QueryInterface* through *IAnotherInterface* to successfully retrieve the *ISomeInterface* again. COM interfaces are also *reflexive*. If you're using the *ISomeInterface* pointer on *CoSomeObject,* you should be able to successfully call *QueryInterface* to retrieve *ISomeInterface* again. Finally, COM interfaces are *transitive*. Let's say you're using *ISomeInterface* on the *CoSomeObject,* and you call *QueryInterface* and successfully retrieve *IAnotherInterface*. Now imagine that you're using *IAnotherInterface* to retrieve the *IUnknown* pointer. If that succeeds, you should be able to call *QueryInterface* through *ISomeInterface* to successfully retrieve the *IUnknown* interface.

The upshot of these rules is that the interfaces on a COM object are peers—you can get from one interface to any other interface that is implemented by an object. The rules of symmetry, transitivity, and reflexivity make it unnecessary for COM client code authors to worry about the order in which interfaces are acquired. If a COM object required interfaces to be acquired in a certain order, any COM code that didn't adhere to that order or that changed the order of acquisition between versions would break.

In addition to the rules of symmetry, transitivity, and reflexivity, COM imposes two other stipulations on interfaces. One stipulation is that COM requires a query for *IUnknown* always to return the same actual pointer value. This requirement allows clients to compare two *IUnknown* pointers to determine whether they both point to the same object. However, it's OK for *Query-*

*Interface* to return different pointers whenever it is called to acquire other interface pointers. As we'll see in a moment, the fact that *QueryInterface* can return different pointers when asked to render the same interface more than once lets you implement objects in a variety of ways, including using tear-offs and aggregation.

The second stipulation is that COM requires the set of interfaces accessible on an object via *QueryInterface* to be static during the lifetime of the object instance. In other words, if you call *QueryInterface* to retrieve *ISomeInterface* once during the life of the object, you should be able to retrieve *ISomeInterface* again at any time during the life of the object. If a query for *ISomeInterface* through *QueryInterface* fails once, the same query must fail for the life of the object. This means that you can't implement *QueryInterface* in such a way that it succeeds only under certain conditions. The main reason for making the available set of interfaces static during the life of the object is that COM doesn't guarantee that all client *QueryInterface* requests will be forwarded to the object when accessed remotely. Client-side proxies can take advantage of this fact to cache the results of *QueryInterface* and avoid excessive client-object communications, thereby reducing the number of round-trips and ultimately increasing the network performance of the object.

So now that you know the COM identity rules, what good are they? The easiest way to make sense of these rules is to remember that all interfaces supported during the life of an object end up being peers. The interfaces form more of a landscape than a hierarchy. These rules are important because if you fail to adhere to them, the remoting layer will yell at you. Additionally, understanding these rules is critical to making sense of the various class composition techniques.

Now we're ready to take a look at how ATL handles *QueryInterface* and examine some class composition techniques to see how they apply to ATL.

## ATL and *QueryInterface*

Before digging too deeply into how ATL handles class composition, we need to quickly review how ATL manages *QueryInterface*. Take a look at the code on the following page, which shows a basic ATL class with some interfaces. The *CSomeATLObj* class has all the parts that make this a living, breathing ATL object, including an implementation of *IUnknown* optimized on the threading model. In addition to providing reference counting, ATL's *IUnknown* implementation provides an implementation of *QueryInterface* inside the class *CComObjectRootBase*.

For *QueryInterface* to work properly, an ATL object needs an interface map. Whenever someone calls *QueryInterface* on an ATL COM object, ATL goes to the interface map to find the interface. ATL maintains object identity because all requests for interfaces filter through this interface map. For example, the following code shows some simple COM classes with two interfaces:

```cpp
class ATL_NO_VTABLE CSomeATLObj :
    public CComObjectRootEx<CComSingleThreadModel>,
    public CComCoClass<CSomeATLObj, &CLSID_SomeATLObj>,
    public ISomeATLObj,
    public IAnotherInterface
{
public:
    CSomeATLObj()
    {
    }

DECLARE_REGISTRY_RESOURCEID(IDR_SOMEATLOBJ)

DECLARE_PROTECT_FINAL_CONSTRUCT()

BEGIN_COM_MAP(CSomeATLObj)
    COM_INTERFACE_ENTRY(ISomeATLObj)
    COM_INTERFACE_ENTRY(IAnotherInterface)
END_COM_MAP()

// ISomeATLObj
public:
    STDMETHOD(AnotherMethod)(BSTR bstr, BSTR* pBstrOut);
    STDMETHOD(SomeMethod)(short x);
// IAnotherInterface
    STDMETHOD(Add)(SHORT x, SHORT y, LONG * pz)
    {
        if(pz == NULL)
            return E_POINTER;

        return E_NOTIMPL;
    }
    STDMETHOD(Subtract)(LONG x, LONG y, LONG * pz)
    {
        if(pz == NULL)
            return E_POINTER;

        return E_NOTIMPL;
    }
};
```

ATL's interface map is comprised of three kinds of macros you can see in this code: the BEGIN_COM_MAP macro, the END_COM_MAP macro, and the COM_INTERFACE_ENTRY macros. When clients ask an object for one of its interfaces via *QueryInterface*, ATL looks to this map to find the interface. The interface map is made up of _ATL_INTMAP_ENTRY structures. These structures essentially pair an interface ID (an IID) to a means of finding a COM interface.

The following code shows the structures that make up the interface map. You'll want to refer to them as we cover the various COM class composition techniques.

```
typedef HRESULT (WINAPI _ATL_CREATORARGFUNC)(void* pv,
    REFIID riid,
    LPVOID* ppv,
    DWORD dw);

struct _ATL_INTMAP_ENTRY
{
    const IID* piid;        // The interface ID (IID)
    DWORD dw;
    _ATL_CREATORARGFUNC* pFunc; //NULL:end, 1:offset, n:ptr
};
```

The _ATL_INTMAP_ENTRY includes the IID, a DWORD utility value, and either a constant (_ATL_SIMPLEMAPENTRY), a pointer to a function, or NULL. If *pFunc* is _ATL_SIMPLEMAPENTRY, ATL interprets the structure member *dw* to be an offset into the object. If *pFunc* is non-null (but not _ATL-_SIMPLEMAPENTRY), the function it points to will be called, passing the pointer to the object as the first parameter and the utility member *dw* as the last parameter. If the last entry in the interface map has a null *pFunc* value, you've reached the end of the map. *InternalQueryInterface* returns E_NOINTER-FACE for any interface not found in the map.

# Interface Map Macros

In the course of figuring out how ATL manages interfaces and *QueryInterface*, we'll look at some fifteen macros for composing COM classes. These macros perform all sorts of interface-switching magic. The ordinary COM_INTER-FACE_ENTRY macro finds an interface's offset within the object. ATL also includes macros to perform tear-offs and aggregation, two of the more arcane methods of composing COM classes.

Before we examine each technique in detail, here's a quick summary of the interface map macros we'll cover:

- **COM_INTERFACE_ENTRY**   Represents the normal interface entry for multiple inheritance.

- **COM_INTERFACE_ENTRY_BREAK**   Enforces a breakpoint when an interface is encountered.

- **COM_INTERFACE_ENTRY_NOINTERFACE**   Disables an interface in a base class.

- **COM_INTERFACE_ENTRY_IID**   Resolves intermediate interfaces (necessary for *IDispatch* and dual interfaces).

- **COM_INTERFACE_ENTRY2**   Another means of resolving intermediate interfaces (necessary for *IDispatch* and dual interfaces).

- **COM_INTERFACE_ENTRY2_IID**   Yet another means of resolving intermediate interfaces (again, necessary for *IDispatch* and dual interfaces).

- **COM_INTERFACE_ENTRY_FUNC**   Maps an arbitrary function to an IID.

- **COM_INTERFACE_ENTRY_FUNC_BLIND**   Maps an arbitrary function to a position in the map.

- **COM_INTERFACE_ENTRY_CHAIN**   Performs *QueryInterface* by delegating to a base class's map.

- **COM_INTERFACE_ENTRY_TEAR_OFF**   Creates a new tear-off.

- **COM_INTERFACE_ENTRY_CACHED_TEAR_OFF**   Creates a cached tear-off.

- **COM_INTERFACE_ENTRY_AGGREGATE**   Returns an interface to an aggregate that was created in a constructor for a given interface.

- **COM_INTERFACE_ENTRY_AGGREGATE_BLIND**   Also returns an interface to an aggregate that was created in a constructor for a given interface.

- **COM_INTERFACE_ENTRY_AUTOAGGREGATE**   Returns an interface to an aggregate that is created on demand.

- **COM_INTERFACE_ENTRY_AUTOAGGREGATE_BLIND**   Also returns an interface to an aggregate that is created on demand.

Throughout the rest of this chapter, we'll study each of these interface map macros in detail.

# ATL's "Normal" Interface Map Macros

The "normal" interface map macros make up the first group of interface macros we'll look at. Many of these macros simply locate an offset into the ATL-based class. Some of the macros add interesting features, such as inserting debug breaks.

## COM_INTERFACE_ENTRY

COM_INTERFACE_ENTRY is the most basic interface map macro. Use this macro whenever you have an interface you want to expose as a plain old vptr. Here's the COM_INTERFACE_ENTRY macro:

```
#define COM_INTERFACE_ENTRY(x)\
    {&_ATL_IIDOF(x), \
    offsetofclass(x, _ComMapClass), \
    _ATL_SIMPLEMAPENTRY},
```

When this macro expands, the interface map contains an _ATL_INTMAP-_ENTRY filled with an IID, the address of the vptr within the class with object identity, and the number 1, which signifies that this is a simple entry (just a vptr within a C++ class). When a client calls *QueryInterface*, ATL looks up the interface. If it's a simple vptr entry, the client gets the address of the vptr. The offsetofclass macro simply performs a static cast on the class's *this* pointer. (*_ComMapClass* is an alias for the class containing the interface map—it's set up during the BEGIN_COM_MAP macro.) Here's the offsetofclass macro:

```
#define offsetofclass(base, derived) \
    ((DWORD)(static_cast<base*>((derived*)_ATL_PACKING))-\
    _ATL_PACKING)
```

As you can see, COM_INTERFACE_ENTRY represents the good old standard *QueryInterface* that most hardcore C++ developers are used to.

## COM_INTERFACE_ENTRY_BREAK

*QueryInterface* lies at the heart of COM. When COM developers find out something intriguing about COM or have a really interesting bug to kill, a call to *QueryInterface* is often involved. Being able to put a breakpoint on a call to *QueryInterface* is important for COM developers. ATL's interface map macros include an entry for breaking on *QueryInterface* requests. Here's the macro.

```
#define COM_INTERFACE_ENTRY_BREAK(x)\
    {&_ATL_IIDOF(x), \
    NULL, \
    _Break}, // Break is a function that issues int 3.
```

COM_INTERFACE_ENTRY_BREAK is also easy to understand. This macro adds an _ATL_INTMAP_ENTRY structure containing the interface's GUID. The *pFunc* field points to the ATL function *_Break*, which simply wraps the function *DebugBreak*. In turn, *DebugBreak* issues an int 3, causing the debugger to break. This macro is useful for debugging client code to find when a client queries for a specific interface. This macro causes the debugger to break, but fails the *QueryInterface*.

## COM_INTERFACE_ENTRY_NOINTERFACE

The intersection between C++ developers and COM developers is quite large. Developers who have a long history with C++ are often accustomed to employing implementation inheritance in their coding practices. When you inherit one class from another, the derived class ends up with whatever's in the base class, including implementations of COM interfaces. Sometimes you implement a class in which you want to disable an interface implemented in a base class. COM_INTERFACE_ENTRY_NOINTERFACE exists for just this purpose— this macro disables an interface in a base class. Here's the macro:

```
#define COM_INTERFACE_ENTRY_NOINTERFACE(x)\
    {&_ATL_IIDOF(x), \
    NULL, \
    _NoInterface}, // NoInterface returns E_NOINTERFACE.
```

When clients query for the interface, ATL searches the interface map for the entry. If ATL finds the entry, this macro causes *QueryInterface* to return E_NO-INTERFACE, thereby disabling the interface.

## COM_INTERFACE_ENTRY_IID

Normally, COM interfaces have IIDs that closely resemble their names. For example, the interface *ISomeInterface* has the IID IID_ISomeInterface. If you define your interfaces using IDL, you'll get interface identifiers such as this when you compile the IDL file. However, you might encounter an interface whose GUID doesn't follow this pattern. If you do come across a situation in which an interface's name is different from its symbolic C++ name, COM_INTERFACE_ENTRY-_IID is for you. Here's the macro:

```
#define COM_INTERFACE_ENTRY_IID(iid, x)\
    {&iid,\
    offsetofclass(x, _ComMapClass),\
    _ATL_SIMPLEMAPENTRY},
```

Use this macro if the IID for your interface is different from the name of your interface. COM_INTERFACE_ENTRY_IID performs the same static cast as COM_INTERFACE_ENTRY when ATL encounters this structure in the interface map.

## COM_INTERFACE_ENTRY2

Sometimes your COM class needs to expose an interface that is ambiguous. The perfect example is a dual interface that can be interpreted as both *IDispatch* and a larger vtable-based interface. This isn't a problem when only one dual interface is implemented on a class. However, you sometimes need to implement multiple dual interfaces on a class. In that case, you need a way to disambiguate the interface. That is, when the client asks for *IDispatch*, which interface should the client get back? Here's the macro:

```
#define COM_INTERFACE_ENTRY2(x, x2)\
    {&_ATL_IIDOF(x),\
    (DWORD)((x*)(x2*)((_ComMapClass*)8))-8,\
    _ATL_SIMPLEMAPENTRY},
```

Like *IUnknown*, *IDispatch* is strongly tied to an object's identity. If you decide you want to implement two dual interfaces on a COM class, you must decide which of the dual interfaces *IDispatch* applies to. If you derive your class from two dual interfaces, you need to expose *IDispatch* using COM_INTER-FACE_ENTRY2, since *IDispatch* can be obtained from either of the interfaces.

COM_INTERFACE_ENTRY2 performs what is sometimes known as a *branching* cast. COM_INTERFACE_ENTRY2's interface entry casts the object's *this* pointer to the intermediate interface. For example, the following code shows how you might implement a COM class with two dual interfaces:

```
class ATL_NO_VTABLE CSomeATLObj :
    public CComObjectRootEx<CComSingleThreadModel>,
    public CComCoClass<CSomeATLObj, &CLSID_SomeATLObj>,
    public IDispatchImpl<IDual1, &IID_IDual1,
        &LIBID_SOMEATLSVRLib>,
    public IDispatchImpl<IDual2, &IID_IDual2,
        &LIBID_SOMEATLSVRLib>
```

*(continued)*

```
{
public:
    CSomeATLObj()
    {
    }

BEGIN_COM_MAP(CSomeATLObj)
    COM_INTERFACE_ENTRY(IDual1)
    COM_INTERFACE_ENTRY(IDual2)
    COM_INTERFACE_ENTRY2(IDispatch, IDual1)
END_COM_MAP()
// function implementations removed for clarity
};
```

The COM_INTERFACE_ENTRY2 macro causes ATL's *QueryInterface* to return *IDual1*'s vpointer when the client requests *IDispatch*.

## COM_INTERFACE_ENTRY2_IID

COM_INTERFACE_ENTRY2_IID provides another way to resolve intermediate interfaces like *IDispatch*. Unlike COM_INTERFACE_ENTRY2, COM_INTER-FACE_ENTRY2_IID lets you resolve the interface entry using a different GUID. Here's the macro:

```
#define COM_INTERFACE_ENTRY2_IID(iid, x, x2)\
    {&iid,\
    (DWORD)((x*)(x2*)((_ComMapClass*)8))-8,\
    _ATL_SIMPLEMAPENTRY},
```

You use this macro in the same way that you use COM_INTERFACE_ENTRY2 except that you can specify a separate IID. For example, imagine having two in-terfaces derive from a single interface, as shown here:

```
[
    object,
    uuid(B8D22023-8E87-11d2-802E-407A76000000),
    helpstring("IBase interface"),
    pointer_default(unique)
]
interface IBaseInterface : IUnknown
{
    [helpstring("method BaseMethod1")] HRESULT BaseMethodOne();
    [helpstring("method MethodTwo")] HRESULT BaseMethodTwo();
};

[
    object,
```

```
    uuid(B8D22027-8E87-11d2-802E-407A76000000),
    helpstring("IDerived1 interface"),
    pointer_default(unique)
]
interface IDerived1Interface : IBaseInterface
{
    [helpstring("method DerivedInterface1Method1")]
        HRESULT DerivedInterface1Method1();
    [helpstring("method DerivedInterface1Method2")]
        HRESULT DerivedInterface1Method2();
};


[
    object,
    uuid(B8D2202A-8E87-11d2-802E-407A76000000),
    helpstring("IDerived2 interface"),
    pointer_default(unique)
]
interface IDerived2Interface : IBaseInterface
{
    [helpstring("method DerivedInterface2Method1")]
        HRESULT DerivedInterface2Method1();
    [helpstring("method DerivedInterface2Method2")]
        HRESULT DerivedInterface2Method2();
};
```

To add this set of interfaces to your COM class, you'd derive your COM class from *IDerived1Interface* and *IDerived2Interface*, as shown here:

```
class CSomeATLObj :
    public CComObjectRootEx<CComSingleThreadModel>,
    public CComCoClass<CSomeATLObj, &CLSID_SomeATLObj>,
    public IDerived1Interface,
    public IDerived2Interface
{
    // Implement the functions here.
};
```

You might then use the COM_INTERFACE_ENTRY2_IID interface macros to implement *QueryInterface,* like this:

```
BEGIN_COM_MAP(CSomeATLObj)
    COM_INTERFACE_ENTRY2_IID(IID_IBaseInterface,
        IBaseInterface,
        IDerived1Interface)
    COM_INTERFACE_ENTRY(IDerived1Interface)
    COM_INTERFACE_ENTRY(IDerived2Interface)
END_COM_MAP()
```

When a client asks for the interface *IBaseInterface*, COM_INTERFACE-_ENTRY2_IID chooses the vptr that belongs to *IDerived1Interface*.

## COM_INTERFACE_ENTRY_FUNC

The final two generic interface map entries from our list on page 198 create a way to hook into ATL's *QueryInterface* mechanism by providing a function for ATL to call whenever a specific interface is requested. Here's the COM-_INTERFACE_ENTRY_FUNC macro:

```
#define COM_INTERFACE_ENTRY_FUNC(iid, dw, func)\
    {&iid, \
    dw, \
    func},
```

The first parameter to the macro is the interface ID. The second parameter to the macro is a DWORD utility value to be passed to the creation function that will be called by ATL. The last parameter to the macro is a pointer to the function to call. If the requested interface is found, the function specified by *func* is called. ATL expects the prototype for the function to look like this:

```
HRESULT WINAPI func(void* pv, REFIID riid, LPVOID* ppv,
    DWORD dw);
```

As the COM class developer, you write this function. When ATL calls this function, ATL passes the class object in the first parameter (*pv*). ATL passes the IID in the second parameter (*riid*). The third parameter, *ppv*, is a place to hold the interface pointer. Finally, the fourth parameter, *dw*, is the parameter specified in the entry. This function's job is to instantiate the interface implementation and return the requested interface to the client.

For example, imagine that you want to implement an interface using a static global class inside our ATL server. You might write a class that looks like the one shown in the following code and then declare an instance of it in your code:

```
class CSomeOtherObj : public ISomeOtherInterface
{
public:
    STDMETHODIMP_(ULONG) AddRef()
    {
        _Module.Lock();
        return 2;
    }
    STDMETHODIMP_(ULONG) Release()
    {
```

```
        _Module.Unlock();
        return 1;
    }
    STDMETHODIMP QueryInterface(REFIID riid, void** ppv)
    {
        *ppv = 0;
        if(riid == IID_ISomeOtherInterface)
        {
            *ppv = static_cast<ISomeOtherInterface*>(this);
            ((IUnknown*)*ppv)->AddRef();
            return S_OK;
        } else
        {
            return E_NOINTERFACE;
        }
    }
    STDMETHODIMP MethodOne(short x, short y, long* pz)
    {
        return S_OK;
    }
    STDMETHODIMP MethodTwo(long x, long y, long* pz)
    {
        return S_OK;
    }
};

CSomeOtherObj someOtherObj;
```

One way to expose this interface as part of your COM class is to use the COM_INTERFACE_ENTRY_FUNC macro in the interface map. First write a function to go in the interface map. The function needs to return an HRESULT and takes a *void\**, an IID, a pointer to a pointer to a void, and a DWORD value. The following code shows the function:

```
HRESULT __stdcall GetSomeOtherInterface(void* pv, REFIID riid,
    void** ppv, DWORD dw)
{
    if(riid == IID_ISomeOtherInterface)
    {
        return someOtherObj.QueryInterface(riid, ppv);
    } else
    {
        *ppv = 0;
        return E_NOINTERFACE;
    }
}
```

Finally, update the interface map to include the interface as shown here:

```
BEGIN_COM_MAP(CSomeATLObj)
    COM_INTERFACE_ENTRY(ISomeATLObj)
    COM_INTERFACE_ENTRY(IAnotherInterface)
    COM_INTERFACE_ENTRY(IDual1)
    COM_INTERFACE_ENTRY(IDual2)
    COM_INTERFACE_ENTRY2(IDispatch, IDual1)
    COM_INTERFACE_ENTRY_FUNC(IID_ISomeOtherInterface,
        0, GetSomeOtherInterface)
END_COM_MAP()
```

You can use the COM_INTERFACE_ENTRY_FUNC macro in several ways. The previous example shows only one, which is your generic hook for exposing interfaces from an ATL-based COM class.

## COM_INTERFACE_ENTRY_FUNC_BLIND

This macro is similar to the COM_INTERFACE_ENTRY_FUNC macro. Instead of filtering out IIDs, however, this macro blindly calls a specified function during interface requests. Here's the macro:

```
#define COM_INTERFACE_ENTRY_FUNC_BLIND(dw, func)\
    {NULL, \
    dw, \
    func},
```

Use this macro whenever you want to insert a generic hook to be called during interface requests. The macro accepts a DWORD and a pointer function as parameters. The DWORD is an optional parameter to pass to the function listed in the macro. The function called through this interface map entry looks just like the one for COM_INTERFACE_ENTRY_FUNC, as shown here:

```
HRESULT __stdcall CallThisForEveryQI(void* pv, REFIID riid,
    void** ppv, DWORD dw)
{
    OutputDebugString("A call to QueryInterface  occurred!\n");
    return S_FALSE;
}
```

To make this hook work, just add the COM_INTERFACE_ENTRY-_FUNC_BLIND macro to the interface map, as shown here:

```
BEGIN_COM_MAP(CSomeATLObj)
    COM_INTERFACE_ENTRY(ISomeATLObj)
    COM_INTERFACE_ENTRY_FUNC_BLIND(0, CallThisForEveryQI)
    COM_INTERFACE_ENTRY(IAnotherInterface)
    COM_INTERFACE_ENTRY(IDual1)
```

```
        COM_INTERFACE_ENTRY(IDual2)
        COM_INTERFACE_ENTRY2(IDispatch, IDual1)
    END_COM_MAP()
```

*CallThisForEveryQI* will then be called during every call to *QueryInterface*.

## COM_INTERFACE_ENTRY_CHAIN

The last normal interface map entry is COM_INTERFACE_ENTRY_CHAIN. This macro gives you a way to link the interface maps of a base class and a derived class. Here's the macro:

```
#define COM_INTERFACE_ENTRY_CHAIN(classname)\
    {NULL,\
    (DWORD)&_CComChainData<classname, _ComMapClass>::data,\
    _Chain},
```

When ATL hits this entry in an object's interface map, ATL looks to the interface map of the class specified in the argument of the macro. This is the macro for you if you want to tie the interface maps between a base class and a derived class together. ATL requires you to do this explicitly, and ATL-based objects don't inherit interface maps from their base classes. (Note that MFC's interface maps automatically chain themselves together.)

That does it for the normal, static-interface macros. Let's now take a look at ATL's support for dynamic interface composition techniques.

# Dynamic Composition Techniques

We've just seen the most common way to implement COM classes: you first inherit a C++ class from some interfaces, and you then implement the union of the functions included in the interfaces. Of course, you need to update the interface map to ensure that the interfaces are actually exposed. With ATL, classes implemented via multiple inheritance of interfaces automatically follow the identity rules. Multiple inheritance isn't the only way to implement COM classes, however. Other ways to compose COM classes include implementing an interface as a tear-off interface or using aggregation. Let's start by looking at tear-off interfaces.

## Tear-Off Interfaces

Imagine that your COM object has to conform to a higher-level protocol. Perhaps this protocol requires 15 interfaces formally, but your implementation can get away with implementing only 5 of them (say the other interfaces manage functionality that you and your client aren't interested in).

If you implement a COM class that uses classic multiple inheritance, the class is always going to lug around that extra vptr overhead. Tear-off interfaces are a mechanism for writing COM classes that create the resources necessary for implementing an interface on demand. In the *CoSomeObject* example illustrated in Figure 8-1, imagine that only the *ISomeInterface* interface needs to be fully implemented at all times and that *IAnotherInterface* is purely optional. So an independent C++ class implements *IAnotherInterface*. Calling *QueryInterface* to retrieve *IAnotherInterface* causes the *CoSomeObject* class to instantiate a new instance of the class implementing *IAnotherInterface*. Because the new tear-off class needs to implement *IUnknown* and preserve the object identity for the client, the new tear-off class gets a back pointer to the class with object identity (in this case, *CoSomeObject*). That way, the new tear-off class can forward *QueryInterface* callbacks to *CoSomeObject* and the client is happy because the COM object follows the rules of identity.

Figure 8-1 illustrates how tear-off interfaces work. *AnotherInterfaceObj* is shown in dashed lines to illustrate that it isn't created until the interface is requested.

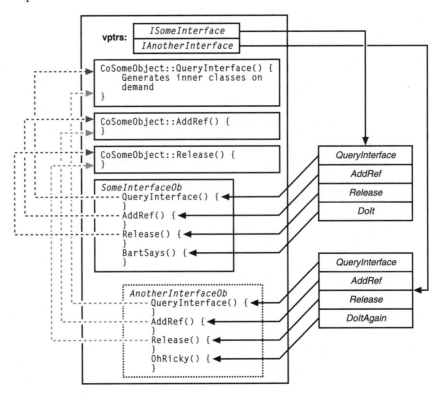

**Figure 8-1**
CoSomeObject *implemented using tear-off interfaces*

Tear-off interfaces are useful in two cases. They're useful whenever you have a large number of interfaces that are purely optional. They're also useful for interfaces that are transient—that is, interfaces with pointers that don't stick around for very long.

Using tear-off interfaces has a certain size cost. The COM-related size overhead of *CoSomeObject* implemented using normal multiple inheritance of interfaces is 12 bytes: 4 bytes for each interface vptr—*ISomeInterface* and *IAnotherInterface*—and 4 more bytes for a reference counter. The size of a multiple inheritance COM class goes up by 4 bytes for every interface it implements. However, the COM-related size of *CoSomeObject* using tear-off interfaces is 20 bytes (when implemented using raw C++ and with all interfaces in use). This includes 4 bytes for the *ISomeInterface* vptr, 4 bytes for *CoSomeObject's* reference count, and 12 bytes for the tear-off class. Each tear-off class needs a back pointer to the managing object, 4 bytes for the vptr, and 4 more bytes for the reference counter. Each additional tear-off class takes up 12 whole bytes. The size of a COM class with tear-off interfaces goes up by 12 bytes for every interface it implements as a tear-off. As a result, the overhead of tear-off interfaces tends to be larger if the interfaces are queried for frequently.

Now that you see how raw tear-off interfaces work, let's take a look at how ATL implements tear-off interfaces.

## Tear-Offs and ATL

ATL supports two kinds of tear-off interfaces—plain, noncached tear-off interfaces and cached tear-off interfaces. ATL's classes for implementing tear-off interfaces include *CComTearOffObjectBase*, *CComTearOffObject*, and *CCom-CachedTearOffObject*. A COM class implementing an interface as a noncached tear-off creates a new instance of the subobject each time the interface is requested. The subobject implementing the tear-off interface stays alive as long as its reference count is greater than 0. A COM class implementing an interface as a cached tear-off creates a new instance of the subobject once, the first time the interface is requested, and caches the object, using the same subobject every time that interface is requested. Tear-off interfaces are interesting because they make heavy use of ATL's creator architecture, which we'll briefly review next. Then we'll examine both noncached and cached tear-offs in more detail.

## ATL's Creators

When you pump out an ATL class using the ATL COM Object Wizard, ATL applies *IUnknown* functions appropriate for the threading model of your class. However, even though your class derives from a class with functions that effectively implement *IUnknown*, that's not enough framework to give your class an *IUnknown* implementation. Remember that the job of *IUnknown* is to provide clients with an interface negotiation mechanism. In addition, *IUnknown* gives the class a way to handle object and server lifetime (via *AddRef* and *Release*). *QueryInterface*, *AddRef,* and *Release* work differently depending on whether the object is tear-off, aggregated, stand-alone, and so on. Also, the construction policy of the object varies depending on how the object is used. ATL lets you defer adding the right implementation of *IUnknown* until the very last minute.

When you write ATL classes, you mix in the correct implementation of *IUnknown* via one of several classes, such as *CComObject*, *CComTearOffObject*, *CComAggObject*, or *CComPolyObject*. These classes hide the construction mechanism, depending on one of the ATL creator classes to handle construction. That is, the construction policy for a certain class is hidden. The creator classes have a static function named *CreateInstance* for implementing the construction mechanism. Rather than use operator *new* directly to handle object construction, ATL relies on the creator classes to mix in the correct behavior. This functionality lets you apply the boilerplate code for aggregation as a mix-in capability to your class. Listing 8-1 shows the main creator class, named *CComCreator.*

```
template <class T> class CComCreator {
public:
    static HRESULT WINAPI
    CreateInstance(void* pv, REFIID riid, LPVOID* ppv) {
        HRESULT hRes = E_OUTOFMEMORY;
        T* p = new T(pv);
        if(p != NULL) {
            p->InternalFinalConstructAddRef();
            hRes = p->FinalConstruct();
            p->InternalFinalConstructRelease();
            if(hRes == S_OK)
                hRes = p->QueryInterface(riid, ppv);
            if(hRes != S_OK)
                delete p;
        } return hRes;
    }
};
```

**Listing 8-1**
*The* CComCreator *class*

Notice how *CComCreator* is a templatized class that accepts a parameter that indicates the type of object to create. Object creation time happens to be the same time your code decides on the aggregation or tear-off status. There are several COM creator helper classes: *CComObject*, *CComAggObject*, *CComTearOffObject*,

*CComCachedTearOffObject*, and *CComPolyObject*. Each supports COM identity and lifetime issues involved in implementing tear-offs and aggregation. Applying *CComTearOffObject* to your class involves your object in a tear-off scenario. Applying *CComAggObject* to your class makes your object support only aggregation. Applying *CComObject* to your class means that your object doesn't support COM aggregation. Applying *CComPolyObject* to your class means that your class supports either kind of instantiation.

To work with a creator class to the C++ COM class, you apply your class wrapped by *CComObject* to one of the creator classes, like this:

```
typedef ComCreator<CComObject<CSomeObject>>  _CreatorClass;
```

Then you can create instances of *CSomeObject*, like this:

```
ISomeInterface* ppv;
CSomeObject::_CreatorClass::CreateInstance(NULL,
    IID_ISomeInterface, ppv);
```

ATL uses this *_CreatorClass* later on in the object map. We'll see that shortly.

We've learned that ATL includes a creator abstraction. But this still doesn't explain how ATL handles identity issues such as tear-off and aggregation. For that we need to review how ATL implements *IClassFactory*.

## ATL and *IClassFactory*

ATL provides an implementation of *IClassFactory* named *CComClassFactory*. *CComClassFactory* has a creation function pointer as a data member. This pointer is named *m_pfnCreateInstance*. The function's signature looks like this:

```
HRESULT FUNC(void* pv, REFIID riid, LPVOID* ppv);
```

The function pointed to by this data member is used to create instances of classes. ATL creators are useful for building this function for use in ATL's *CComClassFactory* implementation of *IClassFactory*. Just as with MFC, ATL has macros for adding a class factory to your class. The macro is named DECLARE_CLASSFACTORY. You use it from within your class to add class factory support. Here's how the DECLARE_CLASSFACTORY macro expands:

```
typedef
    CComCreator<CComObjectCached<CComClassFactory>>
    _ClassFactoryCreatorClass;
```

Notice how DECLARE_CLASSFACTORY uses the *CComCreator* class to hide the creation process. Also notice how the macro uses the *CComObjectCached* class as the helper class. This helper class is similar to *CComObject* except that it manages a single cached object instead of creating new objects.

ATL's tear-off implementation uses this creator architecture to hide the creation policy behind objects. Let's dig in and see how ATL implements tear-off interfaces.

## Noncached Tear-Offs

ATL implements its tear-off interfaces in two phases—the *CComTearOffObjectBase* methods handle the reference count and *QueryInterface*, and *CComTearOffObject* implements *IUnknown*. *CComTearOffObject* implements a tear-off interface as a separate object that is instantiated only when that interface is queried for. The tear-off is deleted when its reference count becomes 0.

As a developer, you only need to concern yourself with the *CComTearOffObjectBase* class, as you need to derive your tear-off object from *CComTearOffObjectBase*. *CComTearOffObjectBase* is templatized on the threading model and the owner object (the class with object identity). Listing 8-2 shows the definition of *CComTearOffObjectBase*.

```
template <class Owner, class ThreadModel = CComObjectThreadModel>
    class CComTearOffObjectBase :
    public CComObjectRootEx<ThreadModel>
{
public:
    typedef Owner _OwnerClass;
    CComObject<Owner>* m_pOwner;
    CComTearOffObjectBase() {m_pOwner = NULL;}
};
```

**Listing 8-2**
*The* CComTearOffObjectBase *class*

Notice how *CComTearOffObjectBase* includes a back pointer to the class with object identity (the data member *m_pOwner*). *CComTearOffObjectBase* uses this data member to maintain the COM identity laws (to call *QueryInterface* on the owner class).

Implementing a tear-off interface using ATL is fairly straightforward. You simply create a tear-off class using *CComTearOffObjectBase*. Then you create the main class (the one with object identity) in the normal way. The tear-off magic happens within the interface map. All you need to do now is use the COM_INTERFACE_ENTRY_TEAR_OFF macro in the interface map.

When a client calls *QueryInterface* for the auxiliary interface, the COM_INTERFACE_ENTRY_TEAR_OFF macro creates a new tear-off object using the normal ATL creation mechanism. The macro uses the *CComTearOffObject* class during the creation process. Here's the COM_INTERFACE_ENTRY-_TEAR_OFF macro:

```
#define COM_INTERFACE_ENTRY_TEAR_OFF(iid, x)\
    {&iid,\
    (DWORD)&_CComCreatorData<\
        CComInternalCreator< CComTearOffObject< x > >\
        >::data,\
    _Creator},
```

This macro takes the interface associated with the tear-off along with the class implementing that interface. When ATL encounters a COM_INTERFACE-_ENTRY_TEAR_OFF macro in the interface map, ATL uses the associated tear-off creator to produce the tear-off object. The following code shows how to implement a tear-off interface in ATL:

```
class CCoreObject;

class CAuxilliary :
    public IUseThisRarely,
    public CComTearOffObjectBase<CCoreObject> {

public:

    CAuxilliary() {
    }

    STDMETHOD(YouDontCallMeEnough)() {
        return S_OK;
    }

    BEGIN_COM_MAP(CAuxilliary)
        COM_INTERFACE_ENTRY(IUseThisRarely)
    END_COM_MAP()
};

/////////////////////////////////////////////////////////////////
// CCoreObject

class ATL_NO_VTABLE CCoreObject :
    public CComObjectRootEx<CComSingleThreadModel>,
    public CComCoClass<CCoreObject, &CLSID_CoreObject>,
    public IDispatchImpl<ICoreObject, &IID_ICoreObject,\
        &LIBID_TEAROFFSLib>,
    public IUseThisALot
```

*(continued)*

```
{
public:
    CCoreObject()
    {
    }

DECLARE_REGISTRY_RESOURCEID(IDR_COREOBJECT)

BEGIN_COM_MAP(CCoreObject)
    COM_INTERFACE_ENTRY(ICoreObject)
    COM_INTERFACE_ENTRY(IDispatch)
    COM_INTERFACE_ENTRY_TEAR_OFF(IID_IUseThisRarely,
        CAuxilliary)
END_COM_MAP()

// ICoreObject
public:
    STDMETHOD(Method2)();
    STDMETHOD(Method1)();

// IUseThisALot
public:
    STDMETHOD(YouCallMeTooMuch)();

};
```

## Cached Tear-Off Interfaces

Implementing a cached tear-off interface in ATL is very similar to implementing a noncached one. The only difference is that you use the COM_INTERFACE-_ENTRY_CACHED_TEAR_OFF macro in the interface map. The difference between the cached and noncached tear-off macros is that the cached tear-off macro uses the *CComCachedTearOffObject* class when creating the tear-off interface. The COM_INTERFACE_ENTRY_CACHED_TEAR_OFF macro looks like this:

```
#define COM_INTERFACE_ENTRY_CACHED_TEAR_OFF(iid,
    x, punk)\
    {&iid,\
    (DWORD)&_CComCacheData<\
        CComCreator<CComCachedTearOffObject<x>>,\
    (DWORD)offsetof(_ComMapClass, punk)\
        >::data,\
    _Cache},
```

To create a cached tear-off, the auxiliary class inherits from *CComCached-TearOffObject*. *CComCachedTearOffObject* implements *IUnknown* for a tear-off interface. *CComCachedTearOffObject* maintains its own reference count on its *IUnknown* and deletes itself when its reference count is 0. Querying for any of the subobject's interfaces increments the reference count of the owner object's *IUnknown*.

When an interface implemented using ATL's cached tear-off interface mechanism is requested, the subobject is instantiated only once. Subsequent requests use the same tear-off object (as opposed to a tear-off interface implemented by a *CComTearOffObject*, which instantiates multiple tear-off objects).

The caveat with cached interfaces is that the class with object identity must implement *FinalRelease* and call *Release* on the cached *IUnknown* for the *CCom-CachedTearOffObject*. This decrements the tear-off's reference count and causes the cached tear-off to delete itself.

That does it for source code tear-off interfaces. Let's finish this chapter with a look at how ATL performs the cruel identity hack known as COM aggregation.

## COM Aggregation (aka Binary Tear-Offs)

Before launching into aggregation, we'd like to clear the air about the purpose behind COM aggregation. You'll usually find the topic of COM aggregation listed in COM textbooks under the heading of "binary reuse." Long ago, when COM was making its public debut, C++ developers mumbled implementation inheritance mantras and lived the implementation inheritance lifestyle, which became popular during the late 1980s and early 1990s. Because COM doesn't support implementation inheritance (as C++ does), COM took a lot of bashing. Folks were calling COM some unflattering names, all because COM didn't support implementation inheritance.

Classic COM documentation (including Microsoft's original COM spec) mentioned COM aggregation as a substitute for run-time binary implementation inheritance. COM aggregation doesn't really solve this problem. Instead, COM aggregation is a way for a COM object to acquire an interface from some other COM object and pass it off as its own interface. However, although aggregation is a way to reuse COM code at the binary level, aggregation makes better sense when viewed as another way to leverage the identity laws. In fact, another way of thinking about aggregation is to consider it as a technique for implementing binary tear-off interfaces. Recall that tear-off interfaces are a way for COM objects to provide interfaces on demand (thereby letting objects avoid carrying all the vptr data around all the time).

As with tear-off implementations, understanding COM identity is key to understanding COM aggregation. Here's the general gist of COM aggregation. Imagine you're implementing the *CoSomeObject* for some client. You know how to implement *ISomeInterface* just fine. However, you don't know how to implement *IAnotherInterface* very well. You want to leverage (leverage is the '90s word for stealing) someone else's implementation. So you license someone else's binary implementation of *IAnotherInterface* (because nobody wants to give away his or her source code for the implementation of *IAnotherInterface*).

To use the binary implementation of *IAnotherInterface*, *CSomeObject* creates an instance of the *AnotherObject* object using the normal COM creation mechanism—*CoCreateInstance*. In calling *CoCreateInstance*, the *CSomeObject* passes in its *IUnknown* pointer as the second parameter to *CoCreateInstance*. In this case, *CoSomeObject* is the controlling object. This *IUnknown* pointer passed into the *AnotherObject* object serves as the back pointer to *CSomeObject* (the class with object identity).

When *CSomeObject* creates an instance of the *AnotherObject* object, *AnotherObject* passes back its *nondelegating IUnknown* (the traditional *IUnknown* that does the regular *QueryInterface* lookup). In addition, the *AnotherObject* object holds on to the back pointer (an *IUnknown* pointer) to the *CSomeObject*. When the client asks for *IAnotherInterface* by calling *QueryInterface* through *CSomeObject*'s *IUnknown* or *ISomeInterface* interface, the *CSomeObject* can't produce the interface, so *CSomeObject* calls *QueryInterface* through the *AnotherObject*'s nondelegating *IUnknown* pointer (the traditional interface lookup mechanism). At this point, the client acquires a working implementation of *IAnotherInterface*. Here's where COM identity steps in.

When the client calls *QueryInterface* through *IAnotherInterface* asking for *ISomeInterface*, *AnotherObject* needs to be able to produce the *ISomeInterface* interface. The only way for *AnotherObject* to be able to do this is to forward the *IUnknown* calls back to the controlling object (*CSomeObject*). The *QueryInterface*, *AddRef*, and *Release* functions provided by *AnotherObject* map to *AnotherObject*'s delegating *IUnknown* functions. That is, the *IUnknown* functions the external client sees simply forward back to *CoSomeObject*'s *IUnknown* functions.

Figure 8-2 illustrates COM aggregation. As you can see in the figure, *AnotherObj*, the aggregatee, maintains the normal *IUnknown* functions. When *AnotherObj* is participating in aggregation, however, only the aggregator uses the traditional query interface call, when it creates the aggregatee. When in aggregation mode, *AnotherObj* forwards all external *IUnknown* method calls back to the controlling object—the one with the identity. The controlling object uses *AnotherObj*'s *QueryInterface* if the controlling object can't produce the requested interface.

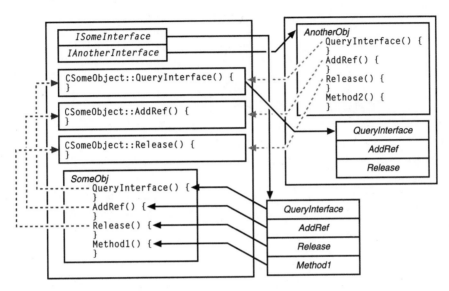

**Figure 8-2**
CoSomeObject *implemented using COM aggregation*

For many developers, understanding COM aggregation is like understanding recursion. If you stare at it long enough, it starts to make sense. COM aggregation requires both parties to agree to a few rules and to implement several lines of boilerplate code. The key to understanding COM aggregation is to understand COM identity. Let's take a look at how ATL handles COM aggregation.

## ATL and Aggregation

ATL adds aggregation support to your object via a simple radio button selection. When you ask the ATL COM Object Wizard to create a COM class for you, the wizard presents the dialog box shown in Figure 8-3.

You can create your COM classes as aggregatable (the default), non-aggregatable, or aggregatable-only. (They can't be created as stand-alone objects.) These radio buttons basically determine the ATL object's construction policy, which is hidden behind ATL's creators as described earlier.

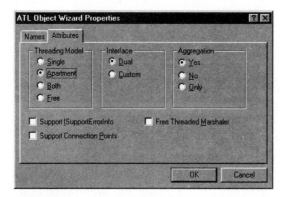

**Figure 8-3**
*Options available through the ATL COM Object Wizard*

The following code shows a plain-vanilla COM class produced by the Object Wizard when the aggregation radio button is checked.

```
class ATL_NO_VTABLE CAggObj :
    public CComObjectRootEx<CComSingleThreadModel>,
    public CComCoClass<CAggObj, &CLSID_AggObj>,
    public IDispatchImpl<IAggObj, &IID_IAggObj, &LIBID_AGGTESTLib>
{
public:
    CAggObj() {}

DECLARE_REGISTRY_RESOURCEID(IDR_AGGOBJ)

DECLARE_PROTECT_FINAL_CONSTRUCT()

BEGIN_COM_MAP(CAggObj)
    COM_INTERFACE_ENTRY(IAggObj)
    COM_INTERFACE_ENTRY(IDispatch)
END_COM_MAP()
};
```

Although you can't see any explicit aggregation support within this generated class, aggregation support is there—it's available by deriving from *CComCoClass*. Deriving from *CComCoClass* gives you default class object and instance creators. *CComCoClass* includes these macros:

```
DECLARE_CLASSFACTORY()
DECLARE_AGGREGATABLE(T) // Your class is passed in as a
                        //  template parameter.
```

We've already seen how the DECLARE_CLASSFACTORY macro works. But how does the DECLARE_AGGREGATABLE macro work? Here's the macro:

```
#define DECLARE_AGGREGATABLE(x) public:\
    typedef CComCreator2<CComCreator<CComObject<x>>,
        CComCreator<CComAggObject<x>>>
        _CreatorClass;
```

Notice that DECLARE_AGGREGATABLE defines a type named _Creator-Class, which is made up of a *CComCreator2* template class that uses your class type as a parameter. Listing 8-3 shows the *CComCreator2* class.

```
template <class T1, class T2>
class CComCreator2
{
public:
    static HRESULT WINAPI CreateInstance(void* pv, REFIID riid,
        LPVOID* ppv)
    {
        ATLASSERT(*ppv == NULL);
        return (pv == NULL) ?
            T1::CreateInstance(NULL, riid, ppv) :
            T2::CreateInstance(pv, riid, ppv);
    }
};
```

**Listing 8-3**
*The* CComCreator2 *class*

*CComCreator2* accepts two template parameters, *class T1* and *class T2*. The *CComCreator2* class has a *CreateInstance* function that accepts a pointer to a controlling unknown, an IID, and a pointer to a pointer—the regular *Create-Instance* signature. The *CreateInstance* function uses either the first or second template parameter, depending on whether the back pointer has a value. Look at the DECLARE_AGGREGATABLE macro shown above. If the class is aggregatable, the creation mechanism chooses between the regular COM creator (using the *CComObject* helper class) or the aggregation creator (using the *CComAggObject* helper class). This mixes in the correct behavior for the class factory, depending on whether the object is being created as an aggregate or as a stand-alone object.

## Polyaggregatable Objects

If you want to create a single class that either can be aggregatable or can run standing alone, use *CComPolyObject*. When an instance of *CComPolyObject* is created, the value of the outer unknown is checked. If the outer unknown is NULL, *IUnknown* is implemented for a nonaggregated object. If the outer unknown is not NULL, *IUnknown* is implemented for an aggregated object.

If you use *CComPolyObject* instead of *CComAggObject*, you get a class that handles both composition options. Then you don't have to use both *CComAggObject* and *CComObject* inside your module to handle the aggregated and nonaggregated cases. This means that only one copy of the vtable and one copy of the functions exist in your module. If your vtable is large, this optimization can substantially decrease your module size. If your vtable is small, however, using *CComPolyObject* can result in a slightly larger module size because it's not optimized for an aggregated or nonaggregated object, as are *CComAggObject* and *CComObject*.

Here's the DECLARE_POLY_AGGREGATABLE macro:

```
#define DECLARE_POLY_AGGREGATABLE(x) public:\
    typedef CComCreator<CComPolyObject<x>> _CreatorClass;
```

This macro defines a single creator class that creates *CComPolyObject* based on your class.

In addition to aggregatable classes, ATL supports aggregatable-only classes as well as nonaggregatable classes.

## Aggregatable-Only Classes

Aggregatable-only classes are generated using the DECLARE_ONLY-_AGGREGATABLE macro:

```
#define DECLARE_ONLY_AGGREGATABLE(x) public:\
    typedef CComCreator2<CComFailCreator<E_FAIL>,
        CComCreator<CComAggObject<x>>>
        _CreatorClass;
```

DECLARE_ONLY_AGGREGATABLE defines a *_CreatorClass* that fails if the object is created in stand-alone mode. The *CComFailCreator* class mentioned above has a *CreateInstance* method that simply fails—no if, ands, or buts.

## Nonaggregatable Classes

Nonaggregatable classes are generated using the DECLARE_NOT_AGGRE-GATABLE macro:

```
#define DECLARE_NOT_AGGREGATABLE(x) public:\
    typedef CComCreator2<CComCreator<CComObject<x>>,
        CComFailCreator<CLASS_E_NOAGGREGATION>>
        _CreatorClass;
```

DECLARE_NOT_AGGREGATABLE defines a _CreatorClass_ that fails if the object is created as an aggregate. With ATL, it's fairly easy to choose an aggregation policy by selecting from one of several macros. The other part of aggregation occurs within the outer object—or the class that manages the object's identity.

## The Outer Objects

The outer object is the final point we'll cover in our examination of how ATL implements aggregates. The first step is getting an inner object that the outer object can aggregate to. This is really just a matter of calling _CoCreateInstance_ in the right place. One option is to create the inner object manually in the ATL class's final constructor function and then release the object's interface pointer in the _FinalRelease_ function, as shown here:

```
class COuterObject : public IOuter {

    HRESULT FinalConstruct() {
        return CoCreateInstance(CLSID_CAgg,
            GetControllingUnknown(), // Below
            CLSCTX_INPROC_SERVER,
            IID_IUnknown,
            (void**)&m_punkInner);
    }
    FinalRelease() {
        m_punkAgg.Release();
        m_punkAutoAgg.Release();
    }

    void    FinalRelease();
    DECLARE_PROTECT_FINAL_CONSTRUCT()
    DECLARE_GET_CONTROLLING_UNKNOWN()
    CComPtr<IUnknown> m_punkInner;
};
```

Using the DECLARE_GET_CONTROLLING_UNKNOWN macro declares a _GetControllingUnknown_ function for getting a pointer to pass as the second parameter of _CoCreateInstance_. The DECLARE_PROTECT_FINAL_CONSTRUCT protects your object from being deleted if the internal

221

aggregated object increments the reference count and then decrements the count to 0 during *FinalConstruct*.

The last step is to make sure that the interface map is filled with correct macros for performing interface lookup. You have two options for managing COM aggregation. The first option is for the outer object to perform controlled aggregation. That is, the controlling outer object filters out interface requests before calling *QueryInterface* on the inner object. The second option is to have the outer object perform blind aggregation. In other words, you can have the outer object blindly forward interface requests to the inner object.

In addition to the option of controlled vs. blind aggregation, you can have the controlling outer object create the inner object or you can have ATL create the inner object for you. ATL provides the following four interface macros for performing each kind of aggregation:

- Controlled aggregation in which the outer object manages the aggregated object

- Blind aggregation in which the outer object manages the aggregated object

- Controlled aggregation in which ATL automatically creates the aggregated object

- Blind aggregation in which ATL automatically creates the aggregated object

Let's first examine normal aggregation, in which the outer object controls interface requests and creates the inner object.

## COM_INTERFACE_ENTRY_AGGREGATE

COM_INTERFACE_ENTRY_AGGREGATE is the first aggregation-oriented macro. This macro enables ordinary aggregation.

```
#define COM_INTERFACE_ENTRY_AGGREGATE(iid, punk)\
    {&iid,\
    (DWORD)offsetof(_ComMapClass, punk),\
    _Delegate},
```

COM_INTERFACE_ENTRY_AGGREGATE takes the interface ID as the first parameter and an *IUnknown* pointer as the second parameter. When ATL encounters this code in an object's interface map during *QueryInterface*, ATL forwards the request to the *IUnknown* pointer represented in the second parameter. This is, of course, assumed to be the *IUnknown* pointer to the inner object.

## COM_INTERFACE_ENTRY_AGGREGATE_BLIND

If you want to let the inner object have at the interface request without having the outer object censor it, put the COM_INTERFACE_ENTRY_AGGREGATE-_BLIND macro in your interface map:

```
#define COM_INTERFACE_ENTRY_AGGREGATE_BLIND(punk)\
    {NULL,\
    (DWORD)offsetof(_ComMapClass, punk),\
    _Delegate},
```

Unlike COM_INTERFACE_ENTRY_AGGREGATE, this macro doesn't take an interface ID as a parameter. When ATL hits this entry in an interface map, ATL blindly forwards interface requests to the inner object.

## COM_INTERFACE_ENTRY_AUTOAGGREGATE

If you don't want to go through the trouble of creating the inner object and you want ATL to create it for you, use the COM_INTERFACE_ENTRY_AUTO-AGGREGATE macro in your interface map:

```
#define COM_INTERFACE_ENTRY_AUTOAGGREGATE(iid, punk, clsid)\
    {&iid,\
    (DWORD)&_CComCacheData<\
        CComAggregateCreator<_ComMapClass, &clsid>,\
        (DWORD)offsetof(_ComMapClass, punk)\
        >::data,\
    _Cache},
```

Notice that in addition to an interface ID and an unknown pointer, this macro has a third parameter that is a class ID. If the unknown pointer is NULL, ATL uses the class ID supplied to the macro to create the inner class.

## COM_INTERFACE_ENTRY_AUTOAGGREGATE_BLIND

You use COM_INTERFACE_ENTRY_AUTOAGGREGATE when you want ATL to create the inner object for you and you also want to forward all interface requests to the inner object. Here's the COM_INTERFACE_ENTRY-_AUTOAGGREGATE_BLIND macro:

```
#define COM_INTERFACE_ENTRY_AUTOAGGREGATE_BLIND(punk, clsid)\
    {NULL,\
    (DWORD)&_CComCacheData<\
        CComAggregateCreator<_ComMapClass, &clsid>,\
        (DWORD)offsetof(_ComMapClass, punk)\
        >::data,\
    _Cache},
```

Like COM_INTERFACE_ENTRY_AGGREGATE_BLIND, COM_INTER-FACE_ENTRY_AUTOAGGREGATE_BLIND forwards interface requests to the inner object. The difference between COM_INTERFACE_ENTRY-_AGGREGATE_BLIND and COM_INTERFACE_ENTRY_AUTOAGGRE-GATE_BLIND is that the latter macro creates the inner object if the unknown pointer is NULL.

### Aggregation Example

To aggregate to another object in the regular way, add the COM_INTERFACE-_ENTRY_AGGREGATE macro as shown here:

```
class COuter : public IOuter,
    :
    BEGIN_COM_MAP(COuter)
        COM_INTERFACE_ENTRY(IOuter)
        COM_INTERFACE_ENTRY_AGGREGATE(IID_IAgg, m_punkInner)
    END_COM_MAP()
    :
};
```

In addition to having the outer object create the inner object during object startup, your other option is to have the object create the inner class only when the inner interface is queried for, using the COM_INTERFACE-_ENTRY_AUTOAGGREGATE macro in the interface map. Using this macro causes the COM object to be created on demand.

As long as the correct entries are in the interface map, ATL will find them when clients call *QueryInterface* and the client will get a pointer to the aggregated object.

# Conclusion

As you saw in this chapter, you can compose COM classes in many ways. As long as you understand and follow the rules of COM identity, you'll live a productive and prosperous life as a COM class author. Unfortunately, COM identity is not given much airtime in the current COM literature. The COM spec from Microsoft covers identity in a few paragraphs. Dale Rogerson's book *Inside COM* (Microsoft Press, 1997) covers the topic in a bit more detail. Be sure to check out Don Box's *Essential COM* (Addison-Wesley, 1997), as it gives quite a good treatment of the notion of COM identity.

As an object implementor, you have a lot more options for creating COM classes once you understand the rules of COM identity. In addition to composing classes by inheriting multiply from several interfaces, one useful way of implementing COM classes is to include tear-off interfaces. This method focuses on composing classes instead of using implementation inheritance to create classes. Tear-off interfaces are handy for creating COM classes whose interfaces are not used by clients frequently or for very long.

In addition, COM specifies the binary equivalent of tear-offs known as COM aggregation. COM aggregation is an interesting way of composing two separate binary objects and fooling the client into thinking it's only one object. Aggregation is a bit hard to swallow using regular C++. Fortunately, ATL has good support for tear-off interfaces. As long as you use the appropriate macros and include entries in your interface map, your objects will conform to the COM spec.

## CHAPTER NINE

# The ATL Wizards in Depth

Up to this point, we've seen how to build COM classes using Microsoft Visual C++. Creating new servers is easy, and adding new classes to those servers is also a breeze because of all the great wizard support from Microsoft. However, even though the wizards do a lot for you, it's not always obvious what they're doing under the hood. This chapter examines the ATL COM AppWizard and the ATL Object Wizard in depth, reviewing and building on the information introduced in Chapter 4. We'll start by examining what the different ATL COM AppWizard options do, and then we'll see what the various options within the ATL Object Wizard do.

## Creating COM Servers

Developing a COM server involves myriad issues, including creating class objects for your COM classes, registering your COM classes in the Registry, providing a way for external clients to get to your class objects, and taking care of the server lifetime issues. For example, if you're creating a COM DLL, you need to write several functions that the COM run time expects to see, including *DllGetClassObject*, *DllRegisterServer*, and *DllUnregisterServer*. You must provide your COM class with a reference count so that it can track the number of outstanding objects it's still serving. You also need to export *DllCanUnloadNow*. If you're creating a COM-based EXE server, you must register your class objects at run time using *CoRegisterClassObject* and check the command line for the */RegServer* or */UnRegServer* switches. An EXE server also needs to maintain a reference count and notify itself when the object reference count drops to 0.

All this requires the developer to pump out a lot of code. As it turns out, much of the code necessary for writing COM code is boilerplate. Of course, that's why there's ATL. ATL takes a load off developers who are creating new COM-based servers by implementing most of the boilerplate code required to develop COM classes and servers.

In addition to supporting basic COM classes, ATL also serves as a light-weight alternative to MFC for writing Microsoft ActiveX controls (which are just COM classes with a bunch of interfaces hanging off of them). Although MFC continues to be the most convenient way to write ActiveX controls using C++ (using Microsoft Visual Basic is probably the most convenient means overall), MFC has a downside. The most difficult-to-swallow aspect of MFC is its run-time DLL, which must accompany an ActiveX control wherever it goes. An ActiveX control usually doesn't need all the functionality available in the MFC DLL. However, the control has to carry around the entire enchilada just to work. For example, ActiveX controls require support for programming concerns such as *IDispatch* and window messaging, but they don't necessarily require everything else MFC provides, such as dialogs.

Because ATL is a template library, the chunks of code absolutely necessary for COM classes to work are brought in via template inheritance rather than normal C++ implementation inheritance. Templates actually copy bits of code into your class. You can customize templates by using template parameters. As a result, code compiled using templates tends to be a bit larger but more self-contained than normal C++ code (so the huge run-time DLL isn't necessary).

Creating a COM-based server in ATL is a simple matter of exercising the ATL COM AppWizard. Just select New from the File menu and choose ATL COM AppWizard. Figure 9-1 illustrates the ATL COM AppWizard.

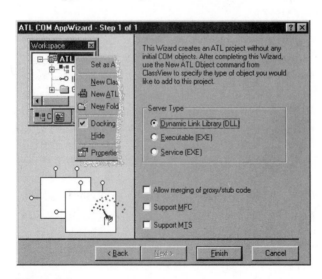

**Figure 9-1**
*The ATL COM AppWizard*

Once you're confronted with this dialog box, you've got several options to choose from. For starters, you can select a COM-based DLL, a COM-based EXE, or a COM-based service. Each of these options produces the correct code for the given context. Let's start by taking a look at what you get with an ATL-based DLL, which is a special type of COM-based DLL.

# ATL-Based DLLs

COM-based DLLs have several distinguishing characteristics. First, COM-based DLLs export a function that the service control manager (SCM) requires in order to locate the class objects within the DLL (*DllGetClassObject*). COM-based DLLs also maintain a reference count on themselves. Clients have the option of flushing the DLL from its process space by calling *CoFreeUnusedLibraries*. When a client calls *CoFreeUnusedLibraries*, COM goes to each DLL in the process space and asks the DLL whether the DLL can be unloaded. COM calls into the DLL's *DllCanUnloadNow* function, which returns S_OK if the DLL can be unloaded and S_FALSE if the DLL can't be unloaded. (The DLL simply checks its reference count.) Finally, COM-based DLL servers are supposed to self-register and self-unregister themselves in the Registry by exporting two functions—*DllRegisterServer* and *DllUnregisterServer*. These are the hooks that COM expects to see in your DLL.

The ATL COM AppWizard's default mode is to create a COM-based DLL. The COM-specific aspects of a DLL include the following four well-known entry points:

- **DllGetClassObject**  This function is required so that the COM run time can retrieve the class object (often known as the *class factory*). The ATL COM AppWizard–generated version of *DllGetClassObject* delegates its work to *CComModule*, which maintains a list of class objects within the server.

- **DllCanUnloadNow**  DLLs export this function so that the COM run time knows whether it can unload the DLL. The ATL COM AppWizard–generated version of *DllCanUnloadNow* delegates its work to *CComModule*, which maintains the reference count of extant objects.

- **DllRegisterServer**  DLLs implement this function for inserting appropriate entries into the Registry. The ATL COM AppWizard–generated version of *DllGetClassObject* delegates its work to *CComModule*, which uses the ATL Registrar component to read the server's Registry script and insert Registry entries.

■ **DllUnregisterServer**   DLLs implement this function for removing a COM class's entries from the Registry. The ATL COM AppWizard–generated version of *DllGetClassObject* delegates its work to *CCom-Module*, which uses the ATL Registrar component to read the server's Registry script and remove Registry entries.

Selecting a COM-based DLL from the ATL COM AppWizard yields the following files for building a COM-based DLL:

■ <project name>.cpp includes the *DllMain* entry point as well as the *Dllxxx* functions COM expects. This file satisfies calls to the well-known functions by delegating to a *CComModule* class that is part of the project.

■ <project name>.def explicitly exports *DllGetClassObject*, *DllCan-UnloadNow*, *DllRegisterServer*, and *DllUnregisterServer*. These are the hooks that COM expects to find inside your DLL.

■ <project name>.idl represents a blank IDL file awaiting some interface definitions.

■ <project name>.rc includes any resources you want to include in your COM-based DLL.

■ stdafx.h is where general *#include* statements go.

■ stdafx.cpp compiles the stdafx.h file.

■ resource.h includes any identifiers your resource script requires.

■ <project name>.clw is used by ClassWizard (if you decide you really can't live without MFC in your project).

Compiling the project yields three more files:

■ <project name>.h includes the C++ versions of the COM interfaces found in <project name>.idl.

■ <project name>_i.c includes the GUIDs defined in <project name>.idl.

■ <project name>.tlb is the binary description of your COM-based server (a type library).

In addition to the source code files listed above, you also get project files for a proxy/stub DLL based on the contents of <project name>.idl. The proxy/stub source code consists of three more files:

- <project name>ps.def

- <project name>ps.mk

- dlldata.c (This file is produced if <project name>.idl has interfaces defined in it.)

As far as clients are concerned, an ATL-based COM DLL is just a regular COM DLL. The difference is that many of the implementation details are handled internally by ATL. Let's take a closer look at the ATL COM AppWizard options.

## MFC Support in ATL

One of the most interesting aspects of ATL is that although ATL is meant to be a lightweight alternative to MFC for creating ActiveX controls, you can include MFC in your ATL-based DLL. Just mark the Support MFC check box before building your DLL. Clicking on Support MFC within the ATL COM AppWizard simply inserts two more lines into stdafx.h:

```
#include <afxwin.h>
#include <afxdisp.h>
// stdafx.h includes MFC by including these
//  two files if you mark the Support MFC
//  check box.
```

Besides adding the include files, the AppWizard links the import library for the MFC run-time DLL into your project.

What can you do once you include MFC in your DLL? You can in fact use almost all of MFC within your COM server. This includes such classes as *CString* and MFC's collection classes. You also get the wrappers for device contexts (the CDC family), the *CMenu* class, *CCmdTarget*, MFC's message-mapping architecture, MFC's window and dialog support, MFC's document/view architecture, and MFC's support for Automation.

If you're a seasoned MFC developer and you're used to having all these goodies, you might find this useful. For example, if you simply must include a dialog inside your COM class, there's no more convenient way than to whip one up using Visual C++'s resource editor and create a *CDialog* class using ClassWizard. Then just include the dialog header wherever you want to display the dialog, create an instance of the dialog class, and call *DoModal*. In addition, many MFC developers are quite used to *CString* and those handy collection classes. It's hard for some developers to give them up. Just mark the Support MFC check box and it's all there for you.

Unfortunately, this MFC support comes at a price. The minute you include MFC support in your ATL-based COM DLL, your COM DLL has to start lugging around the MFC run-time DLL. Wait a minute—that's just the problem COM is trying to solve, isn't it? In addition to this problem, because the MFC AppWizard didn't create the project, there's no Object Description Language (ODL) file. (The MFC AppWizard pumps out an ODL file whenever you check the Automation check box.) Therefore, ClassWizard chokes whenever you want to use it to implement *IDispatch* (by going to the Automation tab). ClassWizard looks for the <project name>.odl file and displays a warning if it's missing. But you do get all the comforts of the MFC classes, and using MFC in your ATL class is sometimes justified—especially if you want to have a whole lot of legacy MFC source code and the MFC DLL will be loaded into memory anyway.

The next check box available through the AppWizard offers the ability to merge the proxy/stubs into your COM DLL.

## Merging Proxy/Stub Pairs

A major goal of COM is for clients to be able to use an object in the same way regardless of its location. To accomplish this feat, COM's remoting architecture uses proxy/stub pairs. Whenever a client calls *QueryInterface* on an object living in another execution context (perhaps another process or even a remote machine), the remoting layer installs an interface proxy on the client side and an interface stub on the server side. On the client side, the proxy looks, feels, and tastes like the COM interface that the client expects. However, rather than talking to the COM object directly (which would happen if the object executed in the same process and thread), the client talks to the proxy. The proxy in turn talks to the remoting layer to make function calls into the other execution context. On the server side, the stub receives calls from the proxy and sets up the call in the other execution context. Then the stub actually calls in to the object to do the work. The stub sends any results back to the proxy, which in turn gets the results back to the client.

> **NOTE**  We first discussed merging proxy/stub pairs in Chapter 4. We're repeating some of the same information here in case you just skimmed that chapter.

Normally, proxy/stub pairs are a product of first compiling some IDL code to get some C source code. Then you take that source code and compile it into a DLL containing the proxy/stub pairs. By default, the ATL COM AppWizard generates the C source code for a proxy/stub DLL based on the contents of the project's IDL file. Of course, this produces a separate proxy/stub DLL for your interfaces. If you like, you can choose to store the proxy/stub pairs inside your COM-based DLL. Do this by checking the Allow Merging Of Proxy/Stub Code option in the ATL COM AppWizard.

Checking Allow Merging Of Proxy/Stub Code generates the same files as a regular COM DLL plus two more files: dlldatax.c and dlldatax.h. Also, the file <project name>.cpp is somewhat larger to handle requests for the proxy. Whether or not you want to merge the proxy/stub objects into your DLL is controlled by the precompiler definition _MERGE_PROXYSTUB. To produce a single DLL that has your COM classes *and* the proxy/stub pair for remoting your interface, simply add dlldatax.c to the project and add _MERGE_PROXY-STUB to the list of precompiler definitions. Depending on your environment (perhaps you're running Windows 95 or Windows 98 without DCOM, for example) you might have to turn off the *#define* _WIN32_WINNT 0x0400 symbol. If you want a separate proxy/stub DLL, you can run NMAKE by itself to produce a separate DLL. The DLL will produce all the correct Registry entries once it is registered.

The ATL COM AppWizard includes one more option as far as DLLs are concerned—creating a Microsoft Transaction Server (MTS) DLL.

## Support MTS

The MTS option adds only a little bit to your project: Microsoft Transaction Server's import library (MTX.LIB) and the GUIDs necessary for doing MTS work. Choosing this option also causes your object to register in the MTS catalog.

# ATL-Based EXEs

Producing an EXE-based server is a little more straightforward than producing a DLL-based server because the Support MFC, Allow Merging Of Proxy/Stub Code, and the Support MTS options are turned off. EXE-based servers run in their own process space, have their own primary thread, and service the message queue. As with DLL-based servers, EXE servers perform the correct contortions to be COM servers.

Instead of exporting the well-known functions for exposing class objects, an EXE server exposes its class objects via the COM API function *CoRegister-ClassObject*. Calls to these functions are hidden within ATL's *CComModule* class. Instead of exporting *DllRegisterServer* and *DllUnregisterServer*, ATL-based EXEs check the command line for */RegServer* or */UnRegServer* to install information in the Registry. Finally, rather than being unloaded passively (as DLLs are), an EXE server watches its reference count go up and down and unloads itself when the reference count drops to 0.

Selecting a COM-based EXE from the ATL COM AppWizard yields the following files:

- <project name>.cpp includes the *WinMain* entry point. The default code generated by the ATL COM AppWizard produces an EXE that runs in the single-threaded apartment. This file also contains the single global instance of the *CExeModule* class that maintains the list of class objects and is responsible for registering information in the Registry.

- <project name>.idl represents a blank IDL file awaiting interface and coclass definitions.

- <project name>.rc includes any resources you want to include in your COM-based EXE server.

- stdafx.h is where general *#include* statements go.

- stdafx.cpp compiles the stdafx.h file.

- resource.h includes any identifiers required by your resource script.

- <project name>.rgs includes the Registry script code necessary to install the AppID for the EXE-based application.

Compiling the project yields three more files:

- <project name>.h includes the C++ versions of the COM interfaces found in <project name>.idl.

- <project name>_i.c includes the GUIDs defined in <project name>.idl.

- <project name>.tlb is the binary description of your COM-based server (a type library).

As with a DLL-based server, an EXE server generated by the AppWizard also includes IDL code. Compiling the EXE yields enough source code to create a proxy/stub DLL capable of remoting the interfaces described within the IDL file.

# ATL-Based Services

The final option for an ATL server is a COM-based Windows NT service. The main difference between a regular EXE server and a Windows NT service is that the AppWizard generates a class named *CServiceModule* derived from *CComModule* to manage the COM and Windows NT service aspects of the server. *CServiceModule* includes four critical member functions necessary for the EXE to run as a service: *Start*, *ServiceMain*, *Run*, and *Handler*.

The server's *WinMain* calls *CServiceModule::Start* to kick off the server. *Start* calls *StartServiceCtrlDispatcher* to connect the main thread of the service to the SCM. *Start* passes *CServiceModule::ServiceMain* as one of the parameters to *StartServiceCtrlDispatcher*.

*CServiceModule::ServiceMain* is called whenever the service is started through Control Panel. *ServiceMain* calls back to the SCM using *Register-ServiceCtrlHandler* to pass *CServiceModule::Handler* to the SCM. The SCM then calls *CServiceModule::Handler*. By default, ATL handles the stop instruction (and posts a WM_QUIT message to itself). *ServiceMain* also calls the API function *SetServiceStatus* to tell the SCM that the service is starting. Finally, *CServiceModule::Run* runs the service. *Run* installs the main thread into the process's multithreaded apartment by calling *CoInitializeEx* and then starting the message pump.

Selecting COM-based service from the ATL COM AppWizard yields the following files:

- <project name>.cpp includes the *WinMain* entry point.

- <project name>.idl represents a blank IDL file awaiting interface and coclass definitions.

- <project name>.rc includes any resources you want to include in your COM-based service.

- stdafx.h is where general #*include* statements go.

- stdafx.cpp compiles the stdafx.h file.

- resource.h includes any identifiers required by your resource script.

- <project name>.rgs includes the Registry script code necessary to install the AppID for the service.

- <project name>.clw is used by ClassWizard (if you decide you absolutely must have MFC in your project).

Compiling the project yields three more files:

- <project name>.h includes the C++ versions of the COM interfaces found in <project name>.idl.

- <project name>_i.c includes the GUIDs defined in <project name>.idl.

- <project name>.tlb is the binary description of your COM-based server (a type library).

As with a DLL-based server, an EXE server generated by the AppWizard also includes IDL code. Compiling the EXE yields enough source code to create a proxy/stub DLL capable of remoting the interfaces described within the IDL file.

That does it for the options available through the ATL COM AppWizard. Let's take a look at the options available through the ATL Object Wizard.

# All the Different Kinds of ATL-Based Classes

In 1996—when ATL first appeared—there were no wizards to generate objects. You had to do it all by hand. When the next version of ATL came out in 1997, Microsoft Visual Studio provided a number of different wizards for generating COM classes (including controls). Visual C++ 6.0 produces even more classes and controls. Here's a survey of the differences between the various classes the ATL Object Wizard produces.

## Simple Objects

The first kind of object on the list is ATL's simple object. A simple object has only the most basic COM support, including the *IUnknown* interface and a class object. From there, you invent new interfaces and add them to your class. You get only a simple object from the wizard, but you can choose from many options for your class. These options are available via the Attributes tab of the ATL Object Wizard properties dialog box.

## The ATL Object Wizard Options

The ATL Object Wizard is an extremely convenient way to add a COM class to your ATL-based server. Just select New ATL Object from the Insert menu. Figure 9-2 illustrates the ATL Object Wizard.

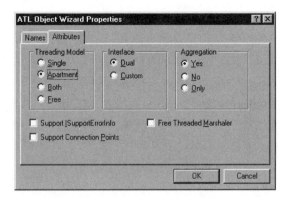

**Figure 9-2**
*The ATL Object Wizard*

The Attributes dialog allows you to select the threading model for your COM class, whether you want a dual (*IDispatch*-based) or a custom interface. The dialog also lets you decide how your class will support aggregation. In addition, the Object Wizard lets you easily include the *ISupportErrorInfo* interface and connection points in your object. Finally, you can choose to aggregate to the Free Threaded Marshaler (FTM).

Let's take a look at ATL's support for the various threading models.

## Apartments and Threading

One key to figuring out COM is to understand that COM is centered on the notion of abstraction—hiding as much information as possible from the client. One piece of information that COM hides from the client is whether the COM class is thread-safe. The client should be able to use an object as it sees fit without having to worry about whether an object properly serializes access to itself. COM uses an apartment to provide this abstraction.

**NOTE** This information on apartments and threading is specific to Windows NT 4.0. The apartment story changes with Windows 2000.

An apartment defines an execution context that houses interface pointers. A thread (an execution context) enters an apartment by calling a function from the *CoInitialize* family: *CoInitialize*, *CoInitializeEx*, or *OleInitialize*. Then COM requires that all method calls to an interface pointer be executed within the apartment that initialized the pointer (for example, from the same thread that called *CoCreateInstance*). Modern COM currently defines two kinds of apartments—single-threaded apartments and multithreaded apartments. Single-threaded apartments can house only one thread, whereas multithreaded apartments can house several threads. A process can have only one multithreaded

237

apartment, but it can have many single-threaded apartments. An apartment can house any number of COM objects.

A COM object created within a single-threaded apartment is guaranteed to have its method calls serialized through the remoting layer. A COM object created within a multithreaded apartment doesn't have this guarantee. A good analogy for instantiating a COM object within a multithreaded apartment is putting a piece of data into global scope where multiple threads can get to it. Putting a COM class within a single-threaded apartment is like having data within the scope of only one thread. The bottom line is that COM classes that want to live in the multithreaded apartment had better be thread-safe, whereas COM classes that are satisfied living in their own apartments need not worry about concurrent access to their data. Access to a COM object living in the same apartment as the client is extremely fast. Accessing a COM object in a different apartment than the client incurs the cost of remoting, which is much slower.

A COM object that lives within a different process space from its client has its method calls serialized automatically via the remoting layer. However, a COM class that lives in a DLL might want to provide its own internal protection (using critical sections, for example) rather than have the remoting layer protect it. A COM class advertises its thread safety to the world via a Registry setting. This named value lives under the CLSID key in HKEY_CLASSES_ROOT, as shown here:

```
[HKCR\CLSID\{some GUID …}\InprocServer32]
@="C:\SomeServer.DLL"
ThreadingModel=<thread model>
```

The *ThreadingModel* can be one of four major values: *Single*, *Both*, *Free*, or *Apartment*. The named value can also be blank. Here's a rundown of what each value indicates:

- *Single* (or blank) indicates that the class executes in the main thread only.

- *Both* indicates that the class is thread-safe and can execute in both apartments. Using this value tells COM to use the same *kind* of apartment as the client.

- *Free* indicates that the class is thread-safe. Using this value tells COM to force the object inside the multithreaded apartment.

- *Apartment* indicates that the object isn't thread-safe and must live in its own single-threaded apartment.

ATL provides support for all current threading models.

Choosing threading models from the Object Wizard inserts different code into your class depending on which model you select. For example, if you select the Apartment option, the Object Wizard derives your class from *CComObject-RootEx* and includes *CComSingleThreadModel* as the template parameter, like this:

```
class ATL_NO_VTABLE CApartmentOb :
    public CComObjectRootEx<CComSingleThreadModel>,
    public CComCoClass<CApartmentOb,
        &CLSID_ApartmentOb>,
    public IDispatchImpl<IApartmentOb,
        &IID_CApartmentOb,
        &LIBID_DLLSVRLib> {
⋮
};
```

The *CComSingleThreadModel* template parameter mixes in the more efficient standard increment and decrement operations for *IUnknown* (because access to the class is automatically serialized). In addition, the Object Wizard causes the class to insert the correct threading-model value in the Registry. Choosing the Single option in the ATL Object Wizard dialog box also causes the class to use the *CComSingleThreadModel* and leaves the threading model value blank in the Registry.

Selecting Both, or the free-threading model, causes the class to use the *CComMultiThreadModel* template parameter, which employs the thread-safe Win32 increment and decrement operations *InterlockedIncrement* and *InterlockedDecrement*. For example, a free-threaded class definition looks like this:

```
class ATL_NO_VTABLE CFreeOb :
    public CComObjectRootEx<CComMultiThreadModel>,
    public CComCoClass<CFreeOb,
        &CLSID_FreeOb>,
    public IDispatchImpl<IFreeOb,
        &IID_IFreeOb,
        &LIBID_DLLSVRLib> {
⋮
}
```

Choosing Both for your threading model causes the Registrar to insert Both as the named value for the threading model in the Registry; choosing Free uses the named value of Free for the threading model in the Registry.

When you're writing the object that will live safely within the multithreaded apartment, please be aware of one caveat: Writing a simple object to live in the multithreaded apartment is a seemingly straightforward matter—simply put locks around the methods that access your object's internal data. However, getting an object to work correctly in the multithreaded apartment is another matter. Writing thread-safe COM code involves potential deadlocks and race conditions that aren't immediately obvious.

For example, most Win32 synchronization mechanisms have thread affinity, which means that the synchronization objects become attached to a thread. This causes difficulties because you can potentially have many threads calling into an object. (You're writing the object to live within the multithreaded apartment.) Imagine writing an object that obtains a lock. That's fine—obtaining a lock within a method call prevents other threads from corrupting the data within the object. Now imagine this method making an outbound call to another object that lives on another thread, and then having the other object make an inbound call into the object holding the lock. The object holding the synchronization object will end up deadlocking. For more information about the intricacies of COM and thread affinity, be sure to read *Effective COM* by Don Box, Keith Brown, Tim Ewald, and Chris Sells (Addison-Wesley, 1999)—particularly Item 34, "Beware Physical Locks in the MTA."

## Dual Interfaces vs. Custom Interfaces

In addition to using the threading model you select for your object, the ATL Object Wizard gives you a chance to choose between a regular custom interface and a dual interface for your object's main incoming interface. A dual interface is an interface whose first functions are the *IDispatch* functions—*GetTypeInfoCount*, *GetTypeInfo*, *GetIDsOfNames*, and *Invoke*—followed by custom interface functions. A regular custom interface is one in which the first functions are simply the *IUnknown* functions followed immediately by the interface functions. When you choose a dual interface, the Object Wizard inserts the correct code to make your main incoming interface a dual interface. The code generated by the Object Wizard derives the class from *IDispatchImpl* and puts an entry in the interface map for *IDispatch*, like this:

```
class ATL_NO_VTABLE CSimpleObjectDefault :
    public CComObjectRootEx<CComSingleThreadModel>,
    public CComCoClass<CSimpleObjectDefault,
        &CLSID_SimpleObjectDefault>,
    public IDispatchImpl<ISimpleObjectDefault,
        &IID_ISimpleObjectDefault,
        &LIBID_EVERYOBJECTKNOWNTOMANSVRLib>
{
    ⋮
BEGIN_COM_MAP(CSimpleObjectDefault)
    COM_INTERFACE_ENTRY(ISimpleObjectDefault)
```

```
        COM_INTERFACE_ENTRY(IDispatch)
END_COM_MAP()
 ⋮
};
```

In addition, the Object Wizard defines your main incoming interface as a dual interface in the IDL, like this:

```
[
    object,
    uuid(DB0C84DF-B372-11D2-803A-B8B4F0000000),
    dual,
    helpstring("ISimpleObjectDefault Interface"),
    pointer_default(unique)
]
interface ISimpleObjectDefault : IDispatch
{
};
```

In contrast, classes generated with the Custom Interface radio button checked simply inherit from the interface described in the IDL and have a single entry in the interface map for that interface.

The last three options are connection points, *ISupportErrorInfo*, and the Free Threaded Marshaler.

### Connection Points and *ISupportErrorInfo*

Adding connections to your COM class is easy. Marking the Support Connection Points check box causes the class to derive from *IConnectionPointImpl*. This option also adds a blank connection map to your class. Adding connection points to your class (for example, an event set) is simply a matter of defining the callback interface in the IDL file and then using the ClassView to create a proxy. The code generated by the Implement Connection Point Wizard available through the ClassView adds the proxy class to the COM class and adds the connection points to the connection point map.

ATL also includes support for *ISupportErrorInfo*. The *ISupportErrorInfo* interface ensures that error information is correctly propagated up the call chain. Automation objects that use the error-handling interfaces must implement *ISupportErrorInfo*. Clicking Support ISupportErrorInfo in the Object Wizard dialog box causes the ATL-based class to derive from *ISupportErrorInfoImpl*.

### The Free Threaded Marshaler

Checking the Free Threaded Marshaler option aggregates the COM Free Threaded Marshaler (FTM) to your class. The class does this by calling *CoCreate-FreeThreadedMarshaler* in the class's *FinalConstruct* function, as shown on the following page.

```
class ATL_NO_VTABLE CATLFTMObj :
    public CComObjectRootEx<CComMultiThreadModel>,
    public CComCoClass<CATLFTMObj, &CLSID_ATLFTMObj>,
    public IDispatchImpl<IATLFTMObj, &IID_IATLFTMObj,
        &LIBID_FTMSVRLib>
{
public:
    CATLFTMObj()
    {
        m_pUnkMarshaler = NULL;
    }

DECLARE_REGISTRY_RESOURCEID(IDR_ATLFTMOBJ)
DECLARE_GET_CONTROLLING_UNKNOWN()

DECLARE_PROTECT_FINAL_CONSTRUCT()

BEGIN_COM_MAP(CATLFTMObj)
    COM_INTERFACE_ENTRY(IATLFTMObj)
    COM_INTERFACE_ENTRY(IDispatch)
    COM_INTERFACE_ENTRY_AGGREGATE(IID_IMarshal,
        m_pUnkMarshaler.p)
END_COM_MAP()

HRESULT FinalConstruct()
{
    return CoCreateFreeThreadedMarshaler(
        GetControllingUnknown(), &m_pUnkMarshaler.p);
}

void FinalRelease()
{
    m_pUnkMarshaler.Release();
}

CComPtr<IUnknown> m_pUnkMarshaler;

// IATLFTMObj
public:
};
```

The FTM allows thread-safe objects to bypass the standard marshaling that occurs whenever cross-apartment interface methods are invoked. That way, threads living in one apartment can access interface methods in another apartment as though they were in the same apartment, thus tremendously speeding up cross-apartment calls. The FTM does this by implementing *IMarshal* for you.

The FTM works like this: When the client asks the object for an interface, the remoting layer turns around and calls *QueryInterface,* asking for *IMarshal.* If the object implements *IMarshal*—which it does because the Object Wizard also adds an entry into the class's interface to handle *QueryInterface* requests for *IMarshal*—and the marshaling request is in process, the FTM copies the actual interface pointer into the marshaling packet. That way, the client receives a real live pointer to the object. The client talks to the object directly, without having to go through proxies and stubs. Of course if you choose this option, all the data in your object had better be thread-safe. Finally, when using the FTM, be sure that your object isn't using any apartment-relative resources—such as interface pointers marshaled for a particular apartment—since that will completely break COM's assumptions about apartments and threading.

**NOTE** You should generally avoid the FTM unless you're 100 percent sure you understand the issues involved.

That wraps up the options you have when creating basic COM classes. Let's take a look at the other kinds of COM classes you can create using the ATL wizards, starting with Developer Studio Add-ins.

## Developer Studio Add-ins

A Developer Studio Add-in is a COM class implementing an interface named *IDSAddIn.* Developer Studio Add-ins are useful for extending the Visual Studio environment as well as automating routine tasks in the Developer Studio environment. For example, you might build a Developer Studio Add-in to help automate your build process.

As many applications do these days, Visual Studio maintains an *object model.* That is, the Developer Studio environment and its components become objects you can control programmatically. For example, you can activate and size windows and even manage projects programmatically. In addition, you can use an Add-in to supply new commands, menu items, and toolbar buttons to the Visual Studio.

The ATL Object Wizard will generate a Developer Studio Add-in shell for you. The main difference between a regular COM class and a Developer Studio Add-in is that the Add-in implements *IDSAddIn,* shown here:

```
interface IDSAddIn : IUnknown
{
    HRESULT OnConnection(IApplication* pApp,
        VARIANT_BOOL bFirstTime,
        long dwCookie,
        VARIANT_BOOL* OnConnection);
    HRESULT OnDisconnection(VARIANT_BOOL bLastTime);
};
```

There's not much to *IDSAddIn*. When Developer Studio creates an instance of your Add-in, Developer Studio calls *QueryInterface* to get *IDSAddIn*. Developer Studio calls *OnConnection* and passes in a pointer to an interface named *IApplication*. This is the top-level pointer to Visual Studio, and it establishes the communication between Visual Studio and the Add-in. When Visual Studio calls your Add-in's *OnDisconnection* method, Visual Studio is informing your Add-in that it's disconnecting from your Add-in.

If you want to, you can add a toolbar button to the Add-in. When you add a toolbar button, the Object Wizard asks you to describe the command on the DevStudio Add-ins And Macro Files property page. In addition to generating the code for connecting the Add-in to the environment, the Object Wizard adds the code required by the Add-in to add a command to the Developer Studio menu and toolbar.

## Internet Explorer Object

The next kind of object to check out is ATL's Internet Explorer object. The main characteristic distinguishing an Internet Explorer object is that it implements the interface *IObjectWithSite*, shown here:

```
IObjectWithSite : public IUnknown
{
    virtual HRESULT SetSite(IUnknown *pUnkSite);
    virtual HRESULT GetSite(REFIID riid,
        void **ppvSite);
};
```

The *IObjectWithSite* interface represents a well-known way to establish communication between a control and its site in the container. Whenever a control needs to exchange interfaces with a container, this is the way to set up the communication. Notice that *GetSite* and *SetSite* both manage *IUnknown* pointers as parameters. This implies that objects implementing *IObjectWithSite* are not tied to a certain kind of site (as opposed to interface pairs such as *IOleControl* and *IOleControlSite*, which exchange specific sites). *IObjectWithSite* is a generic way for controls and containers to establish communication with each other.

## MMC Snap-in

The Microsoft Management Console (MMC) is an Explorer-style console framework for developing server and network management applications. MMC collects small in-process COM objects (called snap-ins) and runs them together under one roof. MMC is already in use today. For example, the Microsoft Transaction Server Explorer runs as an MMC snap-in.

Generating an MMC snap-in component using the Object Wizard yields a standard COM class implementing *IComponent* and *IPersistStreamInit*. An MMC snap-in object implements *IComponent* so that MMC can talk to your object. Here's a rundown of the *IComponent* interface:

- **Initialize**  This function provides an entry point to your object for MMC to use.

- **Notify**  MMC calls this function to notify the snap-in of actions taken by a user (mouse moves, mouse clicks, activation, and so on).

- **Destroy**  MMC calls this function to ask the snap-in to release all references to the console.

- **QueryDataObject**  This function returns a pointer to *IDataObject* that MMC can use to obtain context information for a requested item.

- **GetResultViewType**  This function returns a string representing the type of result pane view MMC will use.

- **GetDisplayInfo**  This function retrieves a RESULTDATAITEM structure representing information about an item in the result pane to be displayed.

- **CompareObjects**  This function compares two *IDataObject* pointers (acquired by MMC through a call to *QueryDataObject*).

In addition to implementing *IComponent*, an MMC snap-in object implements *IPersistStreamInit*. *IPersistStreamInit* derives from *IPersistStream* and adds a function named *InitNew* that clients can use to ask the object to initialize itself. MMC uses a snap-in's *IPersistStreamInit* interface to ask the object to load and save its properties (usually configuration information).

## MTS Component

The final kind of COM class to examine is the MTS component. MTS components are COM classes that know how to interact with Microsoft Transaction Server. Asking the Object Wizard to generate a default MTS component creates a generic COM class that's no different from the Simple Object the Object Wizard creates. When generating an MTS component using the Object Wizard, you can ask the Object Wizard to slip in an implementation of *IObjectControl* for you. In addition, you can ask the Object Wizard to generate a poolable object for you.

When writing components to run under MTS, you always have the ability to retrieve an interface to your object's context wrapper by calling *GetObject-Context* (which retrieves a copy of *IObjectContext* for you). If your object implements *IObjectControl*, your object's context wrapper will notify your object upon activation and deactivation. If you check the Object Wizard's Can Be Pooled check box, the Object Wizard implements *IObjectControl::CanBePooled* so that it returns TRUE. When an object says it can be pooled, MTS will recycle an instance of an object rather than create a new one.

# Conclusion

ATL provides welcome relief to developers of COM objects. Just as MFC more or less renders writing *WndProcs* unnecessary, ATL saves you from repeatedly writing *IUnknown* and the related COM support functions. In addition, the ATL COM AppWizard gives you most of the options you'll want for developing a variety of different servers. All you need to do is become a bit more familiar with the AppWizard and the Object Wizard. (Unfortunately, the ATL documentation doesn't completely describe what each of the check boxes and buttons does.) Once you understand exactly what the AppWizard and Object Wizard options do, you're better prepared to take the fullest advantage of ATL.

If you examine the Object Wizard closely, you'll notice we've left out some COM classes, including the OLEDB templates and the various kinds of ActiveX controls you can produce. The OLEDB templates are beyond the scope of this book. However, we cover the various kinds of ActiveX controls in Chapter 10.

## CHAPTER TEN

# ATL and ActiveX Controls

As you've seen so far, ATL is a great framework for developing plain-vanilla COM classes. By using ATL, you can spend less time worrying about *QueryInterface* and more time reading Dilbert. In addition to being a great framework for developing simple COM classes, ATL is a wonderful framework for developing Microsoft ActiveX controls. This chapter covers the basics of using ATL to develop ActiveX controls.

Even now, some confusion remains about what really constitutes an ActiveX control. In 1994, Microsoft developed some new interfaces in addition to its object linking and embedding (OLE) protocol, packaged these interfaces within DLLs, and called them OLE controls. Originally, OLE controls implemented nearly the entire OLE Embedding protocol. In addition, OLE controls supported the following features:

- Dynamic invocation (Automation)
- Property pages (so the user could modify the control's properties)
- Outbound callback interfaces (event sets)
- Connections (a standard way for clients and controls to hook up the event callbacks)

When the Internet became a predominant factor in Microsoft's business plans, Microsoft announced its intention to plant COM-based controls on Web pages. It was at this point that the size of these components became an issue. Microsoft took its OLE control specification, changed the name from OLE controls to ActiveX controls, and stated that all the features listed above were optional. This meant that under the new ActiveX control definition, a control's only requirement was that it be based on COM (read: the object implements *IUnknown*). Of course, for a control to be useful, it really needs to implement several of the features listed above. So in some cases, ActiveX controls and OLE controls refer to more or less the same animal. In other cases, ActiveX controls can be a little bit lighter and not implement so many of the features. This chapter covers the kinds of ActiveX controls you can create using ATL.

## ATL vs. MFC

Developers have been using MFC to create ActiveX controls since mid-1994. In many ways, MFC is a mature framework for developing controls. Microsoft Visual Studio includes an MFC ActiveX Control Wizard for generating a DLL containing one or more ActiveX controls. For each control that you ask the wizard to generate, you get a class derived from MFC's *COleControl* class and a default property page for the control. The object produced by the wizard implements just about everything required to be a control, including the OLE Embedding protocol, an incoming *IDispatch* interface, an outgoing event interface with connection points, and persistence.

An MFC-based ActiveX control contains all the boilerplate code necessary to be a control and includes many well-defined points for adding features that distinguish your control from other controls. For example, MFC's *COleControl* class implements a function named *OnDraw* that gives you a device context on which you can render your control. The property pages for your control are already wired up correctly—developing a property page for your control is as easy as developing a normal MFC-based dialog box. And adding methods, properties, and events to your control is simply a matter of using the ClassWizard.

One of the downsides of using MFC to create ActiveX controls is that your development effort is then bound to MFC, which can be limiting. For example, sometimes you want your controls to be smaller or to work even if the end user doesn't have the MFC DLLs on his or her system. MFC-based controls include the full complement of OLE control–oriented interfaces and require the MFC library to be available (either through dynamic or static linking). Using MFC to create ActiveX controls also forces you to make certain design decisions. For example, if you decide to use MFC to write an ActiveX control, adding dual interfaces is quite tedious (unless you feel like writing a lot of extra code). In addition, using MFC to create ActiveX controls means the control and its property pages must use *IDispatch* to communicate.

To avoid these issues, you can use ATL to create ActiveX controls. ATL includes the facilities to create full-fledged ActiveX controls, complete with all the features they should have—incoming interfaces, persistent properties, property pages, and connection points, to name a few. Compared to writing an ActiveX control using MFC, ATL provides a lot of flexibility.

As with any other ATL-based COM DLL, the easiest way to create a server to hold your controls is to use the ATL COM AppWizard. Take a look at Chapter 9 for more details on the ATL COM AppWizard. Once the DLL has been generated, just use the Object Wizard to add controls. Visual Studio provides a wide variety of wizards for generating controls. The next section gives you a rundown of the different kinds of controls you can create using ATL.

# Controls by ATL

ATL produces six kinds of controls: a full control, a composite control, an HTML control, and lightweight versions of each of these controls—a "lite" full control (which the Object Wizard calls a "lite control"), a "lite" composite control, and a "lite" HTML control. The Microsoft Visual C++ documentation describes in general terms how these controls differ. For example, the documentation says a full control is an object that supports the interfaces for all containers. A lite control supports the interfaces needed by Microsoft Internet Explorer and includes support for a user interface. A composite control consists of a dialog resource hosting a group of regular Microsoft Windows controls. A lite composite control is a composite control that supports only the interfaces Internet Explorer needs. An HTML control is a control that contains DHTML functionality and has an interface generated by an HTML Web page. Finally, a lite HTML control is a stripped-down HTML control that supports interfaces required by Internet Explorer.

Unfortunately, these descriptions don't tell the whole story. So let's take a deeper look at exactly what's going on here. We'll find out what's at the heart of each control.

## The Full Control

In the old days of COM (six whole years ago), Microsoft defined a technology named OLE controls. As mentioned earlier, OLE controls were COM classes that implemented a host of interfaces—many of them for supporting the OLE Embedding protocol. For example, if you look at MFC's base class for supporting ActiveX controls (*COleControl*), you'll see implementations of over twenty COM interfaces.

In 1996, the OC96 protocol emerged. OC96 changed the definition of a COM-based control from one of these gargantuan COM classes that implements a ton of interfaces to a COM class implementing only *IUnknown*. Microsoft redefined the specification of a control because the size of these executable objects had become a real issue in a browser-centric world. All the classic OLE control interfaces were still valid. They had simply become options. Unfortunately, such a broad definition began to confuse developers.

In addition to the standard OLE control features (embedding, connection points, incoming dispatch interfaces, and so on), the OC96 specification defines such features as delayed activation, windowless controls, hit detection for windowless controls, and quick activation. Most of these features represent optimizations to increase the efficiency and reduce the size of the control.

For example, by employing delayed activation, a control can be instantiated by its container and wait to execute the expensive OLE embedding and activation protocols until the container asks the control to activate. ActiveX controls have historically had their own windows, adding to the instantiation overhead. (The control has to go through the trouble of creating its own window.) As a windowless control, an ActiveX control instead relies on the client's window by communicating with the client through the *IOleInPlaceObject-Windowless* (on the object site) and *IOleInPlaceSiteWindowless* (on the client side) interfaces. Finally, the 1996 control specification defines a means for clients to activate controls quickly (in one round-trip rather than several) through the *IQuickActivate* interface.

A full control is one that implements the entire OLE Embedding protocol as well as all the interfaces necessary for the object to be a control. When you select Full Control from the ATL Object Wizard, ATL gives you a control with the entire embedding and activation protocol added. The Object Wizard generates the following code when asked to create a full control:

```
class ATL_NO_VTABLE CFullATLControl:
    public CComObjectRootEx<CComSingleThreadModel>,
    public IDispatchImpl<IFullATLControl,
        &IID_IFullATLControl, &LIBID_ALLCTLSLib>,
    public CComControl<CFullATLControl>,
    public IPersistStreamInitImpl<CFullATLControl>,
    public IOleControlImpl<CFullATLControl>,
    public IOleObjectImpl<CFullATLControl>,
    public IOleInPlaceActiveObjectImpl<CFullATLControl>,
    public IViewObjectExImpl<CFullATLControl>,
    public IOleInPlaceObjectWindowlessImpl<CFullATLControl>,
    public IPersistStorageImpl<CFullATLControl>,
    public ISpecifyPropertyPagesImpl<CFullATLControl>,
    public IQuickActivateImpl<CFullATLControl>,
    public IDataObjectImpl<CFullATLControl>,
    public IProvideClassInfo2Impl<&CLSID_FullATLControl,
        NULL, &LIBID_ALLCTLSLib>,
    public CComCoClass<CFullATLControl, &CLSID_FullATLControl>
```

```
{
  :
BEGIN_COM_MAP(CFullATLControl)
    COM_INTERFACE_ENTRY(IFullATLControl)
    COM_INTERFACE_ENTRY(IDispatch)
    COM_INTERFACE_ENTRY(IViewObjectEx)
    COM_INTERFACE_ENTRY(IViewObject2)
    COM_INTERFACE_ENTRY(IViewObject)
    COM_INTERFACE_ENTRY(IOleInPlaceObjectWindowless)
    COM_INTERFACE_ENTRY(IOleInPlaceObject)
    COM_INTERFACE_ENTRY2(IOleWindow, IOleInPlaceObjectWindowless)
    COM_INTERFACE_ENTRY(IOleInPlaceActiveObject)
    COM_INTERFACE_ENTRY(IOleControl)
    COM_INTERFACE_ENTRY(IOleObject)
    COM_INTERFACE_ENTRY(IPersistStreamInit)
    COM_INTERFACE_ENTRY2(IPersist, IPersistStreamInit)
    COM_INTERFACE_ENTRY(ISpecifyPropertyPages)
    COM_INTERFACE_ENTRY(IQuickActivate)
    COM_INTERFACE_ENTRY(IPersistStorage)
    COM_INTERFACE_ENTRY(IDataObject)
    COM_INTERFACE_ENTRY(IProvideClassInfo)
    COM_INTERFACE_ENTRY(IProvideClassInfo2)
END_COM_MAP()
  :
};
```

This is a full-blown control implementing all the interfaces necessary to house the control in any container (a Web page, a Microsoft Visual Basic form, an MFC dialog box, and so on). Scanning the control's inheritance list and interface map reveals that the control implements *IFullATLControl* (the default incoming interface generated by the Object Wizard), *IDispatch, IViewObjectEx, IViewObject2, IViewObject, IOleInPlaceObjectWindowless, IOleInPlaceObject, IOleWindow, IOleInPlaceObjectWindowless, IOleInPlaceActiveObject, IOleControl, IOleObject, IPersistStream, IPersistStreamInit, ISpecifyPropertyPages, IQuickActivate, IPersistStorage, IDataObject, IProvideClassInfo,* and *IProvideClassInfo2.* (Notice that connection point support isn't in the list. That's something you can easily add.)

The *IViewObject…, IOleObject, IOleInPlaceObject, IOleInPlaceActiveObject, IPersistStorage,* and *IDataObject* interfaces represent the OLE Document aspects of the control. The other interfaces support the object as a control. This is a full-blown control that implements the complete OLE Embedding protocol, supports the complete OLE control protocol, supports the container in querying for property pages, can persist to streams and storages, and finally can provide type information to the client on demand.

That's a pretty tall order. Let's take a look at what gets left out when you create a lite control.

## The Lite Control

The next option the ATL Object Wizard offers is a lite control. The Object Wizard generates the following code when you select Lite Control:

```
class ATL_NO_VTABLE CLiteATLControl :
    public CComObjectRootEx<CComSingleThreadModel>,
    public IDispatchImpl<ILiteATLControl,
        &IID_ILiteATLControl, &LIBID_ALLCTLSLib>,
    public CComControl<CLiteATLControl>,
    public IPersistStreamInitImpl<CLiteATLControl>,
    public IOleControlImpl<CLiteATLControl>,
    public IOleObjectImpl<CLiteATLControl>,
    public IOleInPlaceActiveObjectImpl<CLiteATLControl>,
    public IViewObjectExImpl<CLiteATLControl>,
    public IOleInPlaceObjectWindowlessImpl<CLiteATLControl>,
    public CComCoClass<CLiteATLControl, &CLSID_LiteATLControl>
{
    ⋮
BEGIN_COM_MAP(CLiteATLControl)
    COM_INTERFACE_ENTRY(ILiteATLControl)
    COM_INTERFACE_ENTRY(IDispatch)
    COM_INTERFACE_ENTRY(IViewObjectEx)
    COM_INTERFACE_ENTRY(IViewObject2)
    COM_INTERFACE_ENTRY(IViewObject)
    COM_INTERFACE_ENTRY(IOleInPlaceObjectWindowless)
    COM_INTERFACE_ENTRY(IOleInPlaceObject)
    COM_INTERFACE_ENTRY2(IOleWindow, IOleInPlaceObjectWindowless)
    COM_INTERFACE_ENTRY(IOleInPlaceActiveObject)
    COM_INTERFACE_ENTRY(IOleControl)
    COM_INTERFACE_ENTRY(IOleObject)
    COM_INTERFACE_ENTRY(IPersistStreamInit)
    COM_INTERFACE_ENTRY2(IPersist, IPersistStreamInit)
END_COM_MAP()
    ⋮
};
```

Notice that the lite control's interface is substantially shorter than that of the full control—it supports all the control-oriented interface implementations but not all the OLE Document interface implementations. The following code illustrates the difference between a full control and a lite control:

```
    ⋮
    public IPersistStorageImpl<CFullATLControl>,
    public ISpecifyPropertyPagesImpl<CFullATLControl>,
```

```
            public IQuickActivateImpl<CFullATLControl>,
            public IDataObjectImpl<CFullATLControl>,
            public IProvideClassInfo2Impl<&CLSID_FullATLControl,
                NULL, &LIBID_ALLCTLSLib>,
    ⋮
    BEGIN_COM_MAP(...)
            COM_INTERFACE_ENTRY(ISpecifyPropertyPages)
            COM_INTERFACE_ENTRY(IQuickActivate)
            COM_INTERFACE_ENTRY(IPersistStorage)
            COM_INTERFACE_ENTRY(IDataObject)
            COM_INTERFACE_ENTRY(IProvideClassInfo)
            COM_INTERFACE_ENTRY(IProvideClassInfo2)
    END_COM_MAP()
    ⋮
```

You can tell from the preceding code that Internet Explorer doesn't require *ISpecifyPropertyPages, IQuickActivate, IPersistStorage, IDataObject, IProvide-ClassInfo,* or *IProvideClassInfo2.*

*ISpecifyPropertyPages* allows a client (Visual Basic, for example) to interrogate the control for a list of property page GUIDs so that the client can host those pages in its own property dialog. *IQuickActivate* allows clients to load and initialize controls in a single round-trip. *IPersistStorage* is part of the whole OLE Embedding protocol and allows objects to persist themselves to a structured storage provided by the client. *IDataObject* is also part of the OLE Embedding protocol proper and is mainly used to transfer presentations (often in the form of a metafile) between a client and an object that live in different process spaces. Finally, *IProvideClassInfo2* gives clients an easy way to get a control's type information.

As it turns out, these interfaces are really there to support a separate design mode (often required by Visual Basic developers), but when developers write controls to send over the Internet, they rarely require this. The size of a bare-bones full control using a Unicode release build is 36,864 bytes. A bare-bones lite control using a Unicode release build is 32,768 bytes. You save about 4000 bytes in overhead alone.

Now let's look at ATL's composite controls.

## The Composite Control

An ATL composite control is relatively straightforward. It's an ActiveX control whose presentation space is represented by a dialog box. Over the years, many folks have used this idea to collect several controls together and make it easy to drop the functionality into an application. Up until now, however, they've had to roll everything by hand. The ATL composite control is a COM object that supports all the COM control interfaces and manages a dialog box full of controls as well.

The Object Wizard generates the following code when you select Composite Control:

```
class ATL_NO_VTABLE CCompositeATLControl :
    public CComObjectRootEx<CComSingleThreadModel>,
    public IDispatchImpl<ICompositeATLControl,
        &IID_ICompositeATLControl,
        &LIBID_ALLCTLSLib>,
    public CComCompositeControl<CCompositeATLControl>,
    public IPersistStreamInitImpl<CCompositeATLControl>,
    public IOleControlImpl<CCompositeATLControl>,
    public IOleObjectImpl<CCompositeATLControl>,
    public IOleInPlaceActiveObjectImpl<CCompositeATLControl>,
    public IViewObjectExImpl<CCompositeATLControl>,
    public IOleInPlaceObjectWindowlessImpl<CCompositeATLControl>,
    public IPersistStorageImpl<CCompositeATLControl>,
    public ISpecifyPropertyPagesImpl<CCompositeATLControl>,
    public IQuickActivateImpl<CCompositeATLControl>,
    public IDataObjectImpl<CCompositeATLControl>,
    public IProvideClassInfo2Impl<&CLSID_CompositeATLControl,
        NULL, &LIBID_ALLCTLSLib>,
    public CComCoClass<CCompositeATLControl,
        &CLSID_CompositeATLControl>
{
BEGIN_COM_MAP(CCompositeATLControl)
    COM_INTERFACE_ENTRY(ICompositeATLControl)
    COM_INTERFACE_ENTRY(IDispatch)
    COM_INTERFACE_ENTRY(IViewObjectEx)
    COM_INTERFACE_ENTRY(IViewObject2)
    COM_INTERFACE_ENTRY(IViewObject)
    COM_INTERFACE_ENTRY(IOleInPlaceObjectWindowless)
    COM_INTERFACE_ENTRY(IOleInPlaceObject)
    COM_INTERFACE_ENTRY2(IOleWindow, IOleInPlaceObjectWindowless)
    COM_INTERFACE_ENTRY(IOleInPlaceActiveObject)
    COM_INTERFACE_ENTRY(IOleControl)
    COM_INTERFACE_ENTRY(IOleObject)
    COM_INTERFACE_ENTRY(IPersistStreamInit)
    COM_INTERFACE_ENTRY2(IPersist, IPersistStreamInit)
    COM_INTERFACE_ENTRY(ISpecifyPropertyPages)
    COM_INTERFACE_ENTRY(IQuickActivate)
    COM_INTERFACE_ENTRY(IPersistStorage)
    COM_INTERFACE_ENTRY(IDataObject)
    COM_INTERFACE_ENTRY(IProvideClassInfo)
    COM_INTERFACE_ENTRY(IProvideClassInfo2)
END_COM_MAP()
};
```

ATL's composite control implements the same interfaces as the full control. The composite control, however, also manages a bunch of regular Windows controls. Notice that the composite control derives from *CComCompositeControl* (instead of the plain-vanilla *CComControl*). *CComCompositeControl* has all the extra code for managing the control's dialog box.

## The Lite Composite Control

A lite composite control is a composite control on a diet. As with a regular composite control, the lite version derives from *CComCompositeControl* so that it can collect some regular Windows controls in a dialog box and manage that dialog box. The following code shows the inheritance list and interface map for an ATL lite composite control:

```
class ATL_NO_VTABLE CLiteCompositeATLControl :
    public CComObjectRootEx<CComSingleThreadModel>,
    public IDispatchImpl<ILiteCompositeATLControl,
        &IID_ILiteCompositeATLControl,
        &LIBID_ALLCTLSLib>,
    public CComCompositeControl<CLiteCompositeATLControl>,
    public IPersistStreamInitImpl<CLiteCompositeATLControl>,
    public IOleControlImpl<CLiteCompositeATLControl>,
    public IOleObjectImpl<CLiteCompositeATLControl>,
    public IOleInPlaceActiveObjectImpl<CLiteCompositeATLControl>,
    public IViewObjectExImpl<CLiteCompositeATLControl>,
    public IOleInPlaceObjectWindowlessImpl<CLiteCompositeATLControl>,
    public CComCoClass<CLiteCompositeATLControl,
        &CLSID_LiteCompositeATLControl>
{
BEGIN_COM_MAP(CLiteCompositeATLControl)
    COM_INTERFACE_ENTRY(ILiteCompositeATLControl)
    COM_INTERFACE_ENTRY(IDispatch)
    COM_INTERFACE_ENTRY(IViewObjectEx)
    COM_INTERFACE_ENTRY(IViewObject2)
    COM_INTERFACE_ENTRY(IViewObject)
    COM_INTERFACE_ENTRY(IOleInPlaceObjectWindowless)
    COM_INTERFACE_ENTRY(IOleInPlaceObject)
    COM_INTERFACE_ENTRY2(IOleWindow, IOleInPlaceObjectWindowless)
    COM_INTERFACE_ENTRY(IOleInPlaceActiveObject)
    COM_INTERFACE_ENTRY(IOleControl)
    COM_INTERFACE_ENTRY(IOleObject)
    COM_INTERFACE_ENTRY(IPersistStreamInit)
    COM_INTERFACE_ENTRY2(IPersist, IPersistStreamInit)
END_COM_MAP()
};
```

You can see that the difference between the regular composite control and the lite composite control is similar to the difference between ATL's full control and its lite control. The full version supports the design-time interface for property pages and the OLE Embedding protocol, whereas the lite version leaves out these interfaces and this functionality. The regular bare-bones composite control compiles to 45,056 bytes, whereas the bare-bones lite version compiles to 40,960 bytes, saving you about 5000 bytes.

The final type of control ATL supports is the HTML control, which we'll turn to now.

## The HTML Control

An HTML control is an ActiveX control that hosts the standard WebBrowser control, specifies its user interface using HTML, and can programmatically access the browser using *IWebBrowser2* (implemented by the WebBrowser control). Here's the inheritance list and interface map the Object Wizard generates for a full HTML control:

```
class ATL_NO_VTABLE CHTMLATLControl :
    public CComObjectRootEx<CComSingleThreadModel>,
    public IDispatchImpl<IHTMLATLControl,
        &IID_IHTMLATLControl, &LIBID_ALLCTLSLib>,
    public IDispatchImpl<IHTMLATLControlUI,
        &IID_IHTMLATLControlUI, &LIBID_ALLCTLSLib>,
    public CComControl<CHTMLATLControl>,
    public IPersistStreamInitImpl<CHTMLATLControl>,
    public IOleControlImpl<CHTMLATLControl>,
    public IOleObjectImpl<CHTMLATLControl>,
    public IOleInPlaceActiveObjectImpl<CHTMLATLControl>,
    public IViewObjectExImpl<CHTMLATLControl>,
    public IOleInPlaceObjectWindowlessImpl<CHTMLATLControl>,
    public IPersistStorageImpl<CHTMLATLControl>,
    public ISpecifyPropertyPagesImpl<CHTMLATLControl>,
    public IQuickActivateImpl<CHTMLATLControl>,
    public IDataObjectImpl<CHTMLATLControl>,
    public IProvideClassInfo2Impl<&CLSID_HTMLATLControl,
        NULL, &LIBID_ALLCTLSLib>,
    public CComCoClass<CHTMLATLControl, &CLSID_HTMLATLControl>
{
    ⋮
};
```

The presentation and user interface for this control are driven by HTML. The HTML source is included in the control's resource. The HTML control loads the HTML into the browser when the control's window is created.

As with the other types of controls, the HTML control also has a stripped-down version, which we'll examine next.

## The Lite HTML Control

The lite HTML control has the same functionality as the regular HTML control. The following code shows the inheritance list and interface map the Object Wizard generates for a default lite HTML control:

```
class ATL_NO_VTABLE CLiteHTMLATLControl :
    public CComObjectRootEx<CComSingleThreadModel>,
    public IDispatchImpl<ILiteHTMLATLControl,
        &IID_ILiteHTMLATLControl,
        &LIBID_ALLCTLSLib>,
    public IDispatchImpl<ILiteHTMLATLControlUI,
        &IID_ILiteHTMLATLControlUI,
        &LIBID_ALLCTLSLib>,
    public CComControl<CLiteHTMLATLControl>,
    public IPersistStreamInitImpl<CLiteHTMLATLControl>,
    public IOleControlImpl<CLiteHTMLATLControl>,
    public IOleObjectImpl<CLiteHTMLATLControl>,
    public IOleInPlaceActiveObjectImpl<CLiteHTMLATLControl>,
    public IViewObjectExImpl<CLiteHTMLATLControl>,
    public IOleInPlaceObjectWindowlessImpl<CLiteHTMLATLControl>,
    public CComCoClass<CLiteHTMLATLControl,
        &CLSID_LiteHTMLATLControl>
{
    ⋮
};
```

The lite version of the HTML control simply omits the design-time support. A bare-bones regular HTML clocks in at 40,960 bytes, whereas a lite HTML control clocks in at 36,864 bytes.

# More Wizard Options for Controls

In addition to the normal options (which you can apply to all COM objects), the ATL Object Wizard gives you several options specific to control creation. First, the ATL Object Wizard lets you subclass your control from a regular control (such as a button control or an edit control). You can specify other options for your control—make the control opaque, give it a solid background, render it invisible at run time, make it act like a button, and so on. In this section, we give you a rundown of the options available in the control's property pages. Figure 10-1 shows the control options available through the ATL Object Wizard's Miscellaneous property page.

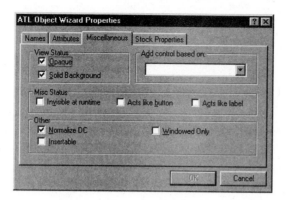

**Figure 10-1**
*The ATL Object Wizard's Miscellaneous property page*

Here's a description of each option:

- **Opaque and Solid Background**   If you want to be sure that none of the container shows behind the control boundaries, select the Opaque checkbox to render your control completely opaque. Choosing this option sets the VIEWSTATUS_OPAQUE bit so that *IView-ObjectExImpl::GetViewStatus* indicates an opaque control to the container. You can also specify a solid background for your control. The Solid Background option sets the VIEWSTATUS_SOLIDBKGND bit so that *GetViewStatus* indicates the control has a solid background.

- **Add Control Based On**   Choose this option to cause your control to subclass from one of the standard window classes. The drop-down list contains window class names defined by Windows. When you choose one of these names, the wizard adds a *CContainedWindow* member variable to your control's class. *CContainedWindow::Create* will superclass the window class you specify.

- **Invisible At Runtime**   Choose this option to make your control invisible at run time. You can use invisible controls to perform operations in the background, such as firing events at timed intervals. Picking this option causes the control to flip the OLEMISC_INVISIBLEAT-RUNTIME bit when it places entries in the Registry.

- **Acts Like Button**   Choose this option to enable your control to act like a button. In this case, the control will display itself as the default button based on the value of the container's ambient property *DisplayAsDefault*. If the control's site is marked as a default button, the control draws itself with a thicker frame. Selecting this option causes the control to flip the OLEMISC_ACTSLIKEBUTTON bit when it places entries in the Registry.

■ **Acts Like Label** Choose this option to enable your control to replace the container's native label. Picking this option causes the control to mark the OLEMISC_ACTSLIKELABEL bit when it places entries in the Registry.

■ **Normalize DC** Choose this option to have your control create a normalized device context when it is called to draw itself. This standardizes the control's appearance but is less efficient than the standard drawing method. This option generates code to override the *On-DrawAdvanced* method (instead of the normal *OnDraw* method).

■ **Insertable** Choose this option to have your control appear in the Insert Object dialog box of applications such as Microsoft Word and Microsoft Excel. Your control can then be inserted by any application that supports embedded objects through the Insert Object dialog box. Choosing this option adds the Insertable key as part of the control's Registry entries.

■ **Windowed Only** Choose this option to force your control to be windowed, even in containers that support windowless objects. If you don't select this option, your control will automatically be windowless in containers that support windowless objects and will automatically be windowed in containers that don't support windowless objects. Choosing this option causes the Object Wizard to generate code to set the flag *CComControlBase::m_bWindowOnly* to TRUE in the constructor. ATL uses this flag to decide whether to query for the container's *IOleInPlaceSiteWindowless* interface during activation.

You can also decide on your object's stock properties up front. In the Stock Properties page, select the stock properties you want the object to support, such as *Caption* or *Border Color*. You can select all the stock properties at once by clicking the >> button. This adds properties to the control's property map.

After you run the ATL COM AppWizard and the Object Wizard, you get a DLL replete with all the hooks necessary to be a COM DLL. The well-known exports that the control exposes include *DllGetClassObject*, *DllCanUnloadNow*, *DllRegisterServer*, and *DllUnregisterServer*. In addition, you get an object that satisfies the main requirements of COM, including a main incoming interface and a class object.

Once you've started a project using one of the wizards, your next step is to get the control to do something interesting. Let's look at an ActiveX control that actually does some real work.

## About the Sample

The sample we'll use here is an ActiveX control that monitors message traffic through a hook procedure, displaying a real-time graph of the message flow over time. The control renders its graph to the screen and has incoming interfaces, so the container can tell the control to start and stop the graph. The control supports both the graph line color and message interval length as properties that can be persisted. Finally, the control supports a default event set for notifying the container how many messages are processed within a certain interval.

The control manages a window hook procedure that keeps track of the number of messages coming through the system over regular intervals. Then the control examines the total number of messages over the interval and draws a little graph to show the amount of message traffic. Figure 10-2 shows the control in action—sampling the message traffic and sending notifications to the client application.

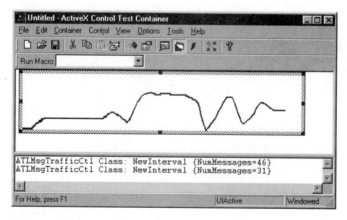

**Figure 10-2**
*The message traffic control in action*

## Basic Control Architecture

The interfaces mentioned in the control listings allow the client and the object to behave as advertised. We'll tackle these interfaces in time, and later chapters will cover them in depth. However, the heart of an ATL-based ActiveX control lies within *CComControl* and its base classes. Let's start by examining the *CComControl* class. This section offers you an overview of ATL's control architecture.

## CComControl

You can find *CComControl* in Microsoft's atlctl.h file under ATL's include directory. *CComControl* is a template class that takes a single class parameter and is defined as shown here:

```
template <class T>
class ATL_NO_VTABLE CComControl :  public CComControlBase,
    public CWindowImpl<T>
{
⋮
};
```

*CComControl* by itself is a lightweight class that doesn't have a lot going on—it derives from *CComControlBase* and *CWindowImpl*. *CComControl* expects the template parameter to be an ATL-based COM object derived from *CComObjectRootEx*. *CComControl* requires the template parameter for various reasons. For example, the class uses the template parameter to call back to the control's *_InternalQueryInterface*.

*CComControl* implements several functions that make it easy for the control to call back to the client. For example, *CComControl* implements a function named *FireOnRequestEdit* that gives controls the ability to tell the client that a specified property is about to change. *FireOnRequestEdit* calls back to the client through the client-implemented interface *IPropertyNotifySink*. This method notifies all connected *IPropertyNotifySink* interfaces that the property specified by a certain DISPID is about to change.

*CComControl* also implements *FireOnChanged*, which is very much like *FireOnRequestEdit* in that it calls back to the client through *IPropertyNotifySink*. However, *FireOnChanged* is useful for telling the control's clients (all clients implementing *IPropertyNotifySink*) that a property specified by a certain dispatch ID (DISPID) has already changed.

*CComControl* implements a function named *ControlQueryInterface* that simply forwards to the control's *IUnknown*. Finally, *CComControl* implements a function named *CreateControlWindow*. The default behavior for this function is to call *CWindowImpl::Create*. (Notice that *CComControl* also derives from *CWindowImpl*.) If you want, you can override this method to do something other than create a single window. For example, you might want to create multiple windows for your control.

Most of the real functionality for *CComControl* exists within the *CComControlBase* and *CWindowImpl* classes. Let's take a look at those classes now.

## CComControlBase

*CComControlBase* is much more substantial than *CComControl*. To start, *CComControlBase* maintains all the pointers the control uses to talk back to the client. *CComControlBase* uses ATL's *CComPtr* smart pointer to wrap its interfaces implemented for calling back to the client. Its member variables include wrappers for *IOleInPlaceSite*, an advise holder for the client's data advise sink, an OLE advise holder for the client's OLE advise sink, and a wrapper for *IOleClientSite*. *CComControlBase* also uses ATL's *CComDispatchDriver* to wrap the client's dispatch interface for exposing its ambient properties.

*CComControlBase* is where you'll find the control's sizing and positioning information, which is maintained as member variables. The other important data member within *CComControlBase* is the control's window handle. Most ActiveX controls are user interface gadgets and therefore maintain a window. *CWindowImpl* and *CWindowImplBase* handle the windowing aspects of an ATL-based ActiveX control.

## CWindowImpl and CWindowImplBase

*CWindowImpl* derives from *CWindowImplBase*, which in turn derives from *CWindow* and *CMessageMap*. As a template class, *CWindowImpl* takes a single parameter upon instantiation. The template parameter is the control that's being created. *CWindowImpl* needs the control type because *CWindowImpl* calls back to the control during window creation to do such things as create the control window.

In addition to wrapping the basic window functionality (wrapping *ShowWindow*, *MoveWindow*, *SendMessage*, and so on), the ATL windowing classes implement a sophisticated message-routing mechanism. We'll take a look at that mechanism when we cover ATL windowing in depth in Chapter 14.

Now you've seen the basic control architecture. Let's take a look at the various tasks involved in developing an ActiveX control, including writing code to render the control, developing an incoming interface, managing properties, and firing events.

# Developing the Control

Implementing an ActiveX control involves a lot of boilerplate code. Look at a basic control's hierarchy and you'll see how much code is necessary for only a bare-bones control. Of course, ATL provides most of that boilerplate code.

The basic infrastructure code for most controls is going to be the same from one control to the next, so it makes sense to move most of the standard code to the library.

Once the control is generated, your job is to add the code that makes the control useful. Among other tasks, you'll need to add drawing code, supply properties (and make these properties persist), and develop a set of meaningful events. We'll look at each issue separately, starting with rendering the control.

## Rendering the Control

ATL's rendering mechanism is very straightforward. *CComControlBase:: OnPaint* sets up an ATL_DRAWINFO structure, including a painting device context. Then ATL calls your control's *OnDrawAdvanced* function. *OnDraw-Advanced* sets up the metafile and then calls your control's *OnDraw* method, which uses the information in the ATL_DRAWINFO structure to know how to draw on the screen. The following code shows the ATL_DRAWINFO structure:

```
struct ATL_DRAWINFO
{
    UINT cbSize;
    DWORD dwDrawAspect;
    LONG lindex;
    DVTARGETDEVICE* ptd;
    HDC hicTargetDev;
    HDC hdcDraw;
    LPCRECTL prcBounds;    // Rectangle in which to draw
    LPCRECTL prcWBounds;   // WindowOrg and Ext if metafile
    BOOL bOptimize;
    BOOL bZoomed;
    BOOL bRectInHimetric;
    SIZEL ZoomNum;         // ZoomX = ZoomNum.cx/ZoomNum.cy
    SIZEL ZoomDen;
};
```

ATL fills this structure for you. When you're drawing on the screen, the most important fields are the *hdcDraw* field and the *prcBounds* field. The other fields are important if you're drawing on a metafile or you need to pay attention to zoom factors and such. The following code shows how the ATL-based message traffic control handles drawing. Notice that when using ATL, you're back to dealing with a raw device context and Graphics Device Interface (GDI) handles.

```
void CATLMsgTrafficCtl::ShowGraph(HDC hDC,
    RECT& rectBound, long nMessages)
{
    HPEN hgraphPen;
    COLORREF rgbGraphLineColor;
```

*(continued)*

```
        OleTranslateColor(m_graphLineColor, NULL,
            &rgbGraphLineColor);
        hgraphPen = CreatePen(PS_SOLID,
            2, rgbGraphLineColor);
        HPEN hOldPen;
        hOldPen = (HPEN)SelectObject(hDC, hgraphPen);

        m_anMessages[m_nCurrentSlot] = nMessages;

        if(m_nCurrentSlot == m_nElements - 1)
        {
            memcpy(m_anMessages,
            m_anMessages + 1,
            (m_nElements - 1)*sizeof(long));
        }
        else
        {
            m_nCurrentSlot++;
        }

        int cx = (rectBound.right - rectBound.left) / m_nElements;
        int cy = (rectBound.bottom - rectBound.top);
        int x = 0;
        int y = 0;
        int i = 0;

        // m_anMessages represents an array showing the number of
        //  messages that came through at any given interval.
        while (i < m_nElements - 1) {
            y = (cy - ((cy * m_anMessages[i]) / m_threshold)) - 2;
            ::MoveToEx(hDC, x, y, FALSE);
            i++;
            x += cx;
            y = (cy - ((cy * m_anMessages[i]) / m_threshold)) - 2;
            LineTo(hDC, x, y);
        }
        SelectObject(hDC, hOldPen);
        DeleteObject(hgraphPen);
    }

HRESULT CATLMsgTrafficCtl::OnDraw(ATL_DRAWINFO& di)
{
    RECT& rc = *(RECT*)di.prcBounds;
    HBRUSH hBrush = CreateSolidBrush(RGB(255, 255, 255));
    FillRect(di.hdcDraw, &rc, hBrush);
    DeleteObject(hBrush);
    Rectangle(di.hdcDraw, rc.left, rc.top, rc.right, rc.bottom);
    ShowGraph(di.hdcDraw, rc, nMessagesToShow);
    return S_OK;
}
```

In ATL, you call your control's *FireViewChange* function to force a redraw of the control. For example, the message traffic control updates itself at regular intervals by responding to the WM_TIMER message, as shown here:

```
LRESULT CATLMsgTrafficCtl::OnTimer(UINT msg, WPARAM wParam,
    LPARAM lParam, BOOL& bHandled)
{
    nMessagesToShow = nMessagesThisInterval;
    nMessagesThisInterval = 0;

    FireViewChange();

    bHandled = TRUE;
    return 0;
}
```

In addition to drawing on a live drawing context, your control will sometimes draw on a metafile owned by the client. For example, when your control is being used in design mode in Visual Studio, the programmer will want to see a rendering of it. When the client calls *IViewObject[Ex]::Draw*, the client is asking the control to draw on a metafile that will be stored. The metafile is a sort of snapshot of the control's current state.

ATL already provides this redraw functionality. When your control needs to redraw for some reason (either to render on the metafile or to draw on the live screen), the code always ends up in the control's *OnDraw* code. This means that the metafile is the same rendering as the one that appears on the live screen. If you want to make your snapshot look different, you can examine the device capabilities of the device context to find out if the device context is a metafile (call the *GetDeviceCaps* API to find this out) and draw accordingly.

Next let's look at what's involved in adding methods to your control.

## Adding Methods

A control is simply another COM class, and as such it has incoming interfaces. Developing an incoming interface for your control is just like developing an incoming interface for any other class. First decide how you'd like your control's clients to interact programmatically, and then add functions to let the client drive your control.

For example, the ATL-based message traffic monitor should obviously have methods for starting and stopping the control. You can add these functions easily using ClassView. When you add the functions using ClassView, Visual Studio updates your IDL file, your control's header file, and your control's source code (.cpp) file. In this example, calling *StartGraph* causes the control to install the message hook and start the timer. *StopGraph* kills the timer and removes the hook procedure. The following code shows the control's IDL and the *StartGraph* and *StopGraph* methods:

```
[
    object,
    uuid(C30CCA3D-A482-11D2-8038-6425D1000000),
    dual,
    helpstring("IATLMsgTrafficCtl Interface"),
    pointer_default(unique)
]
interface IATLMsgTrafficCtl : IDispatch
{
    [id(1), helpstring("method StartGraph")] HRESULT StartGraph();
    [id(2), helpstring("method StopGraph")] HRESULT StopGraph();
};
STDMETHODIMP CATLMsgTrafficCtl::StartGraph()
{
    // TODO: Add your implementation code here
    if(!g_hhook)
    {
        g_hhook = ::SetWindowsHookEx(WH_DEBUG,
            HookWndProc,
            _Module.m_hInst,
            0);
    }

    if(::IsWindow(m_hWnd))
    {
        SetTimer(1, m_interval);
    }
    return S_OK;
}


STDMETHODIMP CATLMsgTrafficCtl::StopGraph()
{
    if(::IsWindow(m_hWnd))
    {
        KillTimer(1);
    }

    if(g_hhook)
    {
        UnhookWindowsHookEx(g_hhook);
        g_hhook = NULL;
    }
    return S_OK;
}
```

## Adding Properties

In addition to having methods, a control's interface often includes functions for accessing and mutating properties. For example, the message traffic control's properties might include the graph line color and the interval over which messages are sampled. Adding properties to the control is a matter of defining them in the control's source code and then providing accessor and mutator functions through the ClassWizard. The following code shows the property accessor and mutator functions listed in the control's IDL file:

```
[
    object,
    uuid(C30CCA3D-A482-11D2-8038-6425D1000000),
    dual,
    helpstring("IATLMsgTrafficCtl Interface"),
    pointer_default(unique)
]
interface IATLMsgTrafficCtl : IDispatch
{
    // Other methods and properties here
    ⋮
    [propget, id(3), helpstring("property Interval")]
    HRESULT Interval([out, retval] long *pVal);
    [propput, id(3), helpstring("property Interval")]
    HRESULT Interval([in] long newVal);
    [propget, id(4), helpstring("property GraphLineColor")]
    HRESULT GraphLineColor([out, retval] OLE_COLOR *pVal);
    [propput, id(4), helpstring("property GraphLineColor")]
    HRESULT GraphLineColor([in] OLE_COLOR newVal);
    // Other methods and properties here
    ⋮
};
```

## Stock Properties

The properties we just mentioned are custom properties; that is, they're specific to the message traffic control. In addition to the control's custom properties, you can define some stock properties for the control. Stock properties are properties with well-known names that any control might have. Examples of stock properties include the control's caption and its background color. Table 10-1 shows all the stock properties the Object Wizard generates, their DISPIDs, their types, and a description of each one.

### Table 10-1   Object Wizard–Supported Stock Properties

| Stock Property | DISPID | Type | Description |
|---|---|---|---|
| *Auto Size* | DISPID_AUTOSIZE | VARIANT_BOOL | Indicates whether the control can be sized; when set to TRUE, *IOleObjectImpl:: SetExtent* returns E_FAIL (meaning that the control can't be sized) |
| *Background Color* | DISPID_BACKCOLOR | OLE_COLOR | Represents the control's background color |
| *Background Style* | DISPID_BACKSTYLE | Long | Represents the control's background style (either transparent or opaque) |
| *Border Color* | DISPID_BORDERCOLOR | OLE_COLOR | Represents the control's border color |
| *Border Width* | DISPID_BORDERWIDTH | Long | Represents the control's border width |
| *Draw Mode* | DISPID_DRAWMODE | Long | Represent the control's drawing mode; that is, manages how the control manages GDI output, such as XOR Pen or Invert Colors |
| *Draw Style* | DISPID_DRAWSTYLE | Long | Represents the control's drawing style, that is, how the control draws lines—dashed, dotted, solid, and so forth |
| *Draw Width* | DISPID_DRAWWIDTH | Long | Represents the width of the pen the control uses to draw lines |
| *Fill Color* | DISPID_FILLCOLOR | OLE_COLOR | Represents the color used to fill the control |
| *Fill Style* | DISPID_FILLSTYLE | Long | Represents the style used to fill the control— solid, transparent, hatched, and so forth |
| *Font* | DISPID_FONT | *IFontDisp\** | Represents the font the control uses when outputting text |

*(continued)*

**Table 10-1** *continued*

| Stock Property | DISPID | Type | Description |
|---|---|---|---|
| *Foreground Color* | DISPID_FORECOLOR | OLE_COLOR | Represents the control's foreground color |
| *Enabled* | DISPID_ENABLED | VARIANT_BOOL | Indicates whether the control is enabled |
| *HWnd* | DISPID_HWND | Long | Represents the control's window handle |
| *Tab Stop* | DISPID_TABSTOP | VARIANT_BOOL | Represents whether the control is a tab stop |
| *Text* | DISPID_TEXT | BSTR | Represents the text the control is to display |
| *Caption* | DISPID_CAPTION | BSTR | Represents the control's caption |
| *Border Visible* | DISPID_BORDERVISIBLE | VARIANT_BOOL | Represents whether the control's border should be visible |
| *Appearance* | DISPID_APPEARANCE | Short | Represents the general appearance of the control, that is, whether the control is three-dimensional or flat |
| *Mouse Pointer* | DISPID_MOUSEPOINTER | Long | Represents the mouse pointer to be shown as the mouse hovers over the control (that is, an arrow, crosshairs, or an I bar) |
| *Mouse Icon* | DISPID_MOUSEICON | *IPictureDisp\** | Represents a graphic image the control is to display when the mouse hovers over the control (that is, a bitmap, an icon, or a metafile) |
| *Picture* | DISPID_PICTURE | *IPictureDisp\** | Represents a graphic image the control is to display (that is, an icon, a bitmap, or a metafile) |
| *Valid* | DISPID_VALID | VARIANT_BOOL | Represents whether the control is valid |

## Property Persistence

Once your control has properties, you might decide to have some of these properties persist. For example, let's say you want to put the message traffic control inside an MFC dialog box. First you pull the component into your project by using Component Gallery, and then you paste an instance of the control into your dialog box. As you develop your dialog box, you decide that the graph line should be a certain color. Of course, the graph line color is one of the control's properties, available through the control's main incoming interface. One option might be to initialize the message traffic control's graph line color in the dialog box's initialization code every time the control starts up. That seems like overkill, though, doesn't it? A better way would be to let the developer configure the control's graph line color and then have the dialog box save the control configuration as part of the dialog resource. This is exactly how ATL's persistence works.

**NOTE** This chapter covers what you need to have to make your properties persist; the next chapter covers how property persistence works.

Making your control's properties persist in ATL involves two steps. First, throw in the ATL implementations of the persistence interfaces you want the client to be able to use. ATL includes the classes *IPersistStorageImpl*, *IPersistStreamInitImpl*, and *IPersistPropertyBagImpl*, which implement the three main COM persistence mechanisms. With these implementations as part of your class, your control's clients can ask the control to persist itself.

The second step to property persistence is to insert the properties into the control's property map. Whenever a client asks to save or load the ATL-based control using one of ATL's persistence mechanisms, ATL looks to the control's property map to transfer the control's properties to and from the storage medium. The property map is a table of property names and DISPIDs and, sometimes, a property page GUID. ATL goes through this table to find which properties to persist and then persists them to the appropriate medium. The following code shows the *ATLMsgTraffic* control inheriting all three persistence interface implementations and a property map:

```
class ATL_NO_VTABLE CATLMsgTrafficCtl :
// More interfaces
⋮
    public IPersistStreamInitImpl<CATLMsgTrafficCtl>,
    public IPersistPropertyBagImpl<CATLMsgTrafficCtl>,
    public IPersistStorageImpl<CATLMsgTrafficCtl>,
// More interfaces
⋮
{
};
```

```
BEGIN_PROP_MAP(CATLMsgTrafficCtl)
    PROP_ENTRY("BackColor", DISPID_BACKCOLOR, CLSID_StockColorPage)
    PROP_ENTRY("GraphLineColor", 4, CLSID_StockColorPage)
    PROP_DATA_ENTRY("_cx", m_sizeExtent.cx, VT_UI4)
    PROP_DATA_ENTRY("_cy", m_sizeExtent.cy, VT_UI4)
    PROP_ENTRY("Interval", 3, CLSID_MainPropPage)
    PROP_PAGE(CLSID_StockColorPage)
END_PROP_MAP()
```

## Property Pages

As you're learning, ActiveX controls are reusable software gadgets (mostly user interface components) built using COM. Even though there's some confusion about what really constitutes an ActiveX control, most folks generally agree that ActiveX controls are COM objects that live within DLLs and implement some sort of visual user interface.

In general, most ActiveX controls have both a presentation state and an internal state. The presentation state of the control is reflected when the control draws itself. The control's internal state is a set of variables exposed to the outside world via one or more interfaces—the properties.

For example, think about the message traffic control we've been building in this chapter. The control has an external presentation state and a set of internal variables for describing the state of the control. The properties of the message traffic control include the graph line color and the sampling interval, among others.

Because ActiveX controls are usually user interface gadgets meant to be mixed into much larger applications, they often find their homes in places like Visual Basic forms and MFC form views and dialog boxes. When a control is instantiated, the client code can usually reach into the control and manipulate its properties by exercising interface functions. When an ActiveX control is in design mode, however, it's usually not practical to access the properties through the interfaces. It would be unkind to force tool developers to go through the interface functions just to tweak some properties in the control. Why should the tool vendor have to provide a user interface for managing properties? That's what property pages are for. Property pages are sets of dialog boxes, some of which belong to Visual C++, that are used for manipulating properties. That way, the tool vendors don't have to keep re-creating dialog boxes for tweaking the properties of an ActiveX control.

## How Property Pages Are Used

Client code usually accesses property pages in one of two ways. The first is for the client to call *IOleObject*'s *DoVerb*, passing in the property verb identifier (named OLEIVERB_PROPERTIES and defined as the number –7). The control then shows a dialog frame with all the control's property pages.

Property pages are a testament to the power of COM. Each single property page is a separate COM object (represented by GUIDs, of course). When a client asks a control to show its property pages via the properties verb, the ActiveX control passes its own list of property page GUIDs into a function named *OleCreatePropertyFrame*. This function enumerates the property page GUIDs, calling *CoCreateInstance* for each property page. The property frame gets a copy of an interface for talking to the control (so the frame can change the properties within the control). *OleCreatePropertyFrame* calls back to the control when the user presses the OK or Apply button.

The second way for clients to use property pages is for the client to ask the control for a list of property page GUIDs. Then the client calls *CoCreateInstance* on each property page and installs each in its own frame. Figure 10-3 shows an example of how Visual C++ uses the message traffic control's property sheets in its own property dialog frame.

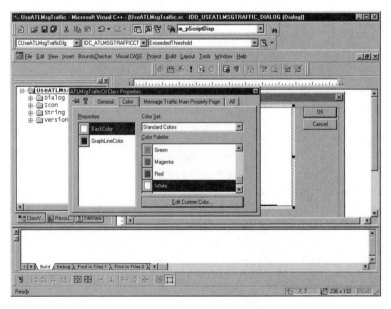

**Figure 10-3**
*Visual C++ using the message traffic control's property page*

This is by far the most common way for clients to use a control's property pages. Notice that the property sheet in Figure 10-3 contains a General tab in addition to the control's property pages. The General property page belongs to Visual C++. The remaining property pages belong to the control (even though they're shown within the context of Visual C++).

For property pages to work correctly, the COM objects implementing property pages need to implement *ISpecifyPropertyPages* and each property page object needs to implement an interface named *IPropertyPage*. With this in mind, let's take a look at exactly how ATL implements property sheets.

# ATL's Property Page Classes

Visual Studio provides a wizard for creating property pages in your ATL project. To create a property page, just select New ATL Object from the Insert menu in Visual C++. The ATL Object Wizard generates a C++ class for you that implements the functions and interfaces necessary for the class to behave as a property page. In addition to generating a C++ class that implements the correct property page interfaces, the ATL Object Wizard makes the property page class part of the project, adding it to the IDL file within the coclass section. The Object Wizard also adds the property page to the object map so that *DllGetClassObject* can find the property page classes. Finally, the Object Wizard adds a new Registry script (so that the DLL makes the correct Registry entries when the control is registered).

ATL's property page classes are composed of several ATL templates: *CComObjectRootEx* (to implement *IUnknown*), *CComCoClass* (the class object for the property page), *IPropertyPageImpl* (for implementing *IPropertyPage*), and *CDialogImpl* (for implementing the dialog box–specific behavior).

ATL's property pages are relatively simple beasts. They really only implement one interface—*IPropertyPage*. The following code shows the *IPropertyPage* interface:

```
interface IPropertyPage : public IUnknown {
    HRESULT SetPageSite(IPropertyPageSite *pPageSite) = 0;
    HRESULT Activate(HWND hWndParent,
        LPCRECT pRect,
        BOOL bModal) = 0;
    HRESULT Deactivate( void) = 0;
    HRESULT GetPageInfo(PROPPAGEINFO *pPageInfo) = 0;
    HRESULT SetObjects(ULONG cObjects,
        IUnknown **ppUnk) = 0;
    HRESULT Show(UINT nCmdShow) = 0;
```

*(continued)*

```
        HRESULT Move(LPCRECT pRect) = 0;
        HRESULT IsPageDirty( void) = 0;
        HRESULT Apply( void) = 0;
        HRESULT Help(LPCOLESTR pszHelpDir) = 0;
        HRESULT TranslateAccelerator(MSG *pMsg) = 0;
};
```

Client code uses this interface to manage the property page. For example, if the property page lives inside the frame created by *OleCreatePropertyFrame*, the property frame uses the interface to perform operations such as applying the new properties when the property frame's Apply button is pushed.

## ATL and the Properties Verb

Let's examine how ATL implements the properties verb. A control shows its property pages in response to the client issuing the properties verb, which it does by calling *IOleObject::DoVerb* using the number defined by OLEIVERB-_PROPERTIES. After the client asks the control to show its property dialog box through *IOleObject::DoVerb*, control ends up in *CComControlBase:: DoVerbProperties*, which simply calls *OleCreatePropertyFrame*, passing in its own *IUnknown* pointer and the list of property page GUIDs. *OleCreateProperty-Frame* takes the list of GUIDs, calling *CoCreateInstance* on each one to create the property pages and arrange them within the dialog frame. *OleCreate-PropertyFrame* uses each property page's *IPropertyPage* interface to manage the property page.

## ATL Property Maps

Understanding how *OleCreatePropertyFrame* works begs the next question— where does the list of property pages come from? ATL generates lists of property pages through its *property maps*, which are macros that help manage property pages. Whenever you add a new property page to an ATL-based control, you need to set up the list of property pages through these macros. Five macros implement property pages: BEGIN_PROPERTY_MAP, PROP_PAGE, PROP_ENTRY, PROP_ENTRY_EX, and END_PROPERTY_MAP. These macros are shown here:

```
struct ATL_PROPMAP_ENTRY
{
    LPCOLESTR szDesc;
    DISPID dispid;
    const CLSID* pclsidPropPage;
    const IID* piidDispatch;
};
```

```
#define BEGIN_PROPERTY_MAP(theClass) \
    typedef _ATL_PROP_NOTIFY_EVENT_CLASS \
    __ATL_PROP_NOTIFY_EVENT_CLASS; \
    static ATL_PROPMAP_ENTRY* GetPropertyMap()\
    {\
        static ATL_PROPMAP_ENTRY pPropMap[] = \
        {

#define PROP_PAGE(clsid) \
        {NULL, NULL, &clsid, &IID_NULL},

#define PROP_ENTRY(szDesc, dispid, clsid) \
        {OLESTR(szDesc), dispid, &clsid, &IID_IDispatch},

#define PROP_ENTRY_EX(szDesc, dispid, clsid, iidDispatch) \
        {OLESTR(szDesc), dispid, &clsid, &iidDispatch},

#define END_PROPERTY_MAP() \
        {NULL, 0, NULL, &IID_NULL} \
    }; \
    return pPropMap; \
}
```

When you decide to add property pages to a COM class using ATL's property map macros, the ATL documentation tells you to put the macros into your class's header file. For example, the following code adds property pages to the *CATLMsgTrafficCtl* class and associates the various properties with the pages:

```
class CATLMsgTrafficCtl :
    // Inheritance list
⋮
{
    ⋮
    BEGIN_PROP_MAP(CATLMsgTrafficCtl)
        PROP_ENTRY("BackColor", DISPID_BACKCOLOR, CLSID_StockColorPage)
        PROP_ENTRY("GraphLineColor", 4, CLSID_StockColorPage)
        PROP_DATA_ENTRY("_cx", m_sizeExtent.cx, VT_UI4)
        PROP_DATA_ENTRY("_cy", m_sizeExtent.cy, VT_UI4)
        PROP_ENTRY("Interval", 3, CLSID_MainPropPage)
        PROP_PAGE(CLSID_StockColorPage)
    END_PROP_MAP()
    ⋮
};
```

ATL's property map macros set up the list of GUIDs representing property pages. Remember that property pages are just COM objects. Notice that the code at the bottom of the preceding page shows a structure named

ATL_PROPMAP_ENTRY and that BEGIN_PROPERTY_MAP declares a static variable of this structure. The PROP_PAGE macro simply inserts a GUID into the list of property pages. PROP_ENTRY inserts a property page GUID into the list and associates a specific control property with the property page. The final macro, PROP_ENTRY_EX, lets you associate a certain dual interface to a property page.

Now let's see how ATL's property pages work with tools such as Visual Basic and Visual C++.

# ATL and Developer Tools

Executing the properties verb isn't the only way for an ActiveX control to show its property pages. As we mentioned before, folks who write developer tools (tools such as Visual Basic and Visual C++) might want programmatic access to a control's property pages. For example, imagine working on a dialog box containing an ActiveX control. When you right-click on the control to view the properties, you get a dialog frame produced by Visual C++ (as opposed to *Ole-CreatePropertyFrame*).

Visual C++ uses the control's *ISpecifyPropertyPages* interface, shown here, to get the list of GUIDs:

```
interface ISpecifyPropertyPages : public IUnknown {
    HRESULT GetPages(CAUUID *pPages);
};

typedef struct tagCAUUID
{
    ULONG       cElems;
    GUID FAR*   pElems;
} CAUUID;
```

ATL implements this interface by cycling through the list of GUIDs (produced by the property map macros) and returning them within the CAUUID structure. Environments such as Visual C++ then use each GUID in a call to *CoCreate-Instance* to create new property pages.

## Pushing the Apply Button

The last interesting part of ATL's property pages to examine is how to implement the *Apply* method. Once it has produced the set of pages (by using *OleCreate-Frame* or some other means), the client code can ask the property page to apply new properties. Remember that the ActiveX control and the property page are separate COM objects, so they need to communicate via interfaces.

When you create a property page using the ATL Object Wizard, ATL overrides the *Apply* function from *IPropertyPage*. The ActiveX control has the necessary interfaces—they were passed into the property page early in the game via a call to *IPropertyPage::SetObjects*. Most property pages respond to the *Apply* function by setting the state of the ActiveX control through the interface provided.

# Property Pages for an ATL-Based Control

Unfortunately, the ATL COM AppWizard doesn't add a default property page to the DLL, which means that you need to do it yourself. Fortunately, there's a wizard for adding property pages to an ATL-based DLL. Just choose New ATL Object from the Insert menu and find the property page object. The wizard adds a dialog template and a C++ class with all the necessary COM goo to be a property page. It's your job to make this property page do something. The ATL property page, however, isn't quite as wizard driven as the MFC-based property page. You need to handle the apply and show operations by hand. This means providing implementations of functions named *Apply* and *Show* to your property page class. Usually the *Apply* function just extracts the state of the controls sitting on the dialog box and walks through the list of interface pointers to the control held by the property page, using the interface pointers to modify the control properties. The *Show* function usually extracts the state of your control and populates the dialog box controls. The following code shows how the ATL-based property page handles the *Apply* function:

```
STDMETHOD(Apply)(void)
{
    long nInterval = GetDlgItemInt(IDC_EDITINTERVAL);
    ATLTRACE(_T("CMainPropPage::Apply\n"));
    for (UINT i = 0; i < m_nObjects; i++)
    {
        IATLMsgTrafficCtl* pATLMsgTrafficCtl;
        m_ppUnk[i]->QueryInterface(IID_IATLMsgTrafficCtl,
            (void**)&pATLMsgTrafficCtl);
        if(pATLMsgTrafficCtl)
        {
            pATLMsgTrafficCtl->put_Interval(nInterval);
            pATLMsgTrafficCtl->Release();
        }
    }
    m_bDirty = FALSE;
    return S_OK;
}
```

*(continued)*

```
STDMETHOD(Show)( UINT nCmdShow )
{
    if(nCmdShow == SW_SHOW ||
       nCmdShow == SW_SHOWNORMAL)
    {
        for (UINT i = 0; i < m_nObjects; i++)
        {
            IATLMsgTrafficCtl* pATLMsgTrafficCtl;
            m_ppUnk[i]->QueryInterface(IID_IATLMsgTrafficCtl,
                (void**)&pATLMsgTrafficCtl);
            if(pATLMsgTrafficCtl)
            {
                long nInterval;

                pATLMsgTrafficCtl->get_Interval(&nInterval);
                SetDlgItemInt(IDC_EDITINTERVAL, nInterval, FALSE);
                pATLMsgTrafficCtl->Release();
            }
        }
    }
    HRESULT hr = IPropertyPageImpl<CMainPropPage>::Show(nCmdShow);
    return hr;
}
```

The second step in providing a property page to the ATL-based control is to make sure the class ID (CLSID) of the property page appears somewhere in the control's property map. Take another look at the code on page 267 to see an example of this. The message map indicates that the standard color property page manages the control's graph line color and the control's main property page manages the control's sampling interval.

# Ambient Properties

In addition to exposing properties to their containers, ActiveX controls can also talk to the container to get information about the environment in which they're operating. These properties, which are held and exposed by the container, are called *ambient properties*. Let's look at how the ambient properties mechanism works.

When the container creates a control, the container and the control exchange interfaces. For example, let's say the control implements an interface named *IOleControl* and the container implements an interface named *IOleControlSite*. The container uses *IOleControl* to talk to the control, and the control uses *IOleControlSite* to talk to the container. In addition to the standard OLE Document/OLE control interfaces, a container might implement a version of *IDispatch*, which exposes the ambient properties to the control.

Here's an example of how the control might use the container's ambient properties. Imagine that you want to make sure your control fits in perfectly with the container. To do that, you need to make sure the control's fill color matches the background of the container. One of the container's ambient properties is its background color. Your control would simply fetch the property from the container and use that as its fill color.

Of course, when you're developing the control, you don't want to deal with the container's ambient properties dispatch interface. (As a developer, you don't want to perform all the work involved in setting up calls to *IDispatch::Invoke*.) Fortunately, ATL provides two easy ways to access a container's ambient properties from a control. The first way is to call *CComControlBase::GetAmbient-Property*. Here's the function signature:

```
HRESULT GetAmbientProperty(DISPID dispid, VARIANT& var)
```

*GetAmbientProperty* takes as its arguments the DISPID of the property you want to retrieve and a VARIANT in which to place the property. *GetAmbientProperty* does all the work of setting up and calling *Invoke* for you.

The second way is to use one of the wrapper functions that ATL conveniently implements for retrieving the various ambient properties. For example, if you want to get the container's background color, you could either call *GetAmbientProperty* and pass in DISPID_AMBIENT_BACKCOLOR as the dispatch ID or call *GetAmbientBackColor*. The advantage of using the wrapper functions is that they unpack the variants for you.

Table 10-2 illustrates the container's ambient properties you can access with ATL's *CComControlBase* class.

### Table 10-2   ATL's Ambient Property Support

| Ambient Property | DISPID | Type | Accessor Function |
|---|---|---|---|
| Appearance | DISPID_AMBIENT-_APPEARANCE | Short | *GetAmbientAppearance* |
| Background Color | DISPID_AMBIENT-_BACKCOLOR | OLE_COLOR | *GetAmbientBackColor* |
| Display Name | DISPID_AMBIENT-_DISPLAYNAME | BSTR | *GetAmbientDisplayName* |
| Font | DISPID_AMBIENT_FONT | *IFont\** | *GetAmbientFont* |
| Font (dispatch version) | DISPID_AMBIENT_FONT | *IFontDisp\** | *GetAmbientFontDisp* |

*(continued)*

**Table 10-2** *continued*

| Ambient Property | DISPID | Type | Accessor Function |
|---|---|---|---|
| Foreground Color | DISPID_AMBIENT-_FORECOLOR | OLE-_COLOR | *GetAmbientForeColor* |
| Locality | DISPID_AMBIENT-_LOCALEID | LCID | *GetAmbientLocaleID* |
| Scale Units | DISPID_AMBIENT-_SCALEUNITS | BSTR | *GetAmbientScaleUnits* |
| Text Alignment | DISPID_AMBIENT-_TEXTALIGNMENT | short | *GetAmbientTextAlign* |
| User Mode | DISPID_AMBIENT-_USERMODE | BOOL | *GetAmbientUserMode* |
| UI Dead | DISPID_AMBIENT-_UIDEAD | BOOL | *GetAmbientUIDead* |
| Show Grab Handles | DISPID_AMBIENT-_SHOWGRABHANDLES | BOOL | *GetAmbientShowGrabHandles* |
| Show Hatching | DISPID_AMBIENT-_SHOWHATCHING | BOOL | *GetAmbientShowHatching* |
| Message Reflection | DISPID_AMBIENT-_MESSAGEREFLECT | BOOL | *GetAmbientMessageReflect* |
| Auto Clip | DISPID_AMBIENT-_AUTOCLIP | BOOL | *GetAmbientAutoClip* |
| Display as Default | DISPID_AMBIENT-_DISPLAYASDEFAULT | BOOL | *GetAmbientDisplayAsDefault* |
| Support Mnemonics | DISPID_AMBIENT-_SUPPORTSMNEMONICS | BOOL | *GetAmbientSupportsMnemonics* |
| Palette | DISPID_AMBIENT-_PALETTE | BOOL | *GetAmbientPalette* |

# Connections and Events in an ATL-Based Control

The last item to look at within a control is how to set up the connection points so that the control can fire events back to the container. This section serves as an overview—Chapter 12 provides more detailed information about connection points.

When you set up an event set for your control, you start by defining the events in the control's IDL file. You then compile the project, which builds the type library. In this example, the control fires an event under two conditions: when the number of events exceeds a certain threshold, and upon each new interval.

The following code shows the message traffic control's event set described in IDL:

```
#include <olectl.h>
// ATLMsgTraffic.idl : IDL source for ATLMsgTraffic.dll
//
// This file will be processed by the MIDL tool to
//  produce the type library (ATLMsgTraffic.tlb) and
//  marshaling code.

import "oaidl.idl";
import "ocidl.idl";

// Interface definitions and such
    ⋮
[
    uuid(1AB5D84F-B593-11D1-8CAA-952EA6C89F6D),
    version(1.0),
    helpstring("ATLMsgTraffic 1.0 Type Library")
]
library ATLMSGTRAFFICLib
{
    importlib("stdole32.tlb");
    importlib("stdole2.tlb");

    [
        uuid(1C4BFAC4-B4A5-11D1-8CAA-FC1024D62D6E),
        helpstring("Event interface for ATLMsgTraffic Control")
    ]
    dispinterface _DATLMsgTrafficEvents
    {
        properties:
            // Event interface has no properties

        methods:
            [id(1)] void ExceededThreshold(long NumMessages,
                long CurrentThreshold);
            [id(2)] void NewInterval(long NumMessages);
    };
```

*(continued)*

281

```
    [
        uuid(1AB5D85D-B593-11D1-8CAA-952EA6C89F6D),
        helpstring("ATLMsgTrafficCtl Class")
    ]
    coclass ATLMsgTrafficCtl
    {
        [default] interface IATLMsgTrafficCtl;
        [default, source] dispinterface _DATLMsgTrafficEvents;
    };
};
```

Once the type library is compiled, you can ask ClassView to create a callback proxy for you by selecting the control's class from ClassView, right-clicking on the class, and selecting Implement Connection Point. Visual Studio displays a dialog box showing all the available event interfaces listed in the control's type library. You select the one(s) for which you want a callback proxy, and Visual Studio writes a proxy for you. The following code shows the ATL-based message traffic control's callback proxy:

```
class CProxy_DATLMsgTrafficEvents :
    public IConnectionPointImpl<T, &DIID__DATLMsgTrafficEvents,
    CComDynamicUnkArray>
{
public:
// methods:
// _DATLMsgTrafficEvents : IDispatch
public:
    void Fire_ExceededThreshold(long NumMessages,
        long CurrentThreshold)
    {
        VARIANTARG* pvars = new VARIANTARG[2];
        for (int i = 0; i < 2; i++)
            VariantInit(&pvars[i]);
        T* pT = (T*)this;
        pT->Lock();
        IUnknown** pp = m_vec.begin();
        while (pp < m_vec.end())
        {
            if(*pp != NULL)
            {
                pvars[1].vt = VT_I4;
                pvars[1].lVal= NumMessages;
                pvars[0].vt = VT_I4;
                pvars[0].lVal= CurrentThreshold;
                DISPPARAMS disp = { pvars, NULL, 2, 0 };
                IDispatch* pDispatch =
                    reinterpret_cast<IDispatch*>(*pp);
```

```
                    pDispatch->Invoke(0x1, IID_NULL,
                        LOCALE_USER_DEFAULT,
                        DISPATCH_METHOD, &disp,
                        NULL, NULL, NULL);
                }
                pp++;
            }
        pT->Unlock();
            delete[] pvars;
        }
        void Fire_NewInterval(long NumMessages)
        {
            // Similar treatment for Fire_NewInterval
        }

    };
```

The callback proxy generated by Visual Studio represents a set of C++-friendly functions that call back to the interface implemented by the client.

Whereas MFC's *IConnectionPointContainer* implementation is hardwired into *COleControl* and each connection point is handled by a connection map, ATL's implementation is handled using multiple inheritance. Your control class inherits from *IConnectionPointContainerImpl* and the proxy generated by ClassView. If you select Supports Connection Points when you start the project, the Object Wizard inserts *IConnectionPointContainerImpl* for you. If you forget to mark the check box, you can just type it in. The following code shows how a connection point mechanism is brought into a control:

```
class ATL_NO_VTABLE CATLMsgTrafficCtl :
{
    ⋮
    public IConnectionPointContainerImpl<CATLMsgTrafficCtl>,
    public CProxy_DATLMsgTrafficEvents<CATLMsgTrafficCtl>
    ⋮
    LRESULT OnTimer(UINT msg, WPARAM wParam,
        LPARAM lParam,
        BOOL& bHandled)
    {
    ⋮
        if(nMessagesToShow > m_threshold)
        {
            Fire_ExceededThreshold(nMessagesToShow, m_threshold);
        }
    ⋮
    }
};
```

That does it for connection points and event sets on the control side. We'll revisit connections and events when we look at integrating controls with their environments in Chapter 13.

## Conclusion

ActiveX controls are a great testament to the power of COM. Through the rules of COM (specifically, the enforcement of standard interfaces and the magic of *QueryInterface*), it's possible to develop a rich user interface architecture, such as that of ActiveX controls.

Remember that it takes a whole lot of code to get an ActiveX control up and running. Specifically, the control needs to implement a host of interfaces, many of which are implemented the same way from one control to another. ATL is useful because it includes most of that boilerplate code in the form of already implemented interfaces. You just need to bring in the right interfaces and you're set.

In this chapter, we took a high-level view of ActiveX controls. ActiveX controls are COM objects that usually implement a user interface component. ActiveX controls maintain an internal state controlled by properties that can be persisted and a visual state represented by the way it renders the control. ATL provides a framework with all the hooks necessary to create COM objects that qualify as ActiveX controls. We'll revisit ActiveX controls from the client side when we look at using ActiveX controls within different development environments in Chapter 13.

In Chapter 11, we'll examine the COM persistence model and you'll find out how ATL implements persistence using property maps.

## CHAPTER ELEVEN

# Persistence

An object is usually created to play a part within the context of an application or to provide some service to a group of applications. If the object has an internal state, programmers might want to save the object's state to nonvolatile storage for later restoration. For example, Microsoft ActiveX controls placed on a container such as Microsoft Visual Basic will have the same properties after closing the container and reopening it (barring catastrophic failure). As with Visual Basic, most desktop applications provide a means of saving their content to a file, database, or other nonvolatile medium. In the past, you might have written such applications without using COM components, streaming the important data and configurations to files in proprietary formats. At that time, the semantics of persistence were homegrown and application specific. Patterns for persistence have since evolved and have been incorporated into the development libraries and technologies we use today. MFC introduced a convenient way for programmers to save instances of C++ objects (with their states) to persistent storage and then load them up again through its *CArchive*, *CFile*, and *CObject* classes. COM specifies several persistence interfaces that define protocols for saving and loading objects and their states in binary or container-defined formats. These interfaces have a rich history that began with OLE Structured Storage. For a more thorough explanation of OLE Structured Storage, see *Inside OLE* by Kraig Brockschmidt (2nd ed., Microsoft Press, 1995).

In this chapter, we'll look at the ATL implementations of COM persistence interfaces and how they are enabled in ATL objects. We'll also step through some common scenarios with hosting applications to show these implementations in action.

# Persistence Interfaces

To understand the ATL COM persistence implementations, let's first look at the interfaces involved and what they are designed to accomplish. Persistence involves three participants: the application, the object being persisted, and an object that handles the read/write operations on the actual data. The application initiates the load or the save by creating an object that implements the *IStream*, *IStorage*, or *IPropertyBag* interface. This interface pointer is then passed off to the persisted object, using one of the *IPersistxxx* interfaces (which the object must implement). The object then uses the interface pointer either to load or to save its state, as requested by the application. Objects can, and typically do, implement more than one persistence interface, allowing the containing application to choose its preferred method. ATL provides implementations for the *IPersistStream*, *IPersistStreamInit*, *IPersistStorage*, and *IPersistPropertyBag* interfaces. Figure 11-1 illustrates how the interfaces match up between the corresponding data object and persisted object.

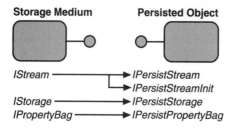

**Figure 11-1**
*Persistence interface pairs*

Here's a summary of the interfaces involved in ATL persistence and what they do:

- **ISequentialStream**   Defines simple read/write semantics for a sequential stream of bytes. This interface is normally implemented as *IStream*, which derives from *ISequentialStream*.

- **IStream**   Implemented on a container's storage medium to enable loading or saving a sequential stream of bytes. *IStream* extends *ISequentialStream* to add transactions, cloning, random access, and locking. COM provides the *CreateStreamOnHGlobal* API to create a stream object implementation on global memory. *IStream* is probably the most widely used data object interface in COM persistence. It can be used in conjunction with the *IPersistStream* and *IPersistStreamInit* interfaces.

■ **IPersist**   Defines a single method, *GetClassID*, which is used to determine the type of object being saved. This type information is used when loading the object to re-create the correct class.

■ **IPersistStream**   Derives from *IPersist*. Provides methods for saving to and loading from an *IStream* provided by the container.

■ **IPersistStreamInit**   Has all the same methods as *IPersistStream*, and adds the *InitNew* method for initializing an object to a default state. Implemented by ATL.

■ **IStorage**   Implemented on the container's storage medium. A storage can be created on a file with COM APIs. Storages are containers for streams and other storages. Microsoft Office applications use this mechanism extensively with the compound document (also known as structured storage) specification. This interface is used with *IPersist-Storage* on the persisted object.

■ **IPersistStorage**   Implemented on an object to enable persistence using the *IStorage* interface. Implemented by ATL.

■ **IPropertyBag**   Specifies reading/writing persisted state as name/value pairs. The application can implement this interface to store the state in any format it chooses. The values themselves must be VARIANT-compatible types. The nice thing about property bags is that the application has control over each data value persisted, instead of a byte stream formatted by the persisted object. The other half of property bag persistence is *IPersistPropertyBag*.

■ **IPersistPropertyBag**   Similar to *IPersistStreamInit*, except an *IPropertyBag** is passed as an argument to *Load* and *Save* instead of an *IStream**. *IPersistPropertyBag* also supports error reporting through the *IErrorInfo* interface. Implemented by ATL.

# ATL Persistence Implementations

ATL provides the *IPersistStreamInitImpl*, *IPersistStorageImpl*, and *IPersistProperty-BagImpl* template classes to enable your object to load and save its state through any client that is capable of providing a stream, a storage, or a property bag. The ATL Object Wizard automatically includes the first two as base classes when inserting a full control. No support is added when inserting a simple object using the Object Wizard; all three of these classes rely heavily on the property map in your object, and the Object Wizard doesn't create property maps for simple objects. You can still use the persistence classes in simple objects—you just have to add the property map manually and do a little extra work by hand. We mentioned the property map in previous chapters, but now we'll add the details necessary for understanding how it fits into the persistence implementation.

## Property Maps Revisited

Property maps are easy to identify in your object header file: just look for the BEGIN_PROP_MAP and END_PROP_MAP macros. These macros declare a static *GetPropMap* function for the class and a static array of ATL_PROPMAP_ENTRY structures within the class, as shown here:

```
#define BEGIN_PROP_MAP(theClass) \
    typedef _ATL_PROP_NOTIFY_EVENT_CLASS \
        __ATL_PROP_NOTIFY_EVENT_CLASS; \
    typedef theClass _PropMapClass; \
    static ATL_PROPMAP_ENTRY* GetPropertyMap()\
    {\
        static ATL_PROPMAP_ENTRY pPropMap[] = \
        {
#define END_PROP_MAP() \
            {NULL, 0, NULL, &IID_NULL, 0, 0, 0} \
        }; \
        return pPropMap; \
    }
```

Between the BEGIN and END macros, several macros insert ATL_PROPMAP_ENTRY data. The data structure has the following members:

```
struct ATL_PROPMAP_ENTRY
{
    LPCOLESTR szDesc;
    DISPID dispid;
    const CLSID* pclsidPropPage;
    const IID* piidDispatch;
    DWORD dwOffsetData;
    DWORD dwSizeData;
    VARTYPE vt;
};
```

The macros used to populate this structure vary depending on whether the property is part of your exposed dispatch interface or is class member data that you want to save as an internal state. The macros related to persistence and the reasons for using them are listed in Table 11-1.

**Table 11-1** **Persistence Macros**

| Macro | Description |
| --- | --- |
| PROP_ENTRY(*szDesc*, *dispid*, *clsid*) | Inserts a property into the map, assuming a single *IDispatch* interface |
| PROP_ENTRY_EX(*szDesc*, *dispid*, *clsid*, *iidDispatch*) | Used for properties in objects with multiple dual interfaces |
| PROP_DATA_ENTRY(*szDesc*, *member*, *vt*) | For internal state not exposed through a dispatch interface; *vt* indicates the VARTYPE of the data |

The PROP_ENTRY macro populates the first three members of the ATL_PROPMAP_ENTRY structure with the parameters passed in and fixes the *piidDispatch* entry at &IID_IDispatch. PROP_ENTRY_EX allows you to specify *piidDispatch*. Both macros leave the *dwOffsetData*, *dwSizeData*, and *vt* members unused (0). Also, the *clsid* parameter can be used to specify the property page associated with the property or &CLSID_NULL if not applicable. This information isn't required for persistence but provides a convenient place to get the property page IDs for a container when it requests them. The PROP_DATA_ENTRY macro initializes only the description, offset, and size of the data member being persisted.

ATL persistence classes use the *GetPropertyMap* static function defined by the BEGIN_PROPERTY_MAP macro to get the first entry in the map and enumerate through the ATL_PROPMAP_ENTRY structures.

## IPersistStreamInitImpl

*IPersistStreamInitImpl* implements and derives directly from *IPersistStreamInit*. It is templatized only on your object C++ class name, which allows ATL access to your overrides and any other inherited members through the *static_cast<T*>(this)* cast operation. This interesting technique is used throughout ATL, and the persistence classes are no exception.

### Saving an Object

To successfully persist your object, the container will first create a stream object— that is, some implementation of *IStream*. Your object doesn't know or care what medium lies beneath the interface, which is one of the reasons we use interface-based programming in the first place. Once the stream is created, the first bit of information your object is asked for is its CLSID. After all, persisted properties must belong to a specific type of object, so the type information must be saved along with the object state. To get the CLSID, containers holding an interface pointer to the object can call *QueryInterface* for *IPersist* and call *GetClassID*. Because *IPersistStreamInit* derives from *IPersist*, *IPersistStreamInitImpl* must also implement the one and only *IPersist* method: *GetClassID*. The implementation of *GetClassID* looks like this:

```
STDMETHOD(GetClassID)(CLSID *pClassID)
{
    *pClassID = T::GetObjectCLSID();
    return S_OK;
}
```

The template parameter *T* is used to access the static *GetObjectCLSID* method in your object. *GetObjectCLSID* is inherited from *CComCoClass*, which you'll see in your object inheritance like this:

```
public CComCoClass<CAtlFullControl, &CLSID_AtlFullControl>
```

Because *CComCoClass* takes the CLSID as a template parameter, it is qualified to supply it to the ATL persistence implementation. All of the ATL persistence classes rely on this method to obtain the CLSID for the persisted object while saving. Once retrieved, the container can utilize the COM API *WriteClassStm (pStream, clsid)* to write the CLSID as the first piece of persisted data describing the object.

So far we haven't used the property map as promised, but we're about to. The container now has the choice of which persistence interface it prefers to use. This is a simple matter of using *QueryInterface* for the *IPersistxxx* interfaces in the order of preference. Assuming *IPersistStreamInit* is the first choice found that the object supports, the *Save* method is called with the *IStream* pointer as a parameter. *IPersistStreamInitImpl* supplies a default implementation as follows:

```
STDMETHOD(Save)(LPSTREAM pStm, BOOL fClearDirty)
{
    T* pT = static_cast<T*>(this);
    return pT->IPersistStreamInit_Save(pStm, fClearDirty,
        T::GetPropertyMap());
}
```

The *fClearDirty* flag is used to set the state of the "dirty" flag in the object after saving but is ignored in the *Save* implementation. ATL keeps tabs on the dirty state in the *m_bRequiresSave* member of *CComControlBase*, which the control indirectly inherits from *CComControl*. If your object doesn't inherit from *CComControl* (for example, it's a simple object), you'll need to manually add this data member in your object header. The dirty state can be checked with the *IPersistStreamInitImpl::IsDirty* method. Moving on with the *Save* operation, *IPersistStreamInit_Save* is called with the *Save* parameters plus the property map pointer. This helper function delegates yet another time to the *AtlIPersistStreamInit_Save* global function, adding a pointer to the object and its *IUnknown* pointer.

```
HRESULT IPersistStreamInit_Save(LPSTREAM pStm,
    BOOL fClearDirty, ATL_PROPMAP_ENTRY* pMap)
{
    T* pT = static_cast<T*>(this);
    return AtlIPersistStreamInit_Save(pStm, fClearDirty, pMap,
        pT, pT->GetUnknown());
}
```

At this point, you might be wondering about all of this indirection. Consider that you could create your own version of the *Save* code by implementing *IPersistStreamInit_Save* yourself. Because this method is called from *IPersistStreamInit::Save* using the cast object pointer, your derived method would be called instead of the default. It's another point of extensibility. Also, delegating the real work to *AtlIPersistStreamInit_Save* can make smaller code when using ATL as a DLL, because the implementation for this global function is found in ATL.DLL for *ReleaseMinSize* builds.

*AtlIPersistStreamInit_Save* writes out the ATL version number and then uses the property map to save each property to the container-supplied stream in turn. The version number is used when the object is loaded from a stream to ensure compatibility between *Load* and *Save* implementations. To get the property value, *AtlIPersistStreamInit_Save* calls *QueryInterface* through the *IUnknown* pointer for the dispatch interface specified in the property map entry, shown here:

```
if(pMap[i].piidDispatch != piidOld)
{
    pDispatch.Release();
    if(FAILED(pUnk->QueryInterface(*pMap[i].piidDispatch,
        (void**)&pDispatch)))
    {
        hr = E_FAIL;
        break;
    }
    piidOld = pMap[i].piidDispatch;
}
```

The *pDispatch* pointer is cached until a different dispatch ID is found in the map. *AtlIPersistStreamInit_Save* checks the map for every entry, because PROP_ENTRY_EX can be used to specify the dispatch interface each property is exposed through. Once a dispatch pointer is obtained, *AtlIPersistStream-Init_Save* calls into the object to get the value using *CComDispatchDriver*. Remember that the dispatch ID for the property was passed in as an argument to the PROP_ENTRY macro. ATL then writes the returned property value to the stream. *CComVariant* is handy for the last step because it has stream read/write capability, as you can see here:

```
if(FAILED(CComDispatchDriver::GetProperty(pDispatch,
    pMap[i].dispid, &var)))
{
    hr = E_FAIL;
    break;
}

hr = var.WriteToStream(pStm);
```

For persisted values placed in the map using PROP_DATA_ENTRY, no dispatch interface is involved. A pointer to the data member is calculated based on the *dwOffsetData* member of ATL_PROPMAP_ENTRY, and the *dwSizeData* member tells ATL how many bytes to write out. The *dwSizeData* member will be 0 for map entries entered using PROP_ENTRY or PROP_ENTRY_EX and nonzero for PROP_DATA_ENTRY entries. The relevant code is shown here:

```
if(pMap[i].dwSizeData != 0)
{
    void* pData = (void*) (pMap[i].dwOffsetData + (DWORD)pThis);
    hr = pStm->Write(pData, pMap[i].dwSizeData, NULL);
    if(FAILED(hr))
        return hr;
    continue;
}
```

After looping through the entire property map, *AtlIPersistStreamInit_Save* exits and the save operation is complete.

## Creating and Loading an Object

With the saved object safely tucked away in persistent storage, the object itself can be released and later re-created. To accomplish re-creation, the container can perform these steps:

1. Create an *IStream* on the storage medium.

2. Read the CLSID of the object from the stream using *ReadClassStm*.

3. Call either *CoCreateInstance* or *CoCreateInstanceEx* to create the object.

4. Call *QueryInterface* through *IPersistStreamInit* for the object.

5. Call *IPersistStreamInit::Load* and pass in the *IStream* pointer.

The ATL implementation of the *Load* function reverses what *Save* did. It loads the ATL version number and then loops through the property map extracting the variant values from the stream using *CComVariant::ReadFromStream*. The values are then used to call into the appropriate dispatch interface on the object and set the property. For raw data values, the data is read directly from the stream into the data member using *dwOffsetData* in the map entry. After loading, the dirty bit is set to FALSE, because the object has a known state.

If an object is being newly created, as when a button is dropped onto a Visual Basic form, *IPersistStreamInit::InitNew* should be called by the container instead of *Load*. *InitNew* does nothing in *IPersistStreamInitImpl* and should be overridden in the object class to put properties into their initial state.

## IPersistStorageImpl

A container might prefer to keep its persisted state in a compound document, or structured storage. Each object is given its own storage to manage as needed to get the persistence job done. To see the results of this, let's create a structured storage using the ActiveX control test container.

1. Launch the test container from the Tools menu in Microsoft Visual Studio.

2. From the Edit menu, choose Insert New Control.

3. Pick the control of your choice from the dialog box and click OK. The control should now be visible.

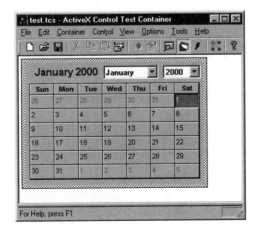

4. Now click on the Control menu and choose Save To Storage.

   **NOTE** There are also menu selections for saving to a stream, known as property bags, which we talked about earlier. We'll look at property bags in more detail right after storages.

5. Enter a file name for the structured storage and click the Save button. The DocFile Viewer applet will open. Folder icons indicate storages, and page icons represent streams.

6. From the Tree menu, choose Expand All. Your file should have one storage and one or more streams beneath it. If you want to look at the actual bytes stored, double-click on a stream. The byte format is, of course, under the control of the object being persisted. To the container, it's just a stream of bytes.

To support this kind of persistence, an object must implement *IPersistStorage*. ATL provides *IPersistStorageImpl*, which is suitable in most cases. If you need to create more than one stream in the provided storage, you'll need to override the default behavior.

## Saving to a Storage

The container kicks off the save process by creating an *IStorage* with one of the structured storage APIs (such as *StgCreateDocfile*) and then calls *QueryInterface* through *IPersistStorage* for the persisted object. As with *IPersistStream*, the CLSID of the object is obtained using *IPersistStorage::GetClassID*. The CLSID can be written directly to the storage using *WriteClassStg*. The container then calls *IPersistStorage::Save*, passing the *IStorage* interface as a parameter. On the object side, *IPersistStorageImpl::Save* then creates a stream named "Contents." This name is hard-coded in *IPersistStorageImpl*; if you want to use a different name, you'll have to override the *Save* method. The resulting *IStream* pointer is then passed to the *IPersistStreamImpl::Save* method for standard stream-based persistence, which we covered in the previous section. When the save operation is complete and the *IPersistStorageImpl::Save* method returns, the container calls *IPersistStorage::SaveCompleted* to indicate the process is complete. *IPersistStorageImpl* reuses the *IPersistStreamInitImpl* code for its read/write functionality.

## Loading from a Storage

To load a persisted object from a storage, the container opens the storage and obtains the *IStorage* interface. It then uses *ReadClassStg* to read the CLSID of the object that the storage belongs to. With the CLSID in hand, the object can be created using either *CoCreateInstance* or *CoCreateInstanceEx* and queried for *IPersistStorage*. *IPersistStorage::Load* is then called, which ATL implements to open the "Contents" stream and hand it off to *IPersistStreamInitImpl::Load*.

If you want to step through the saving and loading action, you'll find once again that the test container is a handy tool.

1. Create an ATL DLL project that contains a full control.

2. Modify the project settings for the debug build (Project–Settings menu, Debug tab) so that the debug executable is the test container. This is a predefined choice—just click the browse button on the edit field and choose ActiveX Control Test Container from the pop-up menu.

3. Build the project in debug mode.

4. Open ATLCOM.H and put breakpoints in the *IPersistStorageImpl* methods.

5. Run the project. The test container application will start.

6. In the test container, insert the control from the Edit–Insert New Control menu.

7. Save the control to storage from the Control menu. You should hit breakpoints *IPersistStorageImpl::GetClassID, Save,* and *SaveCompleted.*

8. Delete the control from the test container (from the Edit menu).

9. Insert the control from storage using the Edit–Insert Control from the Storage menu. You should hit the *IPersistStorageImpl::Load* breakpoint.

## *IPersistPropertyBagImpl*

Property bags enable the container to choose the persistence format. Unlike *IStream* and *IStorage*, *IPropertyBag* has no predefined implementation. The container can choose any format that it can parse to retrieve the CLSID of the object and its name/value pairs representing the properties. Visual Basic form files (.frm) and controls hosted in Web pages are two examples of the use of property bag persistence to save properties as text. A Visual Basic form with a single button on it has this format when persisted:

```
Begin VB.Form Form1
    Caption         =   "Form1"
    ClientHeight    =   3195
    ClientLeft      =   60
    ClientTop       =   345
    ClientWidth     =   4680
    LinkTopic       =   "Form1"
    ScaleHeight     =   3195
    ScaleWidth      =   4680
    StartUpPosition =   3   'Windows Default
    Begin VB.CommandButton Command1
        Caption     =   "Command1"
        Height      =   615
        Left        =   360
        TabIndex    =   0
        Top         =   600
        Width       =   2055
    End
End
```

Each object is enclosed in a Begin/End block with the named values inside. Each named value in the file shown is the result of an *IPropertyBag::Write* call. Write takes the name of the property and a variant value as arguments from the object being saved. Nested objects, such as the button in the file above, are passed to the container as the VT_UNKNOWN type.

Property bag persistence for ATL objects is supplied by the *IPersistPropertyBagImpl* class, from which your object derives. Controls and objects created with the ATL Object Wizard don't derive from this class by default, so you'll have to add the inheritance by hand.

### Adding Property Bag Support

Like the other persistence implementations, *IPersistPropertyBagImpl* relies on the property map. If you're starting with a control generated by the Object Wizard, the map will already be there. Simple objects don't have property maps by default, so you'll need to create the map before we continue. Use the BEGIN-_PROP_MAP and END_PROP_MAP macros to declare the map, and add a BOOL member variable *m_bRequiresSave*. Controls automatically inherit this member from *CComControlBase*.

With the property map in place, you can add property bag support by inheriting from *IPersistPropertyBagImpl*, as shown here:

```
public IPersistPropertyBagImpl<theClass>,
```

The template parameter *theClass* should be replaced with your object C++ class name. Because containers expect *QueryInterface* to successfully return an *IPersistPropertyBag* pointer, you need this entry in the interface map:

```
COM_INTERFACE_ENTRY(IPersistPropertyBag)
```

Your object is now ready for property bag persistence! Let's look at how *IPersistPropertyBagImpl* works.

## Saving to a Property Bag

As with the other persistence interfaces, *IPersistPropertyBagImpl* implements the *IPersist* method *GetClassID*. After retrieving the type information, the container calls the *Save* method, passing in an *IPropertyBag* pointer. *Save* takes an additional BOOL parameter, *fSaveAllProperties*. If FALSE, only those properties that have changed since the last save are persisted. ATL ignores this flag, and all properties are persisted with each call to *Save*. *Save* eventually delegates to *AtlIPersistPropertyBag_Save*, which enumerates the property map to get each property value as a variant. In addition to a value, a text description is needed before you can call *IPropertyBag::Write*. The map stores this value, which you passed in as the first parameter to the PROP_ENTRY macro. Retrieving it is a simple matter of accessing the *szDesc* member of the ATL_PROPMAP_ENTRY structure:

```
HRESULT hr = pPropBag->Write(pMap[i].szDesc, &var);
```

For raw data entries (PROP_DATA_ENTRY), *IPersistPropertyBagImpl* supports a subset of the possible variant types. These include VT_UI1, VT_I1, VT_BOOL, VT_UI2, VT_UI4, VT_INT, and VT_UINT.

We looked at one example of a property bag: the Visual Basic form file. You can also use the test container to save objects to a property bag that is displayed in a list view control. This option is available with the other *Save* selections under the Control menu. Figure 11-2 shows a Microsoft Calendar Control persisted to a property bag in the test container.

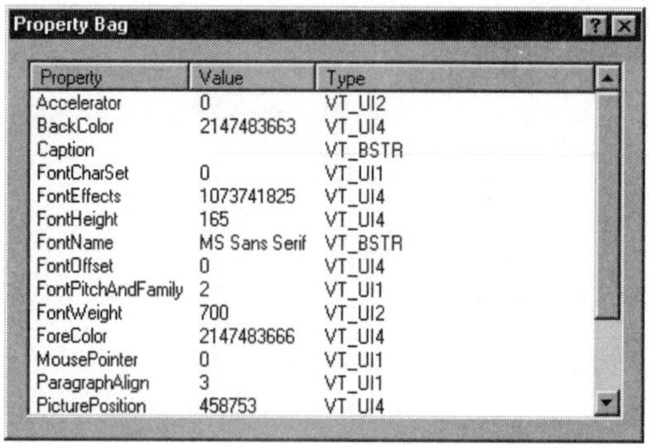


| Property | Value | Type |
| --- | --- | --- |
| Accelerator | 0 | VT_UI2 |
| BackColor | 2147483663 | VT_UI4 |
| Caption | | VT_BSTR |
| FontCharSet | 0 | VT_UI1 |
| FontEffects | 1073741825 | VT_UI4 |
| FontHeight | 165 | VT_UI4 |
| FontName | MS Sans Serif | VT_BSTR |
| FontOffset | 0 | VT_UI4 |
| FontPitchAndFamily | 2 | VT_UI1 |
| FontWeight | 700 | VT_UI2 |
| ForeColor | 2147483666 | VT_UI4 |
| MousePointer | 0 | VT_UI1 |
| ParagraphAlign | 3 | VT_UI1 |
| PicturePosition | 458753 | VT_UI4 |

**Figure 11-2**
*Microsoft Calendar Control persisted to a property bag*

Nonvolatile property bag persistence isn't available in the test container as of this writing, and it doesn't support nested objects. Even so, it's a quick and dirty debugging tool to tuck away in your arsenal.

### Loading from a Property Bag

To restore an object from a property bag, the container can open the file or other property bag storage medium and retrieve the CLSID for the object. This is a container-specific operation that varies between applications. Once the CLSID has been retrieved and the object is created using either *CoCreateInstance* or *CoCreateInstanceEx*, *IPersistPropertyBag::Load* is called to set the properties. As with the other persistence load and save implementations, *Load* delegates to *AtlIPersistPropertyBag_Load*. This global function walks the property map to retrieve each value in turn with the container-provided *IPropertyBag* pointer. *IPropertyBag::Read* takes the property description as an [in] parameter and a variant as an [out] parameter to receive the value. Before calling *Read*, *AtlIPersistPropertyBag_Load* creates an empty variant and invokes the get method on the property. The returned value is unimportant, but the type, shown here, is important:

```
CComVariant var;
if(FAILED(CComDispatchDriver::GetProperty(pDispatch,
    pMap[i].dispid, &var)))
{
    return E_FAIL;
}
```

With the variant correctly typed, the value is read from the container's property bag:

```
HRESULT hr = pPropBag->Read(pMap[i].szDesc, &var, pErrorLog);
```

This process continues for all properties exposed through a dispatch interface in the property map. For raw data values exposed through PROP_DATA-_ENTRY, the process is somewhat different. The following code shows how ATL reads a raw data value from the container:

```
CComVariant var;

if(pMap[i].dwSizeData != 0)
{
    void* pData = (void*) (pMap[i].dwOffsetData + (DWORD)pThis);
    HRESULT hr = pPropBag->Read(pMap[i].szDesc, &var, pErrorLog);
}
```

Notice how the empty *CComVariant var* is used to retrieve the value in *pPropBag->Read*. Because the type of the variant hasn't been specified (VT-_EMPTY by default), the container must decide what type the data is. This can result in errors. For example, the extents of an ATL control are declared in the PROP_DATA_ENTRY macro as type VT_UI4, but they have values small enough to fit in a VT_I2. If the container uses the most efficient type to return the value, the VT_I2 will be copied to the property map declared type VT_UI4, leaving garbage in the upper half of the property value. If the variant *var* is initialized to the type stored in the map, the container can return the correct size value. The corrected code is shown here:

```
CComVariant var;
var.vt = pmap[i].vt;
if(pMap[i].dwSizeData != 0)
{
    void* pData = (void*) (pMap[i].dwOffsetData + (DWORD)pThis);
    HRESULT hr = pPropBag->Read(pMap[i].szDesc, &var, pErrorLog);
}
```

This discrepancy should be fixed in the next version of ATL. As we mentioned in the previous section, only a subset of the variant types is supported for raw data entries in *IPersistPropertyBagImpl*.

# Conclusion

ATL provides convenient implementations for the COM persistence interfaces *IPersistStreamInit*, *IPersistStorage*, and *IPersistPropertyBag*. *IPersistStreamInitImpl* supports saving to and loading from *IStream*. *IPersistStorageImpl* supports *IStorage*. *IPersistPropertyBagImpl* supports *IPropertyBag*. Although primarily targeted for ActiveX controls, a simple object can utilize these features as well by adding a property map and the necessary base class to the object. Most objects should take advantage of all three, unless the object will be used only in a known container environment.

## CHAPTER TWELVE

# ATL and Connection Points

Since the dawn of COM in 1993, developers have been using *incoming* inter-faces to call in to COM objects. Calling in to a COM object by using an incoming interface is a very natural thing to do—it's much like calling methods on a C++ class. Often, however, you want to have a COM object call back out to the client. Once most folks grasp the basic principle behind COM—interfaces and imple-mentations should be treated separately—and understand how to call methods through a COM interface, the next question they ask is how to set up COM objects and clients so that the clients can get callback notifications. COM's connection points were created to answer this question. Though connection points were originally developed for Microsoft ActiveX controls developers, they are now particularly useful for Microsoft Visual Basic and VBScript programmers. In this chapter, we'll look at how two COM objects can set up this communica-tion scheme in which an object written in ATL calls back to the client. We'll first examine how connections work, and then we'll see how ATL implements them.

## How Connections Work

Bidirectional communication between two pieces of software is a common re-quirement. Given two independent software components, it's often useful to have an object notify its client or clients of various goings-on. The classic ex-ample is ActiveX controls, in which the controls notify their clients of special events. Once an object and a client agree on how the object should call back to the client, the client needs a way of connecting its implementation of the callback interface. These interfaces defined by the object and implemented by the client are called *outgoing*, or *outbound*, interfaces.

## Incoming vs. Outgoing Interfaces

Most of the interfaces we've been working with throughout the book have been incoming interfaces—that is, interfaces implemented by a COM object. Incoming interfaces are so named because the interface handles incoming method calls. For clients, acquiring a COM object's incoming interface is a matter of creating the COM object in the usual way (using a function like *CoCreateInstance*) and calling methods on the interface, as shown here:

```
ISomeInterface* pSomeInterface = NULL;
HRESULT hr;

hr = CoCreateInstance(CLSID_SomeObject,
    NULL,
    CLSCTX_ALL,
    IID_ISomeInterface,
    *pSomeInterface);
if(SUCCEEDED(hr)) {
    pSomeInterface->Function1();
    pSomeInterface->Function2();
    pSomeInterface->Release();
}
```

Incoming interfaces are the norm for COM objects, providing a way for clients to call in to COM objects. Figure 12-1 illustrates a COM object with incoming interfaces.

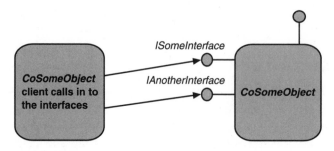

**Figure 12-1**
*A COM object with incoming interfaces*

The other kind of interface, an outgoing interface, is implemented by the client so that the COM object can call the client. When developing bidirectional communication between two objects, the client must implement an interface that's defined by the object. The trick to getting bidirectional communication set up is to get the *lollipop* (the interface implemented by the client) over to the object. Figure 12-2 illustrates an outgoing COM interface.

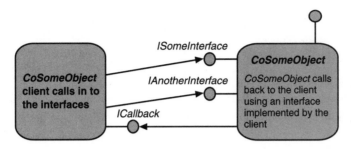

**Figure 12-2**
*An outgoing COM interface*

COM already specifies several standard incoming/outgoing interface pairs that define a connection mechanism. One of the best examples is an interface named *IAdviseSink*. *IAdviseSink* is used in conjunction with the *IDataObject* interface. The *IAdviseSink* and *IDataObject* pair of interfaces is useful for transferring presentations (and other things) between OLE Document objects and OLE Document clients. Here's how the two interfaces work together. Objects implement *IDataObject*. Once clients connect to the object and call *QueryInterface* for *IDataObject*, the client can plug its implementation of *IAdviseSink* in to the client by using *IDataObject::Advise* and begin receiving notifications whenever the data inside *IDataObject* changes. This happens whenever the object calls back to the client's implementations of *IAdviseSink::OnViewChange* or *IAdviseSink::OnDataChange*. The complementary *IAdviseSink* and *IDataObject* interfaces are shown here:

```
interface IAdviseSink : IUnknown
{
    HRESULT OnDataChange(FORMATETC *pFormatetc, STGMEDIUM *pStgmed);
    HRESULT OnViewChange(DWORD dwAspect, LONG lindex);
    HRESULT OnRename(IMoniker *pmk);
    HRESULT OnSave();
    HRESULT OnClose();
};
interface IDataObject : IUnknown
{
    HRESULT GetData(FORMATETC *pformatetcIn,
        STGMEDIUM *pmedium);
    HRESULT GetDataHere(FORMATETC *pformatetc,
        STGMEDIUM *pmedium);
    HRESULT QueryGetData(FORMATETC *pformatetc);
    HRESULT GetCanonicalFormatEtc(FORMATETC *pformatectIn,
        FORMATETC *pformatetcOut);
```

*(continued)*

```
HRESULT SetData(FORMATETC *pformatetc,
    STGMEDIUM *pmedium, BOOL fRelease);
HRESULT EnumFormatEtc(DWORD dwDirection,
    IEnumFORMATETC** ppenumFormatEtc);
HRESULT DAdvise(FORMATETC *pformatetc, DWORD advf,
    IAdviseSink *pAdvSink,
    DWORD *pdwConnection);
HRESULT DUnadvise(DWORD dwConnection);
HRESULT EnumDAdvise(IEnumSTATDATA **ppenumAdvise);
};
```

This is a very specific case of outgoing interfaces. The interfaces and the connection process are understood well by both the client and the object. But now imagine that you're a software designer and you want to create a generalized case of this connection strategy. Perhaps you're inventing a new kind of COM object and you'd like it to be able to call back to its client, but you also want to make the mechanism universal—that is, not specific to the interfaces involved. For example, imagine you want to establish a generic outgoing connection to an object—in much the same way *QueryInterface* lets clients ask for an object's outgoing interface. How would you do it?

Microsoft has taken a shot at solving this problem by defining connectable objects. Microsoft invented connectable objects to connect an ActiveX control to its client so that the control can report events back to its client. After all, ActiveX control events are simply a way for a control to call back to the client. Let's take a look at how connectable objects are used for establishing a connection between two COM objects.

## Connection Point Interfaces

Let's start by examining the COM interfaces involved in connections—*IConnectionPoint* and *IConnectionPointContainer*. The object (rather than the client) implements both these interfaces. These interfaces exist for the sole purpose of connecting an object to its client. Once the connection is made, they drop out of the picture.

Let's look at *IConnectionPoint* first. The following code shows the interface in the raw:

```
interface IConnectionPoint : IUnknown {
    HRESULT GetConnectionInterface(IID *pIID) = 0;
    HRESULT GetConnectionPointContainer(
        IConnectionPointContainer **ppCPC) = 0;
    HRESULT Advise(IUnknown *pUnk, DWORD *pdwCookie) = 0;
    HRESULT Unadvise(DWORD dwCookie) = 0;
    HRESULT EnumConnections(IEnumConnections **ppEnum) = 0;
};
```

You can probably guess the nature of this interface from the function names. Objects can implement this interface so that clients have a way to subscribe to events. Once a client acquires this interface, the client can ask to subscribe to data change notifications via the *Advise* function. Notice that the *Advise* function takes an *IUnknown* pointer, so the callback interface can be any COM interface at all. *IConnectionPoint* also contains the complementary *Unadvise* function. Clients use this function to terminate the connection between the client and the object. We'll see how the other functions are useful a little later in the chapter.

Clients can implement any callback interface and use *IConnectionPoint* to hand the interface over to the object. Once the object has the callback interface (passed via *Advise*'s first parameter), the object can easily call back to the client. This action begs the question of how the client can acquire a connection point in the first place. The answer is through the *IConnectionPointContainer* interface, shown here:

```
interface IConnectionPointContainer : IUnknown {
    HRESULT EnumConnectionPoints(
        IEnumConnectionPoints **ppEnum) = 0;
    HRESULT FindConnectionPoint(REFIID riid,
        IConnectionPoint **ppCP) = 0;
};
```

*IConnectionPointContainer* is an unfortunate name for this interface, especially given the history of ActiveX controls. The name *IConnectionPointContainer* might lead you to conclude that the control container (aka the client) implements this interface. However, it's the object that implements this interface. More descriptive names for this interface might have been *IConnectionPointHolder* or *IConnectionPointCollection* because it holds connection points. At any rate, *IConnectionPointContainer* is the name we have to live with.

As you can tell from the second function, *FindConnectionPoint, IConnection-PointContainer* is the interface a COM client uses to acquire a pointer to an *IConnectionPoint* interface (which the client can then use to establish a connection). Let's take a look at the whole process.

A COM client calls *CoCreateInstance* to create a COM object. Once the client has an initial interface, the client can ask the object if it supports any outgoing interfaces by calling *QueryInterface* for *IConnectionPointContainer*. If the object answers "yes" by handing back a valid pointer, the client knows it can attempt to establish a connection.

Once the client knows the object supports outgoing interfaces (in other words, is capable of calling back to the client), the client can ask for a specific outgoing interface by calling *IConnectionPointContainer::FindConnectionPoint* using the GUID that represents the desired interface. If the object implements that outgoing interface, the object hands back a pointer to that connection point. At that point, the client uses *IConnectionPoint::Advise* to plug in its implementation of the callback interface so that the object can call back to the client.

## Connection Points and IDL

IDL specifically supports defining interfaces as outgoing interfaces. Listing 12-1 shows some basic IDL containing an incoming and an outgoing interface.

```
import "oaidl.idl";
import "ocidl.idl";
    [
        object,
        uuid(04D6A3EE-A7E6-11D2-8039-84DD6A000000),
        helpstring("IIncoming Interface"),
    ]
    interface IIncoming : IUnknown
    {
        HRESULT Method1();
        HRESULT Method2();
    };


[
    uuid(04D6A3E2-A7E6-11D2-8039-84DD6A000000),
    version(1.0),
    helpstring("SomeServer 1.0 Type Library")
]
library SomeServerLib
{
    importlib("stdole32.tlb");
    importlib("stdole2.tlb");

    [
        uuid(04D6A3F0-A7E6-11D2-8039-84DD6A000000),
        helpstring("IEvents Interface")
    ]
    interface IEvents
    {
        HRESULT Event1([in]short x);
        HRESULT Event2([in]BSTR bstr);
    };
```

**Listing 12-1**
*IDL code describing an incoming and an outgoing interface*

```
    [
        uuid(04D6A3EF-A7E6-11D2-8039-84DD6A000000),
        helpstring("SomeObj Class")
    ]
    coclass SomeObj
    {
        [default] interface IIncoming;
        [default, source] dispinterface IEvents;
    };
};
```

When examining this code, you'll notice that the *SomeObj* class involves two interfaces: *IIncoming* and *IEvents*. *IIncoming* has the [default] interface attribute applied to it. This means that when a scripting language uses this coclass, the scripting language understands *IIncoming* as the object's default interface.

Notice also that the *IEvents* interface has the [source] attribute applied to it. The *source* keyword indicates that the *IEvents* interface is an outgoing interface (an interface implemented by the client and called by the object).

Listing 12-2 illustrates the code required to set up and tear down a connection using the interface described in the preceding IDL.

```
#include "SomeSvr_i.c" // Produced by MIDL
#include "SomeSvr.h" // Produced by MIDL

HRESULT ConnectToObject(IUnknown *pObject,
    IEvents *pEventSink,
    DWORD *pdwCookie) {
    IConnectionPointContainer *pcpc = 0;
    HRESULT hr;
    hr = pObject->QueryInterface(IID_IConnectionPointContainer,
        (void**)&pcpc);
    if(SUCCEEDED(hr)) {
        IConnectionPoint *pcp = 0;
        hr = pcpc->FindConnectionPoint(IID_IEvents,
            &pcp);
        if(SUCCEEDED(hr)) {
            hr = pcp->Advise(pEventSink,
                pdwCookie);
            pcp->Release( );
        }
```

**Listing 12-2**
*Using connection points*

*(continued)*

**Listing 12-2** *continued*

```
            pcpc->Release( );
        }
        return hr;
}

HRESULT DisconnectFromObject(IUnknown *pObject,
    DWORD dwCookie) {
    IConnectionPointContainer *pcpc = 0;
    HRESULT hr;
    hr = pObject->QueryInterface(IID_IConnectionPointContainer,
        (void**)&pcpc);
    if(SUCCEEDED(hr)) {
        IConnectionPoint *pcp = 0;
        hr = pcpc->FindConnectionPoint(IID_IEvents,
            &pcp);
        if(SUCCEEDED(hr)) {
            hr = pcp->Unadvise(pdwCookie);
            pcp->Release( );
        }
        pcpc->Release( );
    }
    return hr;
}

class CEventSink : public IEvents
{
public:
    STDMETHODIMP QueryInterface(REFIID riid,
        void** ppv)
    {
        if(riid == IID_IUnknown ||
            riid == IID_IEvents)
        {
            *ppv = static_cast<IEvents*>(this);
            ((IUnknown*)(*ppv))->AddRef();
            return S_OK;
        } else
        {
            return E_NOINTERFACE;
        }
    }
    STDMETHODIMP_(ULONG) AddRef()
```

```
    {
        return 2; // This is a global object.
    }
    STDMETHODIMP_(ULONG) Release()
    {
        return 1; // This is a global object.
    }
    STDMETHODIMP Event1(short x)
    {
        // Handle event 1.
        return S_OK;
    }
    STDMETHODIMP Event2(BSTR bstr)
    {
        // Handle event 2.
        return S_OK;
    }
};

main()
{
    IUnknown* pUnk;
    HRESULT hr;

    hr = CoCreateInstance(CLSID_SomeObject, NULL,
        CLSCTX_ALL, IID_IUnknown,
        (void**)pUnk);

    if(SUCCEEDED(hr))
    {
        CEvents events;
        IEvents* pEvents;
        DWORD dwCookie;

        events.QueryInterface(IID_IEvents, (void**)&pEvents);
        ConnectToObject(pUnk, pEvents, &dwCookie);
        // Do some stuff here that might generate events.
        DisconnectFromObject(pUnk, dwCookie);
    }
}
```

In addition to the normal connection and activation mechanism defined by the ActiveX protocol, COM defines another way to activate controls: through the *IQuickActivate* interface.

## IQuickActivate

ActiveX controls originally started life as OLE controls—COM objects that followed the full OLE Embedding protocol. In addition to the numerous round-trips required by the OLE Embedding protocol to activate the control, OLE controls also required round-trips to hook up the event sink. The result was an extraordinary number of unnecessary round-trips—especially if the control somehow ended up in a different apartment than the client inhabited. To handle this issue of requiring many round-trips to activate a control, the ActiveX specification detailed a new interface named *IQuickActivate,* which bundles all the parameters and handshaking that must go on between the client and the object to perform activation. Instead of taking a ton of round-trips to activate a control, a client activates a control by acquiring the *IQuickActivate* interface from the control, packaging all the parameters in QACONTAINER and QACONTROL structures, and calling *IQuickActivate::QuickActivate.* The following code shows the *IQuickActivate* interface and associated structures:

```
typedef struct   tagQACONTAINER
{
    ULONG cbSize;
    IOleClientSite *pClientSite;
    IAdviseSinkEx *pAdviseSink;
    IPropertyNotifySink *pPropertyNotifySink;
    IUnknown *pUnkEventSink;
    DWORD dwAmbientFlags;
    OLE_COLOR colorFore;
    OLE_COLOR colorBack;
    IFont *pFont;
    IOleUndoManager *pUndoMgr;
    DWORD dwAppearance;
    LONG lcid;
    HPALETTE hpal;
    IBindHost *pBindHost;
    IOleControlSite *pOleControlSite;
    IServiceProvider *pServiceProvider;
} QACONTAINER;

typedef struct   tagQACONTROL
{
    ULONG cbSize;
    DWORD dwMiscStatus;
    DWORD dwViewStatus;
    DWORD dwEventCookie;
    DWORD dwPropNotifyCookie;
    DWORD dwPointerActivationPolicy;
} QACONTROL;
```

```
interface IQuickActivate : public IUnknown
{
    HRESULT QuickActivate([in] QACONTAINER *pQaContainer,
        [out, in] QACONTROL *pQaControl);
    HRESULT SetContentExtent([in] LPSIZEL Sizel);
    HRESULT GetContentExtent([out] LPSIZEL pSizel;
};
```

Using this protocol, clients can quickly activate the objects and more efficiently set up an event sink and a property notify sink. Objects still need to implement connection points, even when clients activate them using *QuickActivate*.

# How ATL Implements Connections

Now that you have the idea behind connection points, let's look at how they work within ATL.

## Setting Up Outgoing Interfaces in ATL

To support the connection points functionality, the object needs to implement *IConnectionPointContainer* and *IConnectionPoint*. ATL's support for connections consists of some template classes and a set of macros. Let's examine how to set up connections using ATL.

Setting up the outgoing interfaces in an ATL-based object involves two steps:

1. Describing the callback interface the client needs to implement

2. Adding the connection support to the object

As with all other interfaces in COM, the callback interfaces for an ATL-based object are described in IDL. For example, imagine you're implementing an object named *CATLConnectionPointsObj* that has an outgoing interface. Normally, you'd add the object to your server by selecting New ATL Object from the Insert menu. The ATL Object Wizard dialog box pops up and asks you to name the object and to specify other aspects of the ATL object, such as the threading model. One of the options you can select is whether the object implements connections. The following code shows the C++ class the wizard creates (with the Support Connection Points option checked).

```
class ATL_NO_VTABLE CATLConnectionPointsObj :
    public CComObjectRootEx<CComSingleThreadModel>,
    public CComCoClass<CATLConnectionPointsObj,
        &CLSID_ATLConnectionPointsObj>,
    public IConnectionPointContainerImpl<CATLConnectionPointsObj>,
```

*(continued)*

```
    public IDispatchImpl<IATLConnectionPointsObj,
        &IID_IATLConnectionPointsObj,
        &LIBID_ATLCONNECTIONPOINTSSVRLib>
{
public:
    CATLConnectionPointsObj()
    {
    }

DECLARE_REGISTRY_RESOURCEID(IDR_ATLCONNECTIONPOINTSOBJ)

DECLARE_PROTECT_FINAL_CONSTRUCT()

BEGIN_COM_MAP(CATLConnectionPointsObj)
    COM_INTERFACE_ENTRY(IATLConnectionPointsObj)
    COM_INTERFACE_ENTRY(IDispatch)
    COM_INTERFACE_ENTRY(IConnectionPointContainer)
END_COM_MAP()
BEGIN_CONNECTION_POINT_MAP(CATLConnectionPointsObj)
END_CONNECTION_POINT_MAP()

// IATLConnectionPointsObj
public:
};
```

Callback interfaces are interfaces described by the object and implemented by the client. When using ATL, the starting place for defining the outgoing interface is within the IDL. Listing 12-3 shows an outgoing interface defined in the IDL.

```
import "oaidl.idl";
import "ocidl.idl";
    [
        object,
        uuid(F4416E5D-AB04-11D2-803A-B8B4F0000000),

        helpstring("IAConnectableObject Interface"),
        pointer_default(unique)
    ]
    interface IAConnectableObject : IUnknown
    {
        [helpstring("method Method1")] HRESULT Method1();
        [helpstring("method Method2")] HRESULT Method2();
    };
```

**Listing 12-3**
*IDL code describing an outgoing interface*

312

```
[
    uuid(F4416E51-AB04-11D2-803A-B8B4F0000000),
    version(1.0),
    helpstring("abcdefg 1.0 Type Library")
]
library ABCDEFGLib
{
    importlib("stdole32.tlb");
    importlib("stdole2.tlb");

    [
        uuid(F4416E5F-AB04-11D2-803A-B8B4F0000000),
        helpstring("_IAConnectableObjectEvents Interface")
    ]
    dispinterface _IAConnectableObjectEvents
    {
        properties:
        methods:
            [id(1)]void OnEvent1();
            [id(2)]void OnEvent2();
    };
    [
        uuid(F3336E5F-AB04-11D2-803A-B8B4F0000000),
        helpstring("_IAConnectableObjectEvents Interface")
    ]
    dispinterface _IAConnectableObjectEvents2
    {
        properties:
        methods:
            [id(1)]void OnEvent3();
            [id(2)]void OnEvent4();
    };


    [
        uuid(F4416E5E-AB04-11D2-803A-B8B4F0000000),
        helpstring("AConnectableObject Class")
    ]
    coclass AConnectableObject
    {
        [default] interface IAConnectableObject;
        [default, source] dispinterface
            _IAConnectableObjectEvents;
        [source] dispinterface _IAConnectableObjectEvents2;
    };
};
```

Notice that this IDL listing includes an incoming interface named *IAConnectableObject*. The IDL also has two outgoing interfaces, named *_IAConnectableObjectEvents* and *_IAConnectableObjectEvents2*.

When the project is compiled, the MIDL compiler produces a type library. The clients of this object use this information to know how to implement the callback interface. Notice in this example that the outgoing interface is a dispatch interface (an instance of *IDispatch*). The outgoing interface doesn't have to be a dispatch interface; however, if it is, your object can call back to a wider variety of clients.

The next step in developing the object is to come up with some way to call through the outgoing interface. The ATL wizards make it easy to add the individual connection points to your application. After compiling the project once to produce the type library, simply select the class to which you want to add connection points inside ClassView and click the right mouse button. Select Implement Connection Point from the context menu. Microsoft Visual Studio will read the type library for your project. Remember that the type library contains binary descriptions of the outgoing interfaces. Visual Studio displays a dialog box asking you to select the interfaces to which you want to add connection points. Simply select the check boxes for those interfaces and click OK. Visual Studio adds the connection points for each outgoing interface listed in the dialog box. Figure 12-3 shows the outgoing interfaces listed in the dialog box.

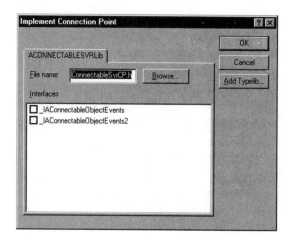

**Figure 12-3**
*Implementing connection points for a control's outgoing interface*

Visual Studio produces the following code for the incoming interface and the outgoing interface described in Listing 12-1 on page 306.

```
class ATL_NO_VTABLE CAConnectableObject :
    public CComObjectRootEx<CComSingleThreadModel>,
    public CComCoClass<CAConnectableObject,
        &CLSID_AConnectableObject>,
    public IConnectionPointContainerImpl<CAConnectableObject>,
    public IAConnectableObject,
    public CProxy_IAConnectableObjectEvents<CAConnectableObject>,
    public CProxy_IAConnectableObjectEvents2<CAConnectableObject>
{
public:
    CAConnectableObject()
    {
    }


DECLARE_REGISTRY_RESOURCEID(IDR_ACONNECTABLEOBJECT)

DECLARE_PROTECT_FINAL_CONSTRUCT()

BEGIN_COM_MAP(CAConnectableObject)
    COM_INTERFACE_ENTRY(IAConnectableObject)
    COM_INTERFACE_ENTRY(IConnectionPointContainer)
    COM_INTERFACE_ENTRY_IMPL(IConnectionPointContainer)
END_COM_MAP()
BEGIN_CONNECTION_POINT_MAP(CAConnectableObject)
    CONNECTION_POINT_ENTRY(DIID__IAConnectableObjectEvents)
    CONNECTION_POINT_ENTRY(DIID__IAConnectableObjectEvents2)
END_CONNECTION_POINT_MAP()


// IAConnectableObject
public:
    STDMETHOD(Method2)();
    STDMETHOD(Method1)();
};
```

What's happening in this code? Notice that the code includes implementations of *IAConnectableObject* and *IConnectionPointContainer* (look for *IAConnectableObject* and *IConnectionPointContainerImpl* in the inheritance list). Notice that *IAConnectableObject* and *IConnectionPointContainer* are also in the interface map. Finally, notice the two proxy classes ( *CProxy_IAConnectableObjectEvents* and *CProxy_IAConnectableObjectEvents2*) and the entries in the connection map for each connection point. These pieces of code represent ATL's implementation of connection points.

Using these tools from within Microsoft Visual C++ is fairly straightforward, and you can use them without understanding the underpinnings. However, you're always better off understanding how ATL implements connection points so that you can make important design decisions and have an easier time debugging the code. Let's take a look at what ATL is doing under the hood, starting with how *IConnectionPointContainer* is implemented.

## ATL and *IConnectionPointContainer*

Remember that the basic premise behind COM is separating interfaces from their implementations. As long as the client gets back the interface (function table) that it requested through *QueryInterface*, the client is happy. That interface might point to some C++-based code, some Visual Basic–based code, some Delphi-based code, or whatever. The client doesn't care what happens behind the interface (as long as it works, of course). When some client code uses *IConnectionPointContainer* and *IConnectionPoint* pointers connected to a COM object implemented using ATL, the client is talking to some C++-based source code written using templates. ATL implements *IConnectionPointContainer* through a template named *IConnectionPointContainerImpl*.

*IConnectionPointContainerImpl* is parameterized with one parameter—the class implementing *IConnectionPointContainer* (that's the ATL-based class you're in the middle of implementing). Remember that the purpose of *IConnectionPointContainer* is to provide a way for clients to ask whether an object supports current outgoing interfaces (each represented by a separate *IConnectionPoint* interface).

*IConnectionPointContainerImpl* maintains a collection of *IConnectionPoint* interfaces using the ATL helper class *CComEnum*. Before diving into *IConnectionPointContainerImpl*, we need to examine a mechanism called *connection maps*, which ATL uses to maintain a collection of connection points. ATL's connection maps are implemented through a set of macros including BEGIN_CONNECTION_POINT_MAP, CONNECTION_POINT_ENTRY, and END_CONNECTION_POINT_MAP. For example, if you want to set up a list of connection points in the *CConnectionObj* class, you'd sandwich the CONNECTION_POINT_ENTRY between the BEGIN_CONNECTION_POINT_MAP and the END_CONNECTION_POINT_MAP, like this:

```
BEGIN_CONNECTION_POINT_MAP(CAConnectableObject)
    CONNECTION_POINT_ENTRY(DIID__IAConnectableObjectEvents)
    CONNECTION_POINT_ENTRY(DIID__IAConnectableObjectEvents2)
END_CONNECTION_POINT_MAP()
```

As with most of the maps described by macros in ATL (and MFC for that matter), ATL's connection map macros define a table. This time, the table simply represents a collection of offsets described by a structure named _ATL-_CONNMAP_ENTRY:

```
struct _ATL_CONNMAP_ENTRY
{
    DWORD dwOffset;
};
```

BEGIN_CONNECTION_POINT_MAP defines a pointer to an array of _ATL_CONNMAP_ENTRY structures and a function for retrieving that pointer:

```
#define BEGIN_CONNECTION_POINT_MAP(x)\
    typedef x _atl_conn_classtype;\
    static const _ATL_CONNMAP_ENTRY* GetConnMap(int* pnEntries) {\
    static const _ATL_CONNMAP_ENTRY _entries[] = {
```

The _ATL_CONNMAP_ENTRY is simply an address that points to an *IConnectionPoint* interface.

The CONNECTION_POINT_ENTRY macro calculates the address of the pointer on the fly using a helper class named *_ICPLocator*, which performs a *QueryInterface*-style operation to find the pointer based on the GUID:

```
#define CONNECTION_POINT_ENTRY(iid){offsetofclass(ICPLocator<&iid>,
    _atl_conn_classtype)-\
    offsetofclass(IConnectionPointContainerImpl<_atl_conn_classtype>,
    _atl_conn_classtype)},
```

Finally, END_CONNECTION_POINT_MAP terminates the array of connection points.

```
#define END_CONNECTION_POINT_MAP() {(DWORD)-1} }; \
    if(pnEntries)*pnEntries =
        sizeof(_entries)/sizeof(_ATL_CONNMAP_ENTRY) - 1;\
        return _entries;}
```

ATL's *IConnectionPointContainerImpl* implements *EnumConnectionPoints* by simply filling the connection point collection and passing back the *IEnumConnectionPoint* interface. *IConnectionPointContainerImpl* uses the connection map's *GetConnPoint* to retrieve the list of connection points and fill the collection of connection points.

*IConnectionPointContainerImpl* implements *FindConnectionPoint* by using the connection map's *GetConnPoint* to retrieve the list of connection points. *FindConnectionPoint* just rips through the list of connection points to find the requested connection point. When *FindConnectionPoint* locates the connection, the function passes back the connection point interface after calling *AddRef* through it. *IConnectionPointContainer* is fairly straightforward. All that's missing now is to see how ATL implements *IConnectionPoint*.

## ATL and *IConnectionPoint*

The last item to examine within ATL's connection point machinery is the proxy classes used to call back to the client. The proxy is where ATL-based COM classes implement *IConnectionPoint*. Listing 12-4 shows the code for the *IAConnectableObjectEvents* proxy.

```
template <class T>
class CProxy_IAConnectableObjectEvents :
    public IConnectionPointImpl<T,
        &DIID__IAConnectableObjectEvents,
        CComDynamicUnkArray>
{
// Warning: this class may be re-created by the wizard.
public:
    VOID Fire_OnEvent1()
    {
        T* pT = static_cast<T*>(this);
        int nConnectionIndex;
        int nConnections = m_vec.GetSize();

        for (nConnectionIndex = 0;
            nConnectionIndex < nConnections;
            nConnectionIndex++)
        {
            pT->Lock();
            CComPtr<IUnknown> sp = m_vec.GetAt(nConnectionIndex);
            pT->Unlock();
            IDispatch* pDispatch =
                reinterpret_cast<IDispatch*>(sp.p);
            if(pDispatch != NULL)
            {
                DISPPARAMS disp = { NULL, NULL, 0, 0 };
                pDispatch->Invoke(0x1, IID_NULL,
                    LOCALE_USER_DEFAULT,
                    DISPATCH_METHOD, &disp,
                    NULL, NULL, NULL);
            }
        }
    }
}
```

**Listing 12-4**
*The connection proxy generated by the ATL Wizard*

```
VOID Fire_OnEvent2()
{
    T* pT = static_cast<T*>(this);
    int nConnectionIndex;
    int nConnections = m_vec.GetSize();

    for (nConnectionIndex = 0;
        nConnectionIndex < nConnections;
        nConnectionIndex++)
    {
        pT->Lock();
        CComPtr<IUnknown> sp = m_vec.GetAt(nConnectionIndex);
        pT->Unlock();
        IDispatch* pDispatch =
            reinterpret_cast<IDispatch*>(sp.p);
        if(pDispatch != NULL)
        {
            DISPPARAMS disp = { NULL, NULL, 0, 0 };
            pDispatch->Invoke(0x2, IID_NULL,
                LOCALE_USER_DEFAULT,
                DISPATCH_METHOD, &disp,
                NULL, NULL, NULL);
        }
    }
}
};
```

The ATL Wizard took a look at the object's type library to learn about the outgoing interfaces. *IAConnectableObjectEvents* is the first outgoing interface listed in the type library. *IAConnectableObjectEvents* is a dispatch interface with two functions: *Event1* and *Event2*.

ATL implements *IConnectionPoint* through a templatized class named *IConnectionPointImpl*. Look back at the ATL proxy in Listing 12-2 and notice that it derives from *IConnectionPointImpl*. *IConnectionPointImpl*'s template parameters include the class implementing *IConnectionPoint* (the proxy class), the GUID of the connection point, and a class that manages the connections.

*IConnectionPointImpl* implements the individual connection points of an ATL-based COM class. *IConnectionPointImpl* doesn't have much state—it maintains the GUID identifying the connection point and a collection of *IUnknown* interfaces that the object uses to call back to the client. That's really all the state required for implementing a connection point. The rest of *IConnectionPointImpl* is implemented as a set of function templates. The two most important functions of *IConnectionPointImpl* are *Advise* and *Unadvise*. When a client wants to subscribe to callbacks, the client calls *IConnectionPoint::Advise*, passing in an unknown pointer. *IConnectionPointImpl* implements *Advise* by inserting the unknown pointer into the collection of callback interfaces and returning the vector position in the *pdwCookie* parameter.

Clients use *IConnectionPoint::Unadvise* to stop receiving callbacks. *IConnectionPointImpl* implements *Unadvise* by looking up the unknown pointer using the *dwCookie* parameter, which happens to be the index into the collection of unknown pointers. If *Unadvise* finds the unknown pointer in the vector, *Unadvise* removes the pointer from the advise list and then releases the pointer.

The rest of the *IConnectionPoint* functions (*GetConnectionInterface, GetConnectionPointContainer,* and *EnumConnections*) aren't used as often. Even so, *IConnectionPoint* implements them just to make sure the interface implementation contract is complete. *IConnectionPointImpl* implements *GetConnectionInterface* by simply returning the GUID representing the connection point. *IConnectionPointImpl* maintains a pointer to the connection point container class (which was passed in as a template parameter). *IConnectionPointImpl* implements *GetConnectionPointContainer* by casting that pointer as *IConnectionPointContainerImpl* to return the *IConnectionPointContainer* vtable. (This, of course, assumes the *IConnectionPointContainer* class is derived from *IConnectionPointContainerImpl*.) Finally, *IConnectionPointImpl* implements *EnumConnections* by filling a *CComDynamicUnkArray*-based class with the unknown pointers known by the object and passing back the *IEnumConnections* interface implemented by the *CComEnum*-based class.

Notice that the proxy classes simply generate calls back to the client by wrapping an *IDispatch*-based interface that the client provides. The proxy sets up all the *IDispatch* cruft so that you don't need to do it by hand. When it comes time to fire either *OnEvent1* or *OnEvent2*, you simply need to call the *Fire_OnEvent1* and *Fire_OnEvent2* members of the *CProxy_IAConnectableObjectEvents* class as shown here:

```
class ATL_NO_VTABLE CAConnectableObject :
    public CComObjectRootEx<CComSingleThreadModel>,
    public IDispatchImpl<IAConnectableObject,
        &IID_IAConnectableObject,
        &LIBID_ACONNECTABLESVRLib>,
    public CComControl<CAConnectableObject>,
    public CComCoClass<CAConnectableObject,
        &CLSID_AConnectableObject>,
    public CProxy_IAConnectableObjectEvents< CAConnectableObject >,
    public CProxy_IAConnectableObjectEvents2< CAConnectableObject >
```

```
{
public:
    CAConnectableObject()
    {
    }

DECLARE_REGISTRY_RESOURCEID(IDR_ACONNECTABLEOBJECT)

DECLARE_PROTECT_FINAL_CONSTRUCT()

BEGIN_COM_MAP(CAConnectableObject)
    COM_INTERFACE_ENTRY(IAConnectableObject)
    COM_INTERFACE_ENTRY(IDispatch)
    COM_INTERFACE_ENTRY_IMPL(IConnectionPointContainer)
END_COM_MAP()

BEGIN_CONNECTION_POINT_MAP(CAConnectableObject)
    CONNECTION_POINT_ENTRY(IID_IPropertyNotifySink)
    CONNECTION_POINT_ENTRY(DIID__IAConnectableObjectEvents)
    CONNECTION_POINT_ENTRY(DIID__IAConnectableObjectEvents2)
END_CONNECTION_POINT_MAP()

// IAConnectableObject
public:

    STDMETHOD(Method2)();
    STDMETHOD(Method1)();

    Void TestEvents()
    {
        Fire_OnEvent1();
        Fire_OnEvent2();
    }
};
```

# Client-Side Event Sink

We need to check out one final feature of ATL before closing the book on connection points: setting up an event sink on the client side. ATL implements an event sink that lets you create an implementation of *IDispatch* for receiving events on the client side.

As an example, the TestEventSink application included on the companion CD includes an event sink that watches the events coming from the ATL message traffic control example in Chapter 10. Figure 12-4 shows the dialog box.

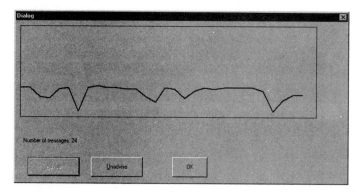

**Figure 12-4**
*Dialog box with event sink*

The class that implements the event sink is named *IDispEventImpl*. To use the ATL-supplied event sink, derive a class from *IDispEventImpl*, instantiate the class, and connect the class to the event source. You can mix the *IDispEventImpl* class into an ATL windowing class (by using multiple inheritance) or you can create the event sink as a stand-alone class. Listing 12-5 illustrates how to use the event sink class to add an event sink to a dialog box. In Listing 12-5, the event sink exists as a nested class within an ATL-based dialog class.

```
class CSinkTestDlg :
    public CAxDialogImpl<CSinkTestDlg>
{
    struct CAtlMsgTrafficEventSink :
        public IDispEventImpl<1,
            CAtlMsgTrafficEventSink,
            &DIID__IATLMsgTrafficCtlEvents,
            &LIBID_ATLMSGTRAFFICLib, 1, 0>
    {
        CSinkTestDlg* m_pSinkTestDlg;

        CAtlMsgTrafficEventSink(CSinkTestDlg* pSinkTestDlg = NULL)
        {
            m_pSinkTestDlg = pSinkTestDlg;
        };

        void __stdcall OnExceededThreshold(long NumMessages,
            long CurrentThreshold)
```

**Listing 12-5**
*Event sink in an ATL dialog class*

```
        {
            MessageBeep(0);
        }


    void __stdcall OnNewInterval(long NumMessages)
    {
        if(m_pSinkTestDlg)
        {
            TCHAR sz[128];

            wsprintf(sz,
                "Number of messages: %ld",
                NumMessages);
            ::SetWindowText(
                ::GetDlgItem(m_pSinkTestDlg->m_hWnd,
                IDC_MSGCOUNT),
                sz);
        }
    }

    BEGIN_SINK_MAP(CAtlMsgTrafficEventSink)
        SINK_ENTRY_EX(1,
            DIID__IATLMsgTrafficCtlEvents,
            1, OnExceededThreshold)
        SINK_ENTRY_EX(1,
            DIID__IATLMsgTrafficCtlEvents,
            2, OnNewInterval)
    END_SINK_MAP()
}; // End of nested class

CAtlMsgTrafficEventSink* m_pAtlMsgTrafficEventSink;

IUnknown* m_pControlUnk;
bool m_bIsSinked;

CAxWindow m_ATLMsgTrafficSite;
    ⋮
};
```

Notice that the sink class has methods for responding to the events the ATL message traffic control throws out. Unfortunately, no wizard support is available yet for reading a component's type information and manufacturing the callback interfaces. We had to define and implement *OnExceededThreshold* and *OnNewInterval* by hand. The event sink map correlates the callback functions with their DISPIDs (1 and 2, respectively). Also notice that the *IDispEventImpl* template takes the name of the callback interface (DIID__IATLMsgTraffic-CtlEvents) and the name of the type library defining the callback interface (LIBID_ATLMSGTRAFFICLib). The event sink uses this information to load the control's type information. The sink class also includes a back pointer to the dialog (because the sink class updates the dialog box every time there's a new interval). Then the dialog class includes a pointer to the control's *IUnknown* pointer, a pointer to the sink, an ATL ActiveX window, and information about whether the dialog box is connected to the object.

The dialog box connects itself to the control during the WM_INITDIALOG handler. The dialog box first creates a *CAxWindow* to host the control and then acquires the control's *IUnknown* pointer. The dialog box also creates an instance of the sink. The dialog box holds on to the event sink and to the control's *IUnknown* pointer—it needs these to connect to the control, as you'll see in a moment. Finally, notice that the dialog box starts the control's message-monitoring graph. Listing 12-6 shows how to create the control and connect the event sink to it.

```
LRESULT CSinkTestDlg::OnInitDialog(UINT uMsg,
    WPARAM wParam,
    LPARAM lParam,
    BOOL& bHandled)
{
    ::SetWindowText(GetDlgItem(IDC_MSGCOUNT),
        "Not sinked");

    ::EnableWindow(GetDlgItem(IDC_ADVISE), FALSE);
    ::EnableWindow(GetDlgItem(IDC_UNADVISE), FALSE);

    RECT rect;
    rect.top = 10;
    rect.left = 10;
    rect.right = 650;
    rect.bottom = 200;

    HRESULT hr;
    m_ATLMsgTrafficSite.Create(m_hWnd, rect,
        _TEXT("{C30CCA3E-A482-11D2-8038-6425D1000000}"),
        WS_CHILD | WS_VISIBLE);
```

**Listing 12-6**
*Creating the control and connecting the sink to the control*

```
        IATLMsgTrafficCtl* pATLMsgTrafficCtl = 0;

        hr = m_ATLMsgTrafficSite.QueryControl(IID_IATLMsgTrafficCtl,
            (void**)&pATLMsgTrafficCtl);
        if(SUCCEEDED(hr))
        {
            hr = pATLMsgTrafficCtl->StartGraph();

            pATLMsgTrafficCtl->QueryInterface(IID_IUnknown,
                (void**)&m_pControlUnk);
            m_pAtlMsgTrafficEventSink =
                new CAtlMsgTrafficEventSink(this);

            if(m_pAtlMsgTrafficEventSink)
            {
                ::EnableWindow(GetDlgItem(IDC_ADVISE), TRUE);
            }
            pATLMsgTrafficCtl->Release();
        }
        return 1;  // Let the system set the focus.

    }
```

The only thing left to do is respond to the Advise and Unadvise buttons. The *OnClickedAdvise* function is called whenever the user presses the Advise button. The event sink class inherits a function named *DispEventAdvise*, which handles all the connection points for you (thank goodness!). Conversely, the *OnClickedUnadvise* function (called when the user presses the Unadvise button) disconnects the sink from the dialog box, at which point the dialog box stops receiving events. The following code shows how to connect and disconnect the dialog box and the advise sink:

```
LRESULT CSinkTestDlg::OnClickedAdvise(WORD wNotifyCode,
    WORD wID,
    HWND hWndCtl,
    BOOL& bHandled)
{
    HRESULT hr;

    if(m_pAtlMsgTrafficEventSink) {
        hr = m_pAtlMsgTrafficEventSink-
>DispEventAdvise(m_pControlUnk);

        if(SUCCEEDED(hr))
```

*(continued)*

```
        {
            m_bIsSinked = TRUE;
            ::EnableWindow(GetDlgItem(IDC_ADVISE), FALSE);
            ::EnableWindow(GetDlgItem(IDC_UNADVISE), TRUE);
        }
    }
    return 0;
}

LRESULT CSinkTestDlg::OnClickedUnadvise(WORD wNotifyCode,
    WORD wID,
    HWND hWndCtl,
    BOOL& bHandled)
{
    HRESULT hr;
    Hr = m_pAtlMsgTrafficEventSink->DispEventUnadvise(
        m_pControlUnk);

    if(SUCCEEDED(hr))
    {
        m_bIsSinked = FALSE;
        ::EnableWindow(GetDlgItem(IDC_ADVISE), TRUE);
        ::EnableWindow(GetDlgItem(IDC_UNADVISE), FALSE);

        ::SetWindowText(GetDlgItem(IDC_MSGCOUNT),
            "Not sinked");
    }
    return 0;
}
```

# Conclusion

While developers have been able to create ActiveX controls using MFC for some time now, using MFC imposes certain design decisions, and your control has to link to the MFC DLL. ATL is a lightweight framework for implementing COM classes. In addition to providing all the machinery for writing basic COM classes, ATL includes the interfaces necessary to implement ActiveX controls. Part of that machinery includes describing interfaces that the client is willing to implement so that the ActiveX control can call back to the client. ATL fully supports this connection mechanism through its *IConnectionPointContainerImpl* and *IConnectionPointImpl* classes.

In Chapter 13, we'll look at how ActiveX controls work in Visual Basic and Visual C++.

## CHAPTER THIRTEEN

# Using ActiveX Controls in Different Development Environments

So far we've seen all the workings of Microsoft ActiveX controls from the control side. In this chapter, we'll look at developing applications using ActiveX controls, especially within varied development environments. We'll take the message traffic control that we developed in Chapter 10 and see how to use it with both Microsoft Visual Basic and Microsoft Visual C++.

## Integrating with Visual Basic

Wait! Don't stop reading because you're a C++ developer! Visual Basic is a powerful tool for developing applications, particularly in the user interface (UI) tier. Visual Basic is one of the most common programming environments in which ActiveX controls appear. In fact, you'll find many more Visual Basic developers than C++ developers—and they all have checkbooks. So it makes sense to learn how they perceive the world and develop software, especially if you want them to use your controls. Let's take a look at how ActiveX controls intermingle with Visual Basic.

### The Nature of Visual Basic

Many C++ developers find that Visual Basic is a handy front-end tool. This viewpoint is certainly justifiable. If you're used to developing Microsoft Windows applications using C++, you'll probably find developing Visual Basic applications much simpler, mainly because Visual Basic takes care of most underlying details for you. When you develop in Visual Basic, you can say goodbye to complex message handlers, messy memory allocation routines, and so forth. However, you do lose some of the flexibility you get with C++.

When creating a new Visual Basic project, you have the choice of creating several types of applications or components, including regular EXEs and DLLs, ActiveX EXEs and DLLs, ActiveX controls, Visual Basic add-ins, ActiveX Document applications, as well as some others. The Visual Basic New Project Wizard will pump out all the boilerplate code, which varies depending on the type of application or component you ask it to generate.

When developing applications using Visual Basic, you might find yourself spending much of your time editing a *form*. A form is basically a window containing UI components. Developing the application involves placing various UI components on the form and writing handlers for the events generated by the controls. Perhaps this definition is a bit oversimplified, but hey—we're C++ programmers. Of course, this sort of development is similar to normal Windows development, except that Visual Basic hides all the grunge.

Because you're familiar with managing dialog boxes using the resource editor in Visual C++, you already know how to work with a Visual Basic form; arranging controls on a Visual Basic form is like working with the Visual C++ resource manager. You get a blank form and Visual Basic's toolbox, which provides all the standard controls (list boxes, group boxes, combo boxes, and so on). In addition to the standard controls, you can use ActiveX controls in your project.

## Including ActiveX Controls in Your Project

To add an ActiveX control to your project, select Components from the Project menu. Visual Basic then finds all the ActiveX controls that have registered themselves in the Registry. Simply choose the ones you want to use in your project, and mark their check boxes. Figure 13-1 shows the Visual Basic Components dialog box for adding controls to your project.

After you select a control, Visual Basic places an icon representing it in the toolbox. Figure 13-2 shows a new control in the toolbox. Once this control is referenced in the project, Visual Basic knows the control's properties and methods (from the control's type information)—and you're free to use it.

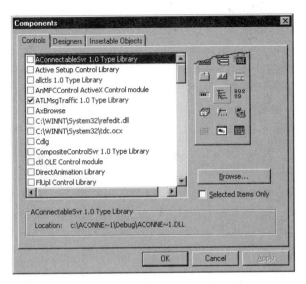

**Figure 13-1**
*The Visual Basic Components dialog box*

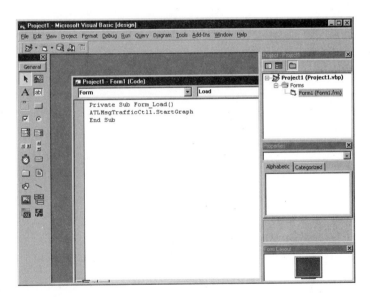

**Figure 13-2**
*A new control in the Visual Basic toolbox*

## Using the Control

The easiest way to use a control in Visual Basic is to select it from the toolbox and drag it onto the form. For example, if you want to use the ATL message traffic control from Chapter 10, simply insert the control in the project. When the control appears in the toolbox, drag it onto the form as you would any other control. Visual Basic renders the control on the form and creates an instance of the control; it's just like using regular controls.

If, for example, you drag the *ATLMsgTraffic* control onto a form, Visual Basic draws the form as shown in Figure 13-3 and creates an instance of the control named *ATLMsgTrafficCtl1*. (You can change the name of this control by editing its properties in the Properties window.)

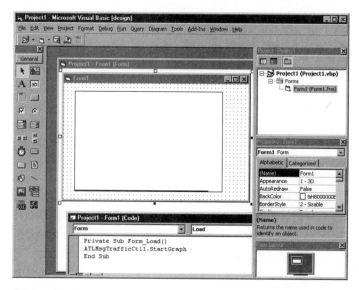

**Figure 13-3**
*The* ATLMsgTraffic *control as it appears in a Visual Basic form*

## Visual Basic and ActiveX Control Methods

After you've placed the control on the form, you can program the control by invoking various methods on it. In Visual Basic, methods are dereferenced using a period. For example, if you want to start the message traffic graph as soon as the Visual Basic form loads, you can do so by invoking the *StartGraph* method when the form loads. Here's the snippet of Visual Basic code showing how to start the graph:

```
Private Sub Form_Load()
ATLMsgTrafficCtl1.StartGraph
End Sub
```

## Visual Basic and Control Properties

Once the control is on the form, you can manipulate the control programmatically. Remember that the control is a COM object with methods and properties. When you made a reference to the object in your Visual Basic project, Visual Basic read the control's type information to determine its properties and methods.

Just as you can adjust the properties of the regular controls on your form, you can adjust the properties of an ActiveX control on the form. The Properties window lists both the stock properties such as foreground and background color and the properties you defined as custom properties.

If you put a breakpoint in the control's loading and saving code while Visual Basic is hosting it, you'll see that Visual Basic uses the *IPersistStreamInit* interface to manage property persistence by default. (Put a breakpoint in your control's property map to see this happen.) Visual Basic takes these properties and saves them in a file named *formname*.frx. For example, if you put the control in a form named MainForm, Visual Basic stores the properties in a file named MainForm.frx.

If your control doesn't implement *IPersistStreamInit*, Visual Basic tries to use the *IPersistPropertyBag* interface to store the properties in the form itself, as shown in this Visual Basic code:

```
Begin ATLMSGTRAFFICLibCtl.ATLMsgTrafficCtl ATLMsgTrafficCtl1
    Height          =   3135
    Left            =   360
    TabIndex        =   0
    Top             =   240
    Width           =   4815
    BackColor       =   -2147483648
    GraphLineColor  =   -2147483642
    Threshold       =   217
    Interval        =   1117
    _cx             =   8493
    _cy             =   5530
End
```

In addition to managing the properties through the Properties window at design time, you can also manipulate the properties programmatically at run time. For example, if you want to set the timing interval for the *ATLMsgTraffic* control programmatically, you can use the following code snippet. This code assumes that the form contains a button named *SetInterval* and an edit control named *Interval*. It takes the value of the data that the user types into the edit box and changes the control's interval property accordingly.

```
Private Sub SetInterval_Click()
    ATLMsgTrafficCtl1.Interval = Val(Interval.Text)
End Sub
```

## Extended Controls

As you've already seen, an ActiveX control is just a COM class that implements a number of interfaces. ActiveX controls use the entire OLE Embedding protocol. It's fairly complex—the container and the control exchange a ton of interfaces, such as *IOleObject*, *IOleControl*, *IDataObject*, and *IOleControlSite*. When a container creates a control, the only information the container has is the properties and methods supported by the control.

To provide a means of manipulating a control with properties and methods that are specific to the container, some containers implement *extended controls*, wrappers to enhance the controls living within that container. For example, many containers would benefit from storing information about the control, such as the size and position of the control on a form; and though these properties aren't normally part of a control, an extended control can store this information. That way, properties such as size and position appear as native properties to the control itself.

By no means is it necessary for the container to implement extended controls; they just offer a convenient way for containers to provide standard functionality (such as size and position properties) on behalf of the control. You can tell whether a container implements an extended control by asking the container through the *IOleControlSite::GetExtendedControl* interface. If the container doesn't implement an extended control, *IOleControlSite::GetExtendedControl* will return the distinguishing HRESULT E_NOTIMPL. Otherwise, *GetExtendedControl* will return the *IDispatch* interface for the extended control managed by the site. Another control can then access any properties of the extended control itself, if necessary.

Visual Basic implements extended controls. The following code shows how the *ATLMsgTraffic* control retrieves this information:

```
STDMETHODIMP CATLMsgTrafficCtl::HasExtendedControl()
{
    HRESULT hr = S_FALSE;
    IOleControlSite* pOleControlSite = 0;

    // Call this only after the control
    //   is fully embedded and active.
    m_spClientSite->QueryInterface(IID_IOleControlSite,
        (void**)&pOleControlSite);
    if(pOleControlSite)
    {
        IDispatch* pDispatch = 0;

        pOleControlSite->GetExtendedControl(&pDispatch);
```

```
        if(pDispatch)
        {
            hr = S_OK;
            OutputDebugString("Found an extended control\n");
            pDispatch->Release();
        }
        pOleControlSite->Release();
    }
    return hr;
}
```

## Visual Basic and Events

The last Visual Basic topic we need to cover is how to hook up event handlers for the controls. Remember that the *ATLMsgTraffic* control defines a default event set that fires two events: *ExceededThreshold* and *NewInterval*. When Visual Basic read the type information about the control, it also retrieved all the information necessary for implementing the event interface. When you select the *ATLMsgTrafficCtl1* object on the form (using the combo box in the upper left-hand corner of the form editor), the combo box in the right-hand corner lists the events generated by the control. Each time you select an event from the combo box in the right-hand corner of the form editor, Visual Basic inserts a stub for the event handler. Visual Basic hooks up to the control using connection points. (See Chapter 12 for more information about connection points.) Of course, you never actually see this process. The following code shows a Visual Basic application responding to events generated by the *ATLMsgTraffic* control by placing strings in a list box named *NormalEvents*.

```
Private Sub ATLMsgTrafficCtl1_ExceededThreshold( _
    ByVal NumMessages As Long, ByVal CurrentThreshold As Long)
    Dim eventStr As String

    eventStr = "Exceeded Threshold: " + Str(CurrentThreshold)
    NormalEvents.AddItem eventStr
End Sub

Private Sub ATLMsgTrafficCtl1_NewInterval( _
    ByVal NumMessages As Long)
    Dim eventStr As String

    eventStr = "New Interval" + Str(NumMessages)
    NormalEvents.AddItem eventStr
End Sub
```

# Integrating with Visual C++

Another home in which ActiveX controls find themselves is a Visual C++ dialog resource. Now that we've seen how ActiveX controls and Visual Basic work together, let's see how to use ActiveX controls in Visual C++.

## Using Component Gallery

The easiest way to add a control to your project is to use Component Gallery. Select Project–Add To Project–Components And Controls from the Visual C++ menu. This opens the Components And Controls Gallery dialog box, which asks if you want to insert standard Visual C++ components or registered ActiveX controls. When you select registered ActiveX controls, Visual C++ searches the Registry for all relevant controls, just as Visual Basic does. When you select a control from the list, Visual C++ uses the control's type library to build a C++ wrapper class around the control. The wrapper class handles all the details of activating the control, including *CoCreateInstance*, and of exchanging all the control and container interfaces. Visual C++ also takes the bitmap representing the control and places it in the resource editor control palette along with the other basic controls. (This, too, is similar to how Visual Basic works.)

Just as Visual Basic allows you to drag a control from the control palette to the form, Visual C++ lets you take a control from the palette and drag it onto a dialog box in your application. When you place the control on a dialog box, the control renders itself using *IViewObject::Draw* so that your dialog template contains a snapshot of how the control normally looks.

You can then use ClassWizard to add a data member to a dialog box that represents the control. Visual C++ makes this easy—it's just like connecting a member variable to a normal Windows control.

## Visual C++ and Methods

When Visual C++ reads the control's type library, Visual C++ retrieves all the information needed to write a wrapper class around your control. The following code shows the wrapper that Component Gallery produces for the *ATLMsg-Traffic* control:

```
class CATLMsgTrafficCtl : public CWnd
{
protected:
    DECLARE_DYNCREATE(CATLMsgTrafficCtl)
public:
```

```
    CLSID const& GetClsid()
    {
        static CLSID const clsid
            = { 0xc30cca3e, 0xa482, 0x11d2, { 0x80, 0x38,
                0x64, 0x25, 0xd1, 0x0, 0x0, 0x0 } };
        return clsid;
    }
    virtual BOOL Create(LPCTSTR lpszClassName,
        LPCTSTR lpszWindowName, DWORD dwStyle,
        const RECT& rect,
        CWnd* pParentWnd, UINT nID,
        CCreateContext* pContext = NULL)
    { return CreateControl(GetClsid(),
        lpszWindowName, dwStyle, rect,
        pParentWnd, nID); }

    BOOL Create(LPCTSTR lpszWindowName, DWORD dwStyle,
        const RECT& rect, CWnd* pParentWnd, UINT nID,
        CFile* pPersist = NULL, BOOL bStorage = FALSE,
        BSTR bstrLicKey = NULL)
    { return CreateControl(GetClsid(),
        lpszWindowName,
        dwStyle, rect,
        pParentWnd, nID,
        pPersist, bStorage, bstrLicKey); }

// Attributes
public:

// Operations
public:
    void SetBackColor(unsigned long newValue);
    unsigned long GetBackColor();
    void StartGraph();
    void StopGraph();
    long GetInterval();
    void SetInterval(long nNewValue);
    unsigned long GetGraphLineColor();
    void SetGraphLineColor(unsigned long newValue);
    long GetThreshold();
    void SetThreshold(long nNewValue);
    void Advise(LPUNKNOWN pATLMsgTrafficCtlEventsCustom,
        long* pCookie);
    void Unadvise(long lCookie);
};
```

You should keep the following points about this class in mind:

- It's based on *CWnd*; in other words, it's an MFC class. In fact, Component Gallery supports only adding controls to a project that uses the ClassWizard.

- A few creation functions will wrap *CoCreateInstance* for you.

- Each of the control's methods and properties are wrapped by normal C++-style functions.

In this example, the *ATLMsgTraffic* control lives inside a dialog box. The control is part of the dialog resource shown in the preceding code. When the dialog box appears, MFC creates all the controls listed in the dialog template and calls *CoCreateInstance* on the GUID listed in the resource:

```
IDD_ABOUTBOX DIALOG DISCARDABLE  0, 0, 255, 197
STYLE DS_MODALFRAME | WS_POPUP | WS_CAPTION | WS_SYSMENU
CAPTION "About useactivexcontrols"
FONT 8, "MS Sans Serif"
BEGIN
    ICON            IDR_MAINFRAME,IDC_STATIC,11,17,21,20
    LTEXT           "useactivexcontrols Version 1.0",
                    IDC_STATIC,40,10,119,8,
                    SS_NOPREFIX
    LTEXT           "Copyright (C) 1999",IDC_STATIC,40,25,119,8
    DEFPUSHBUTTON   "OK",IDOK,198,7,50,14,WS_GROUP
    CONTROL         "",IDC_ATLMSGTRAFFICCTL1,
                    "{C30CCA3E-A482-11D2-8038-6425D1000000}",
                    WS_TABSTOP,7,55,
                    214,135
END
```

Visual C++ then sizes and positions the control using the coordinates listed in the dialog template.

Once the control is loaded and in place, you can start calling methods on the object. For example, if you want the graph to start as soon as the dialog box appears, you might add a call to the control's *StartGraph* function as part of the WM_INITDIALOG processing, as shown in the following code:

```
BOOL CAboutDlg::OnInitDialog()
{
    CDialog::OnInitDialog();
    m_atlctl.StartGraph();
    return TRUE;
}
```

## Visual C++ and Properties

Visual C++ manages a control's properties a bit differently than Visual Basic does. Of course, you can manipulate the control's properties through the C++ wrapper class. (Notice the functions *GetInterval* and *SetInterval* in the C++ wrapper class.) You can also configure the control's properties at design time. When working with the control in a dialog box, highlight the control and activate its property pages by right-clicking and selecting Properties from the context menu or by pressing Alt-Enter. Microsoft Visual Studio retrieves the control's property pages (via the *ISpecifyPropertyPages* interface implemented by the control). Visual Studio calls *CoCreateInstance* on each GUID listed by the control and places each property page inside a dialog box frame, as shown in Figure 13-4.

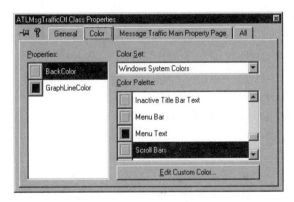

**Figure 13-4**
*The control's property pages in Visual Studio*

As you change the control's properties (such as graph line color or background color), Visual Studio saves these properties in the dialog template. If you look at the resource script, you can see where the properties are stored. The following code from the dialog resource shows how the properties are stored:

```
// From the resource script
IDD_ABOUTBOX DLGINIT
BEGIN
    IDC_ATLMSGTRAFFICCTL1, 0x376, 40, 0,
        0x0000, 0x0000, 0x0300, 0x0000, 0x0013, 0x0000, 0x8000,
        0x0013, 0x0017, 0x8000, 0x0003, 0x0064, 0x0000, 0x0003,
        0x01c9, 0x0000, 0x212d, 0x0000, 0x16a2, 0x0000, 0
END
```

Visual Studio relies on the control implementing *IPersistStreamInit* to handle property persistence. To see this, put a breakpoint on the property map. You'll see that Microsoft Developer Studio uses *IPersistStreamInit* every time you modify the control's properties through the property pages. Unlike Visual Basic, which falls back on *IPersistPropertyBag* if *IPersistStream* is unavailable, Visual Studio can't create your object if your control doesn't expose *IPersistStreamInit*.

## MFC and Ambient Properties

Now let's examine how MFC handles ambient properties—those properties managed by the container but visible to the control. For example, if you want to make the background of your control match the background of the host application, you'd ask the host application what its background is and paint the control with that background.

When a control is running within an MFC-based application, MFC holds on to several ambient properties. As an ActiveX control host, MFC supports autoclipping, message reflection, and mnemonics, so MFC returns TRUE for the following ambient property dispatch IDs (DISPIDs):

- DISPID_AMBIENT_AUTOCLIP
- DISPID_AMBIENT_MESSAGEREFLECT
- DISPID_AMBIENT_SUPPORTSMNEMONICS
- DISPID_AMBIENT_USERMODE

MFC returns FALSE for these two ambient property DISPIDs:

- DISPID_AMBIENT_SHOWGRABHANDLES
- DISPID_AMBIENT_UIDEAD

MFC advertises itself as having a three-dimensional appearance (DISPID_AMBIENT_APPEARANCE). The default ambient background color is the color of the window that is hosting the control, and the default ambient foreground color is the host window's text color.

Now let's take a look at how MFC handles control events.

## MFC and Control Events

When we loaded the *ATLMsgTraffic* control, Component Gallery read the type library. In addition to building the C++ class wrapper, Component Gallery absorbed information about the control's event set. So when you add the control to a dialog box, you can add event handlers. MFC sets up the code so that when the control calls back to the dialog box, the control events can be handled the same way that window messages are handled—even though the events are function calls from the control to the client. Just fire up the ClassWizard and let it add the event handlers for you. Figure 13-5 illustrates this.

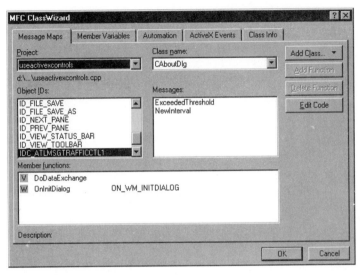

**Figure 13-5**
*Using ClassWizard to add an ActiveX control event handler*

# Conclusion

In this chapter, we discussed how to use ActiveX controls with Visual Basic and Visual C++. Even though ActiveX controls can be quite complex, implementing the interfaces that turn a typical COM object into an ActiveX control doesn't vary much from one control to another. Similarly, integrating ActiveX controls into an environment is fairly straightforward. Both Visual Basic and Visual C++ make it easy to add controls to the project and to treat them like any other Windows control. In the next chapter, we'll look at ATL windowing in more detail.

## CHAPTER FOURTEEN

# ATL Window Classes

In the late 1980s, Microsoft Windows development was an arcane art. Playing in the Windows development arena meant learning the Windows API—a set of functions exported by the Windows system DLLs. Everything in your Windows source code file had to be right or your program wouldn't work. And to top things off, every single Windows application was basically the same underneath the hood. Nearly every Windows application services both the message queue and a window procedure that processes window messages.

Of course, that's why there's MFC, right? MFC exists to save developers from having to constantly rewrite their message loops and window procedures. In MFC, you simply combine a *CWinApp*-derived class and a *CWindow*-derived class and voilà—you have a working Windows application.

Now we're in the age of component development, and folks are assembling systems from a variety of different pieces. At the center of all this component development is COM. When all the components can agree on how to talk to one another, it doesn't matter whether they are built using C++, Java, Microsoft Visual Basic, assembly language, or whatever.

Even though this new component development philosophy has come to pervade the software industry, some things remain constant—such as the need for a user interface. And a windowed interface is the style of user interface in vogue today. So if you're a C++ developer (and you don't succumb to the temptation of using Visual Basic), this means you're still going to need to service the message loop and write window procedures. Of course, you can choose to use MFC to help you. If you don't feel like buying into the whole MFC gestalt, however, there's another framework out there that will hide the message loop and wrap window handles for you—ATL. In this chapter, we'll examine how ATL handles windowing so that you can use it as an effective Windows application development tool (in addition to using it as an effective COM development tool).

Even the purest COM developer has to create a window once in a while. ATL isn't a rapid development environment for user interfaces, but it does provide an extensible variety of windowing classes that help in the creation and use of dialog boxes, control windows, standard windows, and more. The implementations range from the very thin *CWindow* to a complete Microsoft ActiveX control container with *CAxHostWindow*. The ATL window classes provide a reasonable compromise between adding MFC to your ATL project and coding straight to the Win32 SDK. Unlike MFC, ATL defines the message-handling part of a window in a separate class from the window, allowing you to easily create objects that process messages for a window but aren't windows themselves. This granularity promotes message-handling code reuse and enables extensibility.

Figure 14-1 shows the ATL 3.0 window class hierarchy when you use the default template parameters for base classes.

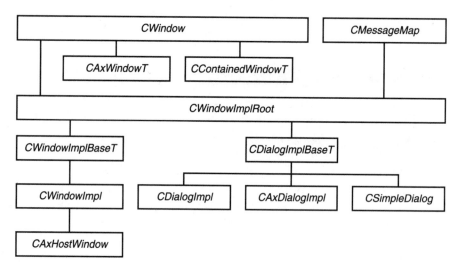

**Figure 14-1**
*ATL 3.0 Window classes*

Many of the classes shown in the diagram have templatized base classes. This chart, however, represents the most commonly used case. Some of these classes you might never use, some aren't directly documented by ATL, and some provide implementation for more derived classes. We'll concentrate on the classes ATL intends for public consumption. In addition to the classes shown in Figure 14-1, the following typedefs are defined:

```
typedef CAxWindowT<CWindow> CAxWindow;
typedef CWindowImplBaseT<CWindow>      CWindowImplBase;
typedef CDialogImplBaseT<CWindow>      CDialogImplBase;
typedef CContainedWindowT<CWindow>     CContainedWindow;
```

These typedefs specify versions of ATL template window classes with *CWindow* as the base class. When using the default template parameters, *CAxWindowT* is equivalent to *CAxWindow*, and so on. ATL window classes are implemented in atlwin.h.

# CWindow

The *CWindow* class is primarily an encapsulation of a window handle and the Win32 APIs that manipulate a window. *CWindow* maintains the handle in the *m_hWnd* public data member. You can pass in an HWND to the constructor, use the *Attach* method, or use operator = to assign the window handle. By default, *CWindow* is constructed with a NULL handle. *CWindow* also provides a *Create* function, which thinly wraps the *CreateWindowEx* API. If *Create* is successful, the *m_hWnd* data member is set to the resulting window handle. Most *CWindow* functions are simple Win32 wrappers, but *CWindow* also provides some more complex methods, such as those that follow:

- **CenterWindow**  Positions the window as centered on any HWND

- **GetDescendantWindow**  Finds an immediate or a distant child with a given control ID

- **ResizeClient**  Resizes a window to accommodate new client rectangle dimensions

- **SendMessageToDescendants**  Multicasts a message to all descendants of a window

- **ModifyStyle**  Adds and removes window styles

- **ModifyStyleEx**  Adds and removes extended window styles

- **GetWindowText**  Returns the window text as a BSTR

- **GetTopLevelParent**  Drills up through parent windows until a window that isn't a child is found

- **GetTopLevelWindow**  Finds the top-level parent, or if the window isn't a child, the top-level owner

Temporary *CWindow* objects are often used to wrap an HWND for the duration of a function call. The following code section constructs a *CWindow* from an existing HWND and retrieves the BSTR version of the window text before returning:

```
BOOL GetDlgItemText(int nID, BSTR& bstrText) const
{
    ATLASSERT(::IsWindow(m_hWnd));

    HWND hWndCtl = GetDlgItem(nID);
    if(hWndCtl == NULL)
        return FALSE;

    return CWindow(hWndCtl).GetWindowText(bstrText);
}
```

Because *CWindow* implements the HWND operator, a *CWindow* object can be used anywhere an HWND is used.

## CWindowImpl

You use *CWindowImpl* to create a new window or to subclass an existing window. You can also create a new window with a window class based on an existing window class, which is known as *superclassing*. As you can see in the class hierarchy, *CWindowImpl* inherits functionality from *CWindowImplBaseT* and *CWindowImplRoot*. Most of the meat is in these parent classes, but normally you'll instantiate only a *CWindowImpl*-derived class. *CWindowImpl* itself implements just one function—*Create*. *CWindowImpl* also inherits *CMessageMap* via *CWindowImplRoot*. *CMessageMap* and the message-map macros define a convenient mechanism for mapping messages to functions. We'll look at message maps in detail later in the chapter.

*CWindowImpl* takes three template parameters. Only the first is required, as shown in the following class definition:

```
template <class T, class TBase =
    CWindow, class TWinTraits = CControlWinTraits>
class ATL_NO_VTABLE CWindowImpl :
    public CWindowImplBaseT< TBase, TWinTraits >
```

Parameter *T* is your class, derived from *CWindowImpl*. *TBase* is the ultimate base class that contains the *m_hWnd* data member and all the Win32 API encapsulation. *CWindow* is typically used for *TBase*, but you could provide your own *CWindow* derivative.

## Traits

The *TWinTraits* template parameter defines a class that encapsulates the desired window styles and extended styles. A trait class must implement two static member functions—*GetWndStyle* and *GetWndExStyle*—as the ATL *CWinTraits* class does here:

```
template <DWORD t_dwStyle = 0, DWORD t_dwExStyle = 0>
class CWinTraits
{
public:
    static DWORD GetWndStyle(DWORD dwStyle)
    {
        return dwStyle == 0 ? t_dwStyle : dwStyle;
    }
    static DWORD GetWndExStyle(DWORD dwExStyle)
    {
        return dwExStyle == 0 ? t_dwExStyle : dwExStyle;
    }
};
```

*CWindowImpl* calls the static members of the class specified by the *TWinTraits* template argument in *CWindowImpl::Create* to determine the actual window styles. The *CWinTraits* class uses template parameters to store the window styles you specify. Note that the *CWinTraits* methods return the template styles only if the caller specifies a 0 value for *dwStyle*. The result is that any styles you specify to the *CWindowImpl::Create* method cause *CWinTraits* styles to be unused. *CWinTraits* is one of two trait classes ATL provides. The other class is *CWinTraitsOR*, which adds the template trait styles to any styles you specify in *Create*. *CWinTraitsOR* generates a style from your creation styles, template parameter styles, and template trait styles. The template parameter styles *t_dwStyle* and *t_dwExStyle* are just like the *CWinTraits* versions. The *CWinTraitsOR* class is shown in the following code section:

```
template <DWORD t_dwStyle = 0, DWORD t_dwExStyle = 0,
    class TWinTraits = CControlWinTraits>
class CWinTraitsOR
{
public:
    static DWORD GetWndStyle(DWORD dwStyle)
    {
        return dwStyle | t_dwStyle |
            TWinTraits::GetWndStyle(dwStyle);
    }
```

*(continued)*

```
static DWORD GetWndExStyle(DWORD dwExStyle)
{
    return dwExStyle | t_dwExStyle |
        TWinTraits::GetWndExStyle(dwExStyle);
}
};
```

ATL defines some common variations of the *CWinTraits* class through the following typedefs:

```
typedef CWinTraits<WS_CHILD | WS_VISIBLE | WS_CLIPCHILDREN |
    WS_CLIPSIBLINGS, 0> CControlWinTraits;

typedef CWinTraits<WS_OVERLAPPEDWINDOW | WS_CLIPCHILDREN |
    WS_CLIPSIBLINGS, WS_EX_APPWINDOW | WS_EX_WINDOWEDGE>
    CFrameWinTraits;

typedef CWinTraits<WS_OVERLAPPEDWINDOW | WS_CHILD | WS_VISIBLE |
    WS_CLIPCHILDREN | WS_CLIPSIBLINGS, WS_EX_MDICHILD>
    CMDIChildWinTraits;

typedef CWinTraits<0, 0> CNullTraits;
```

You can define your own *CWinTraits* variations as well, if you prefer.

## Implementing a Window with *CWindowImpl*

To create a window that uses a completely new window class (*not* a C++ class) or superclasses an existing window class, start by deriving a class from *CWindowImpl*. The following code section shows how to declare a basic application frame window in ATL:

```
class CMainFrame : public CWindowImpl<CMainFrame, CWindow,
    CFrameWinTraits>
{
public:
    CMainFrame();
    virtual ~CMainFrame();

DECLARE_WND_CLASS(NULL);

    BEGIN_MSG_MAP(CMainFrame)
END_MSG_MAP()
};
```

The resulting window will have the predefined ATL frame window traits when created, which means it gets the following styles and extended styles:

```
WS_OVERLAPPEDWINDOW | WS_CLIPCHILDREN | WS_CLIPSIBLINGS,
    WS_EX_APPWINDOW | WS_EX_WINDOWEDGE
```

The window-class macros and message-map macros complete the minimal implementation. We'll talk about those macros soon.

To create the window, use the *CWindowImpl::Create* function as shown here:

```
CMainFrame mainframe;
mainframe.Create(::GetDesktopWindow(),
    CWindow::rcDefault,
    _T("ATL Scribble"), 0, 0, 0);

mainframe.ShowWindow(SW_SHOWNORMAL);
```

The *Create* function takes the handle to the parent window as the first parameter. The second parameter is the initial rectangle. In this case, we're using the default rectangle provided by the static *rcDefault* data member of the *CWindow* class. The remaining parameters are the window name, style, extended style, and control ID (or menu handle). As mentioned earlier, if you specify styles in *Create*, they will override the ones specified in your traits unless you use *CWinTraitsOR*. In the previous code section, we specified 0 for the styles, so our *CFrameWin-Traits* styles are used.

# The Window-Class Macros

To declare a window class, the *CWindowImpl*-derived class needs to supply an implementation of the function *GetWndClassInfo*, which returns a *CWndClassInfo* reference. *CWndClassInfo* is essentially an encapsulation of the WNDCLASSEX structure. *GetWndClassInfo* is called in the *CWindowImpl::Create* function. ATL provides an implementation of *GetWndClassInfo* in the DECLARE_WND-_CLASS( *WndClassName* ) macro. You provide the window class name as an argument to DECLARE_WND_CLASS, and ATL provides defaults for the rest. If you don't want to supply the class name, you can pass in NULL for the class name and ATL will generate one for you. The generated name has the format "ATL:XXXXXXXX," in which X is a hex digit based on the address of the WNDCLASSEX structure contained in *CWndClassInfo*. When you use the macro, the code to declare a new window class named by ATL is trivial:

```
DECLARE_WND_CLASS(NULL);
```

By default, the class gets the class styles CS_HREDRAW | CS_VREDRAW | CS_DBLCLKS and system background color COLOR_WINDOW. To supply your own styles and background color, use the DECLARE_WND_CLASS-_EX( *WndClassName, style, bkgnd* ) macro instead.

If you want to create a window class based on an existing window class, use the DECLARE_WND_SUPERCLASS(*WndClassName, OrigWndClassName*) macro. For example, you might want to extend the Win32 common tab control to encapsulate your own flavor of owner-drawn tabs. You can get all the default common control message processing—plus your own custom processing—by declaring a new tab window class, like this:

```
#include <commctrl.h>
:
DECLARE_WND_SUPERCLASS(_T("InsideATLTabCtrl"),
    _T("SysTabControl32"))
```

# The Message Map

To enable us to process window messages in a *CWindowImpl*-derived class, ATL inherits from the abstract base class *CMessageMap*. *CMessageMap* declares one pure virtual function, *ProcessWindowMessage*. The entire class is shown here:

```
class ATL_NO_VTABLE CMessageMap
{
public:
virtual BOOL ProcessWindowMessage(HWND hWnd, UINT uMsg,
    WPARAM wParam, LPARAM lParam,
    LRESULT& lResult, DWORD dwMsgMapID) = 0;
};
```

Your *CWindowImpl*-derived class must implement the *ProcessWindowMessage* function, which is called from the *WindowProc* function in the *CWindowImpl* base class *CWindowImplBaseT*. If *ProcessWindowMessage* returns TRUE, the message has been handled by your derived class and *WindowProc* shouldn't continue with default message processing. A FALSE return value allows default processing.

## Message-Map Macros

ATL provides a set of macros that implement the *ProcessWindowMessage* function disguised as a message map. You don't need to actually write a *ProcessWindowMessage* function unless the message-map macros don't provide you with enough extensibility. The message map begins with BEGIN_MSG_MAP(*className*) and ends with END_MSG_MAP. These two macros expand to the following implementation of *ProcessWindowMessage*:

```
BOOL ProcessWindowMessage(HWND hWnd, UINT uMsg, WPARAM wParam,
    LPARAM lParam, LRESULT& lResult, DWORD dwMsgMapID = 0)
```

```
{
    BOOL bHandled = TRUE;
    hWnd;
    uMsg;
    wParam;
    lParam;
    lResult;
    bHandled;
    switch(dwMsgMapID)
    {
    case 0:
        break;
    default:
        ATLTRACE2(atlTraceWindowing, 0,
            _T("Invalid message map ID (%i)\n"), dwMsgMapID);
        ATLASSERT(FALSE);
        break;
    }
    return FALSE;
}
```

The top section of this code is from the BEGIN_MSG_MAP macro, and the bottom (after case 0) is from END_MSG_MAP. *ProcessWindowMessage* switches on the message-map ID, which is 0 by default. The ID is there so that message handlers can be logically grouped. By default, all message handlers will go into the *case 0* section. Later in the chapter, you'll find out how to add other groupings (case statements) using alternate message maps. To add a message handler, you can insert a simple *if* statement into the *case 0* section:

```
if(uMsg == WM_DESTROY)
{
    bHandled = TRUE;
    lResult = OnDestroy(uMsg, wParam, lParam, bHandled);
    if(bHandled)
        return TRUE;
}
```

With the code shown here and an *OnDestroy* function that you define, you can handle the WM_DESTROY message. The *OnDestroy* function looks like this:

```
LRESULT OnDestroy(UINT uMsg, WPARAM wParam, LPARAM lParam,
    BOOL& bHandled)
{
    // Do something here.
    bHandled = FALSE;
    return 0;
}
```

To handle a different message, you can just insert another *if* block exactly like the one for WM_DESTROY except with a different message and handler function. Your parameterized code alarm should be going off about now, since the only things that would change are the message ID and the handler function. ATL defines a set of macros that generate the *if* blocks needed to pair messages to handler functions. The complete *ProcessWindowMessage* implementation with the WM_DESTROY *if* block shown in the previous section is generated by the following macros:

```
BEGIN_MSG_MAP(CMainFrame)
    MESSAGE_HANDLER(WM_DESTROY, OnDestroy)
END_MSG_MAP()
```

Message handlers are processed in order from top to bottom until something handles the message or processing falls through, which results in default processing. The *bHandled* parameter is set to TRUE by default before the handler function is called. You can manually set it to FALSE (as *OnDestroy* does) to allow default processing after the handler function returns and *ProcessWindowMessage* exits.

ATL has a large selection of message-handler macros to choose from. The basic types are MESSAGE_HANDLER, NOTIFY_HANDLER, and COMMAND_HANDLER for normal window messages, WM_NOTIFY messages, and WM_COMMAND messages. Ranges of messages are handled using the corresponding macros MESSAGE_RANGE_HANDLER, NOTIFY_RANGE-_HANDLER, and COMMAND_RANGE_HANDLER. The easiest way to add handlers to a message map is to right-click on the class in ClassView and choose Add Windows Message Handler from the context menu. Microsoft Visual C++ then inserts the correct macro based on the message you choose to handle. You can't use ClassWizard to add handlers to ATL message maps. Here's a summary of the available message-handler macros:

- **MESSAGE_HANDLER**   Maps a window message to a handler function

- **MESSAGE_RANGE_HANDLER**   Maps a contiguous range of window messages to a handler function

- **COMMAND_HANDLER**   Maps a WM_COMMAND message to a handler function based on the notification code and the identifier of the menu item, control, or accelerator

- **COMMAND_ID_HANDLER**   Maps a WM_COMMAND message to a handler function based on the identifier of the menu item, control, or accelerator

- **COMMAND_CODE_HANDLER** Maps a WM_COMMAND message to a handler function based on the notification code

- **COMMAND_RANGE_HANDLER** Maps a contiguous range of WM_COMMAND messages to a handler function based on the identifier of the menu item, control, or accelerator

- **NOTIFY_HANDLER** Maps a WM_NOTIFY message to a handler function based on the notification code and the control identifier

- **NOTIFY_ID_HANDLER** Maps a WM_NOTIFY message to a handler function based on the control identifier

- **NOTIFY_CODE_HANDLER** Maps a WM_NOTIFY message to a handler function based on the notification code

- **NOTIFY_RANGE_HANDLER** Maps a contiguous range of WM_NOTIFY messages to a handler function based on the control identifier

## Message Reflection

Windows often need to process their own reflected messages. For example, a tab control might want to handle its tab drawing by processing WM_DRAWITEM messages. ATL message reflection requires a window's parent window to reflect messages back to the child using the REFLECT_NOTIFICATIONS macro. You can put this macro after any other standard message-handler macros in the parent, as shown here:

```
BEGIN_MSG_MAP(CMyDialog)
    MESSAGE_HANDLER(WM_INITDIALOG, OnInitDialog)
    MESSAGE_HANDLER(WM_RBUTTONUP, OnRButtonUp)
    COMMAND_ID_HANDLER(IDOK, OnOK)
    COMMAND_ID_HANDLER(IDCANCEL, OnCancel)
    NOTIFY_HANDLER(IDC_TAB1, TCN_SELCHANGING, OnSelchangingTab1)
    MESSAGE_HANDLER(WM_DESTROY, OnDestroy)
    REFLECT_NOTIFICATIONS();
END_MSG_MAP()
```

REFLECT_NOTIFICATIONS must be present in the parent window's message map to reflect messages back to the child window. The macro expands to call the *ReflectNotifications* function in *CWindowImplRoot*. *ReflectNotifications* validates that the message is important enough to be reflected and then sends the message on to the child with *SendMessage*. Before sending the message to the child, ATL adds the constant OCM__BASE to the message so that the handler in the child can determine it is a reflected message. OCM__BASE isn't defined by ATL, but it is defined in olectrl.h. A partial listing of *ReflectNotifications* is shown here:

```cpp
template <class TBase>
LRESULT CWindowImplRoot< TBase >::ReflectNotifications(UINT uMsg,
    WPARAM wParam, LPARAM lParam, BOOL& bHandled)
{
    HWND hWndChild = NULL;

    switch(uMsg)
    {
    case WM_COMMAND:
        if(lParam != NULL) // Not from a menu
            hWndChild = (HWND)lParam;
        break;
    case WM_NOTIFY:
        hWndChild = ((LPNMHDR)lParam)->hwndFrom;
        break;
    case WM_PARENTNOTIFY:
        switch(LOWORD(wParam))
        {
        case WM_CREATE:
        case WM_DESTROY:
            hWndChild = (HWND)lParam;
            break;
        default:
            hWndChild = GetDlgItem(HIWORD(wParam));
            break;
        }
        break;
    case WM_DRAWITEM:
        if(wParam) // Not from a menu
            hWndChild = ((LPDRAWITEMSTRUCT)lParam)->hwndItem;
        break;

    ⋮

    // More messages omitted here

    default:
        break;
    }

    if(hWndChild == NULL)
    {
        bHandled = FALSE;
        return 1;
    }
```

```
        ATLASSERT(::IsWindow(hWndChild));
        return ::SendMessage(hWndChild, OCM__BASE + uMsg, wParam, lParam);
}
```

The child window handles the reflected message using the standard
MESSAGE_HANDLER macros using the message IDs defined in olectrl.h for
reflected messages, which are listed here:

```
#define OCM__BASE             (WM_USER+0x1c00)
#define OCM_COMMAND           (OCM__BASE + WM_COMMAND)

#ifdef _WIN32
#define OCM_CTLCOLORBTN       (OCM__BASE + WM_CTLCOLORBTN)
#define OCM_CTLCOLOREDIT      (OCM__BASE + WM_CTLCOLOREDIT)
#define OCM_CTLCOLORDLG       (OCM__BASE + WM_CTLCOLORDLG)
#define OCM_CTLCOLORLISTBOX   (OCM__BASE + WM_CTLCOLORLISTBOX)
#define OCM_CTLCOLORMSGBOX    (OCM__BASE + WM_CTLCOLORMSGBOX)
#define OCM_CTLCOLORSCROLLBAR (OCM__BASE + WM_CTLCOLORSCROLLBAR)
#define OCM_CTLCOLORSTATIC    (OCM__BASE + WM_CTLCOLORSTATIC)
#else
#define OCM_CTLCOLOR          (OCM__BASE + WM_CTLCOLOR)
#endif

#define OCM_DRAWITEM          (OCM__BASE + WM_DRAWITEM)
#define OCM_MEASUREITEM       (OCM__BASE + WM_MEASUREITEM)
#define OCM_DELETEITEM        (OCM__BASE + WM_DELETEITEM)
#define OCM_VKEYTOITEM        (OCM__BASE + WM_VKEYTOITEM)
#define OCM_CHARTOITEM        (OCM__BASE + WM_CHARTOITEM)
#define OCM_COMPAREITEM       (OCM__BASE + WM_COMPAREITEM)
#define OCM_HSCROLL           (OCM__BASE + WM_HSCROLL)
#define OCM_VSCROLL           (OCM__BASE + WM_VSCROLL)
#define OCM_PARENTNOTIFY      (OCM__BASE + WM_PARENTNOTIFY)

#if (WINVER >= 0x0400)
#define OCM_NOTIFY            (OCM__BASE + WM_NOTIFY)
#endif
```

These IDs are used directly in the message map of the child window receiving
reflected messages. For example, to handle a reflected WM_DRAWITEM message, the message map looks like this:

```
BEGIN_MSG_MAP(CInsideAtlTabs)
    MESSAGE_HANDLER(OCM_DRAWITEM, OnDrawItem)
    DEFAULT_REFLECTION_HANDLER()
END_MSG_MAP()
```

The DEFAULT_REFLECTION_HANDLER macro is placed in the message
map of the child window to enable default processing for reflected messages.

## Alternate Message Maps

Recall that the default message-map ID declared in BEGIN_MSG_MAP is 0. All message handlers are placed in map zero by default. You can declare additional maps using the ALT_MSG_MAP(*msgMapID*) macro. You might do this to enable a single class to process messages from more than one window. Because *ProcessWindowMessage* takes the message-map ID as a parameter (0 by default), the caller can easily specify a different map ID that corresponds to an ALT_MSG_MAP entry. ALT_MSG_MAP simply adds another case to the switch statement in *ProcessWindowMessage*. Here's what the macro definition looks like:

```
#define ALT_MSG_MAP(msgMapID) \
    break; \
    case msgMapID:
```

You can specify any number of alternate message maps between the BEGIN-_MSG_MAP and END_MSG_MAP macros. To handle messages in an alternate map, just place the normal handler macros after an ALT_MSG_MAP (*msgMapID*) macro. Alternate message maps are primarily used in conjunction with *CContainedWindow* to enable a containing object to process messages for a contained window. *CContainedWindow* takes a message-map ID in the constructor and allows you to specify the message-map ID to change dynamically by using the *SwitchMessageMap* function.

## Chaining Message Maps

Alternate message maps provide a way to group message handlers within a single BEGIN/END macro pair. However, additional message maps can reside in separate *CMessageMap*-derived classes. This mechanism is useful for grouping certain message-handling tasks into a reusable class. You can declare a class that tracks focus messages on any window, like this:

```
template <class T>
class CFocusLogger : public CMessageMap
{
public:
    BEGIN_MSG_MAP(CFocusLogger)
        MESSAGE_HANDLER(WM_KILLFOCUS, OnKillFocus)
        MESSAGE_HANDLER(WM_SETFOCUS, OnSetFocus)
    END_MSG_MAP()

    LRESULT OnKillFocus(UINT uMsg, WPARAM wParam, LPARAM lParam,
        BOOL& bHandled)
```

```
    {
        T* pT = static_cast<T*>(this);
        LogFocusChange(pT->m_hWnd, FALSE);
        bHandled = FALSE;
        return 1;
    }

    LRESULT OnSetFocus(UINT uMsg, WPARAM wParam, LPARAM lParam,
        BOOL& bHandled)
    {
        T* pT = static_cast<T*>(this);
        LogFocusChange(pT->m_hWnd, TRUE);
        bHandled = FALSE;
        return 1;
    }

    void LogFocusChange(HWND hwnd, BOOL bGotFocus)
    {
        // Log to wherever
    }
};
```

The *CFocusLogger* class is used as a base class for your *CWindowImpl*-derived class, as shown here:

```
class CMainFrame : public CWindowImpl<CmainFrame, ...>,
    public CFocusLogger<CMainFrame>
{
public:
    CMainFrame();
    virtual ~CMainFrame();

DECLARE_WND_CLASS(NULL);

    BEGIN_MSG_MAP(CMainFrame)
        CHAIN_MSG_MAP(CFocusLogger)
    END_MSG_MAP()
};
```

The message map then routes messages to *CFocusLogger* by adding the CHAIN_MSG_MAP macro to the map. CHAIN_MSG_MAP calls *Process-WindowMessage* on a *CMessageMap*-derived base class. CHAIN_MSG_MAP will only route messages to a *CMessageMap*-derived class that your class inherits from. ATL provides other chaining macros for cases in which messages need to be routed to *CMessageMap*-derived objects contained in your class as data members.

There are also macros to route messages to alternate message maps in base classes or contained members. Each chaining macro and its purpose is described in the following list:

- **CHAIN_MSG_MAP(*theChainClass*)**   Routes messages to the default message map within a *CMessageMap*-derived base class.

- **CHAIN_MSG_MAP_ALT(*theChainClass, msgMapID*)**   Routes messages to the alternate message map within a *CMessageMap*-derived base class.

- **CHAIN_MSG_MAP_MEMBER(*theChainMember*)**   Routes messages to the default message map within a data member of your class. (The data member must be a class type that derives from *CMessageMap*.)

- **CHAIN_MSG_MAP_ALT_MEMBER(*theChainMember, msgMapID*)**   Routes messages to an alternate message map in a data member of your class. (The data member must be a class type that derives from *CMessageMap*.)

- **CHAIN_MSG_MAP_DYNAMIC(*dynaChainID*)**   Enables you to specify a message-handler object at run time. Your class must derive from *CDynamicChain*, which maintains a map of *CMessageMap* objects to *dynaChainID* numbers. You can add or remove message-handler objects by using *CDynamicChain::SetChainEntry* and *Remove-ChainEntry*. The default message map in the message-handler object is always used. There is no corresponding alternate dynamic-chaining macro.

# *CDialogImpl*, *CAxDialogImpl*, and *CSimpleDialog*

ATL provides classes that support implementing and using modal and modeless dialog boxes. Depending on the level of interaction you need with the dialog box and the type of controls contained in it, you can choose from one of three classes: *CDialogImpl*, *CAxDialogImpl*, and *CSimpleDialog*. A brief description of each follows.

## *CDialogImpl*

This class is used as a base class for implementing a modal or modeless dialog box. *CDialogImpl* provides a dialog box procedure that routes messages to the default message map in your derived class. ActiveX controls are not supported in the dialog box.

## CAxDialogImpl

This class is also used as a base class for implementing a modal or modeless dialog box. *CAxDialogImpl* provides a dialog box procedure that routes messages to the default message map in your derived class. ActiveX controls are supported in the dialog box.

The ATL Object Wizard supports adding a *CAxDialogImpl*-derived class to your project and generates a dialog resource to go with it.

## CSimpleDialog

This class implements a modal dialog box given the resource ID of the dialog box as a template parameter. *CSimpleDialog* has a predefined message map that handles known commands such as IDOK and IDCANCEL, either of which will close the dialog box. *CSimpleDialog* is used for dialog boxes that are simply displayed and then closed by the user, such as an About box.

## Implementing a Dialog Box

The easiest way to create a new dialog box is to use the ATL Object Wizard. Under the category Miscellaneous, you'll see the icon for inserting a dialog box. Running the wizard generates a new class derived from *CAxDialogImpl* and adds a new dialog resource to your project. Because the class is derived from *CAxDialogImpl*, it can contain Windows controls and ActiveX controls.

By default, the dialog box is set up for modal use. This is evident in the following implementation of the IDOK and IDCANCEL command handlers:

```
LRESULT OnOK(WORD wNotifyCode, WORD wID, HWND hWndCtl,
    BOOL& bHandled)
{
    EndDialog(wID);
    return 0;
}

LRESULT OnCancel(WORD wNotifyCode, WORD wID, HWND hWndCtl,
    BOOL& bHandled)
{
    EndDialog(wID);
    return 0;
}
```

*EndDialog* is used only for modal dialog boxes. To make this dialog box modeless, you need to modify the existing code to call *DestroyWindow* instead of *EndDialog*.

You can add message handlers to the dialog box for Windows controls by right-clicking on the dialog box class in ClassView and choosing Add Windows

Message Handler from the context menu, or by right-clicking in the dialog resource in the resource editor and choosing Events from the context menu. You can also use the same procedure to add event handlers for ActiveX controls contained in the dialog box. To see how this is done, let's insert the MS Calendar control in a dialog box and handle an event from it in our derived class. The following steps assume you've already used the Object Wizard to insert a dialog box into your project.

1. Open the dialog resource in the resource editor, and right-click in the dialog box to bring up the context menu. Choose Insert ActiveX Control from the menu.

2. Choose Calendar Control from the list, and click OK, which inserts the control into the dialog box. You might need to resize the dialog box to make everything fit. The resulting dialog box should look something like the one shown here:

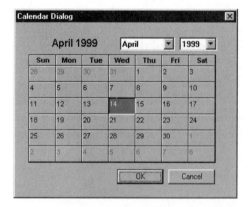

3. Right-click on the dialog box, and choose Events from the menu. When the message and event handlers dialog box appears, click on IDC_CALENDAR1 in the lower right-hand list box to see the events that the calendar control can fire.

4. We'd like to handle the NewMonth event, so click on NewMonth in the list box on the left to select it and then click the Add Handler button. Accept the default method name for the handler.

ATL creates an event sink for the calendar control in the dialog box header file, as shown here:

```
        VOID __stdcall OnNewMonthCalendar1()
        {
            // TODO : Add Code for event handler.
        }
public :

BEGIN_SINK_MAP(CMyDialog)
    // Make sure the Event Handlers have __stdcall calling
    //  convention
    SINK_ENTRY(IDC_CALENDAR1, 0x3, OnNewMonthCalendar1)
END_SINK_MAP()
```

We won't get any events, however, unless we tell the control about our event sink by advising it. We can use the *AtlAdviseSinkMap* function to advise all controls that we're sinking events from. In this case, it's only the one control. We can do the advise in the existing WM_INITDIALOG handler and add a WM_DESTROY handler to do the unadvise. The finished functions are shown here:

```
LRESULT OnInitDialog(UINT uMsg, WPARAM wParam, LPARAM lParam,
    BOOL& bHandled)
{
    HRESULT hr = AtlAdviseSinkMap(this, TRUE);
    _ASSERTE(SUCCEEDED(hr));
    return 1;  // Let the system set the focus.
}

LRESULT OnDestroy(UINT uMsg, WPARAM wParam, LPARAM lParam,
    BOOL& bHandled)
{
    AtlAdviseSinkMap(this, FALSE);
    bHandled = FALSE;
    return 1;
}
```

As written, the event handler for OnNewMonth doesn't do anything. Let's add some code to the event handler to read the *Month* property from the control itself, so we at least know what the month has changed to. Note that ATL has imported the calendar control at the top of the dialog box header file; we can use the interfaces on the control directly. To find out which interfaces and methods are supported, you can use the OLE View utility. Doing so reveals that the control implements an *ICalendar* interface, which has a *Month* property we can read. We can get an *ICalendar* interface pointer for the control using the

*GetDlgControl* function. *GetDlgControl* retrieves an interface pointer for a contained control based on the control ID. Here's the event handler code:

```
VOID __stdcall OnNewMonthCalendar1()
{
    CComPtr<ICalendar> spCal;
    HRESULT hr = GetDlgControl(IDC_CALENDAR1, IID_ICalendar,
        (void**)&spCal);
    if(SUCCEEDED(hr))
    {
        short month = 0;
        hr = spCal->get_Month(&month);
        if(SUCCEEDED(hr))
            ATLTRACE(_T("Month Change: %d\n"), month);
    }
}
```

The event handler now outputs a trace message that displays the current month when the month changes.

## Using a Dialog Box

Creating a dialog box in ATL is probably exactly what you would expect. You can run a modeless dialog box by simply instantiating your dialog box class and calling *DoModal*, like this:

```
#include "mydialog.h"
⋮
CMyDialog dlg;
dlg.DoModal();
```

The dialog box window is destroyed when *EndDialog* is called, typically from the IDOK and IDCANCEL command handlers in your dialog box class. The ATL Object Wizard generates this type of dialog box by default. For simple dialog boxes, you can create a dialog box with only a dialog template. There's no reason to derive a class from *CDialogImpl* or *CAxDialogImpl* if you just want to get an OK/cancel or yes/no confirmation. You specify the dialog resource as a template parameter to *CSimpleDialog*, as shown here:

```
CSimpleDialog<IDD_MYABOUTBOX> dlgAbout;
dlgAbout.DoModal();
```

*CSimpleDialog* has a second BOOL template parameter (not shown here) that controls centering of the dialog box. The dialog box is centered by default. *DoModal* also takes a parameter that specifies the parent window handle, which defaults to the current active window.

A modeless dialog box is created using the *Create* method and typically destroys its window by calling *DestroyWindow* in the IDOK and IDCANCEL handlers. The following code shows how to create a modeless dialog box from your *WinMain* function:

```
#include "mydialog.h"
  ⋮
CMyDialog dlg;
dlg.Create(::GetDesktopWindow());
dlg.ShowWindow(SW_SHOWNORMAL);

MSG msg;
while (GetMessage(&msg, 0, 0, 0))
    DispatchMessage(&msg);
```

# *CAxHostWindow* and *CAxWindow*

Sometimes you want to create a user interface that dynamically includes an ActiveX control in a window, not a dialog box. You might want to specify the type of control at run time as well. ATL supports control containment in a window through its ActiveX hosting window classes, *CAxHostWindow* and *CAxWindow*.

## *CAxHostWindow*

Hosting an ActiveX control involves a lot of interfaces, for which ATL provides default implementations in *CAxHostWindow*. *CAxHostWindow* is found in ATLHOST.H and has the following class declaration:

```
class ATL_NO_VTABLE CAxHostWindow :
    public CComCoClass<CAxHostWindow , &CLSID_NULL>,
    public CComObjectRootEx<CComSingleThreadModel>,
    public CWindowImpl<CAxHostWindow>,
    public IAxWinHostWindow,
    public IOleClientSite,
    public IOleInPlaceSiteWindowless,
    public IOleControlSite,
    public IOleContainer,
    public IObjectWithSiteImpl<CAxHostWindow>,
    public IServiceProvider,
    public IAdviseSink,
#ifndef _ATL_NO_DOCHOSTUIHANDLER
    public IDocHostUIHandler,
#endif
```

*(continued)*

```
public IDispatchImpl<IAxWinAmbientDispatch,
    &IID_IAxWinAmbientDispatch, &LIBID_ATLLib>
```

This isn't your average window implementation. *CAxHostWindow* is both a COM object and a window implementation that can host an ActiveX control. The idea is that ATL registers a window class *AtlAxWin* when you call the global function *AtlAxWinInit*. You can then create a window by using the standard Win32 *CreateWindow* function, as shown here:

```
AtlAxWinInit();
// Create a window that will be subclassed by CAxHostWindow.
DWORD dwStyle = WS_CHILD | WS_VISIBLE;
CRect rcBounds(GetBounds());
HWND hWnd = ::CreateWindow(_T("AtlAxWin"), NULL , dwStyle,
    rcBounds.left,
    rcBounds.top,
    rcBounds.Width(), rcBounds.Height(),
    hParent,
    NULL,
    ::GetModuleHandle(NULL),
    NULL);
```

When the ATL window procedure for the *AtlAxWin* class (*AtlAxWindow-Proc*) gets WM_CREATE, an instance of *CAxHostWindow* is created for you and your HWND is subclassed. You never actually create a *CAxHostWindow* on your own or derive a class from it. To create or load an ActiveX control in the window, you need to use the *IAxWinHostWindow* interface, which ATL defines in ATLIFACE.IDL and implements in *CAxHostWindow*. The interface provides methods to create the ActiveX control or attach an existing control instance. The interface IDL is shown here:

```
interface IAxWinHostWindow : IUnknown
{
    HRESULT CreateControl([in] LPCOLESTR lpTricsData,
        [in] HWND hWnd, [in] IStream* pStream);
    HRESULT CreateControlEx([in] LPCOLESTR lpTricsData,
        [in] HWND hWnd, [in] IStream* pStream,
        [out]IUnknown** ppUnk, [in] REFIID riidAdvise,
        [in]IUnknown* punkAdvise);
    HRESULT AttachControl([in] IUnknown* pUnkControl,
        [in] HWND hWnd);
    HRESULT QueryControl([in] REFIID riid, [out,
        iid_is(riid)] void **ppvObject);
    HRESULT SetExternalDispatch([in] IDispatch* pDisp);
    HRESULT SetExternalUIHandler(
        [in] IDocHostUIHandlerDispatch* pDisp);
};
```

Right now, all we have is an HWND for the window that we got back from *CreateWindow*, but we need an *IAxWinHostWindow* pointer for the *CAxHostWindow* object. *AtlAxWinInit* registers two window messages that we can use to get the *IUnknown* pointer for *CAxHostWindow* and the *IUnknown* pointer for the contained control after we create it. The messages are WM_ATLGETHOST and WM_ATLGETCONTROL. Both return *IUnknown* pointers in the LRESULT. (ATL increments the reference count before returning the pointers to you.) As a convenience, ATL provides a couple of global functions to get the relevant interface pointers using an HWND, as shown in the following code section from ATLHOST.H:

```
ATLINLINE ATLAPI AtlAxGetControl(HWND h, IUnknown** pp)
{
    ATLASSERT(WM_ATLGETCONTROL != 0);
    if(pp == NULL)
        return E_POINTER;
    *pp = (IUnknown*)SendMessage(h, WM_ATLGETCONTROL, 0, 0);
    return (*pp) ? S_OK : E_FAIL;
}

ATLINLINE ATLAPI AtlAxGetHost(HWND h, IUnknown** pp)
{
    ATLASSERT(WM_ATLGETHOST != 0);
    if(pp == NULL)
        return E_POINTER;
    *pp = (IUnknown*)SendMessage(h, WM_ATLGETHOST, 0, 0);
    return (*pp) ? S_OK : E_FAIL;
}
```

Now we can get the *IAxWinHostWindow* pointer for the *CAxHostWindow* object and create a calendar control using this code:

```
CComPtr<IUnknown> spUnk;
HRESULT hr = AtlAxGetHost(hWnd, &spUnk);
if(SUCCEEDED(hr))
{
    CComQIPtr<IAxWinHostWindow> spAxWin(spUnk);
    hr = spAxWin->CreateControl(L"MSCal.Calendar", hWnd, NULL);
}
```

The string that describes the control can be a progID or a CLSID. You can also specify a URL or a raw HTML string prefixed with MSHTML: that results in the creation of the Web browser control. ATL determines what type of string you've passed in to *CreateControl* and reacts accordingly. The ATLCON sample that ships with ATL is a useful test project for these various different description types.

The last parameter to *CreateControl* is an *IStream* pointer. If you specify a non-null value, the control is loaded from that stream using *IPersistStreamInit* on the control. *CreateControlEx* takes an additional parameter for an advise sink interface pointer in case you need to handle events from the control.

*CAxHostWindow* also implements a dual interface named *IAxWinAmbient-Dispatch*, which provides get and set methods for most of the common ambient properties, such as *BackColor*, *Font*, and *UserMode*. The ambient property states are maintained in *CAxHostWindow* data members. You use *AtlAxGetHost* to retrieve the host *IUnknown* pointer and then call *QueryInterface* for *IAxWin-AmbientDispatch*, which you use to set or get ambient properties based on your application preferences.

## CAxWindow

*CAxWindow* encapsulates some of the code used in the previous section to manipulate a *CAxHostWindow*. Instead of creating a window using the Win32 API and the *AtlAxWin* class, simply instantiate a *CAxWindow* and call its *Create* member, which does essentially the same thing. To get any interface implemented by the *CAxHostWindow* object, use *CAxWindow::QueryHost*, which uses pretty much the same *AtlAxGetHost* code we used earlier. Here's the *CAxWindow* implementation:

```
HRESULT QueryHost(REFIID iid, void** ppUnk)
{
    ATLASSERT(ppUnk != NULL);
    HRESULT hr;
    *ppUnk = NULL;
    CComPtr<IUnknown> spUnk;
    hr = AtlAxGetHost(m_hWnd, &spUnk);
    if(SUCCEEDED(hr))
        hr = spUnk->QueryInterface(iid, ppUnk);
    return hr;
}
```

To create a control, use *QueryHost* to get an *IAxWinHostWindow* interface pointer, and then call its *CreateControl* method. Here's an example of how to create a control using *CAxWindow*:

```
CAxWindow m_AxWindow;
m_AxWindow.Create(hwndParent, ...);
CComPtr<IAxWinHostWindow> spHost;
m_AxWindow.QueryHost(&spHost);
hr = spHost->CreateControl(L"MSCal.Calendar", m_AxWindow, NULL);
```

Once created, any interface implemented by the contained control is available through *CAxWindow::QueryControl*. *QueryControl* uses the global *AtlAxGetControl* function we looked at earlier, but it also calls *QueryInterface* for us to get our desired interface pointer.

# Conclusion

The basic ATL windowing classes are convenient enough to make them an attractive alternative to SDK windowing. In addition, Visual C++ offers built-in support to add and remove message handlers and event handlers. The ATL windowing classes are lightweight and granular in their implementation and have the ability to change base classes and separate message-handling implementation from the window object itself. ATL implements a large part of ActiveX control containment for you in the host window classes.

ATL isn't just for COM. As you'll see in the next chapter, ATL can offer you a great way to build Win32 applications using the windowing techniques you just learned, and you'll learn some new tricks as well.

CHAPTER FIFTEEN

# Enumerators and Collections

In COM, collections are objects that contain a logical grouping of items and support a means of navigating these contained items. Although collections can contain simple types, the most common examples are collections of COM objects exposed through application Automation object models. Object models came into vogue as an application extensibility mechanism. By exposing a hierarchy of an application's objects and collections through dispatch interfaces, you can write macros to automate certain tasks. In this chapter, we'll look at the kinds of collections you might find in such an object model.

In 1994, Charlie Kindel described the "Six Commandments of OLE Automation Collections" (see the MSDN article "Implementing OLE Automation Collections" in the online help), which are the foundation of collections in Microsoft Office products (and many other products). Collections are a vital part of the object model in many applications and services. For example, a Microsoft ActiveX Data Object (ADO) recordset has a Fields collection, which is a grouping of *Field* objects, as shown in Figure 15-1.

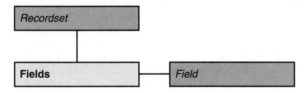

**Figure 15-1**
*Fields collection in ADO*

The properties and methods of a collection object vary depending on the privileges granted to a user of the collection. A collection object usually exposes methods to add, remove, delete, and retrieve items from the collection. The ability to iterate over the items in the collection is inherent to collections. Kindel's article outlines recommended standards for these properties and methods of a collection object. Table 15-1 shows these properties and methods.

**Table 15-1  Standard Properties and Methods of a Collection Object**

| Member | Description | Optional? |
|---|---|---|
| *Add* method | Adds the indicated item to the collection | Yes |
| *Count* property | Returns the number of items in the collection | No |
| *Item* method | Returns the indicated item in the collection; returns VT_EMPTY if the item doesn't exist | No |
| *_NewEnum* property | Returns an object that supports *IEnumVARIANT* (This method isn't visible to users.) | No |
| *Remove* method | Removes the specified item from the collection | Yes |

Although the properties and methods shown in Table 15-1 are fairly standard, in reality the signatures and names for collection properties and methods vary widely across applications. The *Item* method is usually given the predefined dispatch ID DISPID_VALUE, which makes the *Item* method the default member of the collection. The default member is implied when using an object in Microsoft Visual Basic unless another member is specified.

A collection is enumerated using a COM-defined iteration contract, which has a couple of distinct advantages over other enumeration possibilities:

- It provides efficient flow control across the wire when retrieving members of the collection remotely.

- It has built-in support in Visual Basic using the For/Each syntax.

Flow control is supported by the *Next* method, which allows the caller to pull as many items from the enumerator as it wants in a single call. For/Each is a Visual Basic loop statement that makes it simple for Visual Basic users to obtain an enumerator object and manipulate the object using its *IEnumVARIANT* interface.

Imagine a COM object that represents a data acquisition and control board supporting both analog input and analog output. The board could be modeled with a top-level object named *AnalogBoard* that contains two collections: Inputs and Outputs. The Inputs collection contains *Input* objects, and the Outputs collection contains *Output* objects. *Input* and *Output* objects support the *Value* property to read and write the device I/O. A Visual Basic client can read the data from each of the analog *Input* objects in sequence using a For/Each loop, like this:

```
Dim Board1 As New COLLECTIONSERVERLib.AnalogBoard

Private Sub Form_Load()
    Dim AnalogInColl As COLLECTIONSERVERLib.Inputs
    Set AnalogInColl = Board1.Inputs
    Dim AnalogIn As COLLECTIONSERVERLib.Input
    Debug.Print "**** Analog Input Values ****"
    For Each AnalogIn In AnalogInColl
        Debug.Print AnalogIn.Value
    Next

End Sub
```

The *_NewEnum* property returns such an enumerator object to the client. *_NewEnum* also has a predefined dispatch ID: DISPID_NEWENUM. The terms *enumerator* and *iterator* are used interchangeably throughout this chapter.

In the rest of the chapter, we'll look at the ATL classes that help build the collection objects just described and the enumerator objects for those collections.

## Collection Objects in ATL

ATL provides limited assistance in building collection objects through the *ICollectionOnSTLImpl* class. To create a collection object, *ICollectionOnSTLImpl* serves as a base class to your collection object. You can start with a simple object generated by the Object Wizard and add inheritance from *ICollectionOn-STLImpl*, which implements the *Count* property, the *Item* property, and the *_NewEnum* property on a Standard Template Library (STL) sequential container such as a vector or a list. If you need to keep your collection in a map and also support retrieving items by string value, you're probably better off building your own collection implementation from scratch.

You'll need to add the matching IDL for the *ICollectionOnSTLImpl* properties yourself. The text to add to your collection object interface IDL is shown here in bold, inserted in our analog Inputs collection dual interface:

```
interface IInputs : IDispatch
{
    [propget, id(DISPID_NEWENUM)] HRESULT _NewEnum([out,retval]
        LPUNKNOWN* pUnk);
    [propget, id(DISPID_VALUE)] HRESULT Item([in] long Index,
        [out,retval] VARIANT* pvar);
    [propget, id(1)] HRESULT Count([out,retval] long* pcount);
};
```

ATL defines *Item* as a property, not a method. You'll see implementations that declare *Item* and other collection members both ways, depending on how the designer interpreted the spec. Notice that there are no optional *Add* or *Remove* methods. If you need them, you'll have to add their implementations and IDL to your collection object by hand.

*ICollectionOnSTLImpl* derives from an interface you supply—typically your collection object's primary dual interface. The definition of a hypothetical collection class that models analog input on a circuit board might look like this:

```
class ATL_NO_VTABLE CInputs :
    public CComObjectRootEx<CComSingleThreadModel>,
    public CComCoClass<CInputs, &CLSID_Inputs>,
    public ICollectionOnSTLImpl<lots of parameters>
{
    ⋮
}
```

The template parameters to *ICollectionOnSTLImpl* can get a little messy, so we'll look at them one at a time. The template definition for the ATL *ICollectionOnSTLImpl* class is shown here:

```
template <class T, class CollType, class ItemType,
    class CopyItem, class EnumType>
class ICollectionOnSTLImpl : public T
{
    ⋮
}
```

The remaining template parameters for this code are described in the following sections.

## class *T*

This class is the base class for *ICollectionOnSTLImpl*. For our analog Inputs collection, which supports a dual interface *IInputs*, the base class type is defined as follows:

```
IDispatchImpl<IInputs, &IID_IInputs, &LIBID_COLLECTIONSERVERLib>
```

## class *CollType*

*CollType* is the STL collection type that contains the items in the collection. The implementation supports sequential containers such as vectors and lists. Associative containers, such as maps, aren't supported in the current *ICollection-OnSTLImpl* class. Our analog Inputs collection uses an STL vector of *IInput* interface pointers, so the *CollType* parameter is defined as follows:

```
std::vector<IInput*>
```

*ICollectionOnSTLImpl* maintains the STL collection object for you in its *m_coll* data member. You can access *m_coll* directly to populate the collection with initial items. The analog Inputs collection object does this by creating a fixed number of analog input objects and adding them to the STL vector in the constructor, as shown in the following code section:

```
enum {numInputs = 8};

CInputs()
{
    IInput* pIInput = NULL;
    for (int i = 0; i < numInputs; i++)
    {
        CComObject<CInput> *pInput = new CComObject<CInput>;
        if(SUCCEEDED(pInput->QueryInterface(IID_IInput,
            (void**)&pIInput)))
            m_coll.push_back(pIInput);
    }
}
```

The code adds eight analog input objects to the *m_coll* STL container. The destructor must iterate over *m_coll* and release the interface pointers, as illustrated here:

```
~CInputs()
{
    std::vector<IInput*>::iterator it;
    for (it = m_coll.begin(); it != m_coll.end(); it++)
    {
        IInput* pIInput = *it;
        if(pIInput)
            pIInput->Release();
    }
}
```

## class *ItemType*

This parameter describes the type of item contained in the collection and defines the return type for the *Item* property of the collections. Our analog Inputs collection object uses a VARIANT for the *ItemType* parameter. Clients call the *Item* property to retrieve, by numeric index, a single value from the collection. The following code for *ICollectionOnSTLImpl::get_Item* illustrates the use of the *m_coll* STL container to retrieve a collection item of type *ItemType*:

```
STDMETHOD(get_Item)(long Index, ItemType* pvar)
{
    // Index is 1-based
```

*(continued)*

```
        if(pvar == NULL)
            return E_POINTER;
        HRESULT hr = E_FAIL;
        Index--;
        CollType::iterator iter = m_coll.begin();
        while (iter != m_coll.end() && Index > 0)
        {
            iter++;
            Index--;
        }
        if(iter != m_coll.end())
            hr = CopyItem::copy(pvar, &*iter);
        return hr;
    }
```

The returned value is of type *ItemType\**, which is assigned in the *CopyItem::copy* call. *CopyItem* is also specified in a template parameter, which we'll look at next.

## class *CopyItem*

ATL collection and enumerator classes use a helper class to copy a collection item from the STL container to the return value of the *Item* property. The behavior implemented by the *CopyItem* class is also known as a *copy policy*. The class implementing the copy policy must have a static member with this signature:

```
HRESULT copy(/*[out]*/ ItemType* p1, /*[in]*/ STLItemType* p2)
```

The copy policy takes as input the result of dereferencing the STL iterator to retrieve an item and then taking its address, as we see in the following code:

```
if(iter != m_coll.end())
    hr = CopyItem::copy(pvar, &*iter);
```

If the STL container is holding *IInput* interface pointers, the copy policy gets an *IInput\*\** parameter for *p2*. The parameter *p1* is an [out] parameter of the type that the *get_Item* property returns to the client. Typically this is a VARIANT VT_DISPATCH for object collections, so *p2* is a VARIANT\* parameter. Therefore, the purpose of our copy policy is to copy an interface pointer to a VARIANT dispatch pointer. A copy policy class that implements this functionality is shown here:

```
class _CopyVariantFromInterface
{
public:
    static HRESULT copy(VARIANT* pV, IUnknown** pUnk)
    {
        HRESULT hr = (*pUnk)->QueryInterface(IID_IDispatch,
            (void**)&pV->pdispVal);
```

```
        if(SUCCEEDED(hr) )
            pV->vt = VT_DISPATCH;
        return hr;
    }
};
```

We can use the type *_CopyVariantFromInterface* as the *CopyItem* template parameter to *ICollectionOnSTLImpl* for the analog Inputs collection or for any collection that returns a dispatch-based VARIANT from the *Item* property.

## class *EnumType*

The *_NewEnum* property of a collection creates and initializes an enumerator object. The client receives the *IUnknown* pointer for the object as the return value to *_NewEnum*. The code section that follows shows how *ICollection-OnSTLImpl* defines *get__NewEnum*:

```
STDMETHOD(get__NewEnum)(IUnknown** ppUnk)
{
    if (ppUnk == NULL)
        return E_POINTER;
    *ppUnk = NULL;
    HRESULT hRes = S_OK;
    CComObject<EnumType>* p;
    hRes = CComObject<EnumType>::CreateInstance(&p);
    if(SUCCEEDED(hRes))
    {
        hRes = p->Init(this, m_coll);
        if(hRes == S_OK)
            hRes = p->QueryInterface(IID_IUnknown, (void**)ppUnk);
    }
    if(hRes != S_OK)
        delete p;
    return hRes;
}
```

The method creates an enumerator object using *CComObject<EnumType>*. The enumerator is then initialized by passing it a reference to the collection's STL container, *m_coll*. The specification for *EnumType* in the analog Inputs collection is shown here:

```
CComEnumOnSTL<CComIEnum<VARIANT>, &IID_IEnumVARIANT,
    VARIANT, _CopyVariantFromInterface<IInput>,
    std::vector<IInput*> >
```

Code like this can cause technical support engineers to come looking for you. A typedef is highly recommended. ATL provides the *CComEnumOnSTL* enumerator implementation for use as the *EnumType* in *ICollectionOnSTLImpl*. We'll give *CComEnumOnSTL* plenty of attention at the end of the following section on enumerator objects.

# Enumerator Objects

In the introduction to this chapter, we described the properties and methods of a collection object. One of those properties is *_NewEnum*. This property has a COM-defined dispatch ID DISPID_NEWENUM, which is defined as −4. Visual Basic relies on this dispatch ID to retrieve the enumerator object from a collection. The *_NewEnum* property returns an interface pointer to an enumeration object. The enumeration object must conform to the enumeration contract specified by COM. The enumeration contract is defined in the *IEnumxxx* interfaces. *IEnumxxx* isn't an interface itself, but a generic description of the methods required when implementing an enumeration interface. There is no single *IEnumxxx* interface that can completely describe an enumerator for every type of collection. For collections of COM objects, the enumerator is implemented as an object that supports the *IEnumVARIANT* interface. COM defines *IEnumVARIANT* for the common case in which a collection of COM objects that implement *IDispatch* provides an enumerator. *IEnumVARIANT* must be used to enable a Visual Basic client to use For/Each syntax. If you don't care about enabling Visual Basic clients to use For/Each, you can implement the enumerator with an *IEnumxxx* interface for whatever type you like. The contract for an enumerator interface is shown in Table 15-2.

**Table 15-2  Enumerator Interface Methods**

| *IEnumxxx* Method | Description |
| --- | --- |
| *Next* | Retrieves a specified number of items in the enumeration sequence |
| *Skip* | Skips over a specified number of items in the enumeration sequence |
| *Reset* | Resets the enumeration sequence to the beginning |
| *Clone* | Creates another enumerator that contains the same enumeration state as the current one |

A client requests an enumerator object pointer by getting the *_NewEnum* property of the collection. The *_NewEnum* property returns an *IUnknown* pointer, which must be queried for the enumeration interface. Visual Basic always requests *IEnumVARIANT* in a For/Each loop. Once an *IEnumVARIANT* pointer is found, the *Next* method is used to request one or more objects in the collection. Currently, Visual Basic only supports retrieving objects one at a time using *IEnumVARIANT::Next*, but C++ clients can pick an optimum chunk size to retrieve. The enumerator object advances an internal cursor to maintain the current position in the enumeration between calls to *Next*. *IEnumVARIANT::Next* requires the number of elements to be returned as a parameter to the caller. The signature for the *IEnumVARIANT* interface is shown here:

```
interface IEnumVARIANT : IUnknown
{
    virtual HRESULT Next(unsigned long celt,
        VARIANT FAR* rgvar,
        unsigned long FAR* pceltFetched) = 0;
    virtual HRESULT Skip(unsigned long celt) = 0;
    virtual HRESULT Reset() = 0;
    virtual HRESULT Clone(IEnumVARIANT FAR* FAR* ppenum) = 0;
};
```

The methods of an enumeration object are the same, regardless of the type of item being enumerated. However, the *Next* and *Clone* methods require parameters that are typed specifically for the individual enumerator. For clarity, these parameters are shown in bold in the preceding code section. *Next* accepts a pointer to an array (the *rgvar* parameter) that receives items from the enumerator. The array is typed to match the items contained in the collection. *Clone* duplicates the enumerator and returns a pointer of the specific enumerator type, shown in the *ppenum* parameter. Because the implementation of the methods is the same for all *IEnumxxx* interfaces except the types, a template solution is possible. ATL provides this solution in its two types of enumeration classes. One type is for enumerating collections of items contained in a contiguous memory array (*CComEnum* classes) and the other type is for enumerating items contained in an STL sequential container (*CComEnumOnSTL* classes). A collection implemented with *ICollectionOnSTLImpl* needs the STL version.

## *CComEnum* Enumerator Classes

ATL divides the enumerator declaration and implementation across three classes: *CComIEnum*, *CComEnumImpl*, and *CComEnum*. You typically create an instance of a *CComEnum* object and return its *IUnknown* pointer to the client in the *_NewEnum* property of the collection. The two remaining classes serve as base classes to *CComEnum*. A summary of each class follows.

### CComIEnum

*CComIEnum* is an abstract base class that derives from *IUnknown*. *CComIEnum* declares the *Next*, *Skip*, *Reset*, and *Clone* methods using a template parameter that defines the type of items being enumerated. For example, an *IEnumInteger* enumeration interface can be specified in C++ using *CComIEnum<int>*. You're on your own to supply the matching IDL.

### CComEnumImpl

*CComEnumImpl* derives from an *IEnumxxx* base class, typically *CComIEnum*, and supplies the implementations for *Next*, *Skip*, *Reset*, and *Clone* methods.

### CComEnum

*CComEnum* derives from *CComEnumImpl* and *CComObjectRootEx*. *CComEnum* is an ATL COM object that inherits the enumeration interface implementation from *CComEnumImpl*. A *CComEnum* object can be created and returned from *_NewEnum* as the enumerator object.

Figure 15-2 illustrates the enumerator class hierarchy.

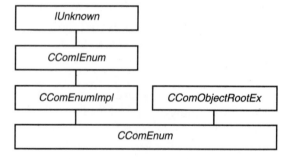

**Figure 15-2**
CComEnum *enumerator class hierarchy*

The template specification for *CComEnum* gives you some control over the hierarchy shown in Figure 15-2. The diagram shows *CComIEnum* as a base class, but you could instead use *IEnumVARIANT* or another predefined *IEnumxxx* interface. *CComIEnum* is a convenient way to define *IEnumxxx* interfaces as needed. We'll look at each class in the hierarchy, starting at the top with *CComIEnum*—which has the fewest template parameters—and working our way down to *CComEnum*.

### CComIEnum<class T>

*CComIEnum* is templatized on the type of item that is being enumerated. In the following code section, you can see how the *Next* and *Clone* methods use the supplied type *T*:

```
template<class T>
class ATL_NO_VTABLE CComIEnum : public IUnknown
{
public:
    STDMETHOD(Next)(ULONG celt, T* rgelt,
        ULONG* pceltFetched) = 0;
    STDMETHOD(Skip)(ULONG celt) = 0;
    STDMETHOD(Reset)(void) = 0;
    STDMETHOD(Clone)(CComIEnum<T>** ppEnum) = 0;
};
```

Déjà vu should be hitting you right about now. This is just a parameterized version of the *IEnumVARIANT* interface you saw earlier in the chapter. You could say that this is the C++ version of the generic *IEnumxxx*. *CComIEnum<VARIANT>* is essentially equivalent to *IEnumVARIANT*. If you're using an enumerator type not defined by COM, you'll need to create the matching IDL as well. *CComIEnum* is usually used as the base class for *CComEnumImpl*.

### CComEnumImpl<class Base, const IID* piid, class T, class Copy>

As you would expect from an ATL class ending with *Impl*, this class implements the interface that it derives from, which is specified in the template parameter *Base*. The base class must comply with the *IEnumxxx* contract, as *CComIEnum* does. The interface ID of the base class is passed in through the *piid* parameter. The parameter *T* is the type of object that the interface enumerates over, and the *Copy* parameter defines the copy policy that will be used to initialize, copy, and destroy items being enumerated. ATL provides copy policy classes for common types through the templatized _Copy class, and you can easily create your own as well. The code for the VARIANT copy policy provided by ATL is shown here:

```
template<>
class _Copy<VARIANT>
{
public:
    static HRESULT copy(VARIANT* p1, VARIANT* p2)
        {return VariantCopy(p1, p2);}
    static void init(VARIANT* p) {p->vt = VT_EMPTY;}
    static void destroy(VARIANT* p) {VariantClear(p);}
};
```

To create a copy policy for a data type not supported by ATL, create a class with all public static members, as in the class above. ATL provides a default copy policy that has no *init* or *destroy* code and that performs a shallow copy:

```
template <class T>
class _Copy
{
public:
    static HRESULT copy(T* p1, T* p2) {memcpy(p1, p2, sizeof(T));
        return S_OK;}
    static void init(T*) {}
    static void destroy(T*) {}
};
```

ATL provides specialized versions of the *_Copy* template class for the following types:

- VARIANT

- LPOLESTR

- OLEVERB

- CONNECTDATA

For collections of COM interface pointers, ATL has the *_CopyInterface* class, which calls *AddRef* on the interface after copying it and releases it in *destroy*, as shown here:

```
template <class T>
class _CopyInterface
{
public:
    static HRESULT copy(T** p1, T** p2)
    {
        *p1 = *p2;
        if(*p1)
            (*p1)->AddRef();
        return S_OK;
    }
    static void init(T** ) {}
    static void destroy(T** p) {if (*p) (*p)->Release();}
};
```

*CComEnumImpl* needs a copy policy to correctly duplicate the enumerated items to your [out] array in the *Next* method. The policy will also be used if *CComEnumImpl* is initialized with a snapshot of the collection items, instead of taking ownership of the items.

Ownership is declared in the *Init* method of *CComEnumImpl*. *Init* is called after *CComEnumImpl* is created to supply the enumerator object with an array of items from the collection. The parameters to *Init* provide pointers to the beginning and end of a contiguous array of items, along with a flag that describes the ownership of the array. The signature for *Init* is shown here:

```
HRESULT Init(T* begin, T* end, IUnknown* pUnk,
    CComEnumFlags flags = AtlFlagNoCopy);
```

The *flags* parameter can be one of three values defined in the *CComEnumFlags* enumeration type, shown here:

```
enum CComEnumFlags
{
    AtlFlagNoCopy = 0,
    AtlFlagTakeOwnership = 2,
    AtlFlagCopy = 3 // Copy implies ownership
};
```

The default is *AtlFlagNoCopy*, which allows the enumerator to use the array passed in to *Init* directly. If the same array is used for enumeration and internal collection state, a client could add or remove items from the array during the lifetime of an enumeration operation—which probably wouldn't be expected by the user of the enumerator. The *AtlFlagTakeOwnership* flag will also result in direct use of the array; however, the array will also be destroyed when the enumerator object is destroyed. The copy policy is used to destroy each item in the array before deleting the array itself. You might use *AtlFlagTakeOwnership* if you create an array on the heap in *_NewEnum* and copy your collection items into it yourself before calling *Init*. The last flag is *AtlFlagCopy*, which signals the enumerator to make a copy of the array in the *Init* method, copying each item to the new array using the copy policy. The copied array is destroyed when the enumerator is destroyed.

### CComEnum<class Base, const IID* piid, class T, class Copy, class ThreadModel = CComObjectThreadModel>

*CComEnum* combines *CComEnumImpl* with *CComObjectRootEx* to implement the enumerator object. *CComEnum* has an interface map with one entry for the base enumeration interface. With the exception of the *ThreadModel* parameter, the template parameters aren't used directly in *CComEnum* but are passed on to *CComEnumImpl*. *CComEnum* doesn't add any new interesting functionality beyond what it inherits from *CComEnumImpl*, but this is the class you'll work with to create an enumerator object. To declare an enumerator type that supports *IEnumVARIANT*, you can use a typedef such as the following.

```
typedef CComEnum< CComIEnum<VARIANT>,
    &IID_IEnumVARIANT,
    VARIANT,
    _Copy<VARIANT> > VariantEnumClass;
```

You can then use the *VariantEnumClass* type with *CComObject* to create an instance of an enumerator object, as shown here:

```
VariantEnumClass *pEnum = new CComObject<VariantEnumClass>;
```

ATL enumerator objects don't override *FinalConstruct*, so using the *new* operator is fine. You can use *CreateInstance* if you prefer. Once the enumerator object has been created, you need to call *Init* to set the array of items that will be enumerated. For *IEnumVARIANT*, you need an array of VARIANTs. The parameters to *Init* are pointers to the first array item and just beyond the last array item, the *IUnknown* pointer of the collection object, and the ownership flag. In the code section that follows, the enumerator is initialized from a dynamically allocated array. The enumerator takes ownership of the array, so you don't have to be concerned about destroying it. Also, the enumerator's copy policy will take care of deleting the VARIANTs contained in the array. This example shows the creation of an *IEnumVARIANT*-compliant enumerator object that enumerates over a collection of objects that implement the *ISimpleObject* interface.

```
typedef CComEnum< CComIEnum<VARIANT>,
    &IID_IEnumVARIANT,
    VARIANT,
    _Copy<VARIANT> > VarEnumClass;

CComObject<VarEnumClass> *pEnum = new CComObject<VarEnumClass>;

// Allocate and initialize an array of VARIANTs.
unsigned int uiSize = sizeof(VARIANT) * m_nCount;
VARIANT* pVar = (VARIANT*) new VARIANT[m_nCount];

// Get IDispatch for each collection item and put it in the array.
for (int i = 0; i < m_nCount; i++ )
{
    VariantInit(&pVar[i]);
    ISimpleObject* pIP = GetCollectionItem((long)i+1);
    pVar[i].vt = VT_DISPATCH;
    if(pIP != NULL)
    {
        hr = pIP->QueryInterface(IID_IDispatch,
            (void**)&pVar[i].pdispVal);
        pIP = NULL;
    }
}
```

```
// Initialize the enumerator and give it ownership of the array.
hr = pEnum->Init(&pVar[0], &pVar[m_nCount],
    this, AtlFlagTakeOwnership);
```

This code is typical of what you might see in the *get_ _NewEnum* property of a collection object. Visual Basic calls *_NewEnum* when it enters a For/Each loop. Visual Basic receives the *IUnknown* pointer of the enumerator (*pEnum*) as an [out] parameter from *_NewEnum*. Visual Basic takes the *IUnknown* pointer and calls *QueryInterface* for *IEnumVARIANT*. With *IEnumVARIANT* in hand, enumeration commences. Each time through the For/Each loop, Visual Basic calls *IEnumVARIANT::Next* to retrieve the next object in the collection. As we mentioned earlier in this chapter, there is currently no support for Visual Basic to retrieve more than one item during a call to *Next*.

## *CComEnumOnSTL* Enumerator Classes

The STL enumerator classes can be used with *ICollectionOnSTLImpl* to implement the enumerator object for the collection. Similar to the non-STL versions described previously, the ATL classes consist of an enumerator interface definition, an implementation, and an object class that is created and returned to the client in the *_NewEnum* property of the collection object. *ICollectionOnSTLImpl* handles all of this. All you need to do is give it the correct type specification for *CComEnumOnSTL*.

### *CComEnumOnSTL<class Base, const IID* piid, class T, class Copy, class CollType, class ThreadModel = CComObjectThreadModel>*

The template parameters for *CComEnumOnSTL* are identical to the parameters for *CComEnum*, with the exception of an additional parameter, *CollType*, that specifies the kind of STL collection that contains the items. *Base* defines the *IEnumxxx* interface the enumerator is implementing, and *piid* is a pointer to the interface ID for *Base*. *T* defines the type of object. The same copy policies described for *CComEnumImpl* also apply to this *Copy* template parameter. Part of the class definition for *CComEnumOnSTL* is shown here:

```
template <class Base, const IID* piid, class T, class Copy,
    class CollType, class ThreadModel = CComObjectThreadModel>
class ATL_NO_VTABLE CComEnumOnSTL :
    public IEnumOnSTLImpl<Base, piid, T, Copy, CollType>,
    public CComObjectRootEx< ThreadModel >
{
    ⋮
}
```

As with the non-STL version, most of the enumerator-specific work is done in the *IEnumOnSTLImpl* class that *CComEnumOnSTL* derives from. Figure 15-3 shows the inheritance tree for a *CComEnumOnSTL* enumerator object that uses *CComIEnum* to define the base interface.

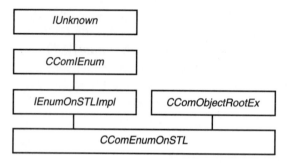

**Figure 15-3**
CComEnumOnSTL *enumerator class hierarchy*

The template parameters are forwarded through to *IEnumOnSTLImpl*, with the exception of the threading model. As you saw earlier in the discussion of *ICollectionOnSTLImpl*, *ICollectionOnSTLImpl::get__NewEnum* creates a new *CComEnumOnSTL* object, initializes it, and returns its *IUnknown* pointer to the caller. The enumerator object is initialized by calling the *Init* method, which *CComEnumOnSTL* inherits from *IEnumOnSTLImpl*.

### IEnumOnSTLImpl <class Base, const IID* piid, class T, class Copy, class CollType>

This class implements the expected *Next*, *Reset*, *Skip*, and *Clone* methods for the *IEnumxxx* interface that you specify as the *Base* template parameter. You can use the same *CComIEnum< T>* class described in the *CComEnum* section. For an *IEnumVARIANT* definition, use *CComIEnum< VARIANT>* for the *Base* parameter. The enumerator is initialized after creation by calling the *IEnumOnSTLImpl::Init* method. *Init* takes a reference to the STL container as a parameter, as shown here:

```
HRESULT Init(IUnknown *pUnkForRelease, CollType& collection)
{
    m_spUnk = pUnkForRelease;
    m_pcollection = &collection;
    m_iter = m_pcollection->begin();
    return S_OK;
}
```

Unlike the *CComEnumImpl* version, there are no options for ownership of the STL container. The enumerator always gets a reference to the caller's STL container in the *Init* call and therefore never owns the container. The *IEnumOnSTLImpl::Clone* method follows suit, only giving out the reference to the container, not copying it. *IEnumOnSTLImpl* caches a pointer to the STL container passed in to *Init*, along with an iterator for the container.

A nice feature of *IEnumOnSTLImpl* is that you don't have to allocate an array of VARIANTs to initialize it when creating an *IEnumVARIANT* implementation. More generally, the *IEnumOnSTLImpl::Next* method uses the copy policy to get a collection item from the STL container, copy it to the type required by the *Next* method return value, and return it to the caller. Because *IEnumOnSTLImpl* has an STL iterator, it can simply dereference the iterator to obtain an item to be copied, regardless of type. In a collection of objects, the STL container holds interface pointers. The copy policy must be prepared to receive the interface pointer for copying and to return a VARIANT VT_DISPATCH. Here's the section of *IEnumOnSTLImpl::Next* just described:

```
T* pelt = rgelt;
while (SUCCEEDED(hr) && m_iter != m_pcollection->end()
    && nActual < celt)
{
    hr = Copy::copy(pelt, &*m_iter);
⋮
}
```

The additional type information passed in for the STL collection in the *CollType* template parameter makes it possible to have an iterator and a return value with different types. In the previous code section, the return value is of type *T*, and *m_iter* is of type *CollType::iterator*. Only the copy policy needs to know how to copy one to the other.

# Conclusion

The ATL enumerator classes provide convenient, reusable implementations for creating enumerator objects. The ATL collection implementation is limited, but it gives us a head start on STL and demonstrates how to use enumerator objects in collections. The best way to get a handle on using the ATL enumerator and collection classes is to look at more examples and then build some code yourself.

## CHAPTER SIXTEEN

# Writing Applications with ATL

Although it is primarily a COM development tool, ATL is also a workable environment for creating Microsoft Win32 applications—but you have to get your hands a little dirty to get the job done. As of this writing, there is no AppWizard support for creating a Win32 EXE in ATL that doesn't have COM server code attached. The lack of a document/view framework, serialization support, and a printing abstraction means you'll have to roll your own if you need them. We'll dedicate this chapter to the creation of a simple ATL application named ATL Scribble, an SDI application that allows you to sketch on a window canvas with your mouse. ATL Scribble will have a menu and a toolbar, and will support persistence to a file. We'll use ATL for all the windowing in the project and the Standard Template Library (STL) for arrays and maps. We'll use the subject–observer design pattern to notify views when the scribble data changes. We'll keep the drawing and message-handling code separate from the windowing classes so that we can reuse it in both a view and a dialog box. The companion CD contains the complete source code for the project. This chapter isn't a tutorial, but we'll highlight the major areas involved in creating a Win32 project with ATL so that you can apply the same concepts to your own applications.

## Creating a Project

You have two AppWizard options for creating a Win32 project that is a suitable starting point for building an ATL application.

The first option is to create an EXE server by using the ATL COM App-Wizard. This choice is good if you think you might want your application to support Automation. Naturally, all the ATL wizards will work right off the bat.

The second option is to create a simple application by using the Win32 EXE Application wizard and then manually add ATL support. This choice involves a little more work if you want to use the ATL object and message wizards because certain files and statements must be present in the project before they will run. The changes required to enable the wizards are described in the following list.

■ Modify stdafx.h to add the necessary ATL headers; atlcom.h is required for the object map macros, and atlwin.h is, of course, for windowing classes. You also need an external reference to a *CCom-Module* instance, *_Module*. The code is as follows:

```
#include <atlbase.h>
extern CComModule _Module;
#include <atlcom.h>
#include <atlwin.h>
```

■ Add an ATL object map to the main .cpp file. The map can be empty. Also add the *CComModule* instance, as shown here:

```
CComModule _Module;

BEGIN_OBJECT_MAP(ObjectMap)
END_OBJECT_MAP()
```

■ Add an IDL file with the same name as the project. The file must have a library block. The file doesn't have to compile, but you must add it to your project under the source files folder. Use the project settings to exclude the IDL file from your build. The file can have the following minimal contents:

```
library AnyNameWillDo
{
};
```

Using the second option, we now have a lightweight application shell to which we can begin adding functionality.

## Creating the Main Frame Window

As mentioned, ATL Scribble is going to be an SDI application, so we'll create a frame window using the ATL *CFrameWinTraits* styles, which we covered in Chapter 14. We'll create a new class derived from *CWindowImpl* named *CMainFrame*. There is no wizard support for creating ATL windowing class derivatives specifically, so we'll have to add a generic class with the New Class dialog box and then modify it. Launch the dialog box by right-clicking on the root node in ClassView, and then choose New Class from the context menu.

Type in *CMainFrame* as the class name and *CWindowImpl* as the base class. Figure 16-1 shows what the fields in the New Class dialog box should contain.

**Figure 16-1**
*The New Class dialog box*

We didn't type in the template parameters for *CWindowImpl* in the edit box because it's so small, so we need to open the mainframe.h header file and add them. We also need to add the message map and the window class name manually using the DECLARE_WND_CLASS macro. After that's done, we can use the wizard bar to add message handlers to the *CMainFrame* message map. A quit message should be posted when the main frame window closes, so we'll override *OnFinalMessage* to do that. ATL calls *OnFinalMessage* when a WM_NCDESTROY message is received. *OnFinalMessage* is a member of *CWindowImplBaseT* and is one of the few virtual functions in ATL. The current state of the mainframe.h header file is shown here:

```
class CMainFrame : public CWindowImpl<CMainFrame, CWindow,
    CFrameWinTraits>
{
public:
    CMainFrame();
    virtual ~CMainFrame();

    DECLARE_WND_CLASS(_T("InAtl:Frame"))
```

*(continued)*

```
BEGIN_MSG_MAP(CMainFrame)
END_MSG_MAP()

void OnFinalMessage(HWND /*hWnd*/)
{
    ::PostQuitMessage(0);
}
};
```

We'll add some code to the *WinMain* function to create the frame window and run a message loop. We'll add a menu resource so that we can specify its handle in the *CWindowImpl Create* function, and we'll also add an icon, which we'll plug into the WNDCLASSEX structure directly. The Win32 project doesn't have a resource file by default, but inserting a resource from the Insert menu will create one that you can then add to the project. (If you plan to use MFC-defined resources such as ID_FILE_OPEN, you'll need to include afxres.h in stdafx.h.) Finally, we have to add a message pump. Our *WinMain* is now functional. Here's the code:

```
int APIENTRY WinMain(HINSTANCE hInstance,
    HINSTANCE hPrevInstance,
    LPSTR     lpCmdLine,
    int       nCmdShow)
{
    lpCmdLine = GetCommandLine();
    HRESULT hRes = CoInitialize(NULL);
    _ASSERTE(SUCCEEDED(hRes));
    _Module.Init(NULL, hInstance, NULL);
    CMainFrame mainframe;
    // Specify the icon in the WNDCLASSEX structure.
    HICON hIcon = LoadIcon(_Module.GetResourceInstance(),
        MAKEINTRESOURCE(IDI_ICON1));
    mainframe.GetWndClassInfo().m_wc.hIcon = hIcon;

    // Menu handle is a parameter to Create.
    HMENU hMenu = LoadMenu(_Module.GetResourceInstance(),
        MAKEINTRESOURCE(IDR_MENU1));
    mainframe.Create(GetDesktopWindow(), CWindow::rcDefault,
        _T("ATL Scribble"), 0, 0, (UINT)hMenu);

    // Make visible.
    mainframe.ShowWindow(SW_SHOWNORMAL);
```

```
    MSG msg;
    while (GetMessage(&msg, 0, 0, 0))
    {
        TranslateMessage(&msg);
        DispatchMessage(&msg);
    }
    _Module.Term();
    CoUninitialize();
    return 0;
}
```

The application now consists of a frame window with a menu and looks like Figure 16-2.

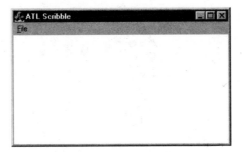

**Figure 16-2**
*ATL Scribble application main frame*

# Adding a Status Bar and a Toolbar

At this point, our application looks pretty plain, so we'll add a toolbar and a status bar to spruce it up. To gain access to the Microsoft Windows common controls, link to the common controls DLL and then add an *InitCommonControls* call to *WinMain*. You can link to the controls using the following *pragma* in the main .cpp file:

```
#pragma comment(lib, "comctl32.lib")
```

ATL ships thin wrappers for most of the standard Windows controls as part of the ATLCON sample. If you haven't seen these control classes, definitely take a few minutes to browse the sample.

> **NOTE** As of this writing, the classes in atlcontrols.h are not documented and are not supported by Microsoft.

To use the control classes, we need to include atlcontrols.h from the ATLCON sample and use the ATLControls namespace. To do this, copy atlcontrols.h into your project directory or set up an include path to the ATLCON sample directory in the Microsoft Visual C++ options. Include atlcontrols.h in mainframe.h and add the *using* statement for the new namespace right after the include statement, like this:

```
#include "atlcontrols.h"
using namespace ATLControls;
```

The status bar class is implemented in *CStatusBarCtrlT<base>*. The class is designed to use *CWindow* as the base class, so atlcontrols.h provides a typedef for that common case, as shown here:

```
typedef CStatusBarCtrlT<CWindow>    CStatusBarCtrl;
```

We'll use the typedef and add a *CStatusBarCtrl* data member to *CMain-Frame*. To create the status bar, add a WM_CREATE handler to *CMainFrame* by using the Wizard Bar. Click the Wizard Bar drop-down button, and choose Add Windows Message Handler. Adding a handler for WM_CREATE generates an empty *OnCreate* handler function, which we'll modify to create the status bar, as shown here:

```
LRESULT OnCreate(UINT uMsg, WPARAM wParam, LPARAM lParam,
    BOOL& bHandled)
{
    m_wndStatusBar.Create(m_hWnd, NULL, NULL, WS_CHILD |
        WS_VISIBLE, ID_STATUS);
    ATLASSERT(m_wndStatusBar.IsWindow());
    m_wndStatusBar.SetSimple();
    m_wndStatusBar.SetText(255, _T("Simple Status Bar"));
    return 0;
}
```

We must position the status bar at the bottom of the frame window and resize the status bar whenever the frame is resized, so we'll add a WM_SIZE handler to *CMainFrame*. The code in *OnSize* simply needs to tell the status bar control to resize itself, which a status bar does by default when it gets a WM_SIZE message. The *OnSize* handler is shown here:

```
LRESULT OnSize(UINT uMsg, WPARAM wParam, LPARAM lParam,
    BOOL& bHandled)
{
    m_wndStatusBar.SendMessage(WM_SIZE);
    return 0;
}
```

The code for adding a toolbar is pretty much like straight SDK code. You have to build an array of TBBUTTON structures and add them to the toolbar control. In the ATL Scribble sample, we use one of the system toolbar bitmaps by calling *LoadStdImages(IDB_STD_SMALL_COLOR)*. We map command IDs to toolbar buttons for ID_FILE_OPEN, ID_FILE_NEW, and ID_APP_ABOUT, which are handled in *CMainFrame* just like the menu commands. Toolbars automatically forward WM_COMMAND messages to their parent, so we get that for free. We'll add three toolbar buttons using the *InitToolBar* function shown here, which is called from *CMainFrame::OnCreate*:

```
void InitToolbar()
{
    m_wndToolBar.Create(m_hWnd, NULL, NULL, WS_CHILD |
        TBSTYLE_FLAT | TBSTYLE_TOOLTIPS, ID_TOOLBAR);
    m_wndToolBar.SetButtonStructSize(sizeof(TBBUTTON));
    m_wndToolBar.LoadStdImages(IDB_STD_SMALL_COLOR);

    TBBUTTON tbb[3];
    ::ZeroMemory(tbb, sizeof(tbb));
    tbb[0].iBitmap = STD_FILEOPEN;
    tbb[0].idCommand = ID_FILE_OPEN;
    tbb[0].fsState = TBSTATE_ENABLED;
    tbb[0].fsStyle = TBSTYLE_BUTTON;

    tbb[1].iBitmap = STD_FILENEW;
    tbb[1].idCommand = ID_FILE_NEW;
    tbb[1].fsState = TBSTATE_ENABLED;
    tbb[1].fsStyle = TBSTYLE_BUTTON;

    tbb[2].iBitmap = STD_HELP;
    tbb[2].idCommand = ID_APP_ABOUT;
    tbb[2].fsState = TBSTATE_ENABLED;
    tbb[2].fsStyle = TBSTYLE_BUTTON;

    m_wndToolBar.AddButtons(3, tbb);
    m_wndToolBar.ShowWindow(SW_SHOW);
}
```

We also added matching menu commands for the File New and About buttons, and WM_COMMAND handlers for these buttons to the *CMainFrame* message map.

We'll want to provide ToolTips for our toolbar buttons as well, so we need to handle TTN_GETDISPINFO and supply ToolTip text in the handler. The message-map entry and handler are listed on the following page.

```
NOTIFY_CODE_HANDLER(TTN_GETDISPINFO, OnTipInfo)

LRESULT OnTipInfo(int idCtrl, LPNMHDR pnmh, BOOL& bHandled)
{
    LPNMTTDISPINFO ptti = (LPNMTTDISPINFO)pnmh;
    if(!(ptti->uFlags & TTF_IDISHWND))
    {
        ptti->hinst = _Module.GetResourceInstance();
        ptti->lpszText = MAKEINTRESOURCE(ptti->hdr.idFrom);
    }
    return 0;
}
```

The handler assumes a string resource exists for each command ID on the toolbar.

## Creating a View

Because we have a toolbar and a status bar taking up space in the client area of the main frame window, we'll go ahead and create a child window that will show the actual drawing strokes. The window will occupy all the usable client area of the frame not covered by the toolbar and the status bar. To create the window, we need to derive a class from *CWindowImpl* with the appropriate styles for a view window. The *CView* class declaration shown here will do the trick:

```
typedef CWinTraits<WS_CHILD | WS_VISIBLE, WS_EX_CLIENTEDGE>
    CViewWinTraits;

class CView : public CWindowImpl<CView, CWindow, CViewWinTraits>
{
public:
    CView();
    virtual ~CView();

    DECLARE_WND_CLASS(_T("InAtl:View"))

    BEGIN_MSG_MAP(CView)
    END_MSG_MAP()
};
```

In the class declaration, we've defined a new window class for our view as well as a default message map. Now all we need to do is add a *CView* data member to *CMainFrame*, create it in *OnCreate*, and size it to the unused client area in the *OnSize* handler. There isn't anything special about the creation code. The *CViewWinTraits* class provides all our styles, so we won't specify any to the *Create* function, as shown here:

```
// Create the view.
m_wndView.Create(m_hWnd, CWindow::rcDefault, _T("View"),
    0, 0, 0);
```

The *OnSize* handler positions and sizes the view to fill the remaining client area in *CMainFrame*. The application frame with the toolbar, status bar, and view is shown in Figure 16-3.

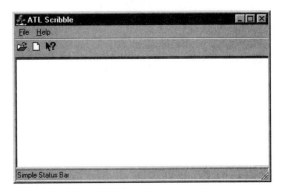

**Figure 16-3**
*ATL Scribble with a toolbar, a status bar, and a view*

# Creating a Document

We need a place to store points when they are generated by mouse clicks. Because ATL Scribble is a simple SDI application, we can create a new class that has a single global instance to contain the points and to handle persistence. Our *CDataModel* class handles these responsibilities. *CDataModel* keeps an STL vector of strokes that represents the sketch. Points are added to the data model using the *Add-Point* method of the global *_DataModel* instance. The data model (subject) also keeps a list of views (observers), which are notified when data changes in the model. You might not need a subject or an observer implementation in a small sample with a single view, but some kind of update mechanism is necessary if multiple views or splitters are allowed in your application. We'll use the update mechanism here to demonstrate. The data model class derives from a *CSubject-Impl* class that maintains and updates a list of observers. *CSubjectImpl* derives from the abstract base class *CSubject*, which defines the following three methods:

```
virtual void AddObserver(CObserver* pObserver) = 0;
virtual void RemoveObserver(CObserver* pObserver) = 0;
virtual void UpdateAllObservers(CObserver* pSender,
    DWORD dwType) = 0;
```

*CSubjectImpl* implements these methods on an STL vector. *CDataModel* contains the application-specific state, which is a vector of strokes. The view adds points when the mouse is dragged and then generates an update by calling *UpdateAllObservers* on the data model. The view subscribes to the data model update list when it is created and removes itself when destroyed. Figure 16-4 shows the class relationships for the data model.

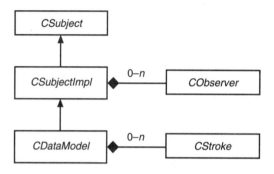

**Figure 16-4**
*Class relationships for the data model*

## Separating the Behavior from the View Window

We might want to have any number of window types that can draw to and render from the same data model. To achieve this, we've encapsulated the drawing and message handling specific to the scribble behavior in a separate base class. *CScribbleImpl* derives from the ATL class *CMessageMap* and our abstract base class, *CObserver*. *CScribbleImpl* takes the derived class name as a template parameter, so it can downcast to get a window handle. We derive *CView* from *CScribbleImpl*. *CView* routes messages to *CScribbleImpl* by adding a CHAIN_MSG_MAP macro to its message map, as shown here:

```
class CView : public CWindowImpl<CView, CWindow,
    CViewWinTraits>, public CScribbleImpl<CView>
{
public:
    CView();
    virtual ~CView();

    DECLARE_WND_CLASS(_T("InAtl:View"))
```

```
BEGIN_MSG_MAP(CView)
    CHAIN_MSG_MAP(CScribbleImpl<CView>)
    MESSAGE_HANDLER(WM_PAINT, OnPaint)
END_MSG_MAP()

LRESULT OnPaint(UINT uMsg, WPARAM wParam, LPARAM lParam,
    BOOL& bHandled)
{
    // Render the point array from the model.
    HDC hdc = GetDC();
    // Delegate to CScribbleImpl.
    DoPaint(hdc);
    ReleaseDC(hdc);
    bHandled = FALSE;
    return 1;
}
};
```

*CView* delegates its painting to *CScribbleImpl* as well. We could have handled WM_PAINT in *CScribbleImpl*, but the code is made more portable by allowing the window to prepare its device context before delegating to *CScribbleImpl:: DoPaint*.

To enable *CScribbleImpl* to get notifications when a point is added or when the data model is modified, we've created an abstract *CObserver* class and derived *CScribbleImpl* from it. *CObserver* has only one function: *OnUpdate*. The data model calls *OnUpdate* for every observer when a sketch point is added. *CScribbleImpl* initiates the update by calling *UpdateAllObservers*, as you can see in the mouse event handlers:

```
LRESULT OnLButtonDown(UINT uMsg, WPARAM wParam, LPARAM lParam,
    BOOL& bHandled)
{
    T* pT = static_cast<T*>(this);
    ::SetCapture(pT->m_hWnd);
    _DataModel.StartStroke();
    m_bStroke = TRUE;
    m_point.x = LOWORD(lParam);
    m_point.y = HIWORD(lParam);
    _DataModel.AddPoint(m_point);
    _DataModel.UpdateAllObservers(this, CDataModel::UPDATE_ALL);
    return 0;
}
```

*(continued)*

```
LRESULT OnMouseMove(UINT uMsg, WPARAM wParam, LPARAM lParam,
    BOOL& bHandled)
{
    if(m_bStroke && (wParam & MK_LBUTTON))
    {
        m_point.x = LOWORD(lParam);
        m_point.y = HIWORD(lParam);
        _DataModel.AddPoint(m_point);
        _DataModel.UpdateAllObservers(this,
            CDataModel::UPDATE_ALL);
    }
    return 0;
}

LRESULT OnLButtonUP(UINT uMsg, WPARAM wParam, LPARAM lParam,
    BOOL& bHandled)
{
    m_bStroke = FALSE;
    ::ReleaseCapture();
    return 0;
}
```

In response to *UpdateAllObservers*, the data model iterates over any subscribed observers and calls *OnUpdate* on each one. *CScribbleImpl* implements *OnUpdate* by simply invalidating the derived classes window, as shown here:

```
void OnUpdate(CSubject* pSubject, CObserver* pSender,
    DWORD dwType)
{
    T* pT = static_cast<T*>(this);
    ::InvalidateRect(pT->m_hWnd, NULL, TRUE);
}
```

When the WM_PAINT message is received by the view, the handler gets a device context and delegates the painting to *CScribbleImpl::DoPaint*, which reads each stroke from the data model and renders it.

## Persistence

If you build an application in ATL, you have to create your own persistence scheme. The ATL Scribble sample uses a simple comma-separated data format for storing the points to a file. The File Open and File Save common dialog boxes provide the file selection user interface. A sketch is persisted by enumerating over the points that define the user's strokes and writing them to the file, as you can see in this section from *CStroke*:

```
void CStroke::Save(FILE* file)
{
    int nPoints = m_points.size();
    _ftprintf(file, _T("%d\n"), nPoints);
    POINTITERATOR it;
    for(it = m_points.begin(); it != m_points.end(); it++)
    {
        POINT pt = *it;
        _ftprintf(file, _T("%d,%d\n"), pt.x, pt.y);
    }
}
```

Of course, you can choose whichever file format you prefer, such as XML.

## What's Missing

We'll stop here with our ATL Scribble application. If you want to add more to the user interface, you'll have to weigh the benefits of writing these features yourself against using MFC. Here are some of the things we didn't include:

- Scroll bars and virtual document size
- Splitter windows
- Printing and print preview
- Drag-and-drop file support

## Conclusion

You can use ATL to provide effective windowing for high-performance Win32 applications. ATL isn't an application framework like MFC, so you do have to work a little harder to get a boilerplate application up and running. The ATLCON sample provides some (unsupported) thin control wrappers, which make programming the common controls cleaner. If you need collections, you should become familiar with STL, which is full of powerful features. We hope to see more application development support from the ATL team in future versions of Visual C++.

## CHAPTER SEVENTEEN

# ATL and Beyond

At this point, it should be clear to you that COM is going to stick around for a while. We COM developers have been on a long, interesting adventure, one that's taken us from developing basic Brockschmidtian COM classes using raw C++ in the early 1990s to using higher leverage tools such as MFC to develop COM-based controls and document applications. COM apartment models appeared in 1995, and ATL came on the scene in 1996, making it much easier to develop simple COM classes. In 1997, we finally witnessed a decent transaction system. And now Microsoft Windows 2000 and COM+ are on the horizon.

Some of you might wonder why we wrote this book about ATL at a time when this thing called "COM+" was just around the corner. Mary Kirtland wrote an article in the September 1997 issue of *Microsoft Systems Journal* proclaiming that COM+ would greatly simplify COM development and perhaps even make C++ "obsolete" by introducing IDL-like constructs into C++ and basic run-time support (such as class factories) into a C++ run-time library. As it turns out, the COM+ advertised in those articles was always just around the corner—the tool and language support probably won't materialize until we're into the next century. The COM+ that is being released with Windows 2000 is based on simplifying the software development model.

The scope of the COM+ version being released with Windows 2000 is different from that of the COM+ concept first announced near the end of 1997. That description of COM+ included extensions to the C++ language as well as a C++ run-time library. The version of COM+ that will appear in Windows 2000 is more a set of run-time services based on the concepts of interception and context-based programming. It's interface-based programming all the way down. COM+ builds on everything that COM already is. So don't worry—interface-based programming still has a lot of life left in it. In fact, many of the really cool new features available in COM+ (through interception and context) are available *because* of interface-based programming.

In this chapter, we'll explain some of the new technologies coming down the pike and how they affect ATL. We'll start off with a look at context-based programming, the main new feature of COM+. Then we'll examine some of the other features becoming available through COM+, including transactions and a new security model.

# Context-Based Programming

We've just spent nearly an entire book examining Microsoft's version of the discipline known as interface-based programming—but hold on! A whole new development paradigm is emerging, and it's called context-based programming.

Before you get too worried, everything you've learned about interface-based development (specifically using ATL) holds true when you're doing context-based development. In fact, context-based development is integral to many aspects of COM development.

To get an idea of what context-based development is all about and to make understanding interception and contexts easier, we'll take a look at COM apartments and see how they affect developers of COM-based software. Interception and context already exist as solid concepts in Microsoft Transaction Server (MTS), and they'll play an important role in COM+ and Windows 2000, in which MTS will become Microsoft Component Services.

## The Long and Winding Road to Thread Management

What a great industry we work in—just when you get a handle on the current technology, something new comes along. After years of developing software using APIs, we moved to an interface-based programming paradigm. And now that we have a handle on interface-based programming, we need to look at new ideas made possible by interception and context. To understand what lies ahead for the collective software development community, let's look back and review how certain aspects of software development have evolved.

Remember when Microsoft Windows NT (or OS/2 if you're a real die-hard) came out? A whole API existed just for managing threads—it let you create threads, start threads, suspend threads, and even kill them if you wanted to. Because of the nature of threads, however, you had to assume that data visible to multiple threads could be accessed by those threads simultaneously. Of course, this accessibility created the possibility of data becoming corrupted.

To solve this problem, the Microsoft Win32 API provided a number of thread synchronization mechanisms, including mutexes, semaphores, events, and critical sections. (Mutexes, semaphores, and events are represented by handles, and critical sections are represented by structures.) These thread synchronization mechanisms all work in more or less the same way. As a thread goes along its merry way, it might decide to access a piece of global data. Before doing so, it tries to acquire a thread synchronization token. If the token is unavailable (that is, another thread acquired it first), the thread trying to acquire the synchronization token has to wait until the other thread frees the token.

The bottom line is that developers need to sprinkle their code with calls to API synchronization functions to make their code thread-safe. Inserting these calls and paying close attention avoids race conditions and deadlock. For example, if a developer uses a critical section to lock out other threads from accessing a resource, a certain function might call *EnterCriticalSection*, access the data, and then call *LeaveCriticalSection*.

One way to simplify the development of multithreaded software is to move the thread synchronization management code into the operating system. As we saw in the last chapter, that's exactly what COM does. In reviewing COM apartments, we'll get to see the concepts of interception and contexts firsthand.

## Apartments and the Concept of Separation

Recall that COM is all about software distribution and integration. The only way to effectively distribute and integrate software components is to decouple the components as much as possible. To this end, the main tenet of COM is to hide from the client as many details about an object's implementation as possible.

As we've seen so far, by separating an object's programmatic interface from its implementation, COM systematically removes knowledge of an object's implementation from the client. Forcing the client to access an object through interfaces truly enforces encapsulation. By shoving the actual location of a server's DLL or EXE into the Registry, COM conceals an object's location from the client. Another detail removed from the client is information about the object's concurrency requirements. Clients should be able to use an object in a thread-intensive environment—whether or not the component was written to be thread-safe.

The mechanism that makes this separation of the client from the object implementation possible is the COM *apartment*. (See page 49 in Chapter 2 for more information about COM apartments.) COM apartments are useful for grouping objects with the same concurrency requirements. Modern COM (Windows NT 4.0) defines two kinds of apartments: a single-threaded apartment (STA) and the multithreaded apartment (MTA). An STA can house only one thread, whereas the MTA can house many threads.

Client threads move into an apartment by calling a variant of *CoInitialize* (*CoInitialize*, *CoInitializeEx*, or *OleInitialize*). After a thread calls *CoInitialize*, it might choose to enter either the MTA or an STA. Then, as the thread executes, it might decide to create a COM object. If it does, when the client calls *CoCreate-Instance*, COM looks in the class's entry in the Registry to find the kind of apartment into which the object wants to move. If the object's advertised apartment is compatible with the calling thread's apartment, the object moves into the same apartment as the calling thread. If the object's advertised apartment is incompatible with the calling thread's apartment, the object moves into a separate apartment, and the client thread has to access the object via a proxy. The proxy (on the client side) and the stub (on the object side) work in concert to serialize calls into the object, avoiding concurrent access to the object's state.

## Interception

You can see the fundamental difference between COM software development during the 1990s and COM development as we head into the next century from the basic example of COM apartments, and it can be summed up in two words: *interception* and *context*.

Recall that in typical C++ development, nothing sits between your client code and the objects the client code creates. When your client code calls operator *new* to get a new object, it gets a raw pointer to the object. COM is all about indirection. When it creates a new COM object, your client code has to go through an API function such as *CoCreateInstance*. By inserting a layer of indirection between the client and the object, COM enables the operating system to intercept creation calls, giving COM the chance to perform intermediate processing such as setting up a separate apartment for the object to live in. For example, recall the process of creating an object that declares itself to be single threaded from a multithreaded environment:

1. A client thread that is running along decides to call *CoCreateInstance*. The class advertises its single-threaded nature by placing the words *Apartment Threaded* in HKEY_CLASSES_ROOT\{...}\ InprocServer32\ThreadingModel.

2. COM examines the Registry and determines first that the client thread is running in the MTA, and second that the object needs to run in an STA.

3. COM finds or creates a compatible environment, places the new object in that environment (an STA), and returns a pointer to a proxy for the client thread.

The proxy switches threads before and after method invocations to ensure that the object is protected and that the object's run-time environment, or apartment, is compatible with the class's requirements.

Notice the big advantage here: the method synchronization inside the object code is provided via the operating system instead of through lots of calls to some threading API.

You can see that if you're familiar with apartments, you already understand the basic notions underlying interception and contexts: COM intercepts calls to an object and makes sure that object lives in an appropriate context. Microsoft Component Services and COM+ in Windows 2000 expand on this idea of interception, layering other services using it.

## How Interception Works in Windows 2000

COM+ and Microsoft Component Services provide advanced services such as concurrency management to components that want them (as does the Windows NT 4.0–style apartment model, in which COM components declare their concurrency requirements in the Registry). Components indicate their desires for these services via declarative attributes stored in the catalog.

Whereas in plain-vanilla COM you advertise the threading requirements of your object in the Registry, in Windows 2000 you use configured components. Instead of having to code certain services in your components, you can tack the services on at deployment by configuring them through deployment tools (as Microsoft Component Services Explorer does now).

Configured components are registered in the Catalog Manager. The Catalog Manager controls the HKEY_CLASSES_ROOT\CLSID entries in the Registry as well as a configuration database. Application-level information, such as the activation type (in-process DLL or surrogate) and details about configuring security, is included in configuring a class. The catalog also includes information about configuring interfaces, methods, and services such as transactions and object pooling.

The basic idea is that services can be layered onto your object by having COM intercept calls to the object. When COM intercepts a method call, it can provide preprocessing and postprocessing for the call, which allows COM to perform such services as setting up a run-time environment for your object (as the apartment architecture does now) and making system calls for you.

For interception to work, COM needs to know what the interface looks like so that it can manufacture the interceptors when necessary. To that end, an interface exposed by a configured component requires a type library or a specially prepared proxy/stub DLL. If you can use type-library marshaling for your interface (that is, your interface is VARIANT-compliant and marked with the Dual or the Ole_Automation attribute), you're good to go. Otherwise, you build a proxy/stub DLL after compiling the IDL code with the */Oicf* switches thrown.

Once the component is deployed, *CoCreateInstance* checks the configuration settings (the auxiliary attribute information) at activation. Depending on how the component is configured, COM will either move the object into the same context as the calling thread or move the object into a different context. But what is a context?

## Contexts

A context is a group of objects within a process. (Wow—sounds like an apartment, doesn't it?) Contexts separate incompatible objects from one another, just as apartments separate objects with different concurrency requirements.

In COM+, every object belongs to exactly one context. Objects that are incompatible (by even a single attribute) live in different contexts. However, a process can contain multiple contexts. (Notice that apartments work in much the same way.)

A call is made between incompatible contexts through an interceptor (a proxy). The proxy is created automatically by COM and implements the same interfaces as the real object. The proxy does whatever it takes to deal with the incompatibilities between two contexts.

Fortunately, contexts are a bit easier to grasp than apartments. Whereas apartments are more or less abstract entities in COM, contexts are represented by real objects inside a process. COM contexts are broken into two pieces: the per-method invocation context (named the *call context*) and the method-independent context (named the *object context*). Each context has properties. As a developer, you can access an object's call context and object context via the API functions *CoGetCallContext* and *CoGetObjectContext*. When you call these functions, interfaces that represent a call context or an object context are returned. Currently, the interface you can retrieve using *CoGetCallContext* is *IServerSecurity*, which provides information about the security settings. Here are the function prototypes for retrieving call contexts as well as the *IServerSecurity* interface:

```
HRESULT CoGetCallContext(REFIID riid, void **ppInterface);

    IServerSecurity : public IUnknown {
    HRESULT QueryBlanket(DWORD* pAuthnSvc,
    DWORD* pAuthzSvc,
```

```
    OLECHAR** pServerPrincName,
    DWORD* pAuthnLevel,
    DWORD* pImpLevel,
    void** pPrivs,
    DWORD* pCapabilities) = 0;
    HRESULT ImpersonateClient(void)=0;
    HRESULT RevertToSelf(void) = 0;
    BOOL IsImpersonating(void) = 0;
};
```

An object's context exposes several interfaces, the most important of which is *IObjectContext*. Here's the prototype for retrieving an object's context and the *IObjectContext* interface:

```
HRESULT CoGetObjectContext([in] REFIID riid,
    [out, retval, iid_is(riid)] void **ppv);

interface IObjectContext : public IUnknown
{
    HRESULT CreateInstance(REFCLSID rclsid,
    REFIID riid,
    LPVOID*ppv) = 0;
    HRESULT SetComplete(void) = 0;
    HRESULT SetAbort(void) = 0;
    HRESULT EnableCommit(void) = 0;
    HRESULT DisableCommit(void) = 0;
    BOOL IsInTransaction(void) = 0;
    BOOL IsSecurityEnabled(void) = 0;
    HRESULT IsCallerInRole(BSTR bstrRole,
    BOOL *bInRole) = 0;
};
```

The context makes several different services available to the object; security is one example. The function *IsCallerInRole* (as shown in the preceding code for *IObjectContext*) enables role-based security. Role-based security lets you assign roles and access rights at deployment time, which in turn allows the objects to examine their callers to determine whether to let callers execute particular functions. This reduces programming complexity significantly—wrapping an object with a context makes it possible to layer orthogonal services on top of your object with the client being none the wiser.

Now let's take a closer look at one of the most important applications of interception and context-based programming—the COM way to handle transactions.

# Microsoft Component Services

One of the most common complaints about COM during the mid-1990s was that many of the services already available through the Common Object Request Broker Architecture (CORBA) were unavailable through COM. Nobody had coded these services to make distributed computing using COM a reality.

Microsoft Transaction Server (MTS) finally emerged from Redmond in 1997. Although people had been writing transaction systems for years, no viable, standard distributed transaction system had been built on COM. To play in the enterprise arena, Microsoft needed something like MTS, which is now called Microsoft Component Services in Windows 2000. In this section, we'll cover how transactions work in general and then how Microsoft Component Services uses interception and context to make writing transaction software easier as well as how Windows 2000 handles issues such as concurrency.

## Transactions

Moving from an understanding of stand-alone systems (which is what many Windows developers have been working with for the last 10 years) to an understanding of distributed transaction systems requires some new thinking. When a simple client application talked to a single database (or some other data source), transactions were simple—either they worked or they didn't. Now that developers are creating distributed systems, transactions have become fairly complex.

A *transaction* is a unit of work done on behalf of a client. It is initiated by some sort of transaction application and can have multiple participants that determine its overall success or failure. For example, consider the process of ordering a product from *Domain.com*. Lots of disparate pieces of the process have to function for the entire operation to be successful—a client's credit must be good, the product has to be available, and the request to ship the product has to be received. Otherwise, the operation isn't completed. Transactions always end in only one of two outcomes: success or failure.

As our example illustrates, a system that can be in a number of states is broken up into lots of little pieces. The state of a transaction system can exist simultaneously in the user tier, the middle tier, and the database, and might need to service many users at the same time. With so many parts to the system, drawing distinct lines between the state transitions is imperative—especially because there can be multiple points of failure. When performing transactions, the system must be able to maintain consistent states and introduce checkpoints along the way so that the users of the system always get accurate answers (that is, the product was shipped from *Domain.com* or it wasn't).

To maintain system integrity and ensure successful transactions, transaction systems introduce four properties for transactions, known collectively as the *ACID* properties. ACID stands for atomic, consistent, isolated, and durable:

■ **Atomic**   The operation can't be interrupted.

■ **Consistent**   The operation always leaves the system in a consistent state—that is, there are no dangling references to resources and no incomplete results.

■ **Isolated**   The operation's outcome doesn't affect other operations.

■ **Durable**   The operation keeps track of changes in the system so that the system can be brought back online immediately even after unusual failures (such as a power loss).

## The Distributed Transaction Coordinator

At the heart of Microsoft Component Services lies the Microsoft Distributed Transaction Coordinator (DTC). One DTC per machine is involved in a transaction. The job of the DTC is to dispense transactions and coordinate work between the client and various resource managers. Resource managers are durable state managers. (Microsoft SQL Server is a good example.)

The DTC has its own API revealed through a number of COM interfaces. In fact, you can program transaction systems manually by using the interfaces exposed by the DTC. A client application programming to the DTC at a lower level typically enlists one or more resource managers on a new transaction. Then the client application submits requests to the resource managers. These state changes are "charged" against the current transaction. When the work is done, the client application closes the transaction through the transaction interface *ITransaction*, shown in the following code. *ITransaction* has two main functions, *Commit* and *Abort*.

```
interface ITransaction : IUnknown {
    HRESULT Commit(
        [in] BOOL fRetaining, [in] DWORD grfTC,
        [in] DWORD grfRM);
    HRESULT Abort(
        [in] BOID *pboidReason,
        [in] BOOL fRetaining,
        [in] BOOL fAsync);
    HRESULT GetTransactionInfo([out] XACTTRANSINFO *pinfo);
};
```

When a transaction closes, the result is either a new system state or the original composite state of the application and all the resource managers involved. Again, here we have the basis of transaction programming—either an operation succeeds in changing the state of the system or it doesn't.

Before moving on to how Microsoft Component Services works, let's take a look at a protocol designed to assure that operations are atomic.

### Two-Phase Commit Strategy

To help ensure atomicity, a transaction system usually employs a two-phase commit strategy when changing the state of the system. The transaction initiator attempts to commit the transaction, initiating the two-phase commit protocol.

Phase one is the vote collection. The transaction manager polls each resource manager, and each votes to commit or abort based on work done within the transaction and whether the state of the system is still intact.

Once all votes have been collected, the transaction enters phase two, called the notification phase. During this phase, the transaction manager notifies all resource managers of the transaction outcome (success or failure), and the resource manager then commits or cancels the changes to keep the system intact.

## Configured Components and Packages

As you learned earlier, the goal of interception and context-based development is to reduce the amount of code you have to write. We'll begin relying on the system to provide extended services, such as security and synchronization, by using declarative attributes. Classes that want extended services declare this desire as part of their registration process. These classes become *configured components.* Configured components are always DLLs, and Microsoft Component Services uses a surrogate to manage remote and local (out-of-process) activation.

As you know, Microsoft Component Services is layered on top of classic COM using interception and contexts. The capability to participate in a transaction, then, is layered onto existing COM objects. The transaction services provided by Microsoft Component Services live in the executive named MTXEX.DLL. When a Microsoft Component Services component registers itself, the component points its *InProcServer32* key toward MTXEX.DLL. So when you call *CoCreateInstance* to retrieve a COM object, the system fires up MTXEX.DLL and the Microsoft Component Services DLL wraps your object.

The Microsoft Component Services catalog also separates classes into *packages.* Packages are analogous to COM applications. They're logical groupings of COM classes sharing activation and security settings. You can set up these logical groupings programmatically or by using the Microsoft Component

Services Explorer. Packaging is a useful deployment tool—it makes it easier to get your application out there.

Once each component is configured within the catalog, Microsoft Component Services can create an interceptor (a proxy) between client and object based on information in the catalog. In this way, each Microsoft Component Services object is protected from concurrent access and has a say about participating in a transaction. Let's first look at how context protects an object from concurrent access and then at how contexts and transactions work in Microsoft Component Services.

## Microsoft Component Services Contexts and Component Synchronization

In earlier chapters, we discussed COM's various apartment models. The original impetus behind apartments was to guard a component from concurrent access by multiple threads if the component wanted that protection. This story changes somewhat with Windows 2000. In Windows 2000, concurrency requirements are identified by a component's configuration and implemented by context and interception.

In Windows 2000, you can configure classes to use system-provided call serialization by using the Synchronization attribute. When a component is configured to require synchronization, COM puts the context in which the component lives into a synchronization boundary called an *activity*. An activity is just a group of one or more contexts in which no concurrent execution is desired. (An activity is similar to an apartment in Windows NT 4.0.) Each context belongs to at most one activity, and each new context belongs to the context creator's activity, a new activity, or no activity. Contexts that share activities share the lock with the creating context, whereas new activities maintain an independent lock. Contexts that reside outside an activity allow concurrency. Table 17-1 shows the effects of the various synchronization attributes.

**Table 17-1  Windows 2000 Synchronization Attributes**

| Synchronization Setting for the New Class | Context in Activity | Share Creator's Activity |
| --- | --- | --- |
| NOT_SUPPORTED | Never | Never |
| SUPPORTED | If creator in activity | If creator in activity |
| REQUIRED | Always | If creator in activity |
| REQUIRES_NEW | Always | Never |

Activities prevent concurrent access to a component in this way: The system maintains a set of activity data structures for each process—each activity maintains its own exclusive lock. Then each context maintains a reference to the activity it belongs to (if it belongs to an activity). When a call is made into the object, the interceptor tries to acquire the activity's lock before invoking the function. Then the interceptor releases the lock after the call finishes to allow other callers to enter the activity.

## Microsoft Component Services Contexts and Transaction Services

When Microsoft Component Services (or Microsoft Transaction Server in Windows NT 4.0 and earlier) creates a transaction object, it inserts an interceptor between your client code and the object. The interceptor exists to establish a proper run-time environment, a context, based on class attributes in the catalog.

Remember that a context is a group of compatible objects within a process. All objects within a single context share a similar worldview—all objects in a single context have compatible attributes such as call synchronization and security settings. In fact, contexts are represented by real living, breathing objects that you can actually touch through interfaces (as we saw in the code for *IObjectContext*). The thread-local storage for a thread running within a Microsoft Component Services context has a pointer to a context object (which you can easily retrieve by calling *GetObjectContext*).

The following code shows how to use the context object to determine whether it's involved in a transaction, use it to do some work, and then let it know about the state of the transaction. The code shows how the transaction services are available through the object's context.

```
STDMETHODIMP CSomeObject::DoSomeStuff(void)
{
    IObjectContext *pObjectContext = 0;
    HRESULT hr = GetObjectContext(&pObjectContext);
    if(SUCCEEDED(hr))
    {
        if(pObjectContext->IsInTransaction())
        {
            hr = this->DoMoreStuff();
            if(SUCCEEDED(hr))
            {
                pObjectContext->SetComplete();
            } else
            {
                pObjectContext->SetAbort();
            }
```

```
        } else
        {
            hr = E_UNEXPECTED;
        }
    pObjectContext->Release();
    }
    return hr;
}
```

Now let's take a closer look at how transaction objects and functions work. Then we'll look at how ATL and Microsoft Component Services fit together.

## Transaction Objects and Functions

All the COM objects we've been running into until now have been regular old COM objects that don't do anything special in terms of transactions. By default, objects run outside transactions. Of course, you can configure a class to support instances running inside a transaction (by adding an attribute to your coclass statement in the IDL or through the Microsoft Component Services Explorer). Once an object is declared as a transaction object, the object can influence the outcome of a transaction.

Remember the *ITransaction* interface we looked at a bit earlier? Whenever you create a transaction COM object (which is wrapped in a transaction context), the context stores a pointer to *ITransaction* as a data member. The resource manager proxies use the *ITransaction* pointer to enlist resource managers in the transaction.

In some cases, a transaction might need to involve multiple transaction objects. To allow this, Microsoft Component Services includes the concept of a *transaction stream*. A transaction stream is a group of contexts that share a transaction. Transaction streams are important because they support the isolated property of ACID operations. The first transaction context created in a transaction stream is called the *root* of the stream. Microsoft Component Services starts a transaction when the first method is called on an object that is involved in a transaction stream, and it ends the transaction when the root object deactivates. The Microsoft Component Services run time tries to commit a transaction when the root object is deactivated.

Microsoft Component Services transactions are based on passive consent. Here's how they work: after an object enters a transaction, it goes about and does its thing. The transaction context maintains a flag that indicates whether or not the object is "happy" with the work the object has done. (The flag can be managed by the object.) When the run time wants to commit a transaction, it examines the flags within the context wrappers. If any of the objects has indicated an inconsistent or "unhappy" state, the run time rolls the transaction back. If and only if all the contexts are "happy" can the transaction roll forward.

In addition to indicating consistency, a flag included by the context wrapper indicates whether or not the object has completed its work. These two flags are controlled through the *IObjectContext* interface, shown here:

```
interface IObjectContext : public IUnknown
{
⋮

    HRESULT SetComplete(void) = 0;
    HRESULT SetAbort(void) = 0;
    HRESULT EnableCommit(void) = 0;
    HRESULT DisableCommit(void) = 0;
⋮
};
```

Each context has two flags, so four permutations are possible. Permutations are managed by the four functions *SetComplete, SetAbort, EnableCommit,* and *DisableCommit*:

- *SetComplete* sets both flags to TRUE, meaning that everything is in a consistent state *and* the object's work is done. If the object is the root object, a setting of TRUE commits the transaction.

- *SetAbort* sets the consistency flag to FALSE and the "done" bit to TRUE, causing the transaction to abort.

- *EnableCommit* sets the consistency flag to TRUE and the "done" bit to FALSE. This setting means everything is fine within the object and that it would be OK to commit the transaction at that point.

- *DisableCommit* sets both flags to FALSE. This tells the system to abort the transaction if the object doesn't get any more calls.

To review, in the Microsoft Component Services model, an object declares its intent to be involved in a transaction. It does so either at deployment time through the Microsoft Component Services Explorer or in the type library. When an object declares its need to be involved in a transaction, a transaction-enabled context joins the object when the object is created. As an object goes about its business, it can choose to set the "happy" and the "done" flags, which ultimately have an impact on the outcome of the transaction.

## Creating Microsoft Component Services Objects Using ATL

As we saw in Chapter 9, the ATL Object Wizard lets you create all sorts of COM classes. One of those classes is an MS Transaction Server Component. An MS Transaction Server Component object is a standard ATL object that derives from the normal ATL COM implementations *CComObjectRootEx* and *CComCoClass*.

The default MS Transaction Server Component object created by the Object Wizard doesn't do anything special. It implements *IUnknown* using the regular ATL mechanism. If you choose to, you can create an object that implements the *IObjectControl* interface, which notifies you when the object is created and destroyed. You can also choose whether or not you want your object pooled when it implements *IObjectControl*.

Microsoft Component Services supports the notion of *just-in-time activation* (JITA), which helps objects maintain isolation and is a useful programming tool for postponing initialization until the first method is called. JITA objects implement *IObjectControl* to receive activation/deactivation notifications. To implement *IObjectControl* when generating an MS Transaction Server Component object, click the ATL Object Wizard's MTS tab and check the Support IObjectControl check box. The wizard yields an object with the *IObjectControl* interface turned on. The following code shows the basic object implementing *IObjectControl*.

```
class ATL_NO_VTABLE CMTSObjectIObjectControl :
    public CComObjectRootEx<CComSingleThreadModel>,
    public CComCoClass<CMTSObjectIObjectControl,
        &CLSID_MTSObjectIObjectControl>,
    public IObjectControl,
    public IDispatchImpl<IMTSObjectIObjectControl,
        &IID_IMTSObjectIObjectControl,
        &LIBID_MTSTESTLib>
{
public:
    CMTSObjectIObjectControl()
    {
    }

DECLARE_REGISTRY_RESOURCEID(IDR_MTSOBJECTIOBJECTCONTROL)

DECLARE_PROTECT_FINAL_CONSTRUCT()
```

*(continued)*

413

```
DECLARE_NOT_AGGREGATABLE(CMTSObjectIObjectControl)

BEGIN_COM_MAP(CMTSObjectIObjectControl)
    COM_INTERFACE_ENTRY(IMTSObjectIObjectControl)
    COM_INTERFACE_ENTRY(IObjectControl)
    COM_INTERFACE_ENTRY(IDispatch)
END_COM_MAP()

// IObjectControl
public:
    STDMETHOD(Activate)()
    {
        HRESULT hr = GetObjectContext(&m_spObjectContext);
        if(SUCCEEDED(hr))
            return S_OK;
        return hr;
    }

    STDMETHOD_(BOOL, CanBePooled)()
    {
        return TRUE;
    }

    STDMETHOD_(void, Deactivate)()
    {
        m_spObjectContext.Release();
    }

    CComPtr<IObjectContext> m_spObjectContext;

// IMTSObjectIObjectControl
public:
};
```

Notice that the class returns TRUE for the *CanBePooled* method. Objects
that return TRUE from *CanBePooled* will be recycled. Announcing that your
object might be pooled lets you recycle objects, which is useful when initializing your object is expensive and generic. One caveat of object pooling is that
the object must be context-neutral between activations, because the next activation could occur in any context, thread, transaction, or client in the process. Deactivating and activating your object is the moral equivalent of resetting
your object.

# Conclusion

Interception and context are wonderful ideas made possible through COM. They teach us in Computer Science 101 how beneficial indirection is, and context and interception are a great example. Because client code never touches an object directly (it touches only the interface), you have an opportunity to inject services by intercepting object method calls and providing object context that's not necessarily part of the object. And the client is none the wiser—it gets the requested interface pointer.

Interception and context remove one more level of detail from the developer's consciousness. So although interception and context don't eliminate the need to write code, they hoist certain critical, bug-prone services to the level of the operating system, thereby letting the developer spend more time in the domain problem space. Currently, transactions are the most common way to add functionality through interception. Look for many services to be layered onto objects this way in the future.

# INDEX

## George Shepherd

George exposes several interfaces to the computer industry, including *IAmADevelopMentorInstructor*, *IAmARogueWaveEngineer*, and *IAmAWriter*. George is coauthor of *Programming Visual C++* (Microsoft Press, 1998) and *MFC Internals* (Addison-Wesley, 1996). In addition, George is a contributing editor to *Microsoft Systems Journal* and *Visual C++ Developers Journal*. You can often find George appearing at conferences such as Software Development, Visual C++ Developers Conference, and WinDev. When not writing, speaking, and coding, George plays his guitars and rides his bicycle. He still prefers to play his Paul Reed Smith between compiles.

## Brad King

Brad is a software engineer at RogueWave Software in North Carolina's Research Triangle Park. He was formally introduced to COM and ATL in Guerilla COM, a DevelopMentor course that George Shepherd was co-instructing (and in which Don Box cut his hair). Prior to RogueWave, Brad worked as a developer for Rockwell Software, participating in the initial OPC (OLE for Process Control) specification draft and writing code for the Logic and HMI groups. He also spent several years at Central Illinois Controls designing measurement/control systems and embedded devices. When he isn't writing code, he likes to swim, run, bike, and go to the beach with his wife, Jenelle; children, Matthew and Amanda; and the family's black lab, Luke.

**T**he manuscript for this book was prepared and submitted to Microsoft Press in electronic form. Text files were prepared using Microsoft Word 97. Pages were composed by Microsoft Press using Adobe PageMaker 6.52 for Windows, with text in Galliard and display type in Helvetica bold. Composed pages were delivered to the printer as electronic prepress files.

*Cover Graphic Designer*
Girvin | Strategic Branding & Design

*Cover Illustrator*
Glenn Mitsui

*Interior Graphic Artist*
Rob Nance

*Principal Compositors*
Paula Gorelick
Barb Levy

*Principal Proofreader/Copy Editor*
Bethany Clement

*Indexer*
Liz Cunningham

# Learn how
# COM+
## can simplify your
## development tasks

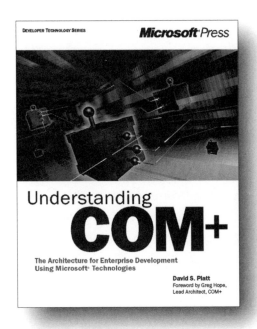

DEVELOPER TECHNOLOGY SERIES

***Microsoft*** *Press*

Understanding
# COM+

The Architecture for Enterprise Development
Using Microsoft· Technologies

**David S. Platt**
Foreword by Greg Hope,
Lead Architect, COM+

**U.S.A.**    **$24.99**
U.K.          £22.99
Canada        $37.99
ISBN 0-7356-0666-8

**W**ouldn't it be great to have an enterprise application's infrastructure so that you could inherit what you need and spend your time writing your own business logic? COM+ is what you've been waiting for—an advanced development environment that provides prefabricated solutions to common enterprise application problems. UNDERSTANDING COM+ is a succinct, entertaining book that offers an overview of COM+ and key COM+ features, explains the role of COM+ in enterprise development, and describes the services it can provide for your components and clients. You'll learn how COM+ can streamline application development to help you get enterprise applications up and running and out the door.

***Microsoft***®

**mspress.microsoft.com**

# Simpler code, faster development.

**MICROSOFT® PROGRAMMING SERIES**

**Microsoft** Press

Programming
Microsoft
**Internet
Explorer** 5

Build Internet and
line-of-business
applications
faster with
Internet Explorer 5

**Scott Roberts**

| | |
|---|---|
| **U.S.A.** | **$49.99** |
| U.K. | £46.99 [V.A.T. included] |
| Canada | $74.99 |
| ISBN | 0-7356-0781-8 |

**W**ith PROGRAMMING MICROSOFT® INTERNET EXPLORER 5, you can build and deploy applications faster, cheaper, and with broader reach than with any other platform. Whether you're simply adding help to a Web page or developing a full-featured Windows® application, you'll get the detailed guidance and practical code samples you need to get productive quickly.

**Microsoft**®

**mspress.microsoft.com**

# MICROSOFT LICENSE AGREEMENT

Book Companion CD

**IMPORTANT—READ CAREFULLY:** This Microsoft End-User License Agreement ("EULA") is a legal agreement between you (either an individual or an entity) and Microsoft Corporation for the Microsoft product identified above, which includes computer software and may include associated media, printed materials, and "online" or electronic documentation ("SOFTWARE PRODUCT"). Any component included within the SOFTWARE PRODUCT that is accompanied by a separate End-User License Agreement shall be governed by such agreement and not the terms set forth below. By installing, copying, or otherwise using the SOFTWARE PRODUCT, you agree to be bound by the terms of this EULA. If you do not agree to the terms of this EULA, you are not authorized to install, copy, or otherwise use the SOFTWARE PRODUCT; you may, however, return the SOFTWARE PRODUCT, along with all printed materials and other items that form a part of the Microsoft product that includes the SOFTWARE PRODUCT, to the place you obtained them for a full refund.

## SOFTWARE PRODUCT LICENSE

The SOFTWARE PRODUCT is protected by United States copyright laws and international copyright treaties, as well as other intellectual property laws and treaties. The SOFTWARE PRODUCT is licensed, not sold.

1. **GRANT OF LICENSE.** This EULA grants you the following rights:

   a. **Software Product.** You may install and use one copy of the SOFTWARE PRODUCT on a single computer. The primary user of the computer on which the SOFTWARE PRODUCT is installed may make a second copy for his or her exclusive use on a portable computer.

   b. **Storage/Network Use.** You may also store or install a copy of the SOFTWARE PRODUCT on a storage device, such as a network server, used only to install or run the SOFTWARE PRODUCT on your other computers over an internal network; however, you must acquire and dedicate a license for each separate computer on which the SOFTWARE PRODUCT is installed or run from the storage device. A license for the SOFTWARE PRODUCT may not be shared or used concurrently on different computers.

   c. **License Pak.** If you have acquired this EULA in a Microsoft License Pak, you may make the number of additional copies of the computer software portion of the SOFTWARE PRODUCT authorized on the printed copy of this EULA, and you may use each copy in the manner specified above. You are also entitled to make a corresponding number of secondary copies for portable computer use as specified above.

   d. **Sample Code.** Solely with respect to portions, if any, of the SOFTWARE PRODUCT that are identified within the SOFTWARE PRODUCT as sample code (the "SAMPLE CODE"):

      i. **Use and Modification.** Microsoft grants you the right to use and modify the source code version of the SAMPLE CODE, *provided* you comply with subsection (d)(iii) below. You may not distribute the SAMPLE CODE, or any modified version of the SAMPLE CODE, in source code form.

      ii. **Redistributable Files.** Provided you comply with subsection (d)(iii) below, Microsoft grants you a nonexclusive, royalty-free right to reproduce and distribute the object code version of the SAMPLE CODE and of any modified SAMPLE CODE, other than SAMPLE CODE, or any modified version thereof, designated as not redistributable in the Readme file that forms a part of the SOFTWARE PRODUCT (the "Non-Redistributable Sample Code"). All SAMPLE CODE other than the Non-Redistributable Sample Code is collectively referred to as the "REDISTRIBUTABLES."

      iii. **Redistribution Requirements.** If you redistribute the REDISTRIBUTABLES, you agree to: (i) distribute the REDISTRIBUTABLES in object code form only in conjunction with and as a part of your software application product; (ii) not use Microsoft's name, logo, or trademarks to market your software application product; (iii) include a valid copyright notice on your software application product; (iv) indemnify, hold harmless, and defend Microsoft from and against any claims or lawsuits, including attorney's fees, that arise or result from the use or distribution of your software application product; and (v) not permit further distribution of the REDISTRIBUTABLES by your end user. Contact Microsoft for the applicable royalties due and other licensing terms for all other uses and/or distribution of the REDISTRIBUTABLES.

2. **DESCRIPTION OF OTHER RIGHTS AND LIMITATIONS.**

   - **Limitations on Reverse Engineering, Decompilation, and Disassembly.** You may not reverse engineer, decompile, or disassemble the SOFTWARE PRODUCT, except and only to the extent that such activity is expressly permitted by applicable law notwithstanding this limitation.

   - **Separation of Components.** The SOFTWARE PRODUCT is licensed as a single product. Its component parts may not be separated for use on more than one computer.

   - **Rental.** You may not rent, lease, or lend the SOFTWARE PRODUCT.

   - **Support Services.** Microsoft may, but is not obligated to, provide you with support services related to the SOFTWARE PRODUCT ("Support Services"). Use of Support Services is governed by the Microsoft policies and programs described in the user manual, in "online" documentation, and/or in other Microsoft-provided materials. Any supplemental software code provided to you as part of the Support Services shall be considered part of the SOFTWARE PRODUCT and subject to the terms and conditions of this EULA. With respect to technical information you provide to Microsoft as part of the Support Services, Microsoft may use such information for its business purposes, including for product support and development. Microsoft will not utilize such technical information in a form that personally identifies you.

- **Software Transfer.** You may permanently transfer all of your rights under this EULA, provided you retain no copies, you transfer all of the SOFTWARE PRODUCT (including all component parts, the media and printed materials, any upgrades, this EULA, and, if applicable, the Certificate of Authenticity), **and** the recipient agrees to the terms of this EULA.

- **Termination.** Without prejudice to any other rights, Microsoft may terminate this EULA if you fail to comply with the terms and conditions of this EULA. In such event, you must destroy all copies of the SOFTWARE PRODUCT and all of its component parts.

3. **COPYRIGHT.** All title and copyrights in and to the SOFTWARE PRODUCT (including but not limited to any images, photographs, animations, video, audio, music, text, SAMPLE CODE, REDISTRIBUTABLES, and "applets" incorporated into the SOFTWARE PRODUCT) and any copies of the SOFTWARE PRODUCT are owned by Microsoft or its suppliers. The SOFTWARE PRODUCT is protected by copyright laws and international treaty provisions. Therefore, you must treat the SOFTWARE PRODUCT like any other copyrighted material **except** that you may install the SOFTWARE PRODUCT on a single computer provided you keep the original solely for backup or archival purposes. You may not copy the printed materials accompanying the SOFTWARE PRODUCT.

4. **U.S. GOVERNMENT RESTRICTED RIGHTS.** The SOFTWARE PRODUCT and documentation are provided with RESTRICTED RIGHTS. Use, duplication, or disclosure by the Government is subject to restrictions as set forth in subparagraph (c)(1)(ii) of the Rights in Technical Data and Computer Software clause at DFARS 252.227-7013 or subparagraphs (c)(1) and (2) of the Commercial Computer Software—Restricted Rights at 48 CFR 52.227-19, as applicable. Manufacturer is Microsoft Corporation/One Microsoft Way/Redmond, WA 98052-6399.

5. **EXPORT RESTRICTIONS.** You agree that you will not export or re-export the SOFTWARE PRODUCT, any part thereof, or any process or service that is the direct product of the SOFTWARE PRODUCT (the foregoing collectively referred to as the "Restricted Components"), to any country, person, entity, or end user subject to U.S. export restrictions. You specifically agree not to export or re-export any of the Restricted Components (i) to any country to which the U.S. has embargoed or restricted the export of goods or services, which currently include, but are not necessarily limited to, Cuba, Iran, Iraq, Libya, North Korea, Sudan, and Syria, or to any national of any such country, wherever located, who intends to transmit or transport the Restricted Components back to such country; (ii) to any end user who you know or have reason to know will utilize the Restricted Components in the design, development, or production of nuclear, chemical, or biological weapons; or (iii) to any end user who has been prohibited from participating in U.S. export transactions by any federal agency of the U.S. government. You warrant and represent that neither the BXA nor any other U.S. federal agency has suspended, revoked, or denied your export privileges.

## DISCLAIMER OF WARRANTY

**NO WARRANTIES OR CONDITIONS.** MICROSOFT EXPRESSLY DISCLAIMS ANY WARRANTY OR CONDITION FOR THE SOFTWARE PRODUCT. THE SOFTWARE PRODUCT AND ANY RELATED DOCUMENTATION ARE PROVIDED "AS IS" WITHOUT WARRANTY OR CONDITION OF ANY KIND, EITHER EXPRESS OR IMPLIED, INCLUDING, WITHOUT LIMITATION, THE IMPLIED WARRANTIES OF MERCHANTABILITY, FITNESS FOR A PARTICULAR PURPOSE, OR NONINFRINGEMENT. THE ENTIRE RISK ARISING OUT OF USE OR PERFORMANCE OF THE SOFTWARE PRODUCT REMAINS WITH YOU.

**LIMITATION OF LIABILITY.** TO THE MAXIMUM EXTENT PERMITTED BY APPLICABLE LAW, IN NO EVENT SHALL MICROSOFT OR ITS SUPPLIERS BE LIABLE FOR ANY SPECIAL, INCIDENTAL, INDIRECT, OR CONSEQUENTIAL DAMAGES WHATSOEVER (INCLUDING, WITHOUT LIMITATION, DAMAGES FOR LOSS OF BUSINESS PROFITS, BUSINESS INTERRUPTION, LOSS OF BUSINESS INFORMATION, OR ANY OTHER PECUNIARY LOSS) ARISING OUT OF THE USE OF OR INABILITY TO USE THE SOFTWARE PRODUCT OR THE PROVISION OF OR FAILURE TO PROVIDE SUPPORT SERVICES, EVEN IF MICROSOFT HAS BEEN ADVISED OF THE POSSIBILITY OF SUCH DAMAGES. IN ANY CASE, MICROSOFT'S ENTIRE LIABILITY UNDER ANY PROVISION OF THIS EULA SHALL BE LIMITED TO THE GREATER OF THE AMOUNT ACTUALLY PAID BY YOU FOR THE SOFTWARE PRODUCT OR US$5.00; PROVIDED, HOWEVER, IF YOU HAVE ENTERED INTO A MICROSOFT SUPPORT SERVICES AGREEMENT, MICROSOFT'S ENTIRE LIABILITY REGARDING SUPPORT SERVICES SHALL BE GOVERNED BY THE TERMS OF THAT AGREEMENT. BECAUSE SOME STATES AND JURISDICTIONS DO NOT ALLOW THE EXCLUSION OR LIMITATION OF LIABILITY, THE ABOVE LIMITATION MAY NOT APPLY TO YOU.

## MISCELLANEOUS

This EULA is governed by the laws of the State of Washington USA, except and only to the extent that applicable law mandates governing law of a different jurisdiction.

Should you have any questions concerning this EULA, or if you desire to contact Microsoft for any reason, please contact the Microsoft subsidiary serving your country, or write: Microsoft Sales Information Center/One Microsoft Way/Redmond, WA 98052-6399.

# Register Today!

Return this
*Inside ATL*
registration card today

## Microsoft®Press
**mspress.microsoft.com**

**OWNER REGISTRATION CARD**

**1-57231-858-9**

## *Inside ATL*

FIRST NAME MIDDLE INITIAL LAST NAME

INSTITUTION OR COMPANY NAME

ADDRESS

CITY STATE ZIP

(    )

E-MAIL ADDRESS PHONE NUMBER

U.S. and Canada addresses only. Fill in information above and mail postage-free.
Please mail only the bottom half of this page.

**For information about Microsoft Press®**
**products, visit our Web site at**
**mspress.microsoft.com**

*Microsoft®Press*